The Reign of Edward II:
New Perspectives

Edward II presided over a turbulent and politically charged period of English history, but to date he has been relatively neglected in comparison to other fourteenth and fifteenth-century kings. This book offers a significant re-appraisal of a much maligned monarch and his historical importance, making use of the latest empirical research and revisionist theories, and concentrating on people and personalities, perceptions and expectations, rather than dry constitutional analysis. Papers consider both the institutional and the personal facets of Edward II's life and rule: his sexual reputation, the royal court, the role of the king's household knights, the nature of law and parliament in the reign, and England's relations with Ireland and Europe.

YORK MEDIEVAL PRESS

York Medieval Press is published by the University of York's Centre for Medieval Studies in association with Boydell & Brewer Limited. Our objective is the promotion of innovative scholarship and fresh criticism on medieval culture. We have a special commitment to interdisciplinary study, in line with the Centre's belief that the future of Medieval Studies lies in those areas in which its major constituent disciplines at once inform and challenge each other.

All enquiries of an editorial kind, including suggestions for monographs and essay collections, should be addressed to: The Director, University of York, Centre for Medieval Studies, The King's Manor, York, YO1 7EP (E-mail: lah1@york.ac.uk).

Publications of York Medieval Press are listed at the back of this volume.

The Reign of Edward II: New Perspectives

Edited by
Gwilym Dodd and Anthony Musson

THE UNIVERSITY *of York*

YORK MEDIEVAL PRESS

First published 2006

A York Medieval Press publication
in association with The Boydell Press
an imprint of Boydell & Brewer Ltd
PO Box 9 Woodbridge Suffolk IP12 3DF UK
and of Boydell & Brewer Inc.
668 Mt Hope Avenue Rochester NY 14620–2731 USA
website: www.boydellandbrewer.co.uk
and with the
Centre for Medieval Studies, University of York

ISBN 978 1 903153 19 2

Transferred to digital printing

A CIP catalogue record for this book is available
from the British Library

Typeset by Pru Harrison, Hacheston, Suffolk

CONTENTS

The editors would like to acknowledge the generosity of the School of History, University of Nottingham, in assisting with the organisation of the colloquium from which are derived the papers in this volume.

ABBREVIATIONS

AA SS	*Acta Sanctorum*
AL	*Annales Londonienses*, in *Chronicles of the Reigns of Edward I and Edward II*, ed. W. Stubbs, 2 vols (1882–3), I
Anonimalle	*The Anonimalle Chronicle, 1307 to 1334*, ed. W. R. Childs and J. Taylor, Yorkshire Archaeological Society Record Series, 147 (1991)
AP	*Annales Paulini*, in *Chronicles of the Reigns of Edward I and Edward II*, ed. W. Stubbs, 2 vols (1882–3), I
BIHR	*Bulletin of the Institute of Historical Research*
BL	British Library
Buck, *Politics, Finance*	M. Buck, *Politics, Finance and the Church in the Reign of Edward II: Walter Stapeldon, Treasurer of England* (Cambridge, 1983)
Bridlington	*Gesta Edwardi de Carnarvon auctore canonico Bridlingtoniensi*, in *Chronicles of the Reigns of Edward I and Edward II*, ed. W. Stubbs, 2 vols (1882–3), II
Brut	*The Brut or Chronicles of England*, ed. F. Brie, Early English Text Society, 121 (1906)
CCR	*Calendar of Close Rolls 1272–1485*, 45 vols (London, 1903–27)
CChR	*Calendar of Charter Rolls 1226–1516*, 6 vols (London, 1903–20)
Chaplais, *Piers Gaveston*	P. Chaplais, *Piers Gaveston, Edward II's Adoptive Brother* (Oxford, 1994)
CFR	*Calendar of Fine Rolls 1272–1509*, 22 vols (London 1911–62)
Conway Davies, *Baronial Oppostion*	J. Conway Davies, *The Baronial Opposition to Edward II* (Cambridge, 1918)
CPR	*Calendar of Patent Rolls 1232–1509*, 52 vols (London, 1891–1916)
EETS	Early English Text Society
EHR	*English Historical Review*
Flores	*Flores Historiarum*, ed. H. R. Luard, Rolls Series 95, 3 vols (London, 1890)
Foedera	*Foedera, conventiones, literae et cujuscunque generis acta*, ed. T. Rymer, 4 vols in 7 (London 1816–30)
Fryde, *Tyranny and Fall*	N. Fryde, *The Tyranny and Fall of Edward II, 1321–1326* (Cambridge, 1979)

GEC	G. E. Cokayne, *The Complete Peerage of England, Scotland, Ireland, Great Britain and the United Kingdom*, ed. V. Gibbs et al., 13 vols (London, 1910–59)
Geoffrey le Baker	*Chronicon Galfridi le Baker de Swynebroke*, ed. E. M. Thompson (Oxford, 1889)
Haines, *King Edward II*	R. M. Haines, *King Edward II: Edward of Caernarfon, His Life, His Reign, and its Aftermath, 1284–1330* (Montreal, 2003)
Hallam, *Itinerary*	E. M. Hallam, *The Itinerary of Edward II and his Household, 1307–1328*, List and Index Society 211 (1984)
Hamilton, *Piers Gaveston*	J. S. Hamilton, *Piers Gaveston, Earl of Cornwall 1307–1312* (Detroit, 1988)
HR	*Historical Research*
Johnstone, *Edward of Carnarvon*	H. Johnstone, *Edward of Carnarvon, 1284–1307* (Manchester, 1946)
JT	*Johannis de Trokelowe et Henrici de Blaneforde, Chronica et Annales*, ed. H. T. Riley (London, 1866)
Lanercost	*Chronicon de Lanercost*, ed. J. Stevenson (Edinburgh, 1839)
Langtoft	*The Chronicle of Pierre Langtoft in French Verse from the Earliest Period to the Death of Edward I*, ed. T. Wright, 2 vols (London, 1868)
Letters, ed. Johnstone	*Letters of Edward, Prince of Wales, 1304–1305*, ed. H. Johnstone (Roxburghe Club, 1931)
Maddicott, *Thomas of Lancaster*	J. R. Maddicott, *Thomas of Lancaster, 1307–1322: A Study in the Reign of Edward II* (London, 1970)
Murimuth	*Adae Murimuth Choninuatio Chronicorum*, ed. E. M. Thompson (London, 1889)
Phillips, *Aymer de Valence*	J. R. S. Phillips, *Aymer de Valence, Earl of Pembroke, 1307–24* (Oxford, 1972)
PROME	*The Parliament Rolls of Medieval England*, ed. C. Given-Wilson et al. (Leicester, 2005), CD-Rom version
Rishanger	*Willelmi Rishanger, quondam monachi S. Albani, et quorundam anonymorum chronica et annales*, ed. H. T. Riley (London, 1865)
RP	*Rotuli Parliamentorum*, ed. J. Strachey et al., 7 vols (London, 1783–1823)
RS	Rolls Series
SAL	Society of the Antiquaries of London
SCCKB	*Select Cases in the Court of King's Bench*, ed. G. O. Sayles, Selden Society, 55, 57, 58, 74, 76, 82, 88 (London, 1936–71)
SR	*Statutes of the Realm*, 11 vols (London, 1810–28)
TNA	The National Archives

Tout, *Place of Edward II*	T. F. Tout, *The Place of Edward II in English History*, 2nd edn (Manchester, 1936)
TRHS	*Transactions of the Royal Historical Society*
Vita	*Vita Edwardi Secundi*, ed. N. Denholm-Young (London, 1957)

Unless otherwise stated, all unpublished documents are in London, The National Archives.

Introduction

J. R. S. Phillips

In the middle of the fourteenth century, the chronicler, Jean le Bel of Liège, who was an admirer of the English crown, who had first-hand knowledge of England and who was writing in the aftermath of the great victories of Edward III, remarked, 'it was commonly believed in England, and had often happened since the time of King Arthur, that a less able king would often come between two valiant monarchs'.[1] Thus Edward I, who was wise, a man of prowess, bold and enterprising and fortunate in war, who conquered the Scots three or four times, was succeeded by Edward II, who did not resemble him either in wisdom or in prowess, who governed savagely and with the advice of others, and who was defeated with all his barons by King Robert of Scotland at the battle of Bannockburn.[2]

The papers which were originally delivered at the symposium on Edward II held at the University of Nottingham on 16 and 17 July 2004 may be allowed to speak for themselves, but a few introductory remarks are needed. The first is that, given the general verdict both of contemporaries and of posterity that the reign of Edward II was an inglorious and disastrous one, it may be asked why there is such an enduring interest in Edward II. In part, perhaps, this reflects the search by historians for significance and for constitutional 'lessons' to be drawn from his reign; but it also reflects the fact that Edward II has never been the 'possession' solely of historians and that other traditions have built up, and continue to build up around him.[3] This may have much to do with the complexity of Edward's character and the difficulty of fitting him into the conventional patterns of medieval kingship, such as the great warrior or the lawgiver. Edward II was neither, and even his posthumous reputation for sanctity, which might with luck have resulted in his canon-

---

1 *Chronique de Jean le Bel*, ed. J. Viard and E. Deprez, vol. I, Société de l'Histoire de France (Paris, 1904), p. 4.
2 Ibid., pp. 4–6: my paraphrase of the text.
3 See, for example, my paper, 'The Reputation of a King: Edward II from Chronicle and Written Record to Compact Disc and Internet', in *European Encounters. Essays in memory of Albert Lovett*, ed. H. B. Clarke and J. Devlin (Dublin, 2003), pp. 37–54; and 'Edward II', in *Oxford Dictionary of National Biography*, ed. H. C. G. Matthew and B. H. Harrison, 60 vols. (Oxford, 2004), XVII, 824–37; and many of the papers in this volume.

ization and placed him on a level of prestige with other holy kings, was ambiguous and overlaid by tales of his moral and other failings. Another cause of fascination is the fact that, although Edward II's reign as king ended in January 1327, his story did not end there. The lurid reports about the brutal, and possibly symbolic, manner of Edward II's death the following September have fuelled a prurient interest in him on the one hand,[4] while on the other the circulation of claims that he had instead survived and escaped from captivity gave him in effect a long 'after-life' which has provided endless scope for further research and speculation.[5]

The papers presented at the symposium challenged many of these earlier conclusions and assumptions. There was a general willingness to reassess Edward II and to engage sympathetically with him and his reign. No one suggested that he should actually be added to the list of 'good kings', but there was also an awareness that Edward II was probably a man of greater ability and more effectively involved in the government of his kingdom than he has been previously considered.[6] One point that came through very clearly was the extent to which Edward II's reputation has been coloured and even manufactured by subsequent writing and propaganda. As Mark Ormrod argues, whether Edward II's relations with Piers Gaveston and possibly other favourites were sexual in nature is beyond objective proof one way or

---

[4] See Mark Ormrod's examination of this theme in 'The sexualities of Edward II' and Ian Mortimer's paper, 'Sermons of sodomy: a reconsideration of Edward II's sodomitical reputation', in this volume.

[5] At the time of writing, the most recent contribution to this debate was my own paper, ' "Edward II" in Italy: English and Welsh Political Exiles and Fugitives in Continental Europe, 1322–1364', in *Thirteenth Century England X*, ed. M. Prestwich, R. Britnall and R. Frame (Woodbridge, 2005), pp. 209–26. This endeavoured to take into account other recent publications by Roy Haines, Paul Doherty, and Ian Mortimer. My own view, put briefly, is that Edward II did die in 1327 and was buried at Gloucester. Ian Mortimer, who is also a contributor to this volume, strongly disagrees with this conclusion and is due to publish a further paper on the subject in November 2005.

[6] There is, however, some interesting evidence that Edward II was in the habit of giving verbal orders without any written confirmation or record. This caused problems, for example, to his former butlers Stephen of Abingdon and Benedict of Fulsham after the accession of Edward III, when they had to account for large quantities of wine supplied for various purposes, for which there was no warrant and which it was therefore hard to prove that they had disposed of honestly: Benedict de Fulsham petitioned Edward III concerning this problem in the 1330 Parliament after the fall of Roger Mortimer: E 175/2/16, m.1 (a roll of petitions submitted to the 1330 Parliament. This previously unpublished membrane can now be found in *PROME* (parliament of November 1330). Edward II may have acted in a similar fashion in more important matters than the disposal of stocks of wine. In reply to Benedict's petition, the council made the very significant remark that 'Il semble au cunsail pur ceo qe tesmoigne est qe le roi le piere soloit faire commandement de bouche saunz autre guarante faire'.

another. What ultimately mattered was the perception both in his lifetime and later that they were sexual.[7] Ian Mortimer's argument that Adam Orleton's charges of tyranny and sodomy against Edward II, which were made in sermons delivered at Wallingford in December 1326, were designed to undermine his political and moral legitimacy and so prepare the way for Edward's deposition, carries conviction.[8]

This short introduction will, however, end as it began, with Jean le Bel. While there were clear differences in achievement and personality between Edward II and both his father Edward I and his son Edward III, as Jean le Bel argued, there are also elements of continuity which should not be forgotten and which must contribute to any final assessment of Edward II. There is no doubt that Edward II was very largely the author of his eventual downfall, but the political, administrative, financial and military problems he inherited from Edward I in 1307 were very significant. Issues such as the abuse of prises and purveyance, for example, were as much a cause of conflict in the early years of the reign as were Edward II's relations with Gaveston. The pressures of war with Scotland began under Edward I and continued almost throughout the reign of Edward II, until 1323 when Edward made a truce with the Scots, for which he got no credit at all. Edward II of course paid the ultimate political price for his perceived failures through his deposition and death in 1327, but the precarious rule of Edward III in his early years should also be remembered. One can only speculate on what would have happened if Edward III had not finally plucked up courage, with the support of William Montague and others in 1330, to launch what amounted to a *coup d'état* to gain control of his own kingdom; or on the possible outcome of the political and financial crisis of 1341, with its uncomfortable echoes of the crises of the previous reign.

---

7 A very good illustration of this is the contemporary or near-contemporary remark by the unknown author of the annals composed at the Cistercian abbey of Newenham in Devon that in 1326 'rex et maritus eius' (presumably a reference to Hugh Despenser the Younger) fled to Wales to escape Mortimer and Isabella. These short annals, which have valuable information on the events between 1326 and 1330, appear in BL, Arundel MS 17, ff. 40–44, under the title *Memorabilia facta tempore Regis Edwardi secundi in Anglia.*

8 As he suggests, there are clear precedents for this kind of charge in the attacks made by the French crown on Boniface VIII and on the Templars. One might add the story of the amphibological message allegedly sent by Orleton to Edward II's gaolers at Berkeley. The story, this time concocted against Orleton rather than by him, has a literary history stretching back via Matthew Paris to the chronicle of Alberic des Trois Fontaines: R. M. Haines, *The Church and Politics in Fourteenth-Century England: the Career of Adam Orleton, c.1275–1345* (Cambridge, 1978), p. 109 and n. 36.

1

The Character of Edward II:
The Letters of Edward of Caernarfon Reconsidered

J. S. Hamilton

Edward of Caernarfon came to the throne as King Edward II upon the death of his father on 7 July 1307. At the time of his accession he was twenty-three years old, and he would reign for twenty years until his deposition in January 1327. In recent years a great deal has been written about the reign in general and Edward's kingship in particular. Much of this recent work has focused on prominent individuals, and questions of character and personality have been of great importance in shaping our understanding of the reign.[1] Interestingly, however, very little has been written about the lengthier portion of Edward's life, prior to his accession. What little that has been written on the early life of Edward II has followed in large part the impressions laid down by Hilda Johnstone. It is now more than half a century since Johnstone wrote her study *Edward of Carnarvon 1284–1307*,[2] yet this slim volume, supplemented by the introduction to Johnstone's earlier edition of the *Letters of Edward, prince of Wales, 1304–1305*,[3] has continued to shape our picture of a diffident, disinterested prince who grew inevitably into an incompetent and unacceptable king. In this paper I wish to return to the letters of Edward of Caernarfon preserved for 1304–5, and in the process to challenge Johnstone's portrayal of an increasingly dissolute prince.

Let me begin this reconsideration of the character of Edward of Caernarfon as presented in the letters of 1304–5 by quoting Johnstone's summary judgement on the prince: 'the general impression . . . conveyed is not that of an heir to the throne anxious to learn the ways of court, camp, and council, or of a great landowner anxious to supervise his possessions, but rather of a somewhat irresponsible country gentleman, living an uneventful and rather monotonous life'.[4]

Nevertheless, a very strong argument can be made for the case that

---

1 Particularly important recent works include Maddicott, *Thomas of Lancaster*; Phillips, *Aymer de Valence*; Fryde, *Tyranny and Fall*; Buck, *Politics, Finance*; Hamilton, *Piers Gaveston*; Chaplais, *Piers Gaveston*; Haines, *King Edward II*.
2 Johnstone, *Edward of Carnarvon*.
3 *Letters*, ed. Johnstone.
4 Ibid., p. xxxvi.

Edward's interests and behaviours were rather conventional and unexceptional. In the very first letter of the collection, for instance, he writes to Adam the poulterer of Reading in order to arrange for four tuns of wine to be available for members of his household who will be coming there for tilting and jousts to be held on the feast of St. Nicholas.[5] Although the prince himself does not seem to have been an active participant in these or other jousts during his father's reign, he was certainly supportive of this thoroughly aristocratic pastime.[6] Indeed, in the following year the desertion of several of the prince's men from Scotland in order to tourney in France greatly enraged Edward I.[7] When Edward of Caernarvon's close companion Piers Gaveston was subsequently sent into exile in the prince's own county of Ponthieu – in part as a result of his participation in the desertion of 1306 – he was provided by the prince with two rather grand tourneying outfits, one of green velvet embroidered with pearls and bearing his arms, and another of green sindon, also bearing his arms.[8] In another of the letters of 1304–5, written to Walter Reynolds on 4 September, the prince ordered the purchase in London of two long swords for his yeomen, along with six small horns, which were all to be sent to him at Windsor Park with haste.[9] The combination of swords and horns seems to point more in the direction of martial than musical pursuits, and it is also perhaps worth noting that, in June, Edward wrote to justice Roger Brabazon seeking to facilitate the release from gaol in London of Mankin the armourer, who is described as 'our well loved'.[10]

---

[5] Ibid., p. 1. It is interesting to note that as late as 15 August 1305 Adam had not been paid, as is made clear in a letter to Walter Reynolds, when the prince reminds his keeper of the wardrobe that the money is owed and must be paid. It seems likely that we hear the prince's own frustrated voice when he adds to the mandate to pay Adam 'dont vous bien sauez et dont nous vous auoms autre foiz comande de paier le, que il ne li coveigne mes returner a nous pur le dit paement'. Ibid., p. 86.

[6] An interesting parallel exists between Edward II and Richard II, who also sponsored, but seems not to have participated in, tournaments. See N. Saul, 'Richard II and Chivalric Kingship', Inaugural Lecture presented at Royal Holloway, University of London (Egham, 1999); J. L. Gillespie, 'Richard II: Chivalry and Kingship', in *The Age of Richard II*, ed. J. L. Gillespie (Stroud, 1997), pp. 115–38.

[7] For evidence of the prince's cognizance of this desertion see Hamilton, *Piers Gaveston*, pp. 33–4. Interestingly, despite her repeated censure of the prince's behaviour, Johnstone has no criticism for the irresponsibility of these youths, remarking that 'they represented the younger generation of families well known in court and camp during Edward I's reign', and had the king not pardoned them 'there would have been scandal in high places': *Edward of Carnarvon*, p. 116.

[8] BL MS Additional 22923 fol. 12v; E 101/369/16 fol. 13v. See Hamilton, *Piers Gaveston*, pp. 35–6.

[9] *Letters*, ed. Johnstone, p. 98.

[10] As Johnstone (*Letters*, ed. Johnstone, p. 37, n. 3) points out, Mankin and his brother Peter were acquitted of charges of theft and homicide after they produced a royal pardon issued at the request of the earl of Lincoln, whose relationship with the prince is discussed below.

Other typically aristocratic preoccupations also feature prominently in his correspondence. There is no question that the prince was interested in horses. On 20 November he wrote a pair of letters concerning the stud of the late earl Warenne, which had recently come into his possession.[11] In each he expressed concern that nothing be removed or damaged on the stud until such time as his own men could measure and survey the lands, and a price be fixed for its value.[12] The following summer, on 16 June, the prince wrote to the archbishop of Canterbury seeking his assistance in remedying a great shortage of stallions on the stud, and inquiring whether the archbishop might not have some 'beal chival' that he would be willing to send to Ditchling in Sussex, as soon as possible, as the breeding season was passing. Similar requests were also sent to John de Northwood, William de Etchingham, and Robert de Burghersh, constable of Dover.[13] The prince's interest in horses and horse breeding is further indicated by a letter dated 17 October in which he authorized the Italian merchant William Person, then in Lombardy, to purchase horses and mares for the prince's use.[14] Concern for both his horses and his men is expressed in a letter of 6 September to the abbot of Reading, thanking him for providing a surgeon to attend to the badly wounded hand of John Lalemand, groom of one of the prince's destriers.[15] A letter of 5 January refers to William Pyrie, who had been sent to Brustwick to obtain two horses, which had been given to the prince by the king, and to return with them to Langley.[16] Another letter, addressed to the sheriffs, bailiffs, and other ministers, on the following day, directs them to provide assistance to Benedict of Calabria, who has been sent to the vicinity of Odiham and Raleigh and is charged with returning to Langley with foals that were a gift to the prince from his stepmother, Queen Margaret.[17] The prince gave as well as received when it came to horses, for a letter of 29 October written to Thomas Inge and Robert de Chishull from Kennington notes that the prince has given two beautiful mares from his stud, along with the foals that they are now carrying and the others that they have recently foaled, to his dear sister Elizabeth, and directs Thomas and Robert to deliver these animals to her.[18]

Finally, something must be said about horses with regard to the very odd letter written to Louis d'Evreux from Langley on 26 May.[19] Johnstone

---

[11] *Letters*, ed. Johnstone, pp. 1, 2.
[12] On 15 March 1305 Edward I ordered Walter de Gloucester, escheator south of Trent, to deliver pasture and meadow in Surrey and Sussex to a value of £38 16s. per annum to the prince. *CCR 1302–7*, p. 245.
[13] *Letters*, ed. Johnstone, p. 31.
[14] Ibid., p. 165.
[15] Ibid., p. 105.
[16] Ibid., p. 160.
[17] Ibid., p. 160.
[18] Ibid., p. 158.
[19] Ibid., p. 11.

suggests that this letter shows the prince to be 'far from contented with his position and his sporting equipment'.[20] However, it seems much more likely – and considerably alters our picture of the prince – that Edward is merely showing a lively wit and a sense of humour when he says 'We are sending you a big trotting palfrey which can hardly carry its own weight, and stands still when it is laden'. He knew what to look for in a mount, and this was not it. He makes this clear elsewhere in his letters, when he writes to Walter Reynolds on 22 June concerning an impending (but ultimately cancelled) visit from the same Louis d'Evreux and his mother, Mary of Brabant, requiring his keeper of the wardrobe to 'purchase for our use two palfreys which are beautiful and suitable for our proper mounting'.[21] The prince's skillful horsemanship seems to have been well established by this time, the author of the *Caerlaverock Roll of Arms* noting in 1300 that 'he managed his steed wonderfully well'.[22]

The prince also showed a keen interest in dogs, particularly greyhounds. On 14 August the prince wrote to John de Foxley, commanding him to send him 'a sparrow hawk for hunting partridges, and a spaniel, and a man who knows well how to handle the hawk'.[23] On 7 September he wrote to thank John Fitzreynold for the greyhounds and other dogs he had sent to the prince, offering '[if] you desire anything that is not prohibited we shall willingly arrange it'.[24] On 15 September he wrote to his sister Elizabeth, requesting that she send her white greyhound to him since he had a beautiful white one himself, and he had 'a great desire to have puppies from them'.[25] It may be with regard to this dog that Edward wrote to Elizabeth's husband, Humphrey de Bohun, earl of Hereford and Essex, on the following day, thanking him for the greyhounds and bow that he had sent.[26] Dogs also figure in the previously mentioned letter of 26 May to Louis d'Evreux, since along with the 'big trotting palfrey which can hardly carry', Edward also claims to be sending to France some 'misshapen greyhounds from Wales, which can well catch a hare if they find it asleep, and running dogs which can follow at an amble, for well we know how you love the joy of lazy dogs'. Once again, the prince's sarcasm appears to point to a genuine appreciation of worthwhile characteristics in a dog, rather than the discontent inferred by Johnstone.

One last interest surfaces in the letters, and that is music. The prince

20 Ibid., p. xxxvii.
21 Ibid., p. 34.
22 *Roll of Arms of Caerlaverock*, ed. T. Wright (1864), p. 18.
23 *Letters*, ed. Johnstone, p. 83. John de Foxley served as a justice under Edward I. Prince Edward also wrote to him on 9 June concerning Foxley's intention to bring an action against John de Caumpeden, serjeant to both the king and prince (p. 26).
24 Ibid., p. 116.
25 Ibid., p. 116.
26 Ibid., p. 117.

appears to have been fond of the newer bowed instruments, such as the Welsh crowth, in contrast to the tastes of his father, who had always been attended by four harpists.[27] There is a letter to the abbot of Shrewsbury, which has been frequently noticed.[28] In it the prince, having heard that the abbot has a talented crowther in his employ, requests that his own minstrel, Richard the Rymer, who wishes to learn this form of minstrelsy, be received into his company and provided for while being instructed in playing the crowth. A letter to Walter Reynolds, written at Tenterden on 1 July, gives some indication of the presence of a variety of musicians within the prince's household, since Reynolds is ordered to procure in London 'a pair of trumpets for our little trumpeters that are good and strong for packing up, and a pair of small kettledrums for Francekin, our kettledrummer, as Jankin our trumpeter, bearer of these letters, will know to select'.[29] Jankin, or Janin, the trumpeter seems to have been attached to the household of the prince since his infancy, and continued to appear in the records as late as 1319.[30] He had been rewarded for his service to the prince in Scotland in 1303–4 with a silver trumpet.[31] The presence of trumpeters and nakerers in the prince's household will come as no surprise, but it should not be over-emphasized or taken as indicative of a lack of *gravitas* – as prince, at least, his employment of and expenditure on minstrels was suitably modest relative to that of his father.

One other aspect of the prince's musical tastes and interests should perhaps be mentioned here, one that points to a more serious form of musical activity. We know that Prince Edward had an organ at his favourite residence at King's Langley, as in 1302–3 payment was made to Master John, the organist of John de Warenne, earl of Surrey, for 15 pounds of tin with which he repaired the prince's organ, in anticipation of a visit in February 1303 by King Edward and Queen Margaret.[32] By 1305 the prince himself apparently employed someone capable of carrying out organ repairs at Langley, as an organ he planned to give to his sister Mary had arrived at Langley broken, and had to be repaired before being shipped on to Amesbury.[33]

---

27 For the musical tastes of father and son, see C. Bullock-Davies, 'Welsh Minstrels at the Courts of Edward I and Edward II', *Transactions of the Honourable Society of Cymmrodorion* (1974 for 1972–73), 104–22.

28 *Letters*, ed. Johnstone, p. 114.

29 Ibid., p. 42.

30 See C. Bullock-Davies, *Register of Royal and Baronial Minstrels* (Woodbridge, 1986), pp. 76–7. Unfortunately, Bullock-Davies made no use of Johnstone's edition of the prince's letters. It is interesting to note that Prince Edward's young half-brothers also had their own minstrels by this time; amusingly, in early July 1306 a payment was made to Martinet the minstrel for repairs to his drum, broken by the two princes, then aged six and not quite five years old. BL MS Add. 37656 fol. 1.

31 BL MS Add. 8835 fol. 130v.

32 E 101/363/18 fol. 5v.

33 *Letters*, ed. Johnstone, p. 134.

Alongside this brief survey of the prince's interests and activities, as revealed in his letters, must be placed his itinerary and some discussion of his household. Johnstone notes critically that the prince's itinerary was rather limited for 1304–5, suggesting to her a lack of purpose. Indeed, she goes further, speculating that 'it is just possible that [his inactivity] is a sign that he was already wearying of responsibilities, and beginning to disappoint his father's hopes',[34] yet it seems unreasonable to expect much divergence from the king's own general patterns of movement at this stage in his life. In any case, Edward spent most of his time in the south and east, generally in the Home Counties. Just over one-fifth of the year was spent at his favourite residence at Langley. Indeed, the roll of letters for 1304–5 shows the prince not only to be frequently resident at Langley, which he had obtained in 1302, but also interested in its upkeep and improvement. On 12 June he wrote to Robert the Parker, his bailiff at Langley, to find the money necessary to pay 'Robert, our carpenter', and other carpenters working on the chamber above the gate of Little London.[35] Exactly one month later, however, the prince wrote to Robert again, ordering that the work cease. This letter of 12 July states that 'the king has charged us to turn out all those who have dwelt at Little London, so that none may dwell there, but the place be kept as it was in the time of our dear mother, whom God absolve'. The only individual specifically named among those who were to be turned out was one Thomas the chaplain.[36] Johnstone concludes from this entry, that 'in the king's opinion, the prince had gathered undesirable companions about him at Langley'.[37] This seems absurd. The eviction refers to only one specific chamber, 'Little London', and not to the entire manor. Moreover, the only denizen of the room specifically named appears to have been a cleric. Is it not a far more reasonable supposition that in fact the king had been apprised of the work at Langley and was disturbed by a violation of his own nostalgic memory of his wife's residence there? This is, of course, the same Edward I who celebrated his late wife with three magnificent tombs as well as the famous Eleanor crosses. Moreover, this order came at a moment in time when the prince had been banished from the king's presence (as discussed below), and was temporarily cut off from financial support by his father. Considerable expenditures on a building programme at this moment would have been contrary to the fiscal privation being enforced upon the prince. Johnstone seems to have found a den of iniquity at Langley merely because she was predisposed

---

[34] Ibid., p. xxxvii.

[35] Ibid., pp. 28–9.

[36] Thomas is otherwise unknown. He is not the prince's confessor, who was the Dominican, John of Lenham. On 21 September the prince wrote from Piribright to Gerard, parson of the church of Stevenage, requesting that he retain Master Thomas Chaplain in his 'latorem presencium'. Ibid., p. 121.

[37] Ibid., p. xliii.

to do so, and subsequent historians have followed her lead rather uncritically.

Returning to the prince's itinerary, a considerable portion of the remainder of the year was spent in close proximity to the king and/or in the vicinity of important political gatherings such as the parliament summoned to meet at Westminster on 28 February and the Westminster parliament of 16 September, which had originally been called for 15 August. In January and February, while resident in London and Eltham, on two occasions he hosted banquets that brought together lay magnates such as the earl of Lincoln, ecclesiastical magnates – both friends such as the Antony Bek, bishop of Durham, and future enemies such as Walter Langton, bishop of Coventry and Lichfield – burgesses, including the mayor of London, and prominent royal officials such as the chancellor.

Although Edward was not often resident in London throughout the rest of the year, the letters show the prince to have been involved in various matters – financial, political, and judicial – impinging upon his own interests in the city of London. These ranged from mandates to the mayor, sheriffs, and citizens of London seeking assistance in payment of various debts and the general advancement of the interests of the Frescobaldi, the release of assorted individuals from gaol, and even a supplication that assistance be given to the Dominicans in London 'as we have great affection for the said Order of friars for many reasons and greatly desire a favourable outcome to such business as touches them'.[38] He was particularly involved in the case of Matilda de Mortimer of Richard's Castle, discussed below. The level and nature of his engagement in London seem entirely appropriate to his status and circumstances in 1304–5.

What of Edward's interest in religion? Again, the letters portray a rather conventional piety, and it is difficult to see the prince disappointing expectations. Fulfilling his public and personal obligations to the church, Edward made two journeys to Canterbury, the first to celebrate the feast of the Purification of the Virgin in February, the second for the feast of the Translation of St Thomas in July. He also spent time at St Albans and Lambeth, and these visits to religious houses should not be dismissed out of hand as merely conventional exercises in hospitality and patronage. In 1300, when Edward had journeyed north to campaign with his father in Scotland for the first time, he had made an extended visit to Bury St Edmunds, where we are told that 'he had been made in chapter one of our brethren, for the regal dignity of the abbey and the monks' abundance of spiritual comforts pleased him. Every day he asked for a monk's allowance, just as the brethren ate in the refectory, to be given to him.'[39]

---

38 Ibid., p. 136.
39 *The Chronicle of Bury St Edmunds, 1212–1301*, ed. A. Gransden (London, 1964), p. 158.

So much for the prince's interests and activities as revealed in his letters. What about his relationships? In referring to the many letters to members of the royal family that survive in this roll, Johnstone concedes that, despite the formulaic nature of much of the material, 'we are still left with traces of contact and sympathy'.[40] I would venture further, and suggest that we can find evidence of several intimate personal friendships, both within and beyond the royal family. More to the point, several of these friendships must challenge the current portrait of Edward as one drawn exclusively to low company and base entertainments. An important distinction can be made between letters written to members of the royal family and leading aristocrats on the one hand, and letters written to administrators, both lay and ecclesiastical on the other. It is almost certainly the case that the voice we are hearing in the majority of the letters, such as the one written to the prior of Twynham on 20 May 1305 – which expresses amazement ('Nous nous mervoillom molt de ceo que vous ne nous auez respundu a la priere que nous vous feismes nadgeres . . .') at the failure to make provision for the prince's clerk, John Makerel, as had been requested exactly six months earlier – is the voice of a clerk who is himself keenly interested in such matters of patronage in his own right, and is not the voice of the prince.[41] However, the opposite appears to be the case in many other letters, where either the tone of the letter, or the nature and quality of the details it contains, make it unlikely to be the product of a clerk, however closely placed he might have been.[42]

The prince's closest relationships, outside those to be found within the intimate circle of his own household, not surprisingly, are found among his family. While the letters directed to his half-brothers Thomas of Brotherton and Edmund of Woodstock on four occasions are indeed nothing more than formulaic, this can hardly be surprising since the boys were only five and four years old respectively in 1304–5.[43] A more genuine concern is to be found in Edward's letters to three of his four surviving sisters and in those to his young stepmother, to each of whom he wrote on a regular, sometimes frequent, basis.

Edward wrote to his sister Elizabeth, countess of Holland, Hereford and

---

[40] *Letters*, ed. Johnstone, p. xxxviii.

[41] Ibid., p. 8, following up on a letter of 20 November 1304 (p. 1).

[42] Johnstone, *Edward of Carnarvon*, p. 96, rightly advised caution in using the letters, even 'those which have "*de l'accent*" '.

[43] Thomas of Brotherton was born on 1 June 1300 and Edmund of Woodstock on 5 August 1301. The lack of content in Edward's correspondence with his half-brothers is neatly contrasted with several letters written to the young princes by their father. In particular, a letter written on 6 May 1305 (from King's Langley, where he was staying with Prince Edward) instructs the two boys to prepare for his arrival for a visit with them at Kempton Park. C 47/19/146, printed in P. Chaplais, 'Some Private Letters of Edward I', *EHR* 77 (1962), 84–5.

Essex, no less than six times, while another four letters concern her affairs.[44]
He wrote on 30 May, from Langley, a letter that begins rather formally, but
ends in a fairly conversational tone, discussing his intervention on her behalf
with the abbess of Barking Abbey. A letter of 1 July may be addressed to Elizabeth, for the tone is very familiar, advising his (unnamed) sister not to be
dismayed by any gossip she hears about himself and the king.[45] This
provides an interesting insight into the prince's mind – surely not a clerk's –
that perhaps the prince did not view the so-called 'Great Quarrel',[46] which
had erupted about two weeks earlier on 14 June, to be as serious as historians
have suggested. Certainly Edward I insisted upon proper respect being
shown to himself and his ministers.[47] Nevertheless, the period of the prince's
discomfiture was not 'wellnigh half a year', but rather a period of no more
than a month. For instance, on 16 July the king ordered Roger le Sauvage,
constable of Windsor Castle, to receive 12 tuns of wine from William Trent,
the king's butler, seven of which were to be delivered to the king's houses in
Windsor Park and put in the cellars there for the use of the prince.[48] Another
letter written by the prince to his sister Elizabeth, on 4 August, illustrates the
on-going reconciliation between the prince and king. Edward acknowledged
the return of John de Haustede and John de Weston to his household,[49] and
prayed his sister to request of the queen that she intercede with the king in

---

44 *Letters*, ed. Johnstone, pp. 14–15, 70, 75, 111, 116, 120, 127, 132–3, 158. It is unclear to
which of Edward's sisters the letter of 1 July (pp. 41–2) is addressed. Elizabeth was
less than two years older than her brother, having been born in August 1282. She
married John, count of Holland, in 1297. She was widowed two years later and,
having returned to England, in 1302 she married Humphrey de Bohun, earl of Hereford and Essex. She died in 1316.

45 'Trescrere soer ne vous esmaez ia de celes noveles que vous nous avez maunde qom
gaungle es parties ou vous estes . . .'. Ibid., p. 41.

46 Discussed ibid., pp. xl–xliv; Johnstone, *Edward of Caernarvon*, pp. 96–102.

47 The incident involving the desertion from the Scottish army in 1306 has been
discussed above, p. 6. Another example of Edward I's insistence on due deference
(with reference back to the Great Quarrel) comes from the record of proceedings
against William de Braose for contempt in the court of the Exchequer from the
autumn of 1305: 'Such contempt and disobedience to the ministers of the lord king,
or to himself, or to his court, are odious to the king. And this was made plain recently
when the lord king removed his first-born and dearest son Edward prince of Wales
from his household for wellnigh half a year, because he had uttered coarse words to a
certain minister of his. Nor did he permit his son to come into his sight until he had
made satisfaction to the said minister for the said transgression.' Quoted in *Letters*,
ed. Johnstone, p. xli, citing *Abbreviatio Placitorum*, pp. 256–7.

48 *CPR 1301–07*, p. 279.

49 The prince had written to Weston on 23 July ordering, upon viewing these letters, his
hasty return to the prince wheresoever he might be, specifically noting that this was
'the will of our lord the king' (*Letters*, ed. Johnstone, pp. 62–3). It is worth noting that
both John de Haustede and John de Weston junior served as household knights of
Edward II throughout the entire reign, receiving their fees and robes as late as the
winter of 1323.

order to obtain the recovery of two more companions, Gilbert de Clare and Piers Gaveston. In a letter of 10 August he addressed her not only in the formulaic language of 'noble dame sa treschere soer,' but also as 'bele soer,' suggesting a genuine intimacy. His subject is also intimate, the cause of Matilda de Mortimer of Castle Richard. As Johnstone discussed at considerable length,[50] Matilda, who had been brought to England and her marriage arranged by Eleanor of Castile, was charged in January 1305 with the poisoning of her husband, Hugh Mortimer of Richard's Castle, and also with instigating the murder of Hugh of Kingsmead. The prince interceded repeatedly and energetically on Matilda's behalf with the mayor and sheriffs of London, the royal justices appointed to hear her case, and the sheriff of Middlesex, responsible for summoning jurors. In this letter, Edward asks his sister to approach the king and urge him to hasten the process of oyer and terminer regarding Matilda's case. In the end, Matilda was pardoned at the request of Queen Margaret. One must wonder, however, if the queen's traditional role as intercessor was not invoked on the prince's behalf in this instance.

Although Joan, countess of Gloucester and Hertford, was twelve years older than Edward, they appear to have had a strong relationship. There are four letters to her, as well as eleven to her husband, Ralph de Monthermer.[51] The first letter written to Joan, dated 22 July, thanks her for having provided the prince with her seal and placed her goods at his disposal while he had been cut off from the king's household. This is an extremely informative letter, especially since the prince reassured her – as he had similarly reassured Elizabeth – that the situation was not as harsh as she may have thought, the king having already ordered that the prince should have a sufficiency of necessaries. Moreover, Ingelard Warle had received back the prince's own seal on the previous day in the archbishop's chambers at Lambeth. Two weeks later, on 6 August, he demurred from an invitation to visit her, citing the king's command that he remain in the vicinity of Windsor, or wherever else the king might ordain, between the present time and parliament, as 'we wish to obey his ordinances an all matters, doing nothing to the contrary'. It is interesting to note that this exchange, like so much medieval correspondence, seems to have been largely oral, communicated by the countess's messenger, Bartholomew du Chastel. In the final letter to Joan in this collection, written on 24 October, Edward notes that he has had letters from Joan concerning a dispute between her husband, Ralph, and Sir Bridowe de Wyhermond. He says that he will give his will and advice to Ralph when he speaks with him, and he very much hopes that the said Bridowe will comport himself in such a manner towards the earl that he will

[50] Ibid., pp. xxxviii–xl.
[51] Ibid., pp. 61, 74, 84, 152.

provide him with an opportunity to pardon him his ill will. This letter points to the very familiar relationship between the prince, Joan, and Ralph. His anticipation of speaking directly with Ralph suggests that this is a frequent event, and the mollifying tone of the letter indicates a genuine regard for his sister's anxious state. The same sensibility is engendered by the letters to Ralph.

Ralph de Monthermer was of somewhat obscure background, having been a squire of Gilbert de Clare, sixth earl of Gloucester and Hertford.[52] Gilbert's widow, Joan of Acre, apparently fell in love with the squire and married him secretly early in 1297. By 1304 the king's initial wrath had cooled (as specifically noted in a letter from the prince on 30 May),[53] and Monthermer was addressed as earl of Gloucester, and was prominent in both the king's armies and his council. In 33 Edward I, Monthermer appears in the witness lists of the royal charter rolls some 27 out of 78 times, or 34.6 per cent.[54] Prince Edward wrote to Monthermer more than to any other magnate,[55] and while some of the letters are merely formulaic, others are considerably more revealing. For instance, a letter of 30 May not only addresses Ralph as 'noble home son trescher frere', but immediately again addresses him as Edward's 'dear brother'.[56] In a letter of 22 June, Edward assures Ralph that he has placed no credence in the merchant Richard Roucyn, nor will he believe any other who speaks ill of the earl. A letter of 21 July is similar to letters to the prince's sisters Elizabeth and Joan, in that it seeks to reassure Monthermer that the king's anger at the prince has subsided, and has in any case been exaggerated: '. . . vous feisom a savoir que nostre seignur le Roy nostre pere ne se tient mie asi mal paye de nous come aucume gentz par auventure vous ount fait entendaunt'. Both the tone and content of the letter point to Ralph's inclusion within the prince's intimate inner circle of friends. A letter of 10 August directs the earl to come to the prince to discuss certain business in person, while another letter just two days later accepts the earl's excuse for failing to visit the prince but reiterates his desire that Ralph should come to him as soon as possible. Similarly, the final letter to Monthermer, written on 17 October, requests that he put aside his indignation against Sir Bridowe de Wyhermond until Ralph and the prince shall have had the opportunity to

---

52 *AL*, p. 133 notes that he attended the funeral of John, earl Warenne, at Lewes in 1304. The chronicler refers to him as 'Comes Gloucestriae, J. Bastard qui dicitur, Radulfus Heanmer'. *GEC*, IX, 140, suggests that he may have been the grandson of William de Meisnilhermer of Tunstal.

53 '. . . molt nous plerroit e graunt ioie aurioms que chere soer feist la volente de nostre cher seignur le Roy nostre pere e la vostre'. *Letters*, ed. Johnstone, p. 15.

54 *The Royal Charter Witness Lists of Edward I (1272–1307)*, ed. R. Huscroft, List and Index Society, 279 (Kew, 2000), 175–83.

55 *Letters*, ed. Johnstone, pp. 6, 15, 34, 60 (twice), 62, 76, 78, 83, 108, 148.

56 Elsewhere in the letters (ibid., p. 70) Edward addresses Agnes de Valence not only as 'treschere cosine', but as figuratively as 'our good mother' and himself as 'your son'.

speak together. The clear picture emerging from this correspondence is of a warm and respectful friendship.

Edward also appears to have had a very cordial relationship with his youngest sister Mary, a nun at Amesbury, to whom he wrote on seven separate occasions.[57] Although several of these letters are merely formulaic *littere de statu*, others suggest a great degree of familiarity existing between the royal siblings. On 7 September he sent her a gift of a greyhound. A week later, on 14 September, he wrote twice to Mary. In the first letter he entreated that she write letters to the Prior and Convent of Bath seeking that they fulfil a request that the prince had made on behalf of the son of his knight, John de Weston. On the same day he wrote again, acknowledging that he had been informed that she had obtained permission from the king for her brother to visit her at Amesbury. He, however, excused himself, citing the impending commencement of parliament, and not knowing when his father might summon him. On 25 September he wrote to apologize once again, but not this time for his failure to visit. Instead, he was apologetic of the failure to dispatch, as promised, several tuns of wine and an organ to his sister at the convent. He had sent orders to London about the wine, but his agents there told him that they did not expect to find any more good wine to purchase. As to the organ, it had arrived at Langley, but it had arrived broken. He went on to say that he had had the organ repaired and would have it shipped to her shortly. This letter is particularly interesting, in part because, if not for the failure to deliver these gifts, we might never have learned of them, and equally for the light it sheds on the depth of the prince's attachment to his sister.

Edward wrote to his young stepmother on eight occasions, and these letters reveal a strong bond between them.[58] The majority of his letters to the queen, including the earliest one, however, are not particularly personal. The prince wrote on 2 July in the hope of obtaining a prebend for his clerk, Walter Reynolds – unsuccessfully as it turned out – and asked the queen to intercede with the king on Reynolds' behalf. On 6 August he wrote with a similar purpose on behalf of his cousin, Henry de Beaumont, who sought a life right in a certain parcel of land held from the king by Westminster Abbey. On the same day he also wrote to the queen with regard to the forest of Odiham. Once again, unfortunately we hear only part of the story, as he sent his yeoman Guillemot Pointz and asked the queen to believe what she should hear from Guillemot's mouth. On 17 August he wrote once again seeking the queen's intercession with the king, this time on behalf of Richard de la Rivere, who would reveal his business to her. Two letters in particular from the prince indicate the strength of his faith in the queen's support and his

[57] Ibid., pp. 16–17, 106, 108, 114, 115, 124, 134.
[58] Ibid., pp. 44–5, 73–4, 88–90, 96, 111, 127.

genuine gratitude for her various efforts on his behalf. The earlier of these letters was written on 6 August and is well known. It acknowledges that the king has allowed the return of the majority of the members of the prince's household, 'and well we know that this was done at your request, for which we are dearly grateful to you, as you know'. The prince then goes on to request, in rather obsequious language ('vous prioms, ma trescher dame e mere, que vncore voillez, sil vous plest, travailler pur nous'), that the queen approach the king to seek the return of two more valets to his household, namely Gilbert de Clare and Piers Gaveston. The following line, which may be the most evocative and emotional statement to be found anywhere in the prince's letters, not only reveals the depth of his feelings for his companions, but also, in this heartfelt revelation, his implicit trust in the queen. He writes, 'but truly, my lady, if we should add those two to the others, we would feel much comfort and alleviation of the anguish which we have endured, and continue to suffer, by the ordinance of our aforementioned lord and father. My lady, will you please take this business to heart, and pursue it in the most gracious manner that you may, so dearly as you love us.' On 1 September the prince wrote to the queen yet again, beginning with fulsome thanks for her previous intercession on his behalf,[59] and then relating that he had sent Sir Robert de Clifford to the king on certain business of his (i.e., the prince's) own. The letter goes on to say that he has charged Robert to reveal this business to the queen prior to discussing it with the king, so that he may know her reaction to the business and what she recommends in terms of presenting these matters to the king, based upon the position in which the prince stands. Edward also expresses his desire to hear, by way of Clifford, if there is anything that the queen wishes of him. This letter provides another tangible sense of the deep trust and faith that by now the prince had developed in the queen and her judgement.

The prince wrote to his cousin Louis d'Evreux on four occasions.[60] The first of these letters, written at Langley on 21 November, is largely a formal letter concerned with business, specifically that of the merchant Stephen of Abingdon. What is significant about the letter is that Louis is requested to intercede with Philip the Fair in all this. The next letter, already mentioned above, is by far the most intriguing in the entire collection. In it Edward claims to be sending Louis a palfrey that cannot carry its own weight, hounds that can only catch sleeping rabbits, deformed Welsh hounds, and even wild Welshmen. It is impossible to take the letter at face value, but equally is it impossible to imagine a clerk, no matter how bored or imaginative, taking the risk of drafting such an insolent letter. This has to be the voice of the prince, one that is playful and ironic. We must also keep in mind that this letter was

---

[59] 'Nous vous mercioms si cherement come nous pooms des travals que vous auez endure pur nous, e du bien que vous auez mis en les busoignes que nous touchent.'

[60] *Letters*, ed. Johnstone pp. 4, 11, 58, 78.

written only shortly before the two men were scheduled to have been together, so this playfulness may have been in anticipation of direct discourse to follow. A third letter was not direct, but seems to have been written to Louis by way of Edward's sister Margaret of Brabant. The final letter, written on 13 August, is once again concerned with business, in this case the forthcoming journey of Amerigo Frescobaldi to France.

Turning from the royal family, there is considerable evidence for Prince Edward's friendships with a variety of leading aristocratic figures of the day, which in many ways is even more significant in revising our impression of the prince.[61] Henry de Lacy, earl of Lincoln, was among the most trusted friends and councillors of Edward I. In 1304–5 he was in near constant attendance at court, witnessing nearly two thirds of all royal charters issued during that year.[62] In the early years of the reign of Edward II, the earl of Lincoln would be a stabilizing influence who commanded the respect of both sides in the political conflicts that swirled around Gaveston.[63] Already in 1304, the regard that Edward of Carnarvon felt for the earl is apparent, but there is an element of trust that may go beyond mere respect. The prince wrote directly to Lacy on seven occasions, most famously on the day he was ejected from his father's presence.[64]

The best known letter to Lincoln was written from Midhurst on 14 June and provides considerable insight into the Great Quarrel. Edward informs the earl that, on account of certain words that were reported to the king as having passed between the prince and the bishop of Chester, the king became so enraged that he banished the prince from his presence and denied all means of royal support (either from the king's household or the exchequer) for his own household. Nonetheless, he states his intention to remain at Midhurst and then to follow his father's household at a distance of some ten or twelve leagues 'so that we may be able to recover his good will, which is our great desire'. He concludes by praying Lincoln that upon his return from Canterbury he will come to the prince, because 'we have great need of your aid and your council'. It is disingenuous of Johnstone to say that 'Prince Edward's own attitude, whether by policy or cowardice, was one of abject subjection',[65] since it is very clear that Edward's 'abject subjection', was indeed a matter of policy in which he shows patience and character rather than cowardice. The use of such charged language as 'abject subjection' fits in

[61] According to the famous caricature of Edward II penned by the chronicler Higden, Edward 'thought little of the company of the nobles, adhering to harlots, singers, actors, carters, diggers, rowers, sailors and practitioners of other mechanical arts'. *Polychronicon Ranulphi Higden*, ed. J. R. Lumby, 9 vols (London, 1865–86), VIII, 298.
[62] *Royal Charter Witness Lists of Edward I*, pp. 175–83.
[63] See Hamilton, *Piers Gaveston*, pp. 46–51, 84–5.
[64] *Letters*, ed. Johnstone, pp. 2, 18–19, 30, 40, 113, 130, 132, 133, 135.
[65] Ibid., pp. xliii–xliv.

with a characterization of Edward II as weak-willed, but it does not fit the evidence presented in the prince's own letters.

Prince Edward's regard for the earl of Lincoln was shown on several other occasions as well. In September the prince asked Lincoln to work with William Langton to represent his interests with regard to Gower in the upcoming parliament. A few weeks later, it was again Lincoln to whom the prince wrote when he learned that the king's council was proposing the dispatch of William Inge to Scotland as a justice. Edward was desperate to retain Inge, who 'knows the entire state of our business as no other', and urged the earl to take council with a delegation comprised of the prince's inner administrative circle, Guy Ferre, William de Bliburgh and Walter Reynolds. It is also interesting to note that Lacy must have had some regard for the competence of the prince's household officials, since he attempted to arrange the transfer of Miles Stapeldon to his own household, something the prince openly sought to prevent.[66] Nevertheless, there are several instances where the prince and earl can be shown to have been working toward a common purpose.[67] This relationship cannot have been one to which the king would have objected.

Another interesting category of letters is comprised of those addressed to Thomas, earl of Lancaster. During his reign as king, Edward II would find Thomas of Lancaster to be his nemesis. As Professor Maddicott has shown, however, the initial falling out between the cousins seems to have taken place in autumn 1308,[68] and the letters of 1304–5 appear to demonstrate a relationship that goes beyond mere formality. Maddicott drew attention to this correspondence,[69] noting that on 22 July the prince wrote to his cousin, asking him to retain one of his servants, Robert le Wayte, while three days he later he returned the favour by writing to the royal justice John Botetourt, requesting that he show favour to the cause of Lancaster and his men. On 7 September Edward asked the earl to intercede with the prior of Kenilworth about an earlier request on behalf of Edward's clerk, Nicholas Baly de Hadenham. Again, the favour was returned on 4 October when Edward wrote to the prior of Burton Abbey, supporting the election of Robert de Langdon. Although Langdon's connection to the earl of Lancaster is not mentioned in the request, it is confirmed to us by the next letter enrolled, which is addressed to the earl and notes that the prince has made the petition at the earl's request. The most

---

66 Ibid., p. 135.
67 For instance, their close cooperation is suggested by the Edward's letter to Isabelle, widow of John Fitzhugh, whose marriage had been granted to the prince's valet John de Stapelton. As Johnstone pointed out, letters patent to the same effect were issued 'at the instance of Henry de Lacy, earl of Lincoln', on the following day. See above, n. 9.
68 Maddicott, *Thomas of Lancaster*, pp. 92–4.
69 Ibid., p. 6.

personal of the letters was written on 22 September, when the prince excuses his cousin from attending him since he is ill, and goes on to offer to travel to Thomas in order 'to see and comfort you'. The cordial relations seem to have extended beyond Thomas to his brother Henry, for on 1 July the prince wrote to Henry of Lancaster's wife Maud, thanking her for 'delibaracione partus sui quem domino significavit' and concluding with a formal clause *de statu* concerning her husband.[70]

Another figure of increasing stature in the reign of Edward I, and one who would play a crucial role in the following reign, was the elder Hugh Despenser, to whom the prince wrote on eight occasions.[71] The elder Despenser would become one of the staunchest supporters of Edward II, but in 1304 he was a trusted councillor and official of Edward I. Like the earl of Lincoln, Despenser was very frequently at court, witnessing nearly half of all the charters issued in 1304–5 (36 out of 78).[72] He also held various offices, such as justice of the forest, and several of Edward's letters to Despenser reflect his official status, rather than a personal relationship. Nevertheless, in a letter of 7 September we gain a sense of the prince's great degree of trust in Despenser. Although no business of any kind is mentioned in the letter, Hugh is urged to come with haste to the prince and also to tell him where he will be on the following Sunday, presumably to facilitate communication between the two. In a slightly later letter of 19 September the prince thanks Despenser for the gift of raisins which 'could not have come at a better time', and makes clear that the exchange of gifts between the two was not unique. It is also important to note, in discussing the prince's regard for Despenser, that he figures prominently in a letter addressed to Guy Ferre, on 3 October, as part of the prince's efforts to prevent having his clerk William Inge sent to Scotland as a justice. Ferre is ordered to take council with Walter Reynolds and William de Bliburgh and to go with them 'to the earl of Lincoln, Sir Hugh le Despenser, and to others of the council of our lord and father *who are our friends . . .*'[73]

To conclude, it is simply not possible to agree with Johnstone when she suggests that 'the general impression . . . conveyed [by the letters of 1304–5] is not that of an heir to the throne eager to learn the ways of court, camp, and council, or of a great landowner anxious to supervise his possessions',[74] when evidence for his interest in such things abounds in the letters. We find him frequently present in and around the court and parliament, and in regular correspondence with a number of leading magnates. His interests are traditional and appropriate to his station. Certainly, as a king, Edward II was

---

[70] *Letters*, ed. Johnstone, p. 41.
[71] Ibid., pp. 19–20, 81, 97, 107–8, 118–19, 122, 123, 137–8.
[72] *Royal Charter Witness Lists of Edward I*, pp. 175–83.
[73] *Letters*, ed. Johnstone, pp. 133–4. Italics added.
[74] Ibid., p. xxxvi.

highly unsuccessful, and he may well have been deeply flawed not only as a king, but as a man. There is, however, no credible evidence in the letters of 1304–5 to project his mature failures back upon his apparently conventional youth, and we must resist the temptation to do so by reading back into his youth characteristics more clearly apparent in his later years.

2

The Sexualities of Edward II

W. M. Ormrod

Let me be clear from the outset: this study does not set out to cast Edward II as a medieval representative of any one modern category of sexual orientation, heterosexual, homosexual, bisexual, whatever. The efforts made in the last few generations of scholarship to 'identify' this king in such a manner are, in the end, both anachronistic and futile: anachronistic because medieval attitudes to sexuality were so different from our own, and futile because the nature of the evidence makes it impossible to tell what Edward actually did – let alone what he thought himself to be doing – whether and when he engaged in emotional and physical contact with women or men. Rather, we are dealing here, of necessity, with *reputations*: with what people thought and said about Edward II's personality, and the place of his sexuality within it, during his lifetime and in the generation after his demise. In some respects, this approach is well established: the idea of a distinction – and tension – between Edward's private life and his public reputation has been a stock-in-trade of historical writing since the Renaissance.[1] Postmodernism, however, has taught us to treat such reputations not as deviations from some scientific truth about the past but as historical phenomena that existed, and exist, in their own right.[2] This article therefore attempts to move beyond the somewhat naïve and sterile positivist debate that aims to claim Edward either as gay or as straight, and instead to examine the reasons why some people in the

---

[1] In his *History of England* (1611), John Speed commented in relation to Edward II's treatment of Piers Gaveston that 'those affections which oftentimes deserve praise in a private person, are subject to much construction in a public': A. Feros, 'Images of Evil, Images of Kings: The Contrasting Faces of the Royal Favourite and the Prime Minister in Early Modern European Political Literature, c. 1580–c. 1650', in *The World of the Favourite*, ed. J. H. Elliott and L. W. B. Brockliss (London, 1999), pp. 205–22 (p. 218). I am grateful to Phil Bradford, Jon Cannon, Bronach Kane, Martyn Lawrence and Danielle Westerhof for information that helped to inform this study, and to Jeffrey Hamilton, Katherine Lewis and Ian Mortimer for their detailed comments on an earlier version. None of them is responsible for errors of fact or judgement that doubtless remain.

[2] In making such a statement I do not suggest that the past exists *only* (or merely) in the texts that articulated such reputations, but instead take the view that texts offer *both* testimony of events *and* a way of understanding perceptions and ideologies of past societies.

22

fourteenth century found it appropriate and necessary to include issues about sexuality in their construction of this king's character and reign.

The decriminalisation of homosexuality in Great Britain in the 1960s and the emergence of a newly visible gay culture in western culture and scholarship during the second half of the twentieth century allowed scholars to address the issue of Edward II's sexuality in a much more direct way than had been possible in the age of Victorian values. Since the 1970s both academic historians and generalist biographers have explicitly declared what had been understood for a long time: namely, that Edward II was, reputedly, homosexual.[3] The celebrated declaration in John Boswell's enormously influential 1980 book that Edward was 'the last overtly homosexual monarch of the Middle Ages' has set the king firmly into a scholarly and populist gay historiography, while new readings of Christopher Marlowe's sixteenth-century historical drama *Edward II* have spawned a whole range of explicit and sometimes eroticised treatments of the king's same-sex relationships in theatre, ballet, film and historical novels.[4] The 'outing' of Edward II, then (as Michael Prestwich presciently noted in 1980), arises not from the discovery of new evidence but from the new visibility of gay sub-culture and its acceptance by the liberal mainstream during the last decades of the twentieth century.[5] There is an interesting and relevant parallel here in the evolution of scholarship on the figure of the Pardoner in Chaucer's *Canterbury Tales*. So huge, now, is the scale and intensity of the work on the Pardoner as homosexual that it is easy to forget that he was only explicitly identified as such in the 1950s, and only began to take off as a serious focus of gay literary studies from about 1980.[6] Such are the ways in which modern cultural politics influence the enterprise of medieval studies.

---

3   The avoidance strategies of nineteenth- and early twentieth-century historians with regard to the issue of the king's sexuality are conveniently summarised by H. Hutchinson, *Edward II* (New York, 1971), pp. 147–8, where one of the earliest explicit discussions of Edward's assumed homosexuality ensues. See also C. Bingham, *The Life and Times of Edward II* (London, 1973), p. 54.

4   J. Boswell, *Christianity, Social Tolerance, and Homosexuality: Gay People in Western Europe from the Beginning of the Christian Era to the Fourteenth Century* (Chicago, 1980), pp. 298–300. For the reception and influence of Boswell's work see C. Dinshaw, *Getting Medieval: Sexualities and Communities, Pre- and Postmodern* (Durham, NC, 1999), pp. 22–34. Among contemporary renderings of the Edward II story, see: Chris Hunt's historical novel *Gaveston* for the Gay Men's Press (London, 1997); Derek Jarman's film, *Edward II* (1991); and John McCabe and David Bintley's ballet, *Edward II* (1995). See also: J. R. S. Phillips, 'The Reputation of a King: Edward II from Chronicle and Written Record to Compact Disc and Internet', in *European Encounters: Essays in Memory of Albert Lovett*, ed. J. Devlin and H. B. Clarke (Dublin, 2003), pp. 37–54; and J. R. S. Phillips in this volume, pp. 220–33.

5   M. Prestwich, *The Three Edwards* (London, 1980), p. 80.

6   See the useful survey in V. L. Bullough and G. Whitehead Brewer, 'Medieval Masculinities and Modern Interpretation: The Problem of the Pardoner', in *Conflicted Iden-*

The postmodern scholarly treatment of Chaucer's Pardoner is pertinent to our study of Edward II in a number of other ways, too. First, there is the very obvious point that the Pardoner is a fiction, a product of Chaucer's imagination based in the poet's acute observation of contemporary society. In what follows, I want to emphasise that the fourteenth-century constructions of Edward II's sexuality, though based in traditions about real people and real events, existed quite independently of any evidence available (then or now) as to the precise nature of the king's human relationships. Secondly, there is still no unanimity on the Pardoner's sexuality: in spite of consistent efforts to identify and appropriate him as the first homosexual in English literature, there is a powerful and resistant strain of scholarship which insists that the Pardoner is (in medieval terms) recognisably heterosexual.[7] So, too, of course, with modern scholarship on Edward II: while many political historians are now inclined to acknowledge that (even if it was not a defining political act) Edward II almost certainly *did* have sex with men, Pierre Chaplais' intervention in the debate in 1994 demonstrated that the king's homosocial relationships are still at least susceptible to being cast in the non-sexualised context of sworn brotherhood.[8] Finally, the Pardoner provides us with a timely example

---

tities and Multiple Masculinities: Men in the Medieval West, ed. J. Murray (New York, 1999), pp. 93–110 (p. 103). Two recent major contributions are: R. S. Sturges, *Chaucer's Pardoner and Gender Theory: Bodies of Discourse* (New York, 2000); G. Burgess, *Chaucer's Queer Nation* (Minneapolis, 2003), pp. 119–59.

[7] R. F. Green, 'The Sexual Normality of Chaucer's Pardoner', *Mediaevalia* 8 (1985), 351–8; H. A. Kelly, 'The Pardoner's Voice, Disjunctive Narrative, and Modes of Effemination', in *Speaking Images: Essays in Honor of V. A. Kolve*, ed. R. F. Yeager and C. C. Morse (Asheville, 2001), pp. 411–44. It is interesting here to note also the resistance of scholarship to the queering of another (in)famous fourteenth-century homosexual, Brunetto Latini: see M. Camille, 'The Pose of the Queer: Dante's Gaze, Brunetto Latini's Body', in *Queering the Middle Ages*, ed. G. Burger and S. F. Kruger (Minneapolis, 2001), pp. 57–86 (pp. 59–64).

[8] For the view that Edward probably did have same-sex encounters, see: Maddicott, *Thomas of Lancaster*, p. 83; Hutchinson, *Edward II*, pp. 147–8; Phillips, *Aymer de Valence*, p. 290; Hamilton, *Piers Gaveston*, pp. 11–17; M. Saaler, *Edward II* (London, 1997), p. 35; J. S. Hamilton, 'Menage à Roi: Edward II and Piers Gaveston', *History Today* 49[6] (1999), 26–31; Haines, *King Edward II*, pp. 42–3 and references at n. 88. For the attempt at refutation, see Chaplais, *Piers Gaveston*, esp. pp. 3, 5, 6–22, 109–14. For sworn brotherhood in general, see M. H. Keen, *Nobles, Knights and Men at Arms in the Middle Ages* (London, 1996), pp. 43–62; E. A. R. Brown, 'Ritual Brotherhood in Western Medieval Europe', *Traditio* 52 (1997), 357–81; A. Bray, *The Friend* (Chicago, 2003). Chaplais' position is questioned by the strain of queer studies that identifies the possibility of the homoerotic in the (merely) homosocial: see R. E. Zeikowitz, *Homoeroticism and Chivalry: Discourses of Male Same-Sex Desire in the Fourteenth Century* (New York, 2003), pp. 1–15. For brotherhood itself as a motif of same-sex, eroticised relationships, see J. Boswell, *Same-Sex Unions in Premodern Europe* (New York, 1994); B.-U. Hergemöller, *Sodom and Gomorrah: On the Everyday Reality and Persecution of Homosexuals in the Middle Ages*, trans. J. Phillips (London, 2001), pp. 66–85; Zeikowitz, *Homoeroticism and Chivalry*, pp. 27–43.

of the way in which postmodern critical studies have transformed our readings of medieval culture and our understanding of medieval attitudes to sex, sexuality and gender. Before we embark on a new kind of exploration of Edward II's sexual identities, it is therefore necessary to say a few things about the theoretical framework within which this enterprise is cast.

In developing a response to the vexed question of how fourteenth-century English political culture constructed the sexuality (or rather, as I shall be arguing, the sexualit*ies*) of Edward II, I have been influenced by the critical theory inclusively labelled gender studies, and more especially by its sub-section, queer studies.[9] I take it as a given that there are useful and valid distinctions to make between *sex* (that is, the biological distinction between female and male), *gender* (the personal sense and/or socialised expression of femaleness/maleness/transgender-ness) and *sexuality* (the type of sexual practice in which one engages and/or with which one 'identifies' – in contemporary terms, the categorisations heterosexual, homosexual, bisexual). But I also assume that sex, gender and sexuality are all, to a greater or lesser degree, social constructs that exist contingently with other forms of cultural signifier – class, race, religion, nationality – and that they therefore consist not in oppositional binaries (male/female, masculine/feminine, straight/gay) but in infinite and unstable gradations over a continuum.[10] This is especially important in the present context because so many theorists have moved away from the 'essentialist' position adopted by gay scholarship in the third quarter of the twentieth century (the idea that sexual identity itself is innate) and tended towards the 'constructionist' view (which stresses the impact of social forces on gender and sexual identity), in the process becoming progressively less persuaded that modern categorisations – 'straight' *versus* 'gay' – are adequate or relevant ways of describing sexualities in the historical past (or, for that matter, in postmodern culture).[11] It needs especially to be remembered in this respect that queer studies, as a pluralist and inclusive cultural theory, tends to resist the idea of a specifically gay 'tradition': it was Foucault, the progenitor of queer studies, who argued that there was really no such thing as homosexual identity before the late nineteenth century; and numerous queer theorists have recently taken issue

---

9 For a helpful summary of the intellectual basis of queer studies and its relationship to medieval studies (in this case, in fact, represented as problematic) see A. J. Frantzen, *Before the Closet: Same-Sex Love from* Beowulf *to* Angels in America (Chicago, 1998), pp. 1–29.

10 See the useful discussion from the point of view of medieval studies by K. Lochrie, P. McCracken and J. A. Schultz, 'Introduction', in *Constructing Medieval Sexuality*, ed. K. Lochrie, P. MacCracken and J. A. Schultz (Minneapolis, 1997), pp. ix–xviii.

11 Boswell's essentialist arguments in *Christianity, Social Tolerance, and Homosexuality* were re-formulated in J. Boswell, 'Categories, Experience and Sexuality', in *Forms of Desire: Sexual Orientation and the Social Constructionist Controversy*, ed. E. Stein (New York, 1992), pp. 133–73.

with Boswell's essentialist position and challenged his use of the term 'gay' in relation to medieval people.[12]

Such arguments may seem, at first sight, to provide vindication for the view adopted by many historians of Edward II to the effect that, since participation in same-sex relationships did not *define* a man as homosexual in Western pre-modern culture, and since there was no precise term to describe what is today called homosexuality, we can simply assume that, in the fourteenth century, there was no real debate on – or, indeed, any real way of debating – the fact that the king may have had sex with other men. That is not the line of thinking adopted here. The queering of a text is not principally about 'outing' its author or its subject, but rather about revealing, and destabilising, the line that contemporaries drew between the hegemonic and the deviant.[13] Queer studies, by recognising the strong desire of heteronormative culture to suppress the story of same-sex love, therefore offers a means of identifying substantive discourses on non-normative sex, gender and sexuality in texts that are usually merely allusive (and often necessarily elusive) about the subject.[14] This is a vitally important strategy in relation to the treat-

---

12 D. Halperin, *One Hundred Years of Homosexuality and Other Essays on Greek Love* (London, 1990), p. 29. See, more generally, the critical discussions of A. Frantzen, 'When Women Aren't Enough', *Speculum* 68 (1993), 445–71; S. Bravmann, *Queer Fictions of the Past: History, Culture, and Difference* (Cambridge, 1997), esp. pp. 46–67. For studies that challenge Foucault by claiming recognisable homosexual/gay identities before the nineteenth century, see, for example, R. Purks MacCubbin, *'Tis Nature's Fault: Unauthorised Sexuality During the Enlightenment* (Cambridge, 1985); Lochrie, McCracken and Schultz, 'Introduction', pp. xiv–xvi. G. Burger and S. F. Kruger, 'Introduction', in *Queering the Middle Ages*, ed. Burger and Kruger, pp. xi–xxiii, point out that much of the work of literary scholars and cultural theorists still tends to assume that the search for a re-casting of Foucault's periodisation should begin at the Renaissance (and, more specifically in an English context, with Shakespeare and Marlowe) (pp. xviii–xx). The idea that there needs to be a teleology of homosexual identity is challenged by Frantzen's arguments about the cultural status of what he decides is best called 'same-sex love' in the early Middle Ages: Frantzen, *Before the Closet*. Both J. Goldberg, *Sodometries: Renaissance Texts, Modern Sexualities* (Stanford, 1992), p. 22 and Dinshaw, *Getting Medieval*, pp. 35–6, while attempting to make connections over time, distance themselves from the notion that there is real continuity in gay culture.

13 See, for example: S. Gaunt, 'Straight Minds/Queer Wishes in Old French Hagiography', in *Premodern Sexualities*, ed. L. O. Fradenburg and C. Freccero (London, 1996), pp. 155–73; K. Lochrie, 'Mystical Acts, Queer Tendencies', in *Constructing Medieval Sexuality*, ed. Lochrie, McCracken and Schultz, pp. 180–200. For a timely questioning of modern assumptions about heteronormativity in the Middle Ages, see K. Lochrie, 'Presidential Improprieties and Medieval Categories: The Absurdity of Heterosexuality', in *Queering the Middle Ages*, ed. Burger and Kruger, pp. 87–96.

14 For the tradition of suppressing the deviant, see J. Dollimore, *Sexual Dissidence: Augustine to Wilde, Freud to Foucault* (Oxford, 1991), p. 31. In this respect, queer theory relies heavily on the notion of the closet, a space that conditions the discourses of both the heteronormative and the queer: E. Kosofsky Sedgwick, *Epistemology of the Closet* (Berkeley, CA, 1990); Frantzen, *Before the Closet*.

ment of what we call homosexuality, given the conventions of 'unmention-ability' that surrounded the sin of sodomy and its specific manifestation in male–male anal penetrative sex.[15] The kinds of readings made possible by queer theory lead me to propose that issues of sex, gender and sexuality were not some kind of distraction from the 'real' political issues of Edward II's reign – favouritism, counsel, faction, tyranny – but, in fact, provided an important discourse through which those very problems could be articulated and their controversial outcomes be justified.

In moving from the proposition to the development of my argument, I want to observe this discourse in not one but two forms. The first, and more obvious, is the politically subversive tradition that emerged around the time of the deposition crisis of 1326–7 and which represented Edward II as a man whose sexual deviancy rendered him unworthy of his royal title. I need to make it clear that I see this construction as part of a wider programme of defamation, traceable well back into Edward's reign, which represented the king's character as defective; and that, although I argue that sexual deviancy may already have been part of this notion of Edward's personal inadequacy by the time of his deposition, I am not necessarily suggesting that the king's supposed homosexual relationships were the sole or primary spur to the emergence of his reputation as a degenerate. The second form of gender discourse that I identify comprises the official line adopted by both Edward II and Edward III and which, as I argue, aimed in a quite assertive manner to counter public speculation about Edward II's sodomy and to rehabilitate him both as heterosexual and as king. This strategy was articulated through the representation of the marriage of Edward II and Queen Isabella as a normal and functional relationship, disrupted not by the intervention of Piers Gaveston and the Despensers but by the queen's own adultery with Roger Mortimer and by her usurpation of kingly power and prerogative in the period between 1327 and 1330. What emerges is an ambiguous and contested debate, in which both subversive and establishment discourses on events in the later 1320s came to be articulated in terms of the contravention of sexual and gender norms variously by Edward II and Isabella of France.

---

[15] For the discourses of 'unmentionability' see: M. Goodich, *The Unmentionable Vice: Homosexuality in the Later Medieval Period* (Santa Barbara, 1979); J. Chiffoleau, 'Dire l'indicible: Remarques sur la catégorie du *nefandum* du XIIe au XVe siècle', *Annales* 45 (1990), 289–324; M. D. Jordan, *The Invention of Sodomy in Christian Theology* (Chicago, 1997), pp. 106, 111, 133, 150–1; J. Cadden, 'Sciences/Silences: The Natures and Languages of "Sodomy" in Peter of Abano's *Problemata* Commentary', in *Constructing Medieval Sexuality*, ed. Lochrie, McCracken and Schultz, pp. 40–57; Dinshaw, *Getting Medieval*, pp. 5–12; M. Hanrahan, 'Speaking of Sodomy: Gower's Advice to Princes in the *Confessio amantis*', *Exemplaria* 14 (2002), 423–46.

*

The first of the two main sections of this study, then, aims to re-assess the tradition that developed during Edward II's lifetime and in the generation after his death on the nature and implications of the king's sexuality. I suggest that there was a quite concerted attempt in the fourteenth century to set Edward II outside the boundaries of normative behaviour – specifically the normative behaviour of a king – and that contemporary culture took it for granted that Edward's stubborn refusal to abide by social convention was manifested in sexual terms. My suggestion is that we may legitimately gender the contemporary descriptions of Edward's personality by exploring the associations that medieval culture made between various forms of intellectual, social and sexual 'queerness'.

The construction of Edward II's personality in fourteenth-century sources has long fascinated historians, since the pen-portraits found in the chronicles and the incidental references gleaned from government records give what appears at first sight to be an unusually vivid, individualised and therefore 'authentic' account of the king's personality, tastes, habits and hobbies.[16] The principal features of Edward's character, according to these sources, were: his excessive love for some and unbridled cruelty to others; his tendency on the one hand to idleness and indolence and on the other to exacting physical exercise; his general debauchery and licentiousness; his preference for low-life company; his enthusiasm for aquatic sports; and his engagement in the rustic arts, specifically those of hedging and ditching. For obvious reasons, these personality traits are grist to the mill of the historical biographer.[17] Very little has previously been done, however, to address the question of what cultural meanings such references might actually have carried for contemporaries: scholars have generally been content to make the observation that the chroniclers cast Edward as a man who flouted established norms of kingly behaviour, courtly protocol and chivalric values, and still remain somewhat uncertain as to what to make of Edward's more outlandish 'eccentricities' (as

16 The relevant texts are: *Vita*, pp. 15, 40; *Polychronicon Ranulphi Higden*, ed. F. C. Hingeston-Randolph and J. R. Lumby, 9 vols (London, 1865–86), VII, 298, 301 (from which derives *Chronicon Henrici Knighton*, ed. J. R. Lumby, 2 vols [London, 1889], I, 40); *Chronica Monasterii de Melsa*, ed. E. A. Bond, 2 vols (London, 1867), II, 286, 355; *Bridlington*, 91; H. Johnstone, 'The Eccentricities of Edward II', *EHR* 48 (1933), 263–7 (p. 267); *AP*, 255; *Flores Historiarum*, III, 146, 229, 331; *AL*, 151; *Lanercost*, p. 210; *Brut*, I, 205; G. L. Haskins, 'A Chronicle of the Civil Wars of Edward II', *Speculum* 14 (1939), 73–81 (p. 75).

17 For comment see, for example: Tout, *Place of Edward II*, pp. 8–23; Johnstone, *Edward of Carnarvon*, pp. 10–11, 149, 152–3; Hutchinson, *Edward II*, pp. 11, 147; Chaplais, *Piers Gaveston*, p. 7; Haines, *King Edward II*, pp. 35–41; C. Valente, 'The "Lament of Edward II"': Religious Lyric, Political Propaganda', *Speculum* 77 (2002), 422–39 (pp. 426–7); Phillips, 'Reputation of a King'.

Hilda Johnstone tellingly called them).[18] I want to propose that a more systematic analysis of these cultural meanings may be derived from the theme I refer to as 'degeneracy', and to suggest that contemporary culture was disposed to assume links between this generalised phenomenon and the more specific sexual offence of sodomy.[19]

The notion of degeneracy is probably best known to political historians of the fourteenth century in the context of the Statute of Kilkenny, that resounding condemnation of the apparently inexorable tendency on the part of the Anglo-Irish political establishment to adopt, and identify with, native Irish dress, manners and culture.[20] But the sense in which the term is today understood ('having lost the qualities proper to the type; having declined to a lower type') clearly had a much wider currency in the later Middle Ages. The word 'degenerate' first appears in English (from the Latin) at the end of the fifteenth century, when it was taken to mean 'out of kynde'.[21] This conveniently links it with the older medieval notion of offence or sin against 'kind' (*cynd* in Old English, *kynde* in Middle English). A number of scholars, particularly Carolyn Dinshaw, have examined the notion of the sin 'against kind' in

---

18 Johnstone, 'Eccentricities of Edward II'. See also R. Horrox, 'Caterpillars of the Commonwealth? Courtiers in Late Medieval England', in *Rulers and Ruled in Late Medieval England: Essays Presented to Gerald Harriss*, ed. R. E. Archer and S. Walker (London, 1995), pp. 1–15 (pp. 4–5).

19 In 1910 Chalfont Robinson argued, through an extensive analysis of the chroniclers' comments, that Edward II was pathologically 'degenerate': J. Chalfont Robinson, 'Was King Edward II a Degenerate?', *American Journal of Insanity*, 66 (1910), 445–64. For discussion of Robinson's views, see: Johnstone, 'Eccentricities of Edward II', p. 265, n. 1; Hutchinson, *Edward II*, p. 148; Haines, *King Edward II*, pp. 46–7. Historians have been understandably reluctant to pick up this idea, partly because of general resistance to the sub-discipline of psychohistory and partly because early twentieth-century assumptions about degeneracy – and particularly about the equation between mental illness and homosexuality – are now so much discredited: for the 'antihomosexual bias of much psychiatric writing', see D. F. Greenberg, *The Construction of Homosexuality* (Chicago, 1988), p. 495. What has been missed, however, is the strong congruity between Robinson's psychoanalytical definition of degeneracy and the late medieval attitude to forms of human behaviour that contravened the natural order.

20 J. F. Lydon, 'The Problem of the Frontier in Medieval Ireland', *Topic: A Journal of the Liberal Arts* 5 (1967), 5–22; J. F. Lydon, 'Nation and Race in Medieval Ireland', in *Concepts of National Identity in the Middle Ages*, ed. S. Forde, L. Johnson and A. V. Murray (Leeds, 1995), pp. 103–24; T. Turville-Petre, *England the Nation: Language, Literature, and National Identity, 1290–1340* (Oxford, 1996), pp. 155–75; R. R. Davies, 'The Peoples of Britain and Ireland 1100–1400: III. Laws and Customs', *TRHS* 6th ser. 6 (1996), 1–23; R. R. Davies, 'The Peoples of Britain and Ireland 1100–1400: IV. Language and Historical Mythology', *TRHS* 6th ser. 7 (1997), 1–24; S. Duffy, 'The Problem of Degeneracy', in *Law and Disorder in Thirteenth-Century Ireland: The Dublin Parliament of 1297*, ed. J. F. Lydon (Dublin, 1997), pp. 87–106; R. Frame, *Ireland and Britain, 1170–1450* (London, 1998), pp. 131–50, 191–220.

21 *OED*, s.v. 'degenerate'.

fourteenth-century England, most specifically in relation to contemporary hostile commentary upon the Lollards, demonstrating that it tended to denote a disposition or action that was thought to contravene the received norms of the dominant culture, be that in a political, social or sexual sense.[22] Degeneracy was obviously an emotive theme in the kind of hierarchical social system to which the medieval elite aspired, and especially so in the fourteenth century, when the sense of stability was so threatened by disconcertingly violent economic and social change.[23] More specifically, and of more immediate relevance to the current discussion, it carried with it specifically gendered and sexualised connotations. Because of the patriarchal nature of the dominant culture, a failure to conform to 'kind' was sometimes observed or articulated as a decline from the masculine to the feminine: in other words, it was assumed that men who did not do what men ought to do were not, in fact, true men.[24] Furthermore, because of the deeply moralistic implications of degeneracy, it was inevitable that one 'proven' offence against the norm led to accusations of others: hence the associations that medieval culture tended to make between treason, tyranny, leprosy, heresy, sorcery and so on.[25] In particular, as Dinshaw and others have noted, there was a predisposi-

---

[22] Dinshaw, *Getting Medieval*, pp. 5–6, 8–9.

[23] The most stimulating contribution to our understanding of medieval (and modern) social theory and its application in fourteenth-century England is S. H. Rigby, *English Society in the Later Middle Ages: Class, Status and Gender* (Basingstoke, 1995).

[24] The point is pursued below. See also, as an example, some recent discussions of the martial role of the medieval knight as a perpetual (and sometimes traumatic) trial of his masculinity: S. Crane, *Gender and Romance in Chaucer's* Canterbury Tales (Princeton, 1994), pp. 16–54; M. Bennett, 'Military Masculinity in England and Northern France c. 1050–c. 1225', in *Masculinity in Medieval Europe*, ed. Hadley, pp. 71–88; K. C. Kelly, 'Menaced Masculinity and Imperiled Virginity in the *Morte Darthur*', in *Menacing Virgins: Representing Virginity in the Middle Ages and Renaissance*, ed. K. C. Kelly and M. Leslie (Newark, NJ, 1999), pp. 97–114; A. Taylor, 'Chivalric Conversation and the Denial of Male Fear', in *Conflicted Identities*, ed. Murray, pp. 179–88.

[25] R. I. Moore, *The Formation of a Persecuting Society: Power and Deviance in Western Europe, 950–1250* (Oxford, 1987); J. Richards, *Sex, Dissidence and Damnation: Minority Groups in the Middle Ages* (London, 1991), pp. 19–21, 59–62; V. L. Bullough, 'Postscript: Heresy, Witchcraft, and Sexuality', in *Sexual Practices and the Medieval Church*, ed. Bullough and Brundage, pp. 206–17; S. Kruger, 'Conversion and Medieval Sexual, Religious, and Racial Categories', in *Constructing Medieval Sexuality*, ed. Lochrie, McCracken and Schultz, pp. 158–79; Dinshaw, *Getting Medieval*, p. 6. The idea that the male favourite worked his influence over the king through the abuse of the magical arts may be of significance in this respect in implying a relationship between sorcery and sodomy. For the favourite as sorcerer, see W. R. Jones, 'The Political Uses of Sorcery in Medieval Europe', *The Historian* 34 (1971–2), 670–87; G. B. Stow, 'Richard II in Thomas Walsingham's Chronicles', *Speculum* 59 (1984), 71–102 (pp. 86–7), L. W. B. Brockliss, 'Concluding Remarks: The Anatomy of the Minister-Favourite', in *The World of the Favourite*, ed. Elliott and Brockliss, pp. 279–309 (pp. 290, 300). For accusations of the sorcery of Piers Gaveston see *AP*, p. 262.

tion to assume that what I am calling degeneracy was accompanied by, or manifested through, acts of sodomy: since sodomy was *the* 'sin against nature', it was a special marker of those whose other actions denoted their general defiance of the natural order.[26]

Let us now apply these ideas to the particular case of Edward II. One aspect of Edward's personality that has caused scholars special difficulty in this respect is the contemporary and near-contemporary comment on his 'love' for his male favourites, Piers Gaveston and Hugh Despenser the younger.[27] In general, and *pace* Boswell, it has been concluded that the comments of fourteenth-century chroniclers on these relationships ought not to be assumed to carry sexual innuendo: it has been argued many a time that those who criticised the king for his intimacy with these men did so not because they were embarrassed by the possibility of sexual impropriety but because they were deeply concerned about the *political* consequences of favouritism.[28] It is worth emphasising in this respect that there is really nothing in the fourteenth-century material to compare with the explicit eroticising of relationships between kings and their favourites found later, in the political discourses of the Renaissance – discourses which, through their own dramatic construction of a sodomitical relationship between Edward II and Gaveston, were in many respects more responsible than any medieval text for prevailing modern and postmodern assumptions about that king's homosexuality.[29] To argue, however, as Michael Prestwich does, that the absence of explicit references to the sexual dimension of the king's male friendships somehow proves that contemporaries did not make such allegations about

26 Dinshaw, *Getting Medieval*, pp. 3–12.
27 *AP*, p. 255; *Flores*, III, 146, 331; *Vita*, pp. 15, 113; *Lanercost*, p. 210; *JT*, p. 64; *AL*, p. 151; Haskins 'Chronicle', p. 75; *Murimuth*, p. 9.
28 Boswell, *Christianity, Social Tolerance, and Homosexuality*, pp. 298–300; Hamilton, *Piers Gaveston*, p. 13; A. Gransden, *Historical Writing in England*, 2 vols (London, 1974–82), II, 1–55, passim; Chaplais, *Piers Gaveston*, p. 7, 110–11; J. Taylor, *English Historical Literature in the Fourteenth Century* (Oxford, 1987), p. 125. Boswell's line is, however, supported by C. Sponsler, 'The King's Boyfriend: Froissart's Political Theater of 1326', in *Queering the Middle Ages*, ed. Burger and Kruger, pp. 143–67 (pp. 146–7); Zeikowitz, *Homoeroticism and Chivalry*, pp. 113–18.
29 L. L. Peck, 'Monopolizing Favour: Structures of Power in the Early Seventeenth-Century English Court', in *The World of the Favourite*, ed. Elliott and Brockliss, pp. 54–70 (pp. 62–5); B. Worden, 'Favourites on the English Stage', in *The World of the Favourite*, ed. Elliott and Brockliss, pp. 159–83; C. Perry, 'The Politics of Access and Representations of the Sodomite King in Early Modern England', *Renaissance Quarterly* 53 (2000), 1054–83; D. Clarke, ' "The sovereign's vice begets the subject's error": The Duke of Buckingham, "Sodomy" and Narratives of Edward II, 1622–28', in *Sodomy in Early Modern Europe*, ed. T. Betteridge (Manchester, 2002), pp. 46–64. For other attitudes to and representations of Edward II before gay liberation, see especially P. Horne, 'The Besotted King and his Adonis: Representations of Edward II and Gaveston in Late Nineteenth-Century England', *History Workshop Journal* 47 (1999), 31–48.

their king is to ignore both the issue of the 'unmentionability' of sodomy in medieval culture, discussed above, and the possibility that the king's relationships with men came to be read as part of a wider discourse of degeneracy.[30] I would suggest, then, that while the chroniclers who wrote in the king's lifetime followed no particular conscious strategy of sexual defamation in their articulations of Edward's friendships, those who followed them in the middle and later fourteenth century may have been more inclined to allow the possibility that the king's 'love' of his favourites was yet another element in his degenerate personality and thus to admit the possibility of a deviant sexual element to those relationships.

One of the most influential of the mid-century chroniclers, Ranulph Higden, might be argued to have implied just this association by drawing together in his memorable pen-portrait of Edward II both an extended comment on the king's penchant for the company of low-life and a severe criticism of his excessive love of favoured courtiers:

> King Edward was . . ., if common opinion is to be believed, most inconsistent in behaviour. For, shunning the company of nobles, he sought the society of jesters, singers, actors, carriage-drivers, diggers, oarsmen, sailors and the practitioners of other kinds of mechanical arts. He indulged in drink, betrayed confidences lightly, struck out at those standing near him for little reason and followed the counsel of others rather than his own. He was extravagant in his gifts, splendid in entertainment, ready in speech but inconsistent in action. He was unlucky against his enemies, violent with members of his household, and ardently loved one of his familiars, whom he sustained above all, enriched, preferred and honoured. From this obsession opprobrium came upon the lover and obloquy to the loved one; scandal was brought upon the people and the kingdom was damaged . . . In the beginning he loved Piers Gaveston . . . [and] because of him he disregarded Isabella, the queen, and paid no attention to the lords of the land . . .[31]

It is fairly obvious that much of this and similar fourteenth-century comment on Edward II's personality fits with the general theme of degeneracy. The idea that Edward enjoyed both the work and the company of manual labourers on land and water seems to have been quite widely circulated, and while it often reads as merely amusing – or 'eccentric' – to a modern audience, it clearly carried much more substantive connotations for contemporaries. When one of Edward's own staff commented in 1315 that no one could expect the king to win battles when he spent his time 'idling, and applying himself to making ditches and digging', the royal exchequer recognised a deeply subversive discourse at work, and formally charged the man with

---

[30] For Prestwich's argument see his article in this volume, pp. 61–75.
[31] *Polychronicon Ranulphi Higden*, VII, 298: translation modified and extended from Phillips, 'Reputation of a King', pp. 39–40.

speaking 'indecent words' (*verba indecencia*) – a striking phrase – against the king.[32] We can identify other parallel references to the idea of degeneracy as articulated by Higden: take, for example, the chronicler's comments on the royal pretender John of Powderham, whose credibility, it was said, was enhanced by Edward's own blatant inability to behave like the kingly Edward I; or see the reference in the articles of deposition of 1327 to the king as 'incorrigible, without hope of reform' ('il est trouve incorrigible sauntz esperaunce de amendement').[33] It is necessary here, however, to move beyond the general idea of Edward's apparently wilful disparagement of his own royal estate and to examine some of the more specific features of the contemporary character sketches of the king that may be said to have commented not merely about his derogation of royal dignity but also about the lack of, and threat to, traditional representations of masculinity. I suggest that this criticism of the king's deficiencies as a man did not in itself carry specific messages about his sexuality, but that the addition, from around the time of the deposition crisis, of the allegation of sodomy had the effect of incorporating into the generalised attack on Edward's loss or lack of manliness a more specific suggestion about his adoption of the submissive, feminised role in male–male sexual relationships.

One of the undesirable characteristics that were imputed to Edward II by Higden and others was his general tendency to immoderate indulgence in the sins of the flesh: Edward is cast in this discourse as lecherous, gluttonous, drunken and generally debauched.[34] Refusing to accept a commitment to a vigorous, self-controlled, moral and chaste way of life was obviously a form of degeneracy, an offence against the obligations of social and political status: according to John Gower, writing a couple of generations after Edward II in the *Vox Clamantis*, a man who submitted himself to lechery rendered himself 'ayein kinde' – metaphorically, as Gower put it, like a fish out of water.[35] Less obviously for modern readers, the biblical and classical repertoire also encouraged medieval culture to see the lecher as betraying gender norms by compromising his own masculinity. In its most extreme form, this idea played on the notion of the predatory Venus, trapping, seducing and then castrating her male prey: we find such an articulation, for example, in the

---

32 Johnstone, 'Eccentricities of Edward II'.
33 W. R. Childs, ' "Welcome, my Brother": Edward II, John of Powderham and the Chronicles, 1318', in *Church and Chronicle in the Middle Ages: Essays Presented to John Taylor*, ed. I. Wood and G. A. Loud (London, 1991), pp. 149–63; *Select Documents of English Constitutional History, 1307–1485*, ed. S. B. Chrimes and A. L. Brown (London, 1961), pp. 37–8; C. Valente, 'The Deposition and Abdication of Edward II', *EHR* 113 (1998), 852–81 (pp. 879–81). The cultural implications of the charge of 'incorrigibility' in the deposition articles of 1327 have yet to be pursued in a systematic way.
34 For further references and comment see: Johnstone, 'Eccentricities of Edward II'; Haines, *King Edward II*, pp. 35–41.
35 Hanrahan, 'Speaking of Sodomy', p. 434.

mid-fourteenth century text, *The Dispute between an Englishman and a Frenchman*, in which the wily women of France, the representatives of Venus, are said to deprive their menfolk (both literally and morally) of their manhood, turning them into mere 'capons'.[36] In a more moderate articulation of the idea, sometimes developed in explicit reference to biblical models such as those of David and Bathsheba or Samson and Delilah, too much involvement in love-making and lasciviousness was simply seen as a dangerous thing, sapping the male of his virility and exposing him to description in gendered terms as *enervatus* (feeble, unmanly) or *effeminatus* (feminine, effeminate).[37] 'Sett nought thyn hert in lecherie of women,' warned a late medieval English version of the *Secreta secretorum*, because this 'makith a man oft femynyne.'[38] Higden's comment that Edward II was 'ready in speech but inconsistent in action' clearly chimes with this idea of effeminisation: it can be equated, for example, with Thomas of Walsingham's famous statement that Richard II's indolent courtiers – the 'knights of Venus' – were better able to defend themselves with their tongues than with their lances.[39] To argue that a text such as Higden constructed Edward II as a voluptuary is thus to suggest that contemporary culture imagined him as having distinct *feminised* attributes which impacted directly on his capacity to do the job of king: the *rex effeminatus*, if one can venture such a concept, is in some ways as self-

36 *Political Poems and Songs Relating to English History*, ed. T. Wright, 2 vols (London, 1859–61), I, 91–3, translated in *The Poems of Laurence Minot, 1333–1352*, ed. T. B. James and J. Simons (Exeter, 1989), pp. 97–9. For comment on this text, see T. Beaumont James, 'John of Eltham, History and Story: Abusive International Discourse in Late Medieval England, France and Scotland', in *Fourteenth Century England II*, ed. C. Given-Wilson (Woodbridge, 2002), pp. 63–80 (p. 64); R. F. Green, 'Further Evidence for Chaucer's Representation of the Pardoner as a Womanizer', *Medium Ævum* 71 (2002), 307–9. For the threat to masculinity posed by medieval understandings of the Venus myth, see the following discussions of the *Roman de la Rose*: S. Kay, 'Venus in the *Roman de la Rose*', *Exemplaria* 9 (1997), 7–37; D. Hult, 'Language and Dismemberment: Abelard, Origen, and the *Romance of the Rose*', in *Rethinking the 'Romance of the Rose': Text, Image, Reception*, ed. K. Brownlee and S. Huot (Philadelphia, 1992), pp. 101–30; A. Minnis, Magister amoris: *The* Roman de la Rose *and Vernacular Hermeneutics* (Oxford, 2001), pp. 165–73, 206 and n. 115.

37 Green, 'Further Evidence', pp. 307–9; W. M. Ormrod, 'Knights of Venus', *Medium Ævum* 73 (2004), 290–305 (p. 295). See the interesting medieval comment on 'excessive coitus' and its deleterious impact ('it weakens the members . . . [and] effeminises the sperm'), in F. Getz, *Medicine in the English Middle Ages* (Princeton, 1998), p. 63 (where, in translation, the verb *enervare* is mistakenly takes to mean 'to enervate' rather than 'to weaken'). I owe this last reference to Katherine Lewis.

38 *Three Prose Versions of the Secreta Secretorum*, ed. R. Steele, EETS ES 74 (London, 1898), p. 14, cited by K. J. Lewis, 'Edmund of East Anglia, Henry VI and Ideals of Kingly Masculinity', in *Holiness and Masculinity in the Middle Ages*, ed. P. H. Cullum and K. J. Lewis (Cardiff, 2004), pp. 158–73 (p. 167).

39 *The St Albans Chronicle: The* Chronica maiora *of Thomas Walsingham*, I: *1376–1394*, ed. J. Taylor, W. R. Childs and L. Watkiss (Oxford, 2003), pp. 814. For discussion of the gender implications of this text see Ormrod, 'Knights of Venus'.

contradictory as is that medieval type more often recognised in Edward II, the *rex inutilis*.[40]

What such a label does not do, however, is to make any direct imputation about deviant *sexuality*: as the references cited above suggest, indeed, the offence against gender norms implicit in the idea of the male's indulgence in lechery could exist within a set of assumptions about sex and sexuality that were entirely heteronormative. Medieval culture did not make the same associations between effeminacy and homosexuality that are contained in modern stereotypes of the camp male: to pick up again on the current debates about Chaucer's Pardoner, we may note that Richard Firth Green has challenged a quarter of a century's queering of this Canterbury pilgrim by arguing that he is a representation of a recognisable medieval type, the 'effeminizing heterosexual'.[41] To cast Edward II as *rex effeminatus* is not, then, necessarily to 'out' him. However, the gendered attributes discerned in these descriptions of the degenerate king also raise interesting possibilities about the degree to which fourteenth-century writers and their audiences related Edward's delight in debauchery with the most obvious and potent biblical reference to excess and sexual deviancy in the story of Sodom and Gomorrah (Genesis 18–19).[42] What follows represents an attempt to link the emergence of explicit references to Edward as 'sodomite' both with a generalised medieval notion of lechery and with the more specific notion of sodomy as an act of male–male anal intercourse. My argument is that, while the early references to Edward's 'sodomitical acts' may well be simply another way of articulating his general inclination to the sins of the flesh, the development, at least from the time of the deposition, of a more specific set of allusions to his participation in same-sex relationships made it possible for contemporaries – at least, those so disposed to do so – to read the king's sodomy as the specific offence of penetrative sex with male partners.

It has long been argued that sodomy is a kind of red herring in the political and sexual history of Edward II, partly because any specific reference to it

---

40 For the *rex inutilis* see J. S. Roskell, *Parliament and Politics in Late Medieval England*, 3 vols (London, 1981–3), I, chap. 1, p. 3; E. Peters, *The Shadow King: Rex* inutilis *in Medieval Law and Literature, 751–1327* (New Haven, 1970).

41 Green, 'The Sexual Normality of Chaucer's Pardoner'; Green, 'Further Evidence'. Modernist notions of 'camp' drew on Freudian representations of homosexual desire as a search for a feminine personality in a male body: for this, and the (generally hostile) reaction of queer theorists and activists in the late twentieth century, see C.-A. Tyler, 'Boys Will Be Girls: The Politics of Gay Drag', in *Inside/Out: Lesbian Theories, Gay Theories*, ed. D. Fuss (London, 1991), pp. 32–70 (pp. 34–7).

42 For discussion of the medieval understanding of sexual abuse supposedly committed by the men of Sodom against the angels in Genesis 19.5, see Boswell, *Christianity, Social Tolerance, and Homosexuality*, pp. 91–117; J. A. Brundage, *Law, Sex and Christian Society in Medieval Europe* (Chicago, 1987), pp. 57, 533–4; Hergemöller, *Sodom and Gomorrah*, p. 8.

comes supposedly well after the king's death and partly because the ambiguities of the word itself make it unclear whether it was being applied to homosexual intercourse or as a generalised term of abuse.[43] I want to take a rather different approach. First, on the matter of chronology: it is true – and, I believe significant – that the explicit charge of sodomy comes later than the observable traditions about Edward's degenerate character outlined above. But they are not so late as some would have us believe. As Roy Martin Haines has recently reminded us, Bishop Adam Orleton was accused in 1334 of inciting Edward II's deposition by denouncing the former king eight years earlier as 'a tyrant and a sodomite'.[44] It is quite possible, indeed, as Ian Mortimer suggests in his contribution to this volume, that the entire idea of Edward as sodomite grew from the organised dissemination of Orleton's sermon and thus stands as an interesting example of the propaganda put out by the supporters of Queen Isabella and Roger Mortimer during the deposition crisis of 1326–7.[45] However, I am inclined to suggest that, whereas Orleton may well have been drawing on a legalistic and high-political tradition in making an equation between political and sexual offence (as, indeed, Adam Usk was to do seventy years later in charging Richard II with sodomy), there also existed – even possibly *before* the deposition – some kind of informal, oral tradition about Edward's sodomy that drew on a set of deep-seated cultural assumptions about degeneracy and its implications about deviancy from both gender and sexual norms.[46] Either way, the comparative slowness with which the charge of sodomy was taken up in formal historical writing is surely explicable in terms of the chroniclers' embarrassment (and often necessary obliqueness) in dealing with this 'unmentionable' offence. In short, there is no particular reason to dismiss the charge of sodomy (in whatever context the word was used) as one that came only late, as a kind of afterthought, to the wider debate on Edward II's personality.

Secondly, of course, there is the vexed question of what this charge of 'sodomy' actually meant. Scholars writing from both straight and queer perspectives have often emphasised that no simple equation can be drawn between sodomy and what we call homosexuality: sodomy was a category of sin (and crime) that encompassed many forms of non-procreative sexual practices between men and women as well as between members of the same sex.[47] The same problem applies to the term *luxuria*, a word often used as seemingly

---

[43] Zeikowitz, *Homoeroticism and Chivalry*, pp. 113–18, argues that accusations of sodomy are a distinctive part of the *late* fourteenth-century writing about Edward II.

[44] Haines, *King Edward II*, p. 42.

[45] See below, pp. 48–60.

[46] For Usk's comment on Richard II see *The Chronicle of Adam Usk, 1377–1421*, ed. C. Given-Wilson (Oxford, 1997), pp. 62–3.

[47] For important discussions of the meaning, and law, of sodomy, see: Brundage, *Law, Sex, and Christian Society*; Goldberg, *Sodometries*, pp. 1–26; Jordan, *Invention of Sodomy*. For the association between sodomy and homosexuality, see variously:

synonymous with sodomy in medieval texts, and which has been elucidated again to denote both a generalised indulgence in the sins of the flesh and the specific act of *coitus masculorum* (male–male anal penetrative sex).[48] Many historians appear to take refuge in this convenient ambiguity as a justification for denying the existence of any positive references to Edward II's homosexuality in fourteenth-century texts.[49] But this is to refuse the possibility, offered by gay theory, of distinguishing between the general and the specific and identifying places where the words sodomy and sodomite can be legitimately applied in precise reference to sex between men.[50] From what has already been said above about the absence of explicitly sexualised connotations in the theme of Edward II's 'love' for his favourites, it should be evident that I am not arguing for a particular predisposition on the part of fourteenth-century English culture to suppose that affective relationships between men were eroticised or, indeed, sexually consummated. However, I do now go on to argue that the knowledge of Edward's very public friendships with Gaveston and (perhaps more particularly) Hugh Despenser the younger, coupled with the general accusation of sodomy current from around the time of the deposition crisis, generated a set of assumptions about the king's sexual practices that were articulated in the narrative of the deposed king's demise at Berkeley in 1327.

If there is one thing that everyone 'knows' about Edward II, it is the gruesome tale of his murder: namely, that his tormentors held him, face-down, on a table and pushed a funnel into his anus, through which they inserted a heated metal rod that was pushed up through his body and twisted around until he collapsed and died. Recently, both Ian Mortimer and Michael Evans, in important discussions of the development of this narrative tradition, have

---

Boswell, *Christianity, Social Tolerance, and Homosexuality*, pp. 328–9; V. L. Bullough, 'The Sin Against Nature and Homosexuality', in *Sexual Practices and the Medieval Church*, ed. V. L. Bullough and J. Brundage (Buffalo, NY, 1982), pp. 55–71.

48 M. D. Jordan, 'Homosexuality, *Luxuria*, and Textual Abuse', in *Constructing Medieval Sexuality*, ed. Lochrie, McCracken and Schultz, pp. 24–39. The importance of the theme of *luxuria* in political rhetoric about Edward III's personal morality around the time of the Good Parliament of 1376 has been productively explored by C. Fletcher, 'Problems of Inconstancy: Morality and Politics in 1370s England', unpublished paper, International Medieval Congress, Leeds, July 2004.

49 Most emphatically in recent scholarship, Chaplais, *Piers Gaveston*, passim. See also M. Prestwich in this volume, pp. 61–75.

50 I have found discussion of the references to sodomy in the late fourteenth century poem *Cleanness* to be especially helpful in this respect: A. J. Frantzen, 'The Discourse of Sodomy in *Cleanness*', *Publications of the Modern Language Association of America* 111 (1996), 451–64; E. B. Keiser, *Courtly Desire and Medieval Homophobia: The Legitimation of Sexual Pleasure in* Cleanness *and its Contexts* (New Haven, 1997), pp. 150, 226. See also, in other contexts: Camille, 'Pose of the Queer', p. 63; Dinshaw, *Getting Medieval*, pp. 7–8 (though in this case noting that the precise form of the same-sex intercourse can be vague).

concluded that the red-hot poker story first emerged from an anti-establishment account circulated, either as a piece of anti-Edwardian propaganda or through popular (and pro-insurrectionist) rumour, in the immediate aftermath of the king's assumed death and burial.[51] In his contribution to this volume, Mortimer reconsiders this material and emphasises the comparative slowness with which this account established supremacy over other competing narratives of the events at Berkeley.[52] My aim here is not to suggest that what I define as an anal rape narrative was either the only or (in terms of written texts) the authoritative version of the events – though Mortimer's emphasis on propaganda raises important and useful questions about the degree to which this most subversive of the accounts of the king's death may itself have been disseminated by his political enemies and usurpers. Instead, I wish to emphasise the very explicit sexual and gender connotations of the narrative, suggesting that it reveals much about the way that generalised assumptions about Edward II's degeneracy, 'tyranny' and 'sodomy' were translated, in the generation after his deposition, into explicit references to his indulgence in same-sex relations.

There are, of course, plenty of explanations as to why such a bizarre method of torture and murder may have been chosen for Edward II, either by its perpetrators or by those who imagined and wrote up the scenes of the king's demise at Berkeley. The chroniclers themselves often make the point that killing the king by means of fatal injury to the internal organs left the body outwardly unmarked, so that his death could be passed off as occurring from natural causes.[53] On the other hand, there are many other, rather more obvious, methods – suffocation and poisoning, for example – that might have been applied or thought up. Even though many scholars have been inclined to admit that the narrative has a sexual connotation, there has been surprisingly little attempt to explore systematically what particular gendered meanings the text may carry. This seems to me to be one of those places where the queering of a text allows us to expose a necessarily implicit sexual discourse and to see very clearly a treatment of the sin of sodomy that is not generalised but specific, focused on the practice of *coitus masculorum*.[54] The anal rape narrative plays on a tradition of (heterosexual) male paranoia about the physical pain and psychological trauma supposedly arising from penetration

---

[51] M. Evans, *The Death of Kings: Royal Deaths in Medieval England* (London, 2003), pp. 119–46 (who favours the idea of rumour); I. Mortimer, *The Greatest Traitor: The Life of Sir Roger Mortimer, 1st Earl of March, Ruler of England, 1327–1330* (London, 2003), pp. 185–95 (who favours the idea of 'propaganda').

[52] See below, pp. 48–60.

[53] For a useful discussion of the circumstances see P. Lindley, *Gothic to Renaissance: Essays on Sculpture in England* (Stamford, 1995), pp. 97–112.

[54] Here I follow the lead, most obviously, of Boswell, *Christianity, Social Tolerance, and Homosexuality*, pp. 298–300.

(penile or other) of the back passage.[55] It can thus be read not only as a piece of heteronormative triumphalism (the sodomite getting his just deserts) but also as a vivid and unsettling representation of the assumed sado-masochistic qualities of homosexuality. If the disturbing eroticism of the murder story is acknowledged, and if the narrative is taken in itself as the articulation of a contemporary discourse about Edward II's sexuality, then it is no longer necessary or valid to hide behind the suggestion that the general charge of sodomy made against Edward II at and after his deposition did not include or imply his participation in male–male penetrative sex.

Furthermore, I would emphasise that the anal rape effectively committed upon the king's body in the Berkeley Castle story significantly casts Edward not as sodomiser but as sodom*ised*. Whereas the tradition of the king's 'love' for his favourites (which I have stressed was not necessarily explicitly eroti-cised in fourteenth-century texts) often casts Edward as the active lover, with the courtier-favourite as the object of infatuation (as, for example, in the passage from Higden quoted above), the anal rape narrative places the king in a submissive role as (unwilling – or willing?) recipient of sexual domina-tion. The possibility that the red-hot poker story carried connotations of the king's subjection to the sexual authority of others provides one context in which to read the later account of the violent death at Hereford in 1326 of Hugh Despenser the younger: according to Jean le Bel (and, via him, Froissart), Despenser's genitals were cut off because 'he was a heretic and a sodomite, even, it was said, with the king'.[56] If the traditions about these two executions are read as complementary (and that is admittedly a big 'if', given the absence of strictly contemporary English references to Despenser's sodomy), then it is possible to suggest that, within the context of the deposi-tion and death of Edward II, propagandists and/or rumour-mongers began to construct the political relationship of king and favourite in the sexualised imagery of a meeting between Hugh's genitals and Edward's anus. This would have arguably been the most subversive of all the possible representa-tions of the king's assumed sexual deviancy. Since medieval culture regarded same-sex intercourse as a depraved version of the heterosexual equivalent, it tended to assume that the parties took up unequal gendered roles, one active, dominant and masculinised, the other passive, submissive and femininised:

---

55 For a historicised discussion of this issue, which extends also into the use of sodomy as a metaphor of social and political discord, see L. Endelman, 'Seeing Things: Repre-sentation, the Scene of Surveillance, and the Spectacle of Gay Male Sex', in *Inside/Out*, ed. Fuss, pp. 93–116.

56 *Chroniques de Jean Froissart*, I, ed. S. Luce (Paris, 1869), p. 34, discussed by Sponsler, 'The King's Boyfriend'. Froissart's dependence on Jean le Bel for this (as for so much else of the early sections of his chronicles) is missed by Sponsler, and has been pointed out to me by Danielle Westerhof, whose University of York Ph.D. thesis also explores other possible meanings of castration within the context of the execution of traitors.

postmodern gay culture appropriates and subverts these stereotypes as 'top' and 'bottom'.[57] The gendering of roles in reference to same-sex relationships during the Middle Ages is especially apparent in the notion that the passive partner was, symbolically or actually, castrated: witness (again) Chaucer's Pardoner, back in the queer reading of the character, who is famously described as 'a gelding or a mare', and who sings falsetto to the ground bass of his assumed 'top', the Summoner. In cases where this kind of role-play was compatible with the partners' relative social status, age and degree of sexual experience, medieval culture sometimes actually found it possible to condone homosexual relationships.[58] By the same token, we can assume that contemporary comment would have found it even more than usually abhorrent to consider the idea of sodomy in relation to a king who imperilled and disparaged his office by making himself the mere catamite of an ambitious courtier. I therefore suggest that a gendered reading of the theme of degeneracy, and of the specific implications of the charge of sodomy, can tell us much about the wider context in which near-contemporary political culture articulated the failure of Edward II's kingship and justified his forcible removal from the throne.

*

The second part of this study considers the manner and significance of the depictions of Edward II's relationship with his wife, Queen Isabella, in political discourse particularly of the second quarter of the fourteenth century. The treatment of these depictions, and their explicit tension with the king's 'queer' relationships as outlined above, has been little discussed by political historians. Only Sophie Menache and Claire Sponsler have provided gendered readings of the relevant sources, and this mainly in relation to those chronicles that attempt to excuse Isabella's actions against her husband.[59] The present study, by contrast, traces the development of a more fraught, and hostile, sense of the queen's role in the politics of the late 1320s. My argument is that the insinuation of Edward II's queerness in the subversive political debate of the 1320s caused the crown to assert the king's 'straightness'

[57] M. Rocke, *Forbidden Friendships: Homosexuality and Male Culture in Renaissance Florence* (Oxford, 1996), pp. 87–111, explores the stereotyping of male-male relationships. See also: Cadden, *Meanings of Sex Difference*, pp. 214–16; G. P. J. Epp, 'The Vicious Guise: Effeminacy, Sodomy, and *Mankind*', in *Becoming Male in the Middle Ages*, ed. J. J. Cohen and B. Wheeler (New York, 1997), pp. 303–20. For the impact of gay liberation on the re-casting of 'sex roles', see T. Carrigan, B. Connell and J. Lee, 'Toward a New Sociology of Masculinity', in *The Masculinity Studies Reader*, ed. R. Adams and D. Savran (Oxford, 2002), pp. 99–118.
[58] G. Ruggiero, *The Boundaries of Eros: Sex Crimes and Sexuality in Renaissance Florence* (Oxford, 1985), pp. 109–45.
[59] S. Menache, 'Isabella of France, Queen of England: A Reconsideration', *Journal of Medieval History* 10 (1984), 107–24; Sponsler, 'The King's Boyfriend'.

through a series of public representations of his marriage, in which the dereliction of heteronormative behaviour was ascribed not to Edward himself but to his queen and to her lover, Roger Mortimer. The particular significance of this debate lies in the fact that it seems to have been picked up and developed after the assumption of personal rule by the royal couple's son in 1330 as a means of rehabilitating the wronged Edward II and re-establishing normalised gender roles in the court of Edward III.

Between the autumn of 1325 and the spring of 1326, Edward II and Queen Isabella chose to 'go public' about their estrangement. The body of correspondence and reports of oral exchanges (some of it surviving in the English royal archive, some preserved in the chronicles) variously between Edward, Isabella, Charles IV of France, the pope, and the English and French episcopates, suggests that the royal couple had become not only significantly more vitriolic in their attacks on each other but also much more readily inclined to make direct political capital out of their domestic disagreements and private grievances.[60] Specifically, this material demonstrates that Edward was prepared, by early in 1326, publicly to admit his wife's adultery with Mortimer: the resulting breakdown of their marriage is made especially clear in the king's letter of March 1326 to Isabella's brother and host, Charles IV, in which Edward beseeches the king of France to assist him in securing the return of the queen and their eldest son and to respond to mutual masculine logic, 'according to reason, good faith and fraternal affection, *without having regard to the wilful pleasure of woman*'.[61] In one sense, the gendered nature of this dispute weighted the argument strongly in Edward's favour, especially after the liaison between Isabella and Roger Mortimer became public knowledge around Christmas 1325: in strictly legal terms it was the queen, not the king, who had formally betrayed the marriage by committing adultery, and Edward was perhaps hoping to play on the neurosis of the French court, which had recently undergone a series of adultery scandals, in calling his errant wife to order.[62] Yet the very fact that Isabella and Mortimer were able

---

60 *Foedera*, II², 148–52, passim; *CCR 1323–7*, pp. 576–82; F. D. Blackley, 'Isabella and the Bishop of Exeter', in *Essays in Medieval History Presented to Bertie Wilkinson*, ed. M. R. Powicke and T. A. Sanquist (Toronto, 1967), pp. 220–35; *Vita*, p. 143; *The French Chronicle of London*, ed. C. J. Aungier, Camden old ser. 28 (London, 1844), p. 49; and references to unpublished chronicles in Haines, *King Edward II*, pp. 168–76. For comment, see R. M. Haines, *Archbishop John Stratford, Political Revolutionary and Champion of the Liberties of the English Church ca. 1275/80–1348* (Toronto, 1986), pp. 161–70; Haines, *King Edward II*, pp. 168–76.

61 *CCR 1323–7*, p. 579 (italics mine).

62 C. T. Wood, *Joan of Arc and Richard III: Sex, Saints and Government in the Middle Ages* (Oxford, 1988), pp. 12–28. The idea that Isabella herself had uncovered and exposed these scandals is reconsidered by E. A. R. Brown, 'Diplomacy, Adultery and Domestic Politics at the Court of Philip the Fair: Queen Isabelle's Mission to France in 1314', in *Documenting the Past: Essays in Medieval History Presented to G. P. Cuttino*, ed. J. S. Hamilton and P. J. Bradley (Woodbridge, 1989), pp. 53–83. Note the rumour of

to find so much support in so many quarters on their subsequent invasion of England, later in 1326, proves very dramatically that moral absolutes did not in themselves determine political action. Isabella's own line of argument followed two strands: first, that she could not reasonably be expected to return to her husband because of the threat of physical violence (an allegation that carried serious implications for the sustainability of the marriage and thus condoned the queen's violation of her wifely duties); and secondly, that the royal marriage had been disrupted not by her own liaison with Mortimer but by the earlier actions of Hugh Despenser, who had sown discord between the king and queen.[63] To this we may tentatively add a third strand, based in the evidence summarised earlier, and which suggests that both the deposition and the death of the discredited Edward II were constructed in pro-Isabella propaganda as due punishment for the former king's indulgence in the vice of sodomy.[64]

The representation of Edward as one wilfully at odds with the laws of nature would undoubtedly have gone a long way to providing the moral justification for Isabella's own very public contravention of gender norms in seizing power during the winter of 1326–7. Like Eleanor of Aquitaine in her marital defiance of Louis VII of France, Isabella justified both her adultery and her political actions by casting doubt on the heteronormativity of her marriage and, *in extremis*, asserting a defiant, independent, *masculinised* role: she became, in Natalie Zemon Davis's famous phrase, a 'woman on top'.[65] Ironically, this very metaphorical position may have served to confirm her husband's own emasculation: like the men of France satirised in *The Dispute between an Englishman and a Frenchman*, the abject, deposed king suffered a kind of castration by falling subject to the domination of his wife. Subsequent chroniclers sympathetic to Isabella's predicament at the time of the deposition were to condone her actions and normalise her gender role by shifting attention from her position as wife of the old king to her responsibilities as

---

Edward II's own supposed adultery with Eleanor de Clare, wife of the younger Despenser (Haines, *King Edward II*, pp. 42–3), whose public construction could be read as some form of pro-Isabellian equalisation of the offences of king and queen.

[63] Mortimer, *The Greatest Traitor*, pp. 140–7.

[64] For the evidence and role of pro-Isabellian or 'Lancastrian' propaganda in the events of 1327, see Gransden, *Historical Writing*, II, 17–19; Taylor, *English Historical Literature*, p. 124; Mortimer, *The Greatest Traitor*, pp. 185–95; Valente, 'The "Lament of Edward II" ', p. 429.

[65] For Eleanor's adultery see: J. C. Parsons, 'Damned if She Didn't and Damned When She Did: Bodies, Babies, and Bastards in the Lives of two Queens of France', in *Eleanor of Aquitaine: Lord and Lady*, ed. B. Wheeler and J. C. Parsons (Basingstoke, 2002), pp. 265–99 (p. 283); T. F. O'Callaghan, 'Tempering Scandal: Benoît de Sainte-Maure's Roman de Troie', in *Eleanor of Aquitaine*, ed. Wheeler and Parsons, pp. 301–17. For 'women on top' see: N. Zemon Davis, 'Women on Top: Symbolic Sexual Inversion and Political Disorder in Early Modern Europe', in *The Reversible World: Symbolic Inversion in Art and Society*, ed. B. Babcock (London, 1978), pp. 147–90.

mother of the new one.[66] But those who witnessed and experienced the harsher realities of the queen mother's regime in the period between the deposition crisis and Edward III's Nottingham coup of 1330 may well have found it rather difficult to come to terms with the view of Isabella as a kind of Marian figure sacrificing all to support her son. It is the suggestion of this study that the 'official' construction of the events of 1326–30 that emerged after Edward III's own seizure of power aimed directly to counter the insinuations of Edward II's degeneracy and sodomy made by Isabella's party in the winter of 1326–7 and to re-assert the public position initially adopted by both king and queen in 1325–6 by commemorating their relationship as a functioning marriage disrupted only by the unwelcome intervention of third parties. The assertion of such an official line has been little remarked because it is usually assumed that Edward III preferred simply to forget the embarrassing events of 1326–7.[67] The argument that follows suggests that he and some of his contemporaries made much more active and conscious efforts to 're-brand' the personal reputation of Edward II, and in this way aimed deliberately to counter the subversive, 'queer' defamations of the king that had circulated during and after the deposition.[68]

One important element in this creative re-writing of the history of his parents' marriage is to be found in Edward III's treatment of his father's mortal remains and memory. Just because Edward III did not petition the pope for the canonisation of Edward II does not mean that he did not subscribe to the notion of his father's status as a political martyr: there is plenty of evidence to show that Edward III and his family formally honoured the memory of the deceased king and were publicly supportive of Gloucester Abbey's active management of the cult of Edward of Caernarfon.[69] I have suggested elsewhere that the theme of martyrdom was an important element in the historical justification of political failure within the English royal family in the later Middle Ages, and that Edward II's posthumous status as a political martyr was a necessary and important part of his own son's re-assertion of the essential maleness of monarchy after the disruption to gender norms during Queen Isabella's usurpation of royal sovereignty.[70] To

---

66 Menache, 'Isabella of France'; Sponsler, 'The King's Boyfriend'.

67 This is the line that I have previously taken on the subject: W. M. Ormrod, *The Reign of Edward III: Crown and Political Society in England, 1327–1377* (London, 1990), pp. 7, 46, 158–9. See also Valente, 'The "Lament of Edward II" ', p. 434.

68 This subject has previously been confined mainly to discussions of the development of chronicle accounts during the reign of Edward III that showed sympathy for the predicament and 'martyrdom' of Edward II. See Gransden, *Historical Writing*, II, 37–42; Taylor, *English Historical Literature*, pp. 27–8, 125–6.

69 For Edward III's patronage of the cult see W. M. Ormrod, 'The Personal Religion of Edward III', *Speculum* 64 (1989), 849–77 (pp. 870–1).

70 W. M. Ormrod, 'Monarchy, Martyrdom and Masculinity: England in the Later Middle Ages', in *Holiness and Masculinity*, ed. Cullum and Lewis, pp. 174–91.

some extent, indeed, Edward III may actually have been prepared to tolerate the popular demonising of his mother as a necessary element of his father's (and his own) rehabilitation. This is the clear inference of the pro-establishment account of the old king's death as told by Geoffrey le Baker in the middle of the fourteenth century. Here, the detailed account of the king's torture and murder – including the detail of the red-hot poker – is trans-formed into a scene reminiscent of the treatment of martyrdom in a medieval saint's life. The villains of this piece are not merely the king's gaolers and murderers: the greatest offence is that of the queen herself, in consigning her husband to such a terrible fate. For Baker, then, Isabella was Jezebel: his narrative fixed a course for a powerful and enduring tradition that con-structed the queen not as heroine but as traitor.[71] While Edward III never, of course, publicly humiliated or punished his mother for the events of 1326–30, a focus on the politics of gender provides some new perspectives on his treat-ment of the dowager queen, and his own management of that history, during the long period between the fall of Mortimer in 1330 and Isabella's own death in 1358.

The crucial text of this royalist re-writing of history is provided by the accusations of treason brought against Roger Mortimer by Edward III's government in the parliament following the Nottingham coup of 1330. The long list of offences recorded on the parliament roll for this session includes the charge that Mortimer had set discord between Edward II and Queen Isabella.[72] The suggestion that the royal marriage had been confounded by the interference of third parties, used by Isabella's party against Hugh Despenser the younger in 1326, was now being appropriated by Edward III as a means of explaining and condoning the uncomfortable circumstances of his own accession. The text further implies that Mortimer had in fact retained Isabella against her will, by persuading her that she stood in danger of her own life if she returned to her husband. A gendered reading of this text allows us to discern the careful reconstruction of past events that was taking place in the regime of the newly independent Edward III. Mortimer's trial was not merely a convenient means of establishing a scapegoat for the misfortunes and evils that had arisen during and since the deposition crisis. It

---

[71] *Geoffrey le Baker*, p. 33. For comment see Mortimer, *The Greatest Traitor*, pp. 191–4. For the theme of the queen as Jezebel, see also N. Vincent, 'Isabella of Angoulême: John's Jezebel', in *King John: New Interpretations*, ed. S. D. Church (Woodbridge, 1999), pp. 165–219.

[72] *RP*, II, 52–3. It is interesting that precisely the same motif cropped up yet again in 1334 in the hostile account of Adam Orleton's involvement in the deposition, which represented the bishop himself as having caused enmity between Edward II and Queen Isabella. See Orleton's response in *Historiae Anglicanae scriptores decem*, ed. R. Twysden (London 1652), pp. 300–6, discussed by R. M. Haines, *The Church and Politics in Fourteenth-Century England: The Career of Adam Orleton c. 1275–1345* (Cambridge, 1978), pp. 165, 176, 189.

was also a way of confounding Isabella's contravention of gender norms. To suggest, as was now done in 1330, that Mortimer had prevented a reconciliation between the royal partners was to ascribe to *him* the dominant role in the adulterous affair and to suggest that Isabella was merely a submissive instrument of his own treason – in other words, to normalise her gender role by casting her as the submissive, feminised victim of a nobleman's unquenchable thirst for power.

It is in the context of this official emphasis on Isabella's subordinate role in the minority regime that we may finally discern some of the longer-term strategies of gender normalisation worked through by Edward III between 1330 and Isabella's death in 1358. Modern scholarship has been anxious to confound the false tradition of Isabella's imprisonment at Castle Rising by emphasising that her son treated her with all the dignity that a dowager queen might expect – particularly one who, as a princess of France, continued occasionally to play a role in the processes of diplomacy between the Plantagenet and Valois courts.[73] This is not to say, however, that Isabella's status as queen mother was not carefully proscribed. Claire Valente has recently pointed to the possibility (and it can only be a possibility, given the lack of a clear provenance) that the poem known as *The Lament of Edward II* was written at the court of Edward III as a kind of admonition to Isabella to accept her subordinate status following the coup of 1330: if this is the case, then the representation of the deceased king in the poem as what Valente calls a 'heterosexual courtly lover' would surely have had particular (and perhaps bitter) resonance.[74] The crucial evidence in respect of Edward III's construction of his mother as loyal and contrite wife, however, is provided by the well-documented details of the queen's devotion to a life of personal piety.[75] There are special features of her own regime, especially those connected with her burial and tomb, which suggest that she, either at her own and her confessors' instigation or, as I am suggesting here, under the direction of her son, used the sacramental repertoire of widowhood to provide some form of expiation for her earlier offences against her royal husband.[76] On her death in 1358, Isabella was buried at the Franciscan

---

73 H. Johnstone, 'Isabella, the She-Wolf of France', *History* 21 (1936), 208–18 (p. 213); M. McKisack, *The Fourteenth Century* (Oxford, 1959), p. 102; J. Vale, *Edward III and Chivalry: Chivalric Society and its Contexts, 1270–1350* (Woodbridge, 1982), p. 50; M. Bennett, 'Isabelle of France, Anglo-French Diplomacy and Cultural Exchange in the Late 1350s', in *The Age of Edward III*, ed. J. S. Bothwell (York, 2001), pp. 215–25.

74 Valente, 'The "Lament of Edward II" ', pp. 432, 434.

75 F. D. Blackley, 'Isabella of France, Queen of England (1308–1358) and the Late Medieval Cult of the Dead', *Canadian Journal of History* 15 (1980), 23–47; Vale, *Edward III and Chivalry*, p. 52; Ormrod, 'Personal Religion', p. 856.

76 Isabella's acknowledged strong devotion to Franciscan modes of piety is frequently acknowledged but the possibility that she adopted the habit of the Poor Clares, became a Franciscan tertiary or observed the life of a vowess have been compara-

convent in London, reputedly dressed in the clothes that she had worn at her wedding half a century earlier, and with the eviscerated heart of her husband interred under the breast of her effigy.[77] If these notable details are correct, then they suggest some very conscious management of gender roles within the royal family – roles that were now being comfortingly normalised, of course, in the public representation of the functional marriage between Edward III and Philippa of Hainault.[78] The emerging courtly 'line' on Isabella's role in the events of 1325–30 was therefore predicated on Roger Mortimer's intrusion into a fictitiously stable royal marriage, on Mortimer's usurpation of the sovereignty that Isabella had sought to invest in her son, and on the symbolic reconciliation worked out between the deceased king and his repentant and submissive widow.

*

In this study, I have tried to move away from the positivist testing of fourteenth-century accounts of Edward II's eccentric social and sexual behaviour and instead to read these accounts as the means by which hostile commentators 'queered' the king, setting him at variance to the dominant contemporary ideologies of kingship, politics, courtliness and gender. I have attempted to suggest that both Edward II and Edward III responded defensively to this subversive strategy by reconstructing gender roles within the royal family in terms that variously criticised and condoned Queen Isabella's betrayal of her marriage bonds and, in particular, re-asserted the threatened masculinity of Edward II and the functionality of his marriage. Those whose

tively little remarked. See McKisack, *Fourteenth Century*, p. 102; Vale, *Edward III and Chivalry*, p. 52.

[77] Blackley, 'Isabella of France', pp. 30–2; F. D. Blackley, 'The Tomb of Isabella of France, Wife of Edward II of England', *International Society for the Study of Church Monuments Bulletin* 8 (1983), 161–4; J. C. Parsons, ' "Never Was a Body Buried in England with Such Solemnity and Honour": The Burials and Posthumous Commemorations of English Queens to 1500', in *Queens and Queenship in Medieval Europe*, ed. A. Duggan (Woodbridge, 1997), pp. 317–37 (pp. 323, 329–30); J. Burden, 'Re-writing a Rite of Passage: The Peculiar Funeral of Edward II', in *Rites of Passage: Cultures of Transition in the Fourteenth Century*, ed. N. F. McDonald and W. M. Ormrod (York, 2004), pp. 13–30 (p. 16).

[78] For normative representations of Philippa's queenship, see W. M. Ormrod, 'Edward III and his Family', *Journal of British Studies* 26 (1987), 398–422 (esp. p. 398); Ormrod, 'Personal Religion', pp. 850, 868; P. Strohm, *Hochon's Arrow: The Social Imagination of Fourteenth-Century Texts* (Princeton, 1992), pp. 95–199; V. Sekules, 'Dynasty and Patrimony in the Self-Construction of an English Queen: Philippa of Hainault and her Images', in *England and the Continent in the Middle Ages: Studies in Memory of Andrew Martindale*, ed. J. Mitchell (Stamford, 2000), pp. 157–74; C. Shenton, 'Philippa of Hainault's Churchings: The Politics of Motherhood at the Court of Edward III', in *Family and Dynasty in Late Medieval England*, ed. R. Eales and S. Tyas (Donington, 2003), pp. 105–21.

duty and strategy it was to vindicate Edward II before and after his demise did so not by creating positive images of gay men but by re-asserting the king's participation in, and conformity to, the normative and dominant culture of heterosexuality.[79] Edward II's sexuality thus arguably emerges as a much more troublesome and long-standing issue for the fourteenth-century crown than most political historians have been inclined to recognise. To search for some definitive answer to the question 'Was Edward II really gay?' seems to me to be of much less interest than to admit and consider the conflicting interpretations that contemporary political culture may have had of the matter. And a gendered reading of such interpretations suggests that the public and political debate provoked by the events of 1325–30 and worked through in the following generation may indeed have been informed, in quite significant and substantive ways, by a competition between the heteronormative and the queer.

[79] Ironically, it may even be that Edward III's own apparent determination to render the notion of the sodomitical king as uncompromisingly subversive – and thus, in effect, as politically 'unmentionable' – contributed, in some inadvertent way, to the increasingly hostile public attitude to homosexuality that has often been seen as a feature of fourteenth-century culture, and thus gave additional negative force to allegations of sodomy when they recurred in the context of political opposition to Richard II in the 1390s. For references and allusions to Richard's indulgence in sodomy, see *The Chronicle of Adam Usk*, pp. 62–3; G. B. Stow, 'Chronicle versus records: the character of Richard II', in *Documenting the Past: Essays in Medieval History Presented to George Peddy Cuttino*, ed. J. S. Hamilton and P. Bradley (Woodbridge, 1989), pp. 155–76 (pp. 160–1); Keiser, *Courtly Desire and Medieval Homophobia*, pp. 150, 226; Hanrahan, 'Speaking of Sodomy'; Zeikowitz, *Homoeroticism and Chivalry*, pp. 118–27; Ormrod, 'Knights of Venus'.

3

Sermons of Sodomy:
A Reconsideration of Edward II's
Sodomitical Reputation

Ian Mortimer

Those who have dealt with the reputation of Edward II's sexuality constitute a whole spectrum of historical commentators. Arguably the least-informed element of that spectrum is composed of those who presume Edward II may be taken as a gay icon, representing the king as a homosexual in order to reinforce arguments about homosexuality in society. Another band consists of those who objectively classify the king as a homosexual in an attempt historically to understand fourteenth-century homosexual identities, presuming that such identities existed. Another consists of those who present Edward II's sexual inclinations in a genuine attempt to understand the personality politics of the fourteenth century. And at the highest end of the spectrum we find a narrow band of writers who are careful about making presumptions about Edward II's personal sexual inclinations but who nevertheless realise that contemporary perceptions of Edward's relationships are of crucial importance to an understanding of the reign, and that the possible homosexual connotations of his acts cannot be ignored. Without any doubt, the essay in this volume by Mark Ormrod now takes pride of place among these.

As Ormrod has shown, there are many methodological parameters to the debate. If one strips out the extraneous arguments concerning the modern politicised understandings of homosexuality, similarly setting aside the presumptions about a repressed homosexual identity in medieval society, one may return to the core evidence and interpret it in the light of what we know about medieval approaches to sexuality generally. This permits a deconstruction of the evidence for Edward II's 'sexuality', the whole complex question being broken down into its constituent elements: his emotional dependence on his favourites, his reputation as a sodomite, immorality and the perceived 'degeneracy' of his behaviour. In this way we may distinguish a number of behavioural aspects which, although they may not have endangered a politically unimportant man, certainly compromised the standing of a man whose political importance was absolute.

In adopting a gendered approach to the evidence for Edward II's supposed sodomy, however, Ormrod presents a cultural context to the accusations of sodomy as opposed to the more usual political one. This raises some important questions, most obvious of which is the implication of the last point in the preceding passage: to what extent were references to Edward's degeneracy a symptom of inadequacy as a king as opposed to inadequacy as a man? Had Edward been a middling sort, say a knight, would any chronicler have focused on his manly shortcomings? In all probablity his 'degenerate' behaviour would not have been cause for attention unless he had become politically important. Hence, when Ormrod writes that 'a failure to conform to 'kind' was sometimes observed or articulated in gendered terms as implying a decline from the masculine to the feminine' it is very important to bear in mind that in Edward II's case 'conforming to kind' meant conforming to expectations of kingship, not just expectations of manliness. This is important, for if we may distinguish between behaviour which is universally 'degenerate' and behaviour which is simply a sign of 'degeneracy' in a king, we may well ask whether the accusations of degeneracy are indicative of political dissent alone or truly indicative of behaviour which would universally be recognised as degenerate.

In trying to answer this question we need to consider the evidence in its precise political context as well as the cultural framework of fourteenth-century society. In particular, we must investigate the information sources for the chroniclers' statements. At first sight this seems impossible, and indeed is a process rarely embarked upon for the simple reason that there is normally insufficient data for there to be any confidence in the conclusions. However, in certain circumstances, when dealing with a specific research question relating to a particular event or individual, it is worth pursuing an information-based approach if only because of the possibility that what was once thought to be a general rumour has a limited and specific – if not unique – source. If that source has an identifiable political motive, then through information-related techniques we may gradually broaden our understanding of how certain stories might have originated. Therefore the following suggestions are made not with a view to their undermining Ormrod's conclusions and stamping another set of views on his but for the purpose of identifying a possible alternative origin for the accusation of sodomy, which would permit different conclusions to be reached about the origins and circulation of the story that Edward was a sodomite.

As Ormrod makes clear, the accusation of 'sodomy' is not one without its complications. Scholars have tended to tiptoe around the difficult subject of its literal male-male-intercourse implications, preferring a non-sexual understanding. Ormrod is bolder, and justifies his boldness through correlating the accusations of sodomy with the supposed 'anal rape' form of murder of the king in 1327. In his words: 'If the disturbing eroticism of the murder story is acknowledged, and if the narrative is taken in itself as the principal articulation of a contemporary discourse about Edward II's sexuality, then it is no longer necessary or valid to hide behind the suggestion that the general charge of sodomy made against Edward II at and after his deposition did not include or imply his participation in male-male penetrative sex.' Therefore, in applying the methodology outlined in the previous paragraph, we need to investigate the evidence underpinning the two narratives which Ormrod suggests correlate: the accusation of sodomy and the 'anal rape' narrative.

THE ACCUSATION OF SODOMY

There are many allusions to Edward's abnormal behaviour dating from before 1326, and several important expressions of disquiet at the personal aspects of his rule, from as early as 1312 (in the case of the *Vita*); but the earliest specific accusation that Edward was a sodomite appears in a sermon preached by Adam of Orleton, Bishop of Hereford, at Oxford in October 1326. To be precise, in 1334 Orleton was accused by John Prickehare, a Winchester cleric, of a number of crimes connected with the fall of Edward II, including that at Oxford he had preached that Edward was a 'tyrant and a sodomite' (*tyrannus et sodomita*), his motive being 'to subvert the status of Edward II'.[1] The same source states that he repeated this accusation at Wallingford in December 1326.

This evidence is interesting for a number of reasons. The most obvious is that the first accusation of Edward being a sodomite dates from before his capture, and therefore before Mortimer, Isabella and their fellow invaders knew whether they would be in a position to depose him. This removes the political accusation from the deposition process of 1327 and firmly places it, as R. M. Haines has said, in the context of publicising the case that it was 'lawful to rebel' against the king.[2] But more importantly, we may observe that in April 1334 – seven-and-a-half years after the Oxford sermon – Orleton was still personally associated with the 'tyranny and sodomy' accusation against Edward. Nor, in his defence, did he deny that he had said these things; rather, he claimed that he was innocent of defaming Edward III's father on the grounds that he had meant Despenser (not the king) was a tyrant and a sodomite (in which light we have to note that John de Shorditch, one of Edward III's most trusted enforcers, was present and a witness to all that was said).[3] In addition the sermon was preached as the word of God to 'copious multitudes' on each occasion, including 'knights and other vassals of the king'. As a result we can see that a key agent – if not the sole one – in overtly publicising the idea that Edward was a sodomite, or confirming public speculation on the matter, was Bishop Orleton, and his means of publicising this information was a sermon.

1 *The Register of Bishop Grandison, Bishop of Exeter*, ed. F. C. Hingeston-Randolph, 3 vols (London, 1894–9), III, 1542.
2 Haines, *King Edward II*, p. 42.
3 *Register of Bishop Grandison*, ed. Hingeston-Randolph, III, 1543.

The foregoing postulation – that Orleton was the original source for the public idea that Edward was a sodomite – is important. In the second of these sermons, preached in December 1326, at Wallingford, Orleton also preached that the reason Isabella would not go near her husband was because he was prepared to kill her if she came near him, and that he carried in his shoe a knife specially for this purpose; and if he did not have his knife with him he would strangle her.[4] This story also appears in the passage preceding the 'anal rape' account of the death in the longer continuations of the French *Brut* chronicle.[5] As Orleton's defence on this point was that he had first heard this in the presence of the Archbishop of Canterbury, and so believed it at the time, it would appear that Orleton's sermon was the original source of the public story that Isabella feared to go near her husband. Further support for this lies in the fact that this story, too, was specifically associated with Orleton in 1334, seven years later. This shows that the author of the longer continuation of the *Brut* was the direct or indirect recipient of information from the second sermon at Wallingford in 1326, and thus also the recipient of the news of the accusation that Edward was a tyrant and a sodomite. As the longer continuation of the *Brut* is the earliest reference to the 'anal rape' form of murder, the latter cannot be said to be independent evidence of the sexual nature of the previous accusation of sodomy. It does not clarify what Orleton meant in 1326, and may have been pure conjecture, imagined by someone in the wake of hearing the accusation of sodomy. In connection with this, it is important to remember that the actual narrative of the 'anal rape' murder has not one but several precedents in the various thirteenth-century chronicle accounts of the death of Edmund Ironside.[6]

The origin of the story that Edward II was a sodomite is only one aspect which we need to consider. We also need to examine the impact of such accusations, and the cultural framework within which accusations of sodomy had previously been made. Although there were many similar accusations in the fourteenth century with political overtones, few compare with those brought against a king. However, if we focus on Orleton as the key mover or principal instigator of the accusation of sodomy, two are immediately important. The first is the accusation of sodomy brought against Pope Boniface VIII in 1303 and the second the charges brought against the Templars in 1308. As is well known, the prime mover behind both of these accusations was Guillaume de Nogaret, chief minister of Philip the Fair. As with the accusations against Edward II, they were highly political charges, brought at key points in the moral destruction of their subjects. They were both, like the accusations against Edward II, anonymous, in that they were accusations of 'sodomy' or

---

4 *Register of Bishop Grandison*, ed. Hingeston-Randolph, III, 1542.
5 For example, BL, MS Royal 20 A iii, fol. 224r–v; MS Royal 20 A xviii, fol. 331v. The English translation appears in *Brut*, I, 252–3.
6 Chaplais, *Piers Gaveston*, p. 112.

being a 'sodomite'; they did not relate to acts of sodomy with someone in particular. They were thus accusations of a subversive or immoral tendency as opposed to a specific illegal event. Obviously, Nogaret's authorship allows us to connect the two earlier accusations, but the later of these also may be connected with Orleton. Orleton travelled five times to Avignon between 1307 and 1317, spending six years out of the kingdom in that period.[7] He would thus have been at Avignon around the time that Nogaret formulated his charges against the Templars. He was constantly at Avignon from March 1314 to May 1317 and so, very familiar by the end of this period with the politics of the papal court. In particular, in 1311 he was responsible for making arrangements for the English delegation to the Council of Vienne, at which the sodomy accusations against the Templars were again aired. It is perhaps in the cultural context of these political accusations of sodomy, brought against politically powerful men with religious or divine as well as secular responsibilities, that we should understand the accusations brought against Edward II in 1326. Lastly, it is not without significance that Nogaret's accusation against Pope Boniface was brought with the specific intention of deposing him. The pope was seized by Nogaret and Cardinal Colonna, and probably would have been deposed had he not died first.

Summing up this appreciation of the 1326 accusation of sodomy, we may say that there are precedents of which Orleton was undoubtedly aware for the political accusation of sodomy in connection with the moral destruction and deposition of those in positions of political and religious authority. He would appear to have used these precedents to undermine the moral integrity of the king in two sermons in 1326. The impact of his sermons seems to have been profound and widespread. Elements were repeated in a chronicle seven years later, and the year after that Orleton was still specifically associated with spreading the accusation that Edward II was a sodomite. After the sermons of 1326 it would appear probable that Edward II's sexual 'offence' become a subject for discussion and elaboration, and may have contributed to the association of his supposed death in Berkeley Castle with the anal rape story told earlier in connection with Edmund Ironside. By the time of the writing of the Meaux Chronicle (1390s),[8] the story had become accepted in some recollections of Edward II's reign, giving rise to the idea that Edward had given himself over 'too much to the vice of sodomy'.[9] It is therefore possible that the popular idea that Edward II engaged in sodomitical acts was entirely and exclusively due to the sermons which Adam of Orleton preached in 1326.

---

7 G. A. Usher, 'The Career of a Political Bishop: Adam de Orleton (c.1279–1345)', *TRHS* 5th series 22 (1972), 33–47 (pp. 33–4).
8 A. Gransden, *Historical Writing in England: c. 1307 to the Early Sixteenth Century* (London, 1982), pp. 356–7.
9 Meaux chronicle quoted in Haines, *King Edward II*, p. 42.

THE ANAL RAPE NARRATIVE

The only evidence we have which suggests that the above is an under-estimate of the strength of popular belief in the period 1326–34 that Edward engaged in sodomitical acts is the story of Edward's murder in an overtly sexual manner: through a metal item inserted into his rectum. Ormrod argues that this should also be considered evidence of a popular understanding that Edward indulged in sodomy. Although the anal rape death was not exclusively associated with Edward, its archetypal character dating from the thirteenth century does not undermine Ormrod's case, for its sexualised nature (if we accept it as such) may be considered a commentary on Edward II at the time of the announcement of his death (less than a year after Orleton's first sermon on his sodomy). Therefore we must turn our attention to the anal rape narrative, to see whether it was indeed common, and whether it could have developed within the information stream initiated by Orleton's sermon or whether it displays characteristics independent of Orleton's propaganda statements.

Original contributions to the chronicle tradition which deal with the death of Edward II begin with accounts written very soon after the event. The principal texts to mention the death are summarised in Table 1. Nine of the twenty-one descriptions either express doubt about the murder or simply state that Edward II 'died' in Berkeley Castle. Taken at face value, this would not strongly support the idea that Edward II's anal rape death was a wide-spread rumour. However, this is a simplistic appreciation of the evidence. Some of the above chronicles are very rare, and express only a single view-point, while others are known from dozens of manuscripts and express a wide variety of view-points. The latter tend also to be dispersed, in that they reflect views of different times and places. Lastly, the various chronicles represented here are spread across seventy years, and therefore do not all have the same connection in time to the rumours of circa 1327–40. A more particular appreciation is necessary.

The shorter *Brut* continuation is probably the earliest unofficial record of the death, being 'composed close to the events it describes'.[10] The editors of the version which has become known as the *Anonimalle Chronicle* suggest that the original continuation text was started in London and came to York as a result of the removal of the government offices there, probably in 1332.[11] This would be consistent with the *Anonimalle Chronicle* giving the correct but rare date of burial (20 December), also noted by the annalist of St Paul's. In addition, since the cause of death is given as illness, it is probable that this passage was composed in its original form before the trial in late 1330 of Roger

10 *Anonimalle*, p. 22.
11 Ibid., p. 20.

Mortimer, whose crimes were said to have included the murder of the ex-king, which every Londoner and every royal clerk at York in 1332 would have known. Thus it almost certainly predates the information 'threshold' of November 1330, when the official cause of Edward II's death (as circulated by the king) was altered from natural causes to murder.

The importance of the shorter *Brut* continuation in the present context is that it is a lay chronicle, written in French. It is very interesting that the copyist of the version known as the *Anonimalle*, who was very probably based at York and possibly involved with royal administration, was not disposed in 1333 to follow Edward III's pronouncements of 1330 and to revise the cause of death from one of illness to one of murder. This is even more important when one realises the extent to which he revised and greatly added to other portions of the text; in other words, the integrity of the original was not a sufficient reason *not* to revise the text. As a result, the *Anonimalle* might be said to reflect a belief that the king died of natural causes which was current in London before 1330 and current – or at least not sufficiently doubted to warrant a major revision – at York in or not long after 1333.[12] The same may be said for the copyists of several other British Library manuscripts, which stick to the story that Edward died of natural causes, while bearing other variations.[13] Some copyists of the shorter *Brut* did update their manuscripts, but the majority did not.[14] Therefore, wherever they were around the

---

[12] Against this one might say that copying was a drudge's function, or a routine activity, perhaps often assigned to junior members of a community, or professional copyists, and thus not requiring revisions. However, in this case there are very significant counter-arguments. The *Brut* in its French form was a lay chronicle, not exclusively copied by monks but much more frequently copied by and for laymen and secular clerks, and thus one cannot presume that the task was delegated to junior members of a community. Second, no event would have rendered the chronicle out of date so much as a failure to record the alternative death of the ex-king, i.e. that he was murdered. In this respect it is important that many of the *Brut* texts would have been purchased to read aloud to an aristocratic audience (Gransden, *Historical Writing*, p. 62) so the outdated element mentioned in the previous point would not have passed unnoticed. But most importantly, there is the simple fact that many later *Brut* continuations were considerably altered, the *Anonimalle* itself being a prime example. Also, where texts were not altered, they did not often receive a gloss like the manuscript of the Peterborough Chronicle, which, where it records a nondescript death, has in the margin 'That Edward was healthy in the evening and dead in the morning, is a fabrication' ('Edwardus vespere sanus in crastino mortuus est inventus'. BL, MS Claudius A v, quoted in R. M. Haines, '*Edwardus Redivivus*: The Afterlife of Edward of Caernarvon', *Transactions of the Bristol and Gloucestershire Archaeological Society* 114 (1996), 65–86 (p. 72).

[13] For instance, BL MS Cleopatra D vii, fol. 174v ('le roi eu maladist illueqes et murust'); MS Harley 200 fol. 77v ('en maladie al chastel de Kenilworth grevousement de graunt dolour & murust'); MS Harley 6359, fol. 83r ('es maledy grevousement de graunt dolour el dist chastiel de Berkelegh et tout apres murust').

[14] Two examples of shorter *Brut* continuations which were changed include the French

country, and whenever they were writing, the majority were not confident that they knew the circumstances of Edward II's death better than that he died of an illness. None repeat Archbishop Melton's pronouncement that he had died of a 'fall' (which perhaps is odd for a continuation circulating around York).[15] In this light it is worth noting that some other authors who used manuscripts of the shorter *Brut* – for example Thomas Gray, the Lanercost author and the Bridlington author – express doubts about the nature of his death. Clearly the Bridlington author saw a shorter *Brut* continuation or similar chronicle – perhaps a longer *Brut* continuation – with a violent and explicit death narrative and refused to believe it. On the strength of these accounts it would appear that the 'anal rape' narrative of Edward II's death would appear not to have been in circulation much before the completion of the longer *Brut* continuation in the mid 1330s, and was treated with scepticism in those places where it was received after that, at least until the circulation of the popular second redaction of Higden's *Polychronicon* in the 1340s.

The circulation of those accounts which became most popular in the fourteenth century – the long *Brut* continuation and Higden's *Polychronicon* – would thus appear to be important media through which the story of the anal rape took hold. Both of these are known from hundreds of manuscripts, about 160 to 170 of each being known. Being specific as to the cause of death, they had much influence on other versions. Coupled with the chronicle of Murimuth (whose account has much by way of detail on the king's captivity), they account for almost every statement regarding the death by every later chronicler. In addition, the *Polychronicon* has no detail which can be said to be 'original', rather it is its wording which is most 'original', being very brief and mentioning an iron implement, like the *Historia Aurea*, rather than a copper one, like the longer *Brut*. It appears that most later 'anal rape' narratives are literary quotations from one or both of these two influential chronicles (the *Brut* and the *Polychronicon*), sometimes used in conjunction with the suffocation element drawn from Murimuth's account. Finally, although Murimuth records that it was 'popularly' (*vulgariter*) said that Maltravers and Gurney killed the king – supporting the notion that the longer *Brut* continuation supports a general rumour – he himself ascribes their method to suffocation, thereby questioning how widespread was the 'anal rape' narrative in 1337 (the date of the first redaction of his chronicle).

As a result of the foregoing discussion, it seems that the rumour of the 'anal rape' narrative of Edward II's death was slow to form and late to become widely accepted, and only became established through the popu-

---

Chronicle of London (see table) and BL MS Domitian A x fol. 87v ('malveisement fust mordre en le chastel de Berkeleye par ces enemys').

[15] *Historical Papers and Letters from the Northern Registers*, ed. J. Raine, RS 61 (London, 1873), p. 355.

larity of two very influential chronicles, both written after 1333. Many of those writing or copying texts in the 1330s did not accept the version of events in the longer *Brut*; many did not even accept that the king had been murdered. Only the gradual demise of this generation left the way clear for the anal 'rape story' to become established as the most widely accepted narrative concerning the death.

CONCLUSIONS

Drawing together the strands of the argument which have been separately examined, it emerges that both information streams for the sodomitical reputation of Edward II were very narrowly based in the years before 1340. The accusation that Edward II was a sodomite was sufficiently narrowly-based in 1326–34 for it to be closely if not uniquely associated with Orleton and his two sermons, during which time we may safely presume that this information was not common knowledge (except in connection with Orleton's sermons). The rumour that Edward II had died from an anal rape torture was sufficiently narrowly-based in the period 1332–39 for every author and copyist except those working on the longer *Brut* to assign the death to natural causes or some other form of murder. Furthermore, the second narrowly-based tradition almost certainly arises within the context of the first, as shown by the longer *Brut* continuator's repetition of Orleton's statements about Queen Isabella's reluctance to see her husband in 1326. All this together suggests a propaganda origin for the accusation, based on Nogaret's charges against Pope Boniface VIII and the Templars, repeated by Orleton and then adapted by the informant of the continuator of the longer *Brut*, perhaps to accentuate both the duplicity of Isabella and the victimisation and suffering of Edward II. Obviously the link between the accusation and the method of murder remains a loose one, but one thing is certain: the sexual nature of the popular story of the death cannot be assumed to be independent corroboration of the supposed sodomitical reputation of Edward II.

In this light it is perhaps worth returning to the political battleground which has so confused popular approaches to Edward II's sexuality. It is inevitable that some will seize upon these findings to suggest that Edward II was not homosexual. It has to be strongly emphasised that the foregoing passages say nothing about Edward II's sexual inclinations or his affections. Indeed, although this note builds on Ormrod's theoretical approach as to Edward's sodomitical behaviour, it does not go anywhere near as far as Ormrod's piece on the matter of degeneracy as a man (his ditch-digging, for example). Therefore, the above arguments that the contemporary evidence for Edward II's association with sodomy is highly (if not entirely) political in origin should not be used to comment on his sexuality per se. It may be argued that political accusation – sodomy – was selected by Orleton not only because it had been proved to work in 1303 and 1308–14 but also because of his perception that Edward II was vulnerable on this precise issue, due to gossip about his affection for various favourites. It would therefore appear most reasonable to conclude that, although the evidence for Edward's engagement in sodomitical practices appears to be more closely related to political propaganda than widespread rumours of his personal behaviour, its very selection as a means of attacking the king is consistent with the degeneracy of the king, as a man as well as a ruler.

Table 1
Principal Accounts which Mention the Death of Edward II, 1327–1400

Chronicle	Approx. date of composition	Date of death of Edward II	Date of burial of Edward II	Cause of death	Murderers?
Anonimalle, p. 135	A shorter *Brut* continuation, copied after 1333. Relevant section probably drafted in annals form before 1330	21 (St Matthew)	20 (vigil St Thomas)	Illness	n/a
Other shorter *Brut* continuations, e.g. BL MS Cleopatra D vii (fol. 174v); BL MS Domitian A x (fol. 87r); BL MS Harley 6359 (fol. 83r)	Copied after 1333. Relevant section probably drafted in annals form before 1330	21 (St Matthew)	21 (jour de St Thomas)	Various, mostly grief-induced illness. MS Dom. x has 'fust mordre'.	(None mentioned in MS Dom. A x)
Alan de Assheborne, 'Lichfield Chronicle', BL MS Cleopatra D ix (fol. 63r)	c.1333, probably drafted in contemp. annals form	21 (die Lune in festo sancti Matt.)	Not stated	Murdered, possibly strangled ('iugulatus')	None mentioned
AP, 333, 337	1330s, probably drafted in contemp. annals form	20 (vigil St Matt.)	20 (xiii Kal Jan)	'died'	n/a
Murimuth, pp. 52–54	1332x1337, notes drafted at the time	22 (x Kal Oct)	Not stated	Suffocation	Maltravers and Gurney
Brut, I pp. 248–9, 253; and other longer *Brut* continuations, e.g. BL MS Royal 20 A xviii (15th century) and MS Royal 20 A iii (14th century)	After 1333 (translated late 14th century)	21 (St Matthew)	Not stated	Red-hot copper rod	Maltravers and Gurney

Source	Date of composition			Manner of death	Agents
Bridlington	Before 1339? It is not clear whether the entry dates from a later 14th-century revision	21 (St Matthew)	20 (vigil St Thomas)	Writer does not believe 'what is now being written'. Used a shorter *Brut*.	n/a
'Woburn chronicle', BL MS Cotton Vespasian E ix (fol. 80r–v)	After 1335, probably drafted in contemp. annals form	21 (xi Kal Oct)	Not stated	'died'	n/a
Polychronicon Ranulphi Higden monachi Cestrensis, ed. C. Babington and J. R. Lumby, 8 vols, RS 41 (1865–6), VIII, 324	2nd redaction, extended to 1340 (1327 redaction ended just before the death of Edward II)	21 (circa fest. St Matt.)	Not stated	Red-hot iron	None mentioned
The French Chronicle of London, ed. C. J. Aungier, Camden OS 28 (London, 1844), p. 58	1343 or later	Not stated	Not stated	'vilement murdriz'	Maltravers and Gurney
Cronica Johannis de Reading ed. J. Tait (Manchester, 1913), p. 78	1346?	Follows *Murimuth*	Follows *Murimuth*	Suffocation and red-hot iron. Based on *Murimuth* and a *Brut*.	None mentioned
Lanercost	1340s	Not stated	21 (St Thomas)	'either by a natural death or the violence of others'	n/a
John of Tynemouth, 'Historia Aurea' in *Chronicon Domini Walteri de Hemingburgh*, ed. H. C. Hamilton, 2 vols, English Historical Society (London, 1848–9), II, 297–8	1346x7?	21 (St Matthew)	Not stated	Red-hot iron. Based on a *Brut*?	None mentioned

Chronicle	Approx. date of composition	Date of death of Edward II	Date of burial of Edward II	Cause of Death	Murderers?
'Chroniculum' in Geoffrey le Baker, p. 172	1347	20 (xx Sept)	21 (xxi Dec)	'died'	n/a
Eulogium historiarum sive temporis, ed. F. S. Haydon, 3 vols, RS 9 (London, 1858–63), III, 199	c.1354–64	20 (xx Sept)	21 (xxi Dec)	'died' (as 'Chroniculum')	n/a
Geoffrey le Baker, pp. 27–34	c.1356	22 (x Kal Oct)	Not stated	Suffocation and red-hot iron. Based on Murimuth and a Brut.	Maltravers and Gurney (following Murimuth and longer Brut)
Robert de Avesbury, 'Gestis Edwardii' in Murimuth, p. 283	1360s?	Not stated	Not stated	'died'	n/a
Thomas Gray, The Scalachronica, ed. H. Maxwell (Glasgow, 1907), p. 74	1363	Not stated	Not stated	'died, in what manner was not known'	n/a
Thomas Walsingham, Historia Anglicana, ed. H. T. Riley, 2 vols, RS 28 (London, 1863–4), I, 189	1370s	21? (circum fest. St Matt.)	Not stated	Murder based on Brut and Murimuth, also quoting Higden.	Maltravers and Gurney (following Murimuth)
Thomas Burton, Chronica Monasterii de Melsa, ed. E. A. Bond, 3 vols, RS 43 (London, 1866–8), II, 354–5	1390s	21 (xi Kal Oct)	Not stated	Murder quoted from Higden.	Thomas Gurney (following Murimuth)
Chronicon Henrici Knighton, ed. J. R. Lumby, 2 vols, RS 92 (London, 1889–95), I, 448	c.1400	22 (x Kal Oct)	20 (xiii Kal Jan)	Killed ('occisus')	Not mentioned

4

The Court of Edward II

Michael Prestwich

It is unlikely that any English monarch has ever seen as much naked flesh on a single occasion as did Edward II when he was at Pontoise in 1313. There, he was entertained by Bernard the Fool and no fewer than fifty-four nude dancers.[1] This event suggests a decadent extravagance, fitting the familiar stereotype of the king. Edward's affection for his favourites and his unkingly tastes for water sports and menial activities imply that his court had an eccentric, or even exotic, quality. The evidence of the household and chamber accounts, and the household ordinance of 1318, makes it possible to test this hypothesis, and to respond to the opinion of those who doubt whether true courts existed at all in this period.

For some historians of the early modern period, the term 'court' is not one which it is appropriate to use in the context of the fourteenth century; for Elton, the court had its origins in the reign of Henry VII, for it was only then that alternative centres of power were destroyed. As a result, 'The Tudor Court as a centre of social and political life springs suddenly into existence with the accession of Henry VIII.'[2] Another argument rests on terminology, with the suggestion that at the start of the fifteenth century 'a member of the royal entourage was known as "a household man", and at the end, as a "courtier" '.[3] It was, it is argued, only in the final quarter of the fifteenth century that the term courtier came to acquire a special connotation.[4] The court of the early modern period was much more than a political institution. A helpful definition is provided by John Adamson: 'For the period between the Renaissance and the French Revolution, "the court" defined not merely a princely residence – a lavish set of buildings and their pampered occupants – but a far larger matrix of relations, political and economic, religious and

---

1 E 101/375/8, fol. 32.
2 G. R. Elton, 'Tudor Government: the Points of Contact. III. The Court', *TRHS* 5th s. 26 (1976), 211–28 (p. 212); and see N. Saul, *Richard II* (London, 1997), pp. 328–33, for comments on this view.
3 D. Starkey, 'Introduction: Court History in Perspective', in *The English Court from the Wars of the Roses to the Civil War*, ed. D. Starkey et al. (London, 1987), pp. 1–24 (p. 73).
4 Starkey, 'Introduction', p. 3 and D. A. L. Morgan, 'The House of Policy: the Political Role of the Late Plantagenet Household, 1422–1485', in *The English Court*, ed. Starkey, pp. 25–70 (pp. 68–9).

artistic, that converged in the ruler's household.'[5] The culture of such courts was distinctive, featuring as it did, among other things, 'the preoccupation with courtly chivalry in all its guises; from jousts and tournaments, to portraiture and the literature of the knightly romance'.[6] Formalities, ceremonial and culture all combined to make up the complexity of the court.

Though medievalists have tended to prefer the terminology of the household to that of the court, it is clearly appropriate for them to write about the latter, since this was a term used by contemporaries.[7] Clerks, however, did not always use words with the accuracy and close sense of meaning that historians want. The *Vita Edwardi Secundi* described the way in which the Ordainers banned Piers Gaveston's followers from the court (*curia*) after their master was sent into exile. The official text of the expulsion, however, used a whole number of different terms. Gaveston's relations were to be 'entirely ousted from the king'. Robert Lewer, archers, and such manner of ribaldry were to be 'ousted from the king's wages'. A number of household knights were to be 'ousted from office and position and out of the service of the king so that they no longer come near him'. Robert Darcy, Edmund Bacon and others were to be removed from the king's household (*oustill*). The only people who were to be ousted specifically from the court were, curiously, the carters.[8] Court appears, therefore, just to be one of a number of effectively synonymous terms that could be used. Accounts frequently use the word court, detailing for example the expenses of members of the royal household when they were 'out of court'. In 1317 two men brought 200 marks from Boston to the court at Fotheringay. However, different terminology might also be used. In the same account Alan Charlton, a household knight, was sent from Lincoln to York to find lodgings for the king and his *familia*, not for his court.[9]

As for courtiers, the author of the *Vita* used the term, calling them *curiales*. He warned them not to despise the barons. The courtier was typified by this writer as proud and insolent, imbued with malice, constantly striving to outdo his betters.[10] The concept of the Renaissance courtier might not have been fully developed, but the *curialis* was much more than a straightforward household man.

---

5   J. Adamson, 'Introduction: The Making of the Ancien-Régime Court 1500–1700', in *The Princely Courts of Europe 1500–1750*, ed. J. Adamson (London, 1999), pp. 7–41 (p. 7). I am grateful to my colleague Dr Natalie Mears for lending me this book, drawing my attention to other works, and for advice about the nature of the early modern court.

6   Adamson, 'Introduction', p. 19.

7   M. Vale, *The Princely Court. Medieval Courts and Culture in North-West Europe* (Oxford, 2001), pp. 24–33, provides an important discussion.

8   *Vita*, p. 21; *AL*, 199–200.

9   SAL, MS 121, fols 7, 14.

10   *Vita*, pp. 28, 56–7.

The household, however, undoubtedly formed the core of the royal court. It was formed of two main sections, the hall and the chamber, the latter being the more private section.[11] Most of the accounts of the various departments were presented through the wardrobe; the chamber, however, kept its own separate accounts. The size of the royal household varied somewhat in the course of Edward II's reign; reforms in 1318 and in the 1320s aimed to reduce numbers. The lists of those who were in receipt of robes is the best indication of the total size; in the summer of 1317 there were 477 of them, with an additional forty-six squires who, it was noted, were not present at the time of the distribution. This number included sixty-eight bannerets and knights, and seventy squires. It was not just such élite personnel who were given robes (or the monetary equivalent); the list also included the staff of the kitchen and its associated departments, along with twenty-seven sumptermen, thirty-two palfreymen, and sixteen carters. It did not, however, contain any huntsmen.[12] The number of additional personnel can only be guessed at, but there must have been lower servants of various kinds present, as well as some members of the families of household staff. This royal establishment was far larger than those possessed by great magnates in this period; for example, the earl of Lincoln, who died in 1311, is thought to have had a total of 184 in his household.[13] There was one exception, however. The household of Thomas of Lancaster rivalled that of the king. Thomas retained a similar number of bannerets and knights to his cousin Edward II. Another indication of the scale of his entourage is that in 1318–19 he issued letters to about 750 individuals, many of them summoning his men to attend on him.[14]

While the formal membership of the household is relatively easy to establish, the identity of the courtiers, the *curiales*, is not so simple to determine. Charter witness lists pose well-known problems, and do not provide clear proof that those named in them were present when a grant was made. Some notable court figures, such as Piers Gaveston and Hugh Audley, witnessed remarkably few charters. In contrast, the younger Despenser's career as a court favourite can be plotted accurately from his appearance on witness lists. It is also reasonable to deduce from the frequent appearance on the lists of Humphrey de Bohun, earl of Hereford, Aymer de Valence, earl of Pembroke, and John of Brittany, earl of Richmond, that they were frequently attendant at court. Walter Reynolds, archbishop of Canterbury, appeared with remarkable frequency.[15] Below these exalted ranks of earls and bishops,

---

11 This distinction is analysed by Vale, *Princely Court*, pp. 56–68.

12 SAL, MS 120, fols 86 ff. The issue of robes is discussed by Vale, *Princely Court*, pp. 109–10.

13 C. M. Woolgar, *The Great Household in Medieval England* (London, 1999), p. 12.

14 Maddicott, *Thomas of Lancaster*, pp. 44–5.

15 J. S. Hamilton, 'Charter Witness Lists of the Reign of Edward II', in *Fourteenth Century England I*, ed. N. Saul (Woodbridge, 2000), pp. 1–17.

however, this type of evidence is less valuable, and there is no easy way to discover who, apart from those in receipt of fees and robes, were the regular frequenters of Edward's court.[16]

The court was itinerant, and full details of its comings and goings can be worked out. On average, it spent sixty-eight days a year in London or Westminster, but there were considerable variations year by year. In 1318–19 (the regnal year ran from July to July) the king and court were not in London at all; in 1320–21 they were there for 121 days. The fact that parliament was summoned to meet at Westminster more often than anywhere is one explanation for the king's presence at his palace there. His itinerary suggests that King's Langley was his preferred place of residence. Curiously, at the end of the reign he was spending time not at Westminster, where he had a great palace, but at the Tower, which was a slightly run-down if grandiose castle. In 1325 he was there for a month, from late February until late March. In general, castles were not particularly favoured, though in September, October, November and December, 1312, and January, February, March and April of the following year, Edward spent a long time at Windsor, with occasional interludes at Westminster. He was again there from 29 July to 16 September in 1313. Some of the places he stayed seem far from obvious as royal residences; he was, for example, at Fen Ditton in Norfolk from 18 September until 1 October 1315. No doubt this was a reflection of the delight that the king took in boating.[17] What is abundantly clear from the itinerary is that there was no regular court routine; there could be no Westminster or London season as a matter of course. This contrasts with the courts of more modern periods, for such a routine was central to their operation. The Tudor court's peregrinations were confined to the hot summer months, when it became essential to leave London.

For the Tudor historian David Starkey, an important part of the background of the early modern court was the way in which its physical surroundings had developed in the fourteenth and fifteenth centuries from the king's single private apartment, the Chamber, 'a bedsit that struggled to contain too many conflicting functions', into a more specialized suite of rooms.[18] The slick phraseology fails to disguise a misunderstanding. In fact, the medieval palace of Westminster was large and complex. Henry III's palace had two halls, a great chamber (later known as the Painted Chamber), with at least one other chamber below it, a knights' chamber, the queen's chamber with its own chapel, and two other chapels, as well as wardrobes and other smaller rooms. By Edward II's reign the palace possessed, in addition, a new Green Chamber, and two White Chambers, in one of which the

---

[16] There are similar difficulties in identifying the courtiers of the Tudor period: see Elton, 'Tudor Government: The Points of Contact. III. The Court', pp. 213–17.

[17] Calculations based on the details given in Hallam, *Itinerary*.

[18] Starkey, 'Introduction: Court History in Perspective', p. 73.

king slept. There was also an additional suite which had been constructed for Edward I's queen, Eleanor.[19] This may not have amounted to the full complexity of the enormous Tudor palace of Whitehall, but it was far from a single, if very large, bedsit.

Ceremonies and the etiquette associated with them were an important part of court culture in later periods. There are, unfortunately, no treatises which set these out for Edward II's court; the earliest ordinance of this type, detailing rank and ceremonial, dates from 1337, and derives from the court of James II of Majorca.[20] The fact that they were not written down, however, does not mean that there were no formalities in court life. The household ordinance of 1318, drawn up in an attempt at reform, provides some hints in the accounts it gives of the various offices of the household. Eight valets of the chamber were to make beds, carry and maintain torches, and perform other tasks. It was noted that they ate before the king, in the chamber. There were to be thirty mounted sergeants at arms, four of whom, nominated by the king, assisted the usher of the chamber. They even slept outside the door of the chamber, as close to it as they could. The king was to have a bodyguard of twenty-four archers. There were to be two sergeant cooks to provide for the king, one for the main meal, and one for dinner. Five grooms of the king's kitchen were then to do the work at their instruction. One was to collect all the foodstuffs needed for the king's chamber, meat, fish, bread, wine, ale, and spices. Another was to serve as ewer, and a third as potager. The remaining two were to deal with the roasts and other courses. The king was to have four good courses and no more, as were the queen and any lords dining; others in the household were to have three, though boys were entitled to only two. People at dinner were to be served according to their rank. There was a clear hierarchy of officials, with a high degree of specialisation of function. The ordinance also noted that there were to be two trumpeters, and two other minstrels (sometimes more, sometimes fewer) who were to perform before the king when he chose. It also optimistically ordered the removal of criminals and prostitutes from the court. For such an instruction to have been included suggests that in practice the court was a magnet for such people.[21]

Scraps of other evidence offer further hints about the nature of ceremonial in Edward's court. The mode of address, for example, is revealed by the *Vita Edwardi Secundi*, which tells of an edict that no one should call the king's favourite by his name, Piers Gaveston, but all should style him earl of Cornwall.[22] It may have been acceptable in a later age for Queen Elizabeth to

19 *History of the King's Works: The Middle Ages*, ed. H. M. Colvin, R. A. Brown, A. J. Taylor, 2 vols (London, 1963), I, 501–6.

20 Vale, *Princely Court*, 61–2, 202–4; W. Paravicini, 'The Court of the Dukes of Burgundy. A Model for Europe?', in *Princes, Patronage and the Nobility*, ed. R. G. Asch and A. M. Birke (Oxford, 1991), pp. 69–102 (p. 99).

21 Tout, *Place of Edward II*, pp. 284, 291–2, 303–4, 309, 313.

22 *Vita*, p. 3.

use nicknames, but it was not appreciated when Edward's favourite teased the earls with rude epithets instead of referring to them by title. Well-informed as the *Vita* was, it reveals little more about the etiquette of court life. Household accounts are more informative than chronicles in revealing some of the ceremonies which might take place at court. Payment of forty marks to the herald king Robert and other minstrels, who performed in the Friary at York to celebrate the purification of Margaret, countess of Cornwall, provides one example.[23] At New Year, there was surely much jollity at a feast at which someone would be 'king of the bean'. In 1317–18 this duty, or honour, fell to William de la Beche, who, as a result, received a present of a silver-gilt goblet worth £7 13s. from the king.[24] Thomas Ughtred, who in later life would be a very tough customer, was paid twenty marks for some service performed when the king went to eat, which suggests a high degree of ceremonial.[25] Just as in the early modern court, there were ceremonies associated with the king's bed. One entry reveals that Jack le Coppehouse, a chamber valet, was paid twenty shillings, an appreciable sum, as a gift for 'what he did when the king went to bed'. Another such payment was made to Giles Beauchamp, knight, who received £5 'for that done at the king's chamber when he went to bed', and to pay for his travel back to his home.[26] The royal *coucher* was clearly an occasion of some formality. Surely less solemn was the custom, also known from Edward I's reign, of dragging the king from his bed on Easter Monday morning. If he was caught in this way, then he paid a ransom, set at £20 in 1311.[27] The bed itself was surrounded by curtains, for which 600 hooks were purchased on one occasion.[28]

Christmas and New Year were occasions for presents. At Christmas 1317 twenty-four knights received silver-gilt goblets, worth up to £7 each. These were not, with the exception of John de Vaux, household knights, and it is hard to see why they were particularly singled out for favour. The queen did well, with an enamelled silver-gilt bowl, with foot and cover, worth £17, as a New Year's present. Rings, worth up to £10 each, went to the king's niece, Elizabeth de Burgh, his sons Edward and John, and Margaret, widow of Piers Gaveston. The latter's daughter Joan got a ring worth thirty-two shillings.

[23] BL, Cotton Nero C.VIII, fol. 84v.
[24] SAL, MS 120, fol. 92v. In the next year there is a similar entry, with a goblet given to John de Weston, a squire of the household. The scribe, however, has not written Faba, but Paba, presumably in error: SAL, MS 121, fol. 67.
[25] SAL, MS 122, p. 41. I have used page numbering for this manuscript, as the foliation is barely visible, and the page numbers clear.
[26] SAL, MS 122, pp. 28, 65. The final entry of these seems garbled: Beauchamp received his money 'de doun pur ceo fait en la couche chambre le roi qant il ala coucher pur ses dispenses an alant vers son pais'.
[27] BL, Cotton Nero C.VIII, fol. 86; J. C. Parsons, *Eleanor of Castile. Queen and Society in Thirteenth-Century England* (New York, 1995), p. 50.
[28] BL, MS Add. 9951, fol. 5v.

Even at that price, it was gold with two emeralds and three pearls. The list of ladies who received presents was similar in the following year, but it also included Edward's sister Mary, a nun at Amesbury, who received a ring worth £13 13s. 4d., which was gold with six emeralds – not perhaps quite appropriate for one of her calling, but given Mary's extravagant habits, no doubt much appreciated.[29]

The chapel was a major focus for ceremonies, which went beyond the normal hearing of mass. Edward II was a man of wholly conventional religious attitudes; the chapel services were an important part of his daily routine. A substantial staff served the king's religious needs, with a confessor, an almoner, and nine clerks of the royal chapel. Alms-giving was important. In addition to normal gifts, a 'great penny' was presented in alms every day on behalf of the queen, which was then bought back for 7d., so that it could be re-used.[30] On special feast days gold florins were given as alms.[31] There was also the blessing of the sick, those suffering from the king's evil, though in Edward II's case the numbers, compared to those of his father's reign, were very low. In 1320–1 he blessed seventy-nine sick, and between 8 July and 19 October 1322 thirty-six.[32] Few of the sick can have been as fortunate as Matilda of Newark, who came to court seeking a cure and went away, if not necessarily better, at least richer by half a mark.[33] Other religious ceremonies included that of the appointment of a boy bishop on St Nicholas' day.[34]

Cultural patronage was an important aspect of the courts of later periods, and the concept of a 'court style' is one which has proved attractive to some art historians.[35] It was certainly possible for a medieval court to play a leading role in this sense. Henry II's court had been a centre of literary and scholarly endeavour, and Henry III's architectural activities, notably the rebuilding of Westminster Abbey, have shown the considerable potential influence of royal patronage. Edward, there is no doubt, was very interested in building. Early in the reign the building of the splendid great tower at Knaresborough castle can be linked directly to the king, for the chief mason had to leave the site on four occasions to seek out the king, 'in order to find out his express wishes and intentions regarding the works'. The king also was responsible for designing buildings in Nottingham castle.[36] There was nothing evidently distinctive about the style of these buildings, though the

---

[29] SAL, MS 120, fol. 67ff.

[30] SAL, MS 121, fol. 8v.

[31] SAL, MS 120, fol. 3v; 121, fol. 11.

[32] BL, Stowe 553, fol. 118.

[33] SAL, MS 121, fol. 10v; Vale, *Princely Court*, p. 245.

[34] SAL, MS 121, fol. 9.

[35] For an excellent critical discussion, see N. Coldstream, *The Decorated Style. Architecture and Ornament 1240–1360* (London, 1994), pp. 186–92.

[36] *History of the King's Works*, II, 689, 761.

plan of the Knaresborough tower was remarkable, featuring as it did a grand ceremonial stair. In broader terms, there is surprisingly little work that can be directly connected with the king's patronage. Some work simply continued what had already been begun, such as the building of St Stephen's chapel at Westminster. William Hurley was a royal carpenter, but his finest work was not done for the king: it was he who would be responsible for the great Octagon at Ely. When a couple of Irish friars visited London in 1323, they were more impressed by the Painted Chamber at Westminster, a work of Henry III and Edward I's day, than by any more recent building.

Edward admired pictures. He clearly liked one of John the Baptist bought from John the Painter of Lincoln, for it was to be kept in his chamber. His tent on the 1322 Scottish expedition was decorated with a picture of the evangelists. Inevitably, these have not survived, so their quality is unknown.[37] There is nothing to suggest that there were court painters, or a court school. Adam of Garstrete was the painter of three pictures bought to decorate the chapel of the king's younger brothers in 1311, but he was not a permanent employee of the crown.[38] Some works made political points. A tapestry was bought from a London mercer, Thomas of Stepney, depicting the king and the earls, which was to be brought out for solemn feasts.[39] Scenes from the life of Edward I were painted in the lesser hall at Westminster by John of St Albans.[40] John was a man of other talents; on one occasion he danced on a table before the king, which made Edward roar with laughter.[41]

There are fine manuscripts from this period, but none that can be identified with a court style; the closest to it was perhaps a London style. It is dangerous to assume that because a book is particularly splendid, it must have originated in the court. It cannot be proven, for example, that the Queen Mary psalter was a court product. When a royal official, Walter Milemete, had a fine book made to present to the future Edward III in 1327, he appears to have gone to various London craftsmen in their workshops.[42] The artistic patronage of the court under Edward II cannot, of course, be discounted, because so little survives, but at the same time there is nothing to demonstrate that the court was in the forefront of artistic and architectural development.

Edward's court was not a literary centre. One very notable chronicle, the *Vita Edwardi Secundi*, was very probably written by a royal official, possibly

---

[37] SAL, MS 120, f. 13v; BL Stowe 553, fol. 32.
[38] Vale, *Princely Court*, p. 266.
[39] SAL, MS 121, fol. 8. The tapestry cost £30, and its border of green cloth a mere 6s. 3d.
[40] *History of the King's Works*, I, 508.
[41] SAL, MS 122, p. 55. The entry states that John 'lui fist tres grantement rire'; his reward was 50s.
[42] *Queen Mary's Psalter*, ed. G. F. Warner (London, 1912); *The Treatise of Walter de Milemete*, ed. M. R. James (Roxburghe Club, Oxford, 1913).

John Walwyn, who had inside knowledge of the court. With its highly critical tone, it was very clearly not the product of royal patronage.[43] There is evidence for the possession of books at court, but not for their production. The chamber accounts at the end of the reign show that Edward gave Hugh Despenser the younger a big book containing a Tristram romance, and it has been suggested that the fourteen romances, with one French psalter, issued from the privy wardrobe in 1324 were intended for Edward's own use. The king himself used to be thought to have written a poem in his captivity, but this is now doubted; it looks like a literary exercise written later.[44]

The court must have been a sumptuous place. This is demonstrated above all by the quantities of gold and silver plate, with many jewels, that were carefully listed in annual inventories. At Newcastle in 1312 many of the king's horses and much of his plate was captured by Thomas of Lancaster from Piers Gaveston, in whose custody they were. Partial inventories survive from this event, and the wardrobe account books also provide lists of the royal plate. As well as great quantities of goblets, often of silver-gilt with enamelled decoration, there were items such as that remarkable biological rarity, a griffon's egg, which had been made into a pitcher with silver-gilt mounts.[45] The king himself used pairs of splendid knives with either silver enamelled or ebony handles at dinner; these cost about twelve shillings each. They never seemed to last very long, for replacements were bought frequently.[46] There was a constant process of renewal of the royal plate, as older pieces were sent to London goldsmiths to be melted down for the manufacture of new and no doubt more splendid ones.

Entertainment was an important element in court life. The author of the *Vita Edwardi* suggested that it was because of Walter Reynolds' skill in putting on theatrical entertainments that the king had promoted him, so that he became not merely treasurer, but archbishop of Canterbury.[47] The household accounts, however, give no details of any play-acting. Payments to minstrels provide glimpses of what took place. The purification of Margaret de Clare, wife of Piers Gaveston, early in 1312 was celebrated with a performance by a group of minstrels who were handsomely rewarded with a gift of forty marks. In 1312 there was an act by an Italian snake-charmer. In 1313–14 a singer, Master William de Milly, was paid the remarkably high wages of two shillings a day, the same as a knight would receive.[48] The many

---

43 For recent comment on the *Vita*, see C. Given-Wilson, *Chronicles. The Writing of History in Medieval England* (London, 2004), pp. 167–73.

44 SAL, MS 122. p. 92; C. Valente, 'The "Lament" of Edward II: Religious Lyric, Political Propaganda', *Speculum* 77 (2002), 422–39.

45 SAL, MS 120, fol. 95v.

46 BL, MS Add. 17362, fols 10, 10v; SAL, MS 121, fols 6, 7, 8v.

47 *Vita*, p. 45.

48 C. Bullock-Davies, *A Register of Royal and Baronial Domestic Minstrels 1272–1327* (Woodbridge, 1986), pp. 32, 116, 143.

surviving references to organists, harpers and fiddlers, along with drummers and others, give an impression that the musical life of the court was extremely active, but of course, there is no way that what was played can be reconstructed.

There was a very human side to the court and household. Records of gifts made on other occasions suggest a good style of personnel management, with small personal acts of generosity. When Oliver de Bordeaux, one of the household squires, married in 1318, he and his wife each received from the king a ring worth thirty shillings.[49] A gift of twenty shillings to John Spayn, a page of the chamber, on the occasion of his marriage to Alice Maure in 1319, is another example of the king looking after those in his entourage.[50] This gift was paltry in comparison to the £50 given to Peter the Surgeon, for curing a groom who had been bitten by one of the royal chargers.[51] A personal touch emerges with the payment to William Wytherwood, one of the household purveyors, of thirty shillings, a substantial sum, because the king was so delighted with the crabs and prawns he brought him. 'He said he had not anything so much to his taste for a long time.'[52]

One notable feature of Edward's court, which finds many parallels in later periods, was the succession of royal favourites, from Piers Gaveston at the start of the reign to the younger Depenser in the final years. It has often been assumed that the role of such favourites resulted from the king's own sexual preferences. If this was so, it might be expected that this would be reflected in the manners and style of the court, and that there might be criticism of this. There had been such attacks in an earlier period. Orderic Vitalis condemned the court of William Rufus and its widely followed fashions. 'Foul catamites, doomed to eternal fire, unrestrainedly pursued their revels and shamelessly gave themselves up to the filth of sodomy.' 'They parted their hair from the crown of the head to the forehead, grew long and luxurious locks like women, and loved to deck themselves in long, over-tight shirts and tunics.' Archbishop Anselm's pointed condemnations of the effeminate manners of Rufus's court find no early fourteenth-century parallel. Edward II's court attracted no such condemnation from contemporaries. It was not seen as a nest of corruption where men 'revel in filthy lusts like stinking goats'.[53]

The court was a public place, and it would not have been easy for the king and his favourites to engage in homosexual affairs unnoticed. Contemporary attitudes had changed since the late eleventh century; the church's condemnation of homosexuality was fiercer. The issue was one which came to the

---

49 SAL, MS 120, fol. 93v.
50 BL, MS Add. 17362, fol. 32v.
51 BL, MS Cotton Nero C.VIII, f. 4.
52 SAL, MS 121, p. 79.
53 *The Ecclesiastical History of Orderic Vitalis*, ed. M. Chibnall, 6 vols (Oxford, 1969–80), IV, 189; F. Barlow, *William Rufus* (London, 1983), p. 103.

fore early in the reign with the condemnation of the Templars, for in many cases the interrogation of members of the order revealed homosexual practices.[54] It would have been extraordinary if the king had been openly gay while this was happening.[55] When a royal messenger, a man in a position to know what went on at court, was accused in 1315 of slandering the king, it is striking that homosexuality was not among the accusations.[56] Edward took a normal pleasure in his family; he gave a very substantial gift of £100 to Eble des Montz when he brought news of the birth of the king's second son, John of Eltham, in 1316.[57] There is nothing in the household accounts to suggest that the king was not heterosexual in his tastes. As Roy Haines has pointed out, the evidence of the accounts points rather to the possibility that Edward had an affair with his niece, Eleanor de Clare, the younger Despenser's wife. The two are linked in an unusual way in a wardrobe account for 1319–20, which mentions medicines bought for them when they were ill. The chamber accounts later in the reign show sugar bought at the king's instructions to make sweets for Eleanor. Edward also gave her caged goldfinches, and on one brief visit to her he gave her the very substantial sum of 100 marks.[58] No other ladies feature in such a way, and while the entries can be interpreted as the king sensibly keeping his lover's wife happy, the alternative explanation, that Despenser was willingly handing his wife over to the king to keep him happy, seems at least as plausible. Such an affair with his niece would make sense of the remark made by Robert of Reading in his chronicle, that Edward was engaged in 'illicit and sinful unions', and rejecting the 'sweet conjugal embraces' of Queen Isabella.[59] The accusation of an affair with Eleanor was made more explicitly by a Hainault chronicler, who could have picked up the information from someone in the queen's entourage. It would, however, be going too far to follow one recent commentator, who suggests wife-swapping between the king and Despenser, and argues that Isabella's anger with the king was because of his 'allowing his favourite into her bed'.[60]

Although there is nothing in the accounts to support accusations of homosexuality, there are entries which suggest that other charges against the king may have more warrant. In the household accounts for 1311–12 there is mention of purchases of iron, and of plaster, 'for the king's private works'.[61] This may well mean no more than works authorised by the king, but the

---

54 For example, *AL*, p. 192.
55 Bertha Putnam described the year books of Edward II as 'the gayest of law books', but this was a phrase which meant something rather different in 1950 than it does today: *The Place of Legal History of Sir William Shareshull* (Cambridge, 1950), p. 117.
56 H. Johnstone, 'The Eccentricities of Edward II', *EHR* 48 (1933), 264–7.
57 SAL, MS 120, fol. 52.
58 BL, MS Add. 17362, f. 18; SAL, MS 122, pp. 15, 28, 40.
59 *Flores*, III, 229.
60 P. Doherty, *Isabella and the Strange Death of Edward II* (London, 2003), pp. 101–2.
61 BL, Cotton MS Nero C. VIII, fol. 57.

entry is none the less unusual, and could reflect Edward's liking for do-it-yourself activities. At the close of the reign there are some curious entries in the Chamber accounts. There is much detail of expenditure on the small fleet of royal ships, but what are unusual are the entries recording that, for example, Adam Cogg, master of one of the barges, ate in the king's room for four days in June 1325. A little later there were ten of the royal sailors dining in this way, and a couple of carpenters also ate in the king's room. Nor are these the only such examples.[62] What, and how much, should be read into this can only be left to the imagination, but it strongly suggests that the accusations that the king enjoyed the company of the low-born were not unfounded.

In contrast to those of Edward I's day, there is startlingly little evidence in the accounts about hunting. This could be the result of an organisational change which took the hunting establishment out of the household accounts, but it probably also reflects the king's distaste for the activity. Nor, in contrast to the court of Edward III, or the English courts of the early modern period, does there appear to have been much attention paid to the cult of chivalry. In the early years of the reign, under Piers Gaveston's influence, a number of tournaments were held. That at Kennington in 1308, when the victor was declared King of the Greenwood, was a royal event. Subsequently, however, tournaments were abandoned as a part of court life.[63] There was no parallel in Edward's reign to the great Feast of the Swans in 1306, at which he had himself been knighted, nor to the masques which were a feature of Edward III's court.

The court was central to the politics of the reign. The role of successive royal favourites endowed it with an unusual character, as these men were capable of establishing an extraordinary mastery. In the early part of the reign one way to obtain favours from the king was to approach Piers Gaveston first, as a letter the latter wrote to John Darcy in 1308 shows:

> And as far as your request that we should request our lord the king that you be granted the wardship and marriage of the son and heir of sir John Moriet, who has died, know that sir Hugh Despenser asked for it three days before your letter reached me, and the king has granted it and others to him. But as soon as you spy out something else for you, we will do all we can to ensure that you shall have it, to the best of our ability.[64]

A letter from the Italian Biagio Aldobrandini, a member of the Frescobaldi banking house, to two other members of the firm in 1313, shows that another

[62] SAL, MS 122, pp. 4, 6, 7, 30.
[63] J. R. V. Barker, *The Tournament in England 1100–1400* (Woodbridge, 1986), pp. 46–7; *AP*, 264.
[64] Maddicott, *Thomas of Lancaster*, p. 335.

Italian, Antonio Pessagno, came to take what Biagio regarded as a similar position to that previously occupied by Gaveston:

> He is now in such a condition that he fears nobody, and what he wants is made in the court . . . he does what he wants and he pleases everybody and is so generous in the court towards the great and the small that everybody likes him . . . Mr Aymer de Valence helps him and backs him with all his forces and he runs as never did the earl of Cornwall, and the court is led according to his judgement and will, so you can see how things can be changed.[65]

In the final stages of the reign, it was of course the younger Despenser who exercised a complete domination over the court, as ample evidence shows.

The fevered character of court politics is suggested by an extraordinary story produced by Bartholomew Badlesmere, who served as household steward. He stated that the younger Despenser tried to bring into an alliance with him Richard de Grey, John Giffard and Robert Shirland, by showing them a parchment which began by stating that homage and allegiance were owed more to the crown, than to the person of the king. This was a document originally produced in 1308 by the earl of Lincoln, and it is generally assumed that there was no truth behind Badlesmere's attempt to smear Despenser, particularly when Grey, asked about it, said weakly that he had 'found it in his wallet among other papers'. Badlesmere may have planted it there, but Grey, Giffard and Shirland were all knights of the royal household, and it is not unlikely that Despenser may have been engaged in manoeuvres of this sort.[66]

The events of a single year, 1317, show how the court might be a hotbed of political intrigue. It was at court in February of that year that the plot was hatched for the abduction of Thomas of Lancaster's wife, Alice.[67] There were complex court manoeuvres over the election of a new bishop of Durham. There were various candidates. The monks had one, Henry de Stamford. The queen had one, Louis de Beaumont. The earl of Lancaster had another, John of Kinnardesley. Beaumont was a young man, whose brother Henry was a powerful figure at court. Not surprisingly, his candidature was successful. As Beaumont was on his way to be consecrated, however, he and the two cardinals with him were kidnapped by Gilbert de Middleton. There was what amounted to a small-scale rising in the north, but Beaumont was set free and Middleton was eventually dealt with. The connections and links that underlay Middleton's act went back to the court. Robert de Sapy was a royal

65 R. W. Kaeuper, 'The Frescobaldi of Florence and the English Crown', *Studies in Medieval and Renaissance History* 10 (1973), 41–95 (pp. 82–3). In this quotation I have changed 'Mister Amari from Valenza' to 'Aymer de Valence'.

66 *Parliamentary Texts of the Later Middle Ages*, ed. N. Pronay and J. Taylor (Oxford, 1980), pp. 162–3; Maddicott, *Thomas of Lancaster*, pp. 281–2.

67 Maddicott, *Thomas of Lancaster*, pp. 190–1.

household knight, in charge of Durham during the vacancy, and he was clearly anxious to delay the consecration. He first entered into a deal with John de Eure to try to prevent Beaumont's installation before Michaelmas. This fell through, and Sapy then turned to Middleton, another household knight. Further, Middleton was aggrieved because his relative, John de Swinburne, also a household knight, had been imprisoned in Nottingham castle for criticising the king and his failure to defend the north. There were therefore three household knights, men present on a regular basis at court, involved in an intrigue to prevent a man with different court connections, Louis de Beaumont, from becoming bishop.[68]

Discontent on the part of the household knights is further indicated by a curious incident which happened in this same year of 1317, when a woman dressed theatrically rode into the king's hall at Westminster during a banquet. After riding round, she approached the king's table – perhaps the new one bought for 33s. 4d.[69] – and put a letter in front of him. The letter criticised the king for not treating his established knights properly and for promoting worthless men in their place. It turned out that one of the household knights had put her up to this.[70]

All politics, however, did not centre upon the court. The opposition of Thomas, earl of Lancaster, could almost be interpreted in terms of court versus country. Thomas withdrew from the court late in 1308, when he ceased witnessing royal charters, and even when he played an active part in government from 1314 to 1316 it does not seem that he involved himself again in court affairs. Even though he witnessed over 40 per cent of royal charters in 1314–15, he kept his distance. In 1315 he held a council at Doncaster, along with the archbishop of York, to discuss the defence of the north – quite independently of king, court and parliament.[71] If a definition of the court is that all political life should centre upon it, as was argued by Elton, then Edward's court evidently fails. Such a definition, however, is hardly convincing, and even Elton has to allow the appearance in the sixteenth century of 'mini-alternatives', 'court-like centres'.[72]

The court of Edward II was not the exotic establishment that Bernard the Fool surely hoped it was when he assembled his troop of nude dancers. The reality that is revealed by the accounts is conventional, and perhaps even rather dull. The distinctive Decorated style of the period in architecture,

[68] M. C. Prestwich, 'Gilbert de Middleton and the Attack on the Cardinals, 1317', in *Warriors and Churchmen in the Middle Ages: Essays Presented to Karl Leyser*, ed. T. Reuter (London, 1992), pp. 179–94.

[69] SAL, MS 121, fol. 7.

[70] *JT*, 98–9.

[71] Maddicott, *Thomas of Lancaster*, pp. 92, 168–9; Hamilton, 'Charter Witness Lists of the Reign of Edward II', p. 11.

[72] Elton, 'Tudor Government: the Points of Contact. III. The Court', p. 212.

mirrored in painting, was not the product of court patronage or leadership. The court was not a literary centre, nor is there any evidence that it led the way in fashion. The ceremonial of the royal chapel, of the hall and of the chamber have left few traces in the records, but there is nothing to suggest that it was particularly distinctive or innovatory. In many ways Edward may not have been conventional, but there was little power to his personality. His eccentricities may have led him to invite sailors to dine in his chamber, but his tastes did not transform the institution of the court.

5

Household Knights and Military Service under the Direction of Edward II

Alistair Tebbit

Historians of the twelfth and thirteenth centuries have concluded that the system of retaining knights was devised principally to provide a pool of skilled fighting men who could be called upon to serve in royal campaigns. Household knights nearly always formed the nucleus of the king's heavy cavalry in major armies. It has also been recognized that they were useful in providing military leadership. Many acted as constables of strategically important castles and some were given command of small and medium sized forces. It is likely that most English kings took a very active interest in supervising the military activities of household knights. Aside from occupying positions of responsibility, they were, in any case, his most trusted liege men. By implication, an examination of the activities of household knights in the context of war is likely to reveal something of a king's style and quality of rule. However, the military side of household service under Edward II has been almost entirely ignored.[1] The existence of a considerable body of work in relation to the household knights of earlier kings and their contribution, often highly significant, to the waging of royal wars makes this all the more apparent.[2] The ignominious defeat at Bannockburn will probably always stain Edward's reputation, but not until other aspects of his conduct as a military commander have been considered can he be properly judged. The purpose of this paper is to take a step towards that end by examining how effectively he directed the knightly retinue.

Household knights formed the core of the cavalry in major expeditions, much as they had done under Edward I. In 1310–11, 1319 and 1322 a very

---

[1] Conway Davies made a brief reference to their military contribution in his *Baronial Opposition*, p. 223.

[2] See, for example, J. O. Prestwich, 'Military Household of the Norman Kings', *EHR* 96 (1981), 1–35; M. Chibnall, 'Mercenaries and the *Familia Regis* under Henry I', *History* 62 (1977), 15–23; S. D. Church, *The Household Knights of King John* (Cambridge, 1999), pp. 39–73; R. F. Walker, 'The Anglo-Welsh Wars, 1217–67: with special reference to English military developments' (unpublished D.Phil. thesis, University of Oxford, 1954), pp. 66–90; M. C. Prestwich, *War, Politics and Finance* (London, 1972), pp. 41–61; and R. Ingamells, 'The Household Knights of Edward I', 2 vols (unpublished Ph.D. thesis, University of Durham, 1992), I, pp. 69–114.

high proportion of the knightly retinue served.[3] However, the military value of household knights operating within large armies in Scotland ought to be questioned, as should Edward's decision to use them in the manner he did. It would undoubtedly have required a far more confident and capable commander than Edward to have moved away from the military methods employed by his father in Scotland,[4] but it still seems remarkable that after two fruitless expeditions (1310–11 and 1319), and one that was utterly disastrous (1314), there was no realization among Edward and his subordinates that the strategies they employed, and the composition of the armies they commanded, in Scotland were ineffective. The manner in which household knights were used collectively and in conjunction with other heavy cavalry resources contributed significantly to these failures. The evidence for 1322, a campaign that was conceived and executed on very similar lines to earlier expeditions, makes this clear. Household knights mustered with their retainers and the rest of the army, marched across the border, and then returned ignominiously some weeks later without seeing any fighting. Edward never seems to have come to terms with the fact that the knightly retinue and other heavily mounted elements were of little practical use against an enemy who evaded pitched battle at all costs unless it was offered on ground that was distinctly unfavourable to heavy cavalry, as was the case, of course, at Bannockburn.

By giving the knightly retinue a central role in protecting the north of England from the incursions of the Scots between 1315 and 1318, Edward demonstrated a great deal more imagination as a commander. So great was the number of household knights involved that we can be left in little doubt that Edward was using them to guarantee manning levels and to provide competent and reliable leadership on the west and east Marches. Some caution ought to be exercised, however, in arguing that the participation of these individuals was entirely due to their membership of the household. Most household knights who guarded the borders of England held lands in

---

3   In 1310–11 twenty-six out of the thirty-four household knights retained at the time campaigned (BL Cotton MS Nero C. VIII, fols 2–37); in 1319 thirty-six out of fifty-one (E 101/378/4, fols 19r–29v); and in 1322 thirty out of thirty-five (BL Stowe MS 553, fols 56–61). It is very likely that the knightly retinue mustered in large numbers for the Bannockburn campaign in 1314, but the wage roll for that year does not survive and we can, therefore, only assume that the army was organized in similar fashion to the others of the reign.
4   The armies Edward II led into Scotland broadly resembled those of his father. For example, the invasion army of 1322 described in detail in Fryde, *Tyranny and Fall*, pp. 119–34, is very similar in terms of composition to that which won the battle of Falkirk in 1298. For details of the latter army, see M. Prestwich, *Edward I* (New Haven, 1997), pp. 479–80. Furthermore, the strategy did not change. The objective, as far as is revealed in the composition of the armies and in the events of Bannockburn, was to bring the Scots to battle, as at Falkirk when the heavy English heavy cavalry made the weight of their arms felt in combination with archers.

the region, and an important factor in motivating them was probably a desire to protect these interests. Equally, though, it is likely that Edward was trying to exploit the natural desire of northern knights to be involved in the war, by directing their efforts in a more coherent fashion through the household system. In any case, these individuals were supported by the employment of numerous other household knights who had no landed interests in the region and whose participation can only really be explained by their household connection.

To understand this fully we need to look at the evidence in detail. Between 1315 and 1318 Edward retained twenty-seven men with significant interests in the north, particularly in Cumberland and Northumberland, and in Scotland (the lands beyond the border had been lost, of course, by this stage).[5] At any given moment during this period the total strength of the knightly retinue varied between approximately fifty and sixty men. Not all twenty-seven knights served at the same time during the period under discussion, but most did, and it is clear that the proportion of the retinue with interests in the north was very significant. If we look at the knightly retinue of 1312–13 the point is further underlined. Only seven men with similar landed backgrounds can be found serving, from a total of thirty-seven household knights.[6] It is difficult to believe that the retention of such large numbers of northern knights between 1315 and 1318, a time when the region was under its severest pressure from the Scots, was mere coincidence.

In the same period, household knights were highly active as the commanders of key northern strongholds and of cavalry forces patrolling the frontier. It can be shown that household knights provided nearly all the key subordinates to the three *chevetaignes* (Pembroke, Lancaster and Arundel) who held overall command in the north between 1315 and 1318, a fact that has been overlooked.[7] Not surprisingly, northern household knights led the way. John de Felton held the important yet vulnerable castle of Alnwick throughout the period. From this position he stood for four years in the

---

5   These were the bannerets Gilbert de Umfraville, earl of Angus, William de Ros, Henry FitzHugh, Henry FitzWilliam, Ralph FitzWilliam, Adam de Swinburn, Nicholas de Menill and Simon Ward; and the simple knights John de Felton, John de Fenwick, Andrew de Harclay, Gilbert de Middleton, John de Lilleburn, John de Vaux, Edmund Darel, John and Thomas de Heselarton, Robert de Leyburn, Edmund Bacon, John de Castre, William de Felton, Thomas de Richmond, Roger Mauduit, David de Betoign, Dougal Macdowell, Hugh de Eland and Adam de Everingham (E 101/378/6; E 101/377/1; E 101/376/7, fol. 54; SAL, MS 120, fols 58r–61r, 82r–86v; SAL, MS 121, fols 36r–38v, 55, 62).

6   These were Gerard de Salveyn, Robert de Felton, Adam de Swinburne, Roger Mauduit, William de Felton, William Olyfard (or Oliphant) and William de Vescy (E 101/375/8, fols 33r–37r).

7   See C. McNamee, *The Wars of the Bruces: Scotland, England, and Ireland 1306–1328* (East Linton, 1997), pp. 123–65, for the fullest account of the defence of the north.

vanguard of English defences in Northumberland. He was first appointed as constable in November 1314, the fortress having fallen into the king's hands following the death of Henry de Percy.[8] From July 1315 to January 1316 he was paying the wages of eleven men-at-arms and eleven hobelars.[9] In January the garrison was strengthened and Felton now had three knights, twenty-seven men-at-arms and forty hobelars under his command.[10] The garrison remained at this level of manning until December, when Felton made a contract with the king's banker, Anthony Pessagano, to retain a force of fifty men-at-arms and forty hobelars in future.[11] This arrangement continued until at least July 1318.[12] Felton was finally relieved of his command in November 1318, when the castle was returned to the Percy family.[13]

Other northerners connected to the knightly retinue played similar roles. Adam de Swinburn served as sheriff of Northumberland and constable of the town and fortress of Newcastle. He was appointed in October 1315 and led a major cavalry force of eighty men-at-arms and eighty hobelars on the March between November 1316 and August 1317.[14] The household banneret Henry FitzHugh came, with a retinue of seven knights and thirty-three squires, to serve under the earl of Arundel, the overall commander in the north from November 1316.[15] FitzHugh stayed on the March with his forces between December 1316 and July 1317, and then with twenty men-at-arms until September 1318.[16] Another household banneret, William de Ros of Helmsley, also served on the March under Arundel in the same period. He led a force of fifty men-at-arms. In July 1317 he was appointed constable of Warkworth castle, which he held with thirty men-at-arms and eleven hobelars.[17] Ralph FitzWilliam, yet another royal banneret, was paid to retain sixty men-at-arms and deploy them on the March for its safe keeping in 1316.[18] The soon-to-be-infamous household knight Gilbert de Middleton appears to have been at least gainfully employed in 1316. He was compensated for the loss of several horses while on royal service.[19] Also, the household banneret Simon

8 Percy had an heir of the same name, but he was a minor (*CFR 1307–19*, p. 219).
9 E 101/376/7, fol. 62r.
10 E 101/14/39.
11 SAL, MS 120, fol. 45r.
12 SAL, MS 121, fol. 20.
13 *CFR 1307–19*, pp. 378–9.
14 *CFR 1307–19*, p. 261; E101/376/7, fol. 115r; SAL, MS 120, fol. 45r; SAL, MS 121, fol. 32r.
15 McNamee, *Wars of the Bruces*, p. 149.
16 SAL, MS 120, fol. 44v; SAL, MS 121, fol. 21v.
17 SAL, MS 120, fol. 44r; *Calendar of Documents Relating to Scotland*, ed. J. Bain (1881–8), G. G. Simpson and J. D. Galbraith, 5 vols (Edinburgh, 1986) (hereafter *CDS*), III, no. 576.
18 E 101/376/7, fol. 62r.
19 Ibid., fol. 62r; E 101/14/39.

Ward was employed as keeper of the town of Berwick until October 1315, when he became sheriff of York.[20]

On the west March local household knights were also very prominent as leaders of forces deployed to oppose the Scots. Robert de Leyburn is a striking example. In March 1316 he was commissioned to array infantry in Westmorland, and in August he was involved in raising a footman from every vill in the county.[21] As constable of Cockermouth castle, he controlled a force of eleven men-at-arms and twenty hobelars from December 1316 to March 1317, and then a slightly reduced force until August.[22] John de Castre served as a key figure in the garrison of Carlisle in 1315–16, alongside Andrew de Harclay, another individual who was connected, if only briefly, in 1314–15, to the household.[23] As Leyburn had been for Westmorland, Castre was commissioned in March 1316 to array foot in Cumberland, and in August was ordered to choose a footman from every vill in the county.[24] In February 1316 he was appointed sheriff of Cumberland and keeper of Carlisle, strategically the most important town on the western March, and held both offices until June 1318.[25] In July 1316 representatives of the Bardi paid him 400 marks for expenses he had incurred in munitioning Carlisle,[26] and from 1316 to 1318 he had over seventy hobelars at his disposal in the town.[27] The royal knight Thomas de Richmond was also very active on the western March, with a considerable retinue. He and twenty of his men had their horses valued at Cockermouth in July 1315, prior, presumably, to performing military service.[28]

But perhaps the most telling evidence for a coordinated household effort being made between 1315 and 1318 can be seen in the arrival on the frontier of royal knights whose landed interests were predominantly outside the north, and who, therefore, must have been serving at the specific request of the king. The Worcestershire knight John de Wysham was very prominent. Since December 1310 he had been constable of St Briavels castle and keeper of the Forest of Dean.[29] He first arrived at Berwick in the summer of 1315, with three squires.[30] By October 1315 Wysham had replaced Simon Ward as

---

[20] E 101/376/7, fol. 115r; *Northern Petitions*, ed. C. M. Fraser, Surtees Society, 144 (1981), p. 60.

[21] *CPR 1313–17*, p. 460; *CFR 1307–19*, p. 296.

[22] SAL, MS 120, fol. 44v; SAL, MS 121, fol. 21v.

[23] E 101/376/7, fol. 117r.

[24] *CPR 1313–17*, p. 460; *CFR 1307–19*, p. 296.

[25] Ibid., pp. 270, 344, 363.

[26] *CDS*, III, no. 497.

[27] McNamee, *Wars of the Bruces*, p. 156.

[28] E 101/14/15.

[29] *CPR 1307–13*, p. 355; *CFR 1307–19*, p. 76.

[30] E 101/376/7, fol. 10r.

keeper of Berwick, when the latter was made sheriff of York.[31] Wysham had been serving as 'marshal of the town' under Ward, and it was soon after Ward's appointment at York that he was described as keeper.[32] In July 1316 he made a contract with Edward to hold the town in return for 600 marks per annum, from which he was to take his wages and those of the garrison.[33] It should be remembered that Berwick was blockaded at this time, from the sea by Flemish mercenaries and from the landward side by the Scots, who were making efforts to take the town by siege.[34] Wysham's importance to the English cause at this moment should not be under-estimated; he had been entrusted with the safeguarding of a place that, if lost, would have provided the Scots with an ideal base for ever deeper raids into England. His tenure of Berwick appears to have ended in June 1317, when Edward ordered him to take a number of hostages from the townspeople (the intention was presumably to guarantee the loyalty of the population in the face of increasing Scottish pressure) before handing the town back to the keeping of the mayor and returning to the royal court at York with the hostages.[35] However, Edward sent him back in October with ten men-at-arms to bolster the strength of the garrison in the face of further Scottish depredations in the vicinity of the town.[36] Edward's gratitude to Wysham for his services can be seen in a grant for life to him, in May 1318, of the lucrative castle and honour of Knaresborough.[37]

Many more southern household knights were brought into service against the Scots in the aftermath of Bannockburn. In July 1315 the earl of Pembroke was overall commander in the north. Household knights, many from the south, provided a key part of his force. Pembroke mustered his forces at York in the summer of 1315 before advancing north, and he was joined by royal favourite Bartholomew de Badlesmere, the household knights Oliver de Ingham, Robert de Haustede the Younger, Robert de L'Isle and John de Hardeshull, and the northern retainers Roger Mauduit, John de Eure and William de Felton.[38] Roger Damory was serving at the time as constable of Knaresborough castle and he too joined Pembroke on the northern Marches, bringing with him eight knights, fourteen squires and nine hobelars.[39] Hugh Audley the Elder later became prominent as a local commander. With John de Cromwell, the steward of the household, Audley raised horse and foot

31 *CFR 1307–19*, p. 261.
32 *CDS*, III, no. 427; *Northern Petitions*, p. 60.
33 SAL, MS 120, fol. 44r.
34 McNamee, *Wars of the Bruces*, pp. 213, 216–18.
35 *CPR 1313–17*, p. 671.
36 SAL, MS 121, fol. 19r.
37 *CFR 1307–19*, p. 362.
38 E 101/15/6.
39 E 101/376/7, fol. 61v; *CCR 1313–18*, p. 493.

from Yorkshire in readiness for Lancaster's summer campaign of 1316.[40] When Arundel succeeded Lancaster as *chevetaigne* Audley served under him at Newcastle. He commanded six knights and fourteen men-at-arms in the garrison from December 1316 to June 1317, and by July 1317 he was serving as constable of the castle there.[41]

During his absence from the Scottish war between 1314 and 1319 it is plain, from the evidence above, that Edward made genuine efforts to strengthen the defence of the north by deploying much of the knightly retinue. His commitment of many powerful royal retainers indicates that he was not indifferent to the plight of the region. However, it is also the case that the strategy Edward and his commanders used, in which household knights played the central role, was largely ineffective in protecting the region. The emphasis was on defending strong-points along the frontier, but the Scots were more interested in ravaging the surrounding countryside, or by-passing border castles and towns altogether and raiding deep into England.[42] Under the command of the *chevetaignes*, household knights, based in their fortresses and lacking large numbers of mobile troops, could do little to stop this from happening.

Household knights played a more successful role under Edward's direction in suppressing the revolt of Llywelyn Bren in Glamorgan in early 1316. As was the case for the defence of Scotland, this episode demonstrates how Edward relied on the knightly retinue to provide not just manpower but also leadership when military crises arose.[43] The first step that Edward took to deal with Llywelyn occurred on 6 February, when he appointed two of his favourites, the household knights Hugh Audley the Younger and William de Montague, as joint commanders of the royal army being raised to deal with the revolt.[44] It must be acknowledged that their authority appears to have been superseded when, on 11 February, Humphrey de Bohun, earl of Hereford was appointed as captain of the forces marching against the rebels.[45] This was hardly surprising. The death of Gilbert de Clare, earl of Gloucester at the battle of Bannockburn had left Hereford as perhaps the most powerful magnate in the Welsh March. As such he was the logical person, in the absence of Edward, to take overall command of armies that were operating in such close proximity to his own lands. Indeed, it seems distinctly possible

---

[40] SAL, MS 120, fol. 14v. This expedition was aborted after Lancaster quarrelled with Edward, see Maddicott, *Thomas of Lancaster*, pp. 183–9.

[41] SAL, MS 120, fol. 46r; *CDS*, III, no. 570.

[42] For more on the question of whether castles in this period were particularly useful from a military perspective, see M. C. Prestwich, 'English Castles in the Reign of Edward II', *Journal of Medieval History* 8 (1982), 159–78.

[43] Edward was at Lincoln and then Clipston for the duration of the campaign, see Hallam, *Itinerary*, pp. 136–8.

[44] *CPR 1313–17*, p. 384.

[45] *CPR 1313–17*, p. 432.

that he asserted his right to do so after discovering the appointment of Audley and Montague. Both were no more than simple knights of the household, and Audley had been serving as a lowly household squire as recently as October 1312.[46]

But despite the apparent relegation of Audley and Montague from overall command, the latter continued to play a key role and would later lead a powerful force into Glamorgan from the east while Marcher lords such as John Giffard of Brimpsfield, the Mortimers and the earl of Hereford moved against Llywelyn from their respective lordships.[47] By 12 February, Montague was sharing command of his army with another royal favourite, Bartholomew de Badlesmere.[48] Their force was made up of 150 men-at-arms and 2,000 foot, all of whom were in the king's pay.[49] A number of these 150 men-at-arms were almost certainly household knights and their retainers. The likelihood of this emerges in evidence found in letters of protection issued by the king on 6 February. On this day, the same day that Montague and Audley had been appointed as commanders, Edward issued letters of protection to Montague and seven other individuals going on the campaign. All of these seven were members of the knightly retinue.[50] On 16 February another royal knight, Humphrey de Littlebury, was issued with a protection and on the same day, and also on 21 February, further protections were issued to nine followers of household knights.[51]

Other royal knights lent their support to the expedition by a variety of means. On 9 February John de Wysham, the constable of St Briavels castle and keeper of the Forest of Dean, was ordered, along with the sheriff of Somerset and Dorset and the sheriff of Gloucester, to give whatever money and victuals he had in his hands to the king's clerk, Master Stephen le Blount.[52] Blount was employed to settle the expenses incurred by the army and he seems to have been at the heart of the administration of the forces under the command of Montague and Badlesmere throughout the campaign. On 12 February Blount, Richard de la Rivere and the household knight Robert de Sapy were appointed commissioners of array in the Forest of Dean

---

46 *CFR 1307–19*, p. 147.
47 I. Mortimer, *The Greatest Traitor* (London, 2003), pp. 73–6; *Calendar of Ancient Correspondence Concerning Wales*, ed. J. G. Edwards (Cardiff, 1936), pp. 68–9.
48 *CCR 1313–18*, p. 265.
49 *Calendar of Chancery Warrants, 1244–1326*, p. 440.
50 They were John de la Beche, Edmund Bacon, Robert de L'Isle, William de Argentein, Oliver de Ingham, Roger Damory and John de Bures (*CPR 1313–17*, p. 384).
51 William le Cauf, Alexander Robert and John de Patemere who went with Humphrey de Littlebury, received protections, as did Adam de Iminghagh going with William de Montague, Robert de Bereford going with Oliver de Ingham, Andrew de Bernham going with John de la Beche, Geoffrey le Keu going with Roger Damory, and Thomas and Richard Gorge going with Edmund Bacon (*CPR 1313–17*, pp. 442–3).
52 *CCR 1313–18*, p. 265.

and elsewhere in Gloucestershire. They were charged with raising 1,000 foot soldiers, who were to be marched at the King's wages under the command of Montague and Badlesmere.[53] While it is the case that Montague and Badlesmere were nominally under the control of the earl of Hereford it is plain that they were leading a royal army independent of the Marcher lords. Their forces had been recruited from lands outside the March by officials appointed by the king and were supported by money and supplies raised from lands in England. The members of the army were in receipt of the king's wages and the force was spear-headed by a relatively small but significant element of the royal knightly retinue. By contrast, the Marcher lords led troops raised from their own lands and presumably paid for them from their own resources.[54]

The evidence from the Llywelyn Bren campaign shows that Edward was keen to use members of the knightly retinue to form the senior element of an independent force. Edward I, during his wars with the Welsh in 1276 and 1283, had used household troops as independently operating units.[55] The case of 1316, though, is rather different. The size of the force under household supervision was much greater, and it consisted of a large foot component of around 2,000 men. In 1277 and 1282 the units were around 100 men strong and were formed mainly of mounted household troops (i.e. household bannerets, knights, squires and sergeants). Edward II clearly chose household men to organize and lead this major force because he trusted them to perform effectively, and it is clear from the swift defeat of Llywelyn's rebellion that his judgement was sound.

During his reign there were moments when Edward looked to the knightly retinue as a key military resource with which to counter his domestic enemies. Full civil war was narrowly averted in 1308 and 1312, and it is noticeable how Edward relied on household knights on both occasions for military support. In 1321–2, when civil war did break out, Edward's knightly retainers were exceptionally active on his behalf. Precisely how household knights were employed on these three occasions, and the success of relying on them, is our next concern.

Within six months of succeeding his father, Edward had damaged his relations with most of the magnates to the point where he faced armed opposition. Explanations for how this situation arose in the spring of 1308 have been widely debated by historians and it is not the intention here to tread over the

---

53 *CPR 1313–17*, p. 433. A fragment of an account that Blount made illustrating payments for victuals, has survived, and probably relates to the campaign (E 101/376/16).

54 The men of south and west Wales served against Llywelyn at their own expense (*CPR 1313–17*, p. 433).

55 J. E. Morris, *The Welsh Wars of Edward I* (Oxford, 1901), p. 86.

old arguments.[56] What is of bearing to the present discussion, however, is that the majority of earls had decided by April 1308 to use the threat of violence as one method of persuading Edward to exile Piers Gaveston. As we shall see, this threat of armed action led the king to employ the knightly retinue to counter his opponents' forces.

Edward suspected that the earls were raising troops in the early months of 1308 under the cover of tournaments. This is revealed by the banning on 9 February of one such event at Croydon, just prior to the coronation, and another that was due to take place at Stamford before the opening of a parliament on 28 April.[57] His suspicions were well founded. When the magnates arrived for the parliament at Westminster they came armed with a large force and demanded Gaveston's exile.[58] However, Edward had been aware of impending trouble and had already made preparations. Central to these was the appointment of close royal adherents, principally members of the knightly retinue, to the keeping of important royal castles, mainly in the south and the Midlands, and the removal from office of men whose loyalty was dubious.[59] The household knight Robert de Haustede the Younger had already been appointed constable of Windsor castle on 12 December 1307, but it was not until 12 March that significant changes in personnel were made.[60] Nicholas de Segrave, who on the same day was appointed marshal of England, was made constable of Northampton castle.[61] John de Segrave the Elder was made keeper of Nottingham, the steward of the household, Robert FitzPayn, was appointed constable of Winchester, Nicholas de Kingston was made sheriff of Gloucester and constable of the castle there, John de Cromwell was appointed constable of the Tower of London and William Latimer constable of Rockingham castle. Also, Piers Gaveston received the keeping of Berkhamsted and Hugh Despenser the Elder was entrusted with castles at Chepstow, Devizes and Marlborough.[62] Apart from the latter two, all the appointees mentioned above were in the knightly retinue or connected to the royal household.

In addition, Edward required the newly appointed constables to improve the defences of their castles. Robert de Haustede the Younger, constable of Windsor, was ordered on 28 February to make extensive repairs to the walls,

---

56 Maddicott, *Thomas of Lancaster*, pp. 67–73.
57 *CCR 1307–13*, p. 52. Edward was crowned at Westminster Abbey on 25 February, a week later than planned: *Foedera*, II[1], 43.
58 Phillips, *Aymer de Valence*, p. 28; *Vita*, p. 5.
59 As has been pointed out, three of those who lost office on 12 March were Payn Tibetot, Robert de Clifford and John Botetourte. They had affixed their seals to the so called 'Boulogne Declaration' in January and were therefore probably assumed by Edward to be hostile (Maddicott, *Thomas of Lancaster*, p. 77).
60 *CFR 1307–19*, p. 10.
61 *CPR 1307–13*, p. 51.
62 *CFR 1307–19*, pp. 18–19; *CPR 1307–13*, pp. 51, 58.

towers and bridges of the castle,[63] and on 6 April the keepers of fifty-one royal castles, including all those mentioned above, were ordered to fortify them, 'so that no danger arise through want of fortification or guard'.[64] What is most striking about Edward's preparations, particularly those made in conjunction with household knights, is their defensive nature. There is no evidence to suggest that Edward tried to raise large numbers of troops to oppose the earls, as he would on future occasions. Indeed, his behaviour from late March suggests that he had developed something of a 'fortress mentality'. Largely ensconced at Windsor, he surrounded himself with his favourites and household knights. His physical seclusion there was augmented by his destruction of two nearby bridges over the Thames at Kingston and at Staines in May.[65] To some extent, isolation was inevitable. Opposition to Edward was perhaps more united in the spring of 1308 than at any later date in the reign, with the exception of 1326. The earls of Pembroke, Hereford, Gloucester, Warwick, Lincoln, Surrey and Arundel were all party to demands for Gaveston's removal at the Westminster parliament in late April. No matter how well organized the household retinue was, even if allied with other resources, it was unlikely to have been effective against the combined resources of the earls. It is hardly surprising that Edward acquiesced to the opposition's demands on 18 May and agreed to Gaveston's exile.

Civil war came much closer in 1312 and household knights played a role in events. Edward used them more extensively than in 1308, although again with mixed success. Conflict had arisen once more over the place of Gaveston at court, after his return from exile in defiance of the Ordinances.[66] Edward, knowing that the return of Gaveston would provoke the barons, fled to York with his favourite in January 1312 in order to evade his opponents, who were mainly located in London, working on the implementation of the Ordinances.

It seems likely that Edward had been preparing this move for some weeks. As we shall see, he had been issuing military orders, many of which involved royal knights, since December, and he continued planning with the household retinue in mind throughout the early months of 1312. He also moved the centre of government to York soon after his arrival there in early January. Adam de Osgodby, the keeper of the chancery rolls, and numerous chancery clerks were ordered to join Edward and set up the workings of their office in the abbey church of St Mary's.[67] Once again, the military emphasis was on defensive measures, although on this occasion the preparations seem to have been rather more comprehensive than those made in 1308. Not surprisingly, given his presence there, Edward concentrated on securing his northern

---

[63] *CCR 1307–13*, p. 22.

[64] *CCR 1307–13*, p. 29.

[65] Maddicott, *Thomas of Lancaster*, p. 78.

[66] *Vita*, p. 21.

[67] *CCR 1307–13*, pp. 448–9.

fortresses. However, the most important royal castles in the Midlands and the south were not neglected. On 10 December Edward entrusted to the household knights William de Vaux, Edmund Bacon and John de la Beche the castles of Knaresborough, Wallingford and Nottingham respectively.[68] The household banneret Gerard de Salveyn, who had been sheriff of York and keeper of York castle since March 1311, seems to have been particularly important to Edward at this time. He had been sent to the continent as an escort to Piers Gaveston while the latter was in exile.[69] When Salveyn returned he was given responsibility for improving the defences at York castle. Two springalds, two unspecified siege engines (*ingenia*) and thirteen crossbows were manufactured there. In addition, 1,000 crossbow bolts were produced, and thirty quarrels for use with the springalds under his supervision.[70]

Defences were improved elsewhere by royal knights. On the 29 January the sheriff of Nottingham, Ralph de Crophill, was ordered to build a 'peel' on the western side of Nottingham castle as quickly as possible, under the instructions of the constable and royal knight, John de la Beche. Much was also done to improve the security of the Tower of London, by its constable John de Cromwell. On the 8 February the sheriffs of London were ordered by Edward to pay, without delay, to Thomas, the king's engineer, a sum from the farm of the city that was deemed sufficient by Cromwell for the building of four *ingenia* and six springalds. And on 28 March repairs were ordered for the towers, garnistures, engines and springalds of the Tower, under Cromwell's supervision. On 28 January Edward ordered the constables of numerous royal fortresses to stock up on provisions without delay and to ensure that the castles were safely guarded. The household knights Edmund de Mauley (the current steward), Nicholas de Segrave, Robert de Mauley, Hugh Audley the Elder and John de Wysham were recipients of these orders for the corresponding castles of Bristol, Northampton, Bolsover and Horeston, Shrewsbury and Stafford, and St Briavels. In addition, the royal knights Robert de Kendale, Warin de L'Isle, John de la Beche and John de Cromwell were ordered to take delivery of large quantities of victuals from their local sheriffs for their respective charges of Dover, Windsor, Nottingham and the Tower. Edward had clearly decided that royal castles were worth defending and that household knights were the best individuals to command the most important of them.[71]

As the earls again began to raise troops under the cover of more tournaments Edward's military strategy, however, did not evolve beyond placing household knights and other allies in key castles and ensuring that those

---

[68] *CFR 1307–19*, p. 118.
[69] Ibid., p. 97.
[70] BL Cotton MS Nero C. VIII, fols 64v–65r.
[71] *CCR 1307–13*, pp. 396, 399–400, 417, 402.

places were well provisioned. There is no evidence that foot levies were recruited, or that magnates loyal to Edward were asked to raise troops. Consequently, when Lancaster attacked Edward at Newcastle on 4 May the latter probably only had a few men to oppose him. Certainly, this is the impression one inevitably gains, given the ease with which Lancaster forced his way into the town and compelled Edward to flee. With no army, it also proved impossible for Edward to relieve Scarborough castle where Pembroke, Warenne, Percy and Clifford had trapped Gaveston. His surrender was assured, a development which probably sealed his fate. Edward seems to have misjudged the likely tactics of the magnates. Their interest was in pursuing Gaveston, not in capturing royal castles. If Edward, accompanied by Gaveston, had ordered his household knights to muster in the north and asked them to bring retainers and levies from their respective areas, rather than dispatching them to various fortresses across England, he would surely have been in a much stronger position to oppose the barons. The opposition magnates would have been forced into the unenviable dilemma of whether or not to attack Edward directly. Had they done so, the conflict would have been transformed into a full civil war. It is hard to believe that more moderate earls like Pembroke and Warenne would have been prepared to do this. Instead, though, the retinue remained scattered and impotent and the magnates were not required to commit themselves decisively.

The revolt of many former and some current household knights in 1321–2, best epitomized by the conduct of the household steward, Bartholomew de Badlesmere, has received much attention recently from one historian.[72] But despite his having been betrayed by many retainers, Edward's faith in the value of households knights appears to have been unshaken. The retinue was reformed with many new recruits in the second half of 1321 and was subsequently deployed *en masse* against Edward's enemies between November 1321 and March 1322.[73] Indeed, the contribution that Edward's knightly retinue made to defeating the 'contrariants' was hugely significant, a fact that has been largely ignored.

It was Edward's recall of the exiled Despensers in November 1321 that heralded the second outbreak of violence that year between him and his opponents. The knightly retinue swiftly moved into action under Edward's direction. Many household knights and other individuals with recent connections to the *familia* were initially sent to seize the lands of rebels who were removed from the areas where the contrariant forces were assembling. In late

---

[72] M. C. Prestwich, 'The Unreliability of Household Knights in the Early Fourteenth Century', in *Fourteenth Century England* II, ed. C. Given-Wilson (Woodbridge, 2002), pp. 1–11.

[73] See BL Stowe MS 553, fols 65r, 66r, 105r, 108r, for a full list of household knights at this time.

November John de Haustede was ordered to take possession of Roger Damory's lands in Essex, Hertfordshire and Suffolk.[74] On 6 and 7 December Oliver de Ingham and the household sergeant, Robert le Ewer, were given writs of aid to seize the lands of all the major rebels in Oxfordshire, Berkshire, Wiltshire and Gloucestershire.[75] In late December John Howard and, again, John de Haustede were ordered to seize the lands of contrariants in Essex and Norfolk and Suffolk. Another household knight, Nicholas de la Beche, was given custody of the earl of Hereford's castle at Plescy in Essex on 30 December.[76] These were positive developments, from Edward's perspective, for two reasons. First, the rebels were denied the manpower and financial resources that could be extracted from those lands; and second, the king was now able to exploit the estates for his own benefit. We know that Edward raised money from the confiscated lands of the Marcher lords in February, to finance the army he would lead against Lancaster, and it seems likely that he was engaged in a similar practice at this stage.[77]

While lands were being seized the knightly retinue was also busy raising troops in various parts of the country, either to crush insurgents locally, or to form part of the army that Edward planned to lead against the rebels in the Welsh March. In late November writs of aid were issued to various retainers to assist them in the raising of horse and foot. These were given to John de Somery and John de Segrave the Elder for Warwickshire, Leicestershire and Staffordshire, Oliver de Ingham and Robert le Ewer for Wiltshire and Berkshire, and John Howard for Norfolk. In addition, on 2 January Ralph de Grendon was ordered to raise 1,000 footmen in Warwickshire.[78]

By January, Edward was ready to go on the attack against the Marcher lords, and it is clear, from extensive evidence, that household knights were crucial to the success of this part of the campaign. While Edward gathered his army in the Midlands, royal forces from north Wales and Cheshire invaded the lands of the rebellious Marcher lords. Men connected to the household led these forces. The role of the Welsh knight Gruffydd Llwyd in this offensive has been described before, but his previous connection to the knightly retinue has not.[79] Llwyd's intervention was without doubt very useful in splitting the contrariant army when it became apparent to its commanders

---

74 *CFR 1319–27*, p. 81.
75 *CPR 1321–24*, p. 40.
76 *CFR 1319–27*, pp. 84–5.
77 Fryde, *Tyranny and Fall*, p. 92.
78 *CPR 1321–24*, pp. 40, 45.
79 J. G. Edwards, 'Sir Gruffydd Llwyd', *EHR* 30 (1915), 589–601; J. Beverley Smith, 'Gruffydd Llwyd and the Celtic Alliance, 1315–18', *Bulletin of the Board of Celtic Studies* 26 (1974–6), 463–78; J. Beverley Smith, 'Edward II and the Allegiance of Wales', *WHR* 8 (1976–77), 139–71. Llwyd was retained by Edward as a knight in 1314–15 (E 101/378/6), a fact which illustrates another dimension to his long association with the king.

that they faced attack from behind, and not just from Edward.[80] The estates of John de Charlton, lord of Powys, Edward's former chamberlain and household banneret, were singled out for assault, together with those of the Mortimers.[81] Charlton appears to have abandoned the main rebel army in mid-January in order to defend his lands. However, Llwyd was not alone. Robert de Sapy, a household knight, was also operating in the area, and was probably just as important. Charlton was trapped in la Pole castle in mid-January and it is likely that Sapy was the commander of the besieging force. The castle fell quickly, and on the 18 January Sapy's name was at the head of a list of two others in royals orders, one of whom was Llwyd, as authorized to receive Charlton into the King's will.[82] Furthermore, on the 19 January Sapy, not Llwyd, was given sole custody of the entire lordship of Powys, including la Pole castle. Sapy was supported in nearby Shropshire by another household knight, John de Felton, who was also operating independently against the insurgents at this time, seizing rebel strongholds and lands. On the 18 January he was ordered to take control of Red Castle, and on the 22 January, the manor of Hodnet.[83]

The main royal army that assembled in January 1322 was built around a core formed by the knightly retinue. In this sense the composition of the army of January 1322 is not significantly different from that of the armies that Edward led against the Scots. Wage rolls for the campaign have not survived, but the participation of the knightly retinue is apparent through other forms of evidence. For example, a considerable number of household knights were in receipt of protections, at this time, for going on the royal service in the Welsh March. Edmund de Kendale and John de Say received protections on 4 January, by the testimony of the steward of the household, Gilbert Pecche, as did Thomas le Ercedekne on 6 January. Also in receipt were John Inge, John de Cromwell and Alan de Charlton on the 6 January; Edmund Bacon and John de Bures on 7 January; and Henry de Staunton, Walter de Beauchamp, Robert de Morby and John Sturmy on 15 January.[84] We know, also, that Edward later dispersed nine household knights across the March to seize the confiscated lands of rebels, a task which we shall discuss in more detail. It is likely that all nine were in Edward's company on the campaign before being sent on this mission. These were: William de la Beche, Walter le Gras, Robert de Morby, John de Siggeston, John de Dene, Richard le Marshal, Humphrey de Littlebury, Alan de Charlton and Robert de Sapy.[85] In all, twenty-one

---

[80] Edward arrived at Shrewsbury on the 14 January (Hallam, p. 220).
[81] For further details of Charlton's career, see R. Morgan, 'The Barony of Powys, 1275–1360', *Welsh History Review* 10 (1980–1), pp. 1–32.
[82] *CPR 1321–24*, p. 48.
[83] *CFR 1319–27*, pp. 89–90.
[84] *CPR 1321–24*, pp. 65–8.
[85] *CFR 1319–27*, pp. 91–3.

household knights were clearly involved in the campaign against the Marcher lords, out of a total of thirty-five retained at the time. Edward was wise to use large numbers of household knights. They provided experienced leaders and valuable manpower for the forthcoming campaign and their presence also demonstrated the new unity of the retinue after recent defections. This must have been valuable in encouraging others to join the King.

Many of the household knights who were not involved in fighting the Marcher lords were, in any case, engaged against the rebels in other places. There seems, for example, to have been considerable skirmishing in the south-west and in northern parts of the Midlands, both areas where many of the contrariants held lands. That royal forces were directed against them in those areas indicates that the contrariants were active there in opposing the king. Household knights provided leadership in the fighting. John de Beauchamp of Somerset and Richard Lovel were commissioned on 7 February to raise horse and foot in Somerset and Dorset and to march against the rebels there. And in Staffordshire, Warwickshire, Leicestershire, Rutland and Northamptonshire Oliver de Ingham and Ralph de Grendon were similarly empowered to raise forces and to direct them against the king's enemies.[86]

With the surrender of the Mortimers on 22 January 1322, resistance in the Welsh March collapsed. However, it was important from Edward's perspective, given Lancaster's menacing presence in the north, that the rebellion was crushed once and for all across the region and neighbouring districts. He turned to knightly retainers to finish the task by placing them in areas that had previously served as centres of power for the rebels. As has been mentioned above, Edward did this by committing the lands of rebel Marcher lords to the custody of household knights. The orders, which were issued on 23 January, were directed to twelve individuals, nine of whom were in the knightly retinue.[87] It was probably both useful and necessary that royal knights were employed. Men with military skills and resources were needed in order to stabilize volatile areas. Household knights were ideal for the task and were given seniority over the royal clerks who accompanied them. The clerks were only given responsibility to survey the confiscated lands and chattels, and, of course, raise revenues from the estates.[88]

The role that the knightly retinue played in asserting royal control over

---

[86] *CPR 1321–24,* p. 69.

[87] *CFR 1319–27,* pp. 91–3.

[88] A royal clerk accompanied each knight to his area of responsibility. For example, John de Siggeston was in the company of Master William de Holyns and Richard le Marshal with Master Benedict de Normanton (*CFR 1319–27,* pp. 91–3). The knight was termed the custodian and clearly had ultimate authority locally. The clerk's subservience was emphasized further by the fact that it was the knight who was authorized by the King to pay the clerk's wages from local revenues rather than *vice versa* (*CCR 1318–23,* p. 415).

rebel lands extended to places other than the Welsh March. On 22 January Nicholas de la Beche was ordered to take custody of the manors of the earl of Hereford in Essex. On 15 January John de Say took custody of the castle of Bridgewater, and on 8 February John Sturmy seized Berkeley. Simon de Driby, who had been appointed keeper of the castle and town of Gloucester and keeper of St Briavels castle and the Forest of Dean, was given custody on 13 February of various rebel lands in Herefordshire and Gloucestershire, most notably those of the earl of Hereford and John Giffard de Brimpsfield, and on 18 February Richard Lovel took control of the estates of Maurice de Berkeley, Thomas de Gurney and various minor rebels in Gloucestershire and Wiltshire.[89]

Edward was not content with merely placing household knights in charge of contrariant lands. He also gave them a central role in suppressing the remaining insurgents. Knightly retainers were authorized to pursue and arrest those implicated in the rebellion. Most were issued with writs of aid. These were intended to compel local officials and inhabitants into providing assistance to household knights in their hunt for the fugitives. No doubt severe penalties were incurred if cooperation was not provided to the bearers. As early as 3 January 1322 Nicholas de la Beche was commissioned to arrest contrariants in Essex, but the greatest flurry of suppressive activity involving household knights took place in the aftermath of the collapse of the revolt in the March and west Midlands.[90] Ralph de Grendon was appointed to arrest insurgents in Warwickshire on 15 January. On 22 January Grendon, who had previously been ordered to bring his Warwickshire foot to the King at Shrewsbury during the main campaign, was ordered to remain where he was with his forces and to instead arrest insurgents. On 8 February John de Say was given a writ of aid for the arrest of various rebels in the south-west. Similar writs were issued for use in the same region, to Richard Lovel on 14 February, and to Nicholas de Grey on 21 February.[91] On 18 February all the household knights who were soon to be appointed to the keeping of rebel lands in the March were ordered to identify the names of recent insurgents within their respective areas of responsibility, and to identify which individuals should be taken hostage.[92] On 16 March Robert de Morby was authorized to arrest various Welsh insurgents, as was Gilbert de Glencarny on 22 March.

Between 12 and 18 March more writs of aid were given, to knights pursuing rebels in the north Midlands and Yorkshire. John de Somery's remit extended to Warwickshire, Leicestershire, Derbyshire, Worcestershire, Nottinghamshire and Staffordshire, and Ralph de Grendon's to Warwick-

---

[89] *CFR 1319–27*, pp. 90, 94, 96, 97.
[90] *CPR 1321–24*, p. 46.
[91] *CPR 1321–24*, pp. 51, 53, 62.
[92] *CCR 1318–23*, p. 422.

shire, Robert de Leyburn's to Lancashire, Humphrey de Littlebury's to Lincolnshire, Thomas Ughtred's to Yorkshire. Nicholas de Grey and John de Hardeshull were given responsibility for Derbyshire and Leicestershire. Emphasis was also given to pursuing rebels in East Anglia. John Haustede was ordered to search for John de Botetourte the Elder on 13 March, and on the 16 March to arrest various contrariants in Norfolk and Suffolk. Similar orders were given to Nicholas de la Beche on the same day, for rebels hiding in Essex.[93]

Edward's household knights, with the authority of the King expressed through writs of aid, probably created a climate of fear as they combed the Welsh March and areas of southern and central England for insurgents. But just how successful they were in capturing the most important rebels is less clear. John Botetourt managed to escape abroad and John Mautravers evaded capture in the south-west, where he became a significant irritant by launching attacks on the estates of royal supporters.[94] However, many of the rebels who were eventually executed met their ends in the south-west and the Midlands and it is likely that they were captured by the household knights who had been appointed to hunt them down.[95]

Household knights had little involvement in the war against the Bruces and their allies in Ireland, for two main reasons. First, the war with the Scots in northern England was probably seen as a more pressing place to employ household knights. It is always worth remembering that the Bruce invasion of Ireland coincided with the Scottish raids of northern England. These touched the heartlands of Edward's realm and dealing with them was always likely to be a priority. And second, it is likely that most of the knightly retinue, even if requested, would have been reluctant to fight in a region where the vast majority had no vested interest and where Edward never campaigned in person.[96] The minimal involvement of household knights in fighting the Bruces in Ireland, however, did not prevent one man from enjoying considerable success. The career of John de Athy is of interest in it own right, but its relevance to this essay is that it demonstrates extremely well Edward II's ability to recruit capable household knights and to employ them advantageously.

The day before John de Athy joined the household (28 March 1317) he had been appointed captain of the fleet that was due to sail from Bristol to Youghal. Athy's task was to transport an army, led by Roger Mortimer of

---

93 *CPR 1321–24*, pp. 77, 81–2.
94 Fryde, *Tyranny and Fall*, pp. 151, 177.
95 For example, John Giffard of Brimpsfield and Henry de Teye were executed at Gloucester, and Henry de Wilington and Henry de Montfort at Bristol (ibid., p. 61).
96 It is worth noting that the knightly retinue was very Anglocentric in its composition. John de Athy, Alan FitzWarin and Theobald de Verdun were the only retainers to have strong connections with the Anglo-Norman colony.

Wigmore, that had been raised to combat the Bruce threat in Ireland.[97] After delivering Mortimer safely in early April, Athy's orders required him to remain at sea with a flotilla of four ships and guard the routes between Ireland and Scotland, and at the same time pursue enemy shipping.[98] With these limited resources he was remarkably successful. His capture and execution of the infamous Scottish pirate, Thomas Dun, was probably critical in improving communications and supply routes between England and Ireland.[99] Dun's ships were attacked by Athy and Geoffrey de Coigners on 2 July and after a fierce battle, during which forty pirates were killed, Dun was taken alive.[100] The removal of Thomas Dun from the seas by Athy may also have obstructed plans for Scottish and Welsh cooperation against the English. J. Beverley Smith has shown how Dun was active on the north coast of Wales in 1316 at the same time as Edward Bruce explored ways of building alliances with discontented native Welsh.[101]

Athy remained in the household until at least 1323 and continued to be active on behalf of the crown in Ireland and on the neighbouring seas throughout his career as a royal retainer.[102] Indeed, he was given considerable authority by Edward to act in the region as he saw fit. In April 1317 he was appointed to receive rebellious Ulstermen into the King's peace, and in July was appointed keeper of the Isle of Man.[103] His remit for receiving former rebels back into the king's peace was widened in June 1318 to include all Irish and Scots who had fought against the English. In addition, he was appointed admiral and captain of ships and men destined for service in the 'west', and authorized to press sailors into service.[104] In this period it is clear that Athy was the most significant figure involved in the English strategy for dealing with the Scots and Irish rebels on the seas and coast lines of northeastern Ireland.

This impression is reinforced by evidence for his activities in late 1318 and 1319 and by the sheer quantity of royal orders directed towards senior royal officials who were required to aid him. For example, the recaptured and strategically important castle of Carrickfergus was entrusted to him. He was officially appointed constable in March 1319, but seems to have been in charge there since at least early February, and perhaps soon after it was recaptured

---

[97] P. R. Dryburgh 'The career of Roger Mortimer, first earl of March' (unpublished Ph.D. thesis, University of Bristol, 2002), pp. 54–5.

[98] *CPR 1313–17*, pp. 574–5, 632; SAL, MS 120, fols 45r, 53v.

[99] For details of Thomas Dun's career and his impact on the Irish Sea theatre see McNamee, *Wars of the Bruces*, pp. 173–6, 180–4, 190–1.

[100] *Chartulary of St Mary's, Dublin*, ed. J. T. Gilbert, 2 vols (RS, 1886), II, 355.

[101] Beverley Smith, 'Gruffydd Llwyd and the Celtic Alliance', p. 473.

[102] BL Stowe MS 553, fols 65r, 66r.

[103] *CPR 1313–17*, pp. 574–5, 636; *CFR 1307–19*, p. 332.

[104] *CPR 1317–21*, pp. 164–5, 195.

in October/November 1318.[105] The importance of this post and the confidence placed in Athy by Edward are reflected well by the personal interest he took in making sure that the castle was very well garrisoned and had ample supplies. Edward's orders in these matters were directed to his highest officials in Ireland, the justiciar Alexander Bicknor, archbishop of Dublin, and the treasurer Master Walter de Islip.[106] During late 1318 and 1319 these men regularly and promptly reimbursed him from the Irish exchequer for the expenses he had incurred in purchasing and transporting victuals from Dublin and Drogheda to Carrickfergus.[107]

Edward clearly feared that Carrickfergus might fall again to the Scots and that more of his enemies would attempt to cross the sea from Scotland in the summer of 1319.[108] Athy, as constable, was obviously at the heart of preventing this. On 27 February Edward ordered the chamberlain of Carmarthen to send to Carrickfergus 100 marks' worth of victuals, and on the same day ordered him to provide a 'great ship' for service there with a crew from the town of Carmarthen. The day before the order was issued the sheriff of Devon had also been told to dispatch five ships with twice the normal complement of sailors to Carrickfergus. It is clear from the wording of the orders that Athy, who is described as 'admiral of the king's ships in Ireland', had advised Edward that these particular resources were essential for the security of the castle and nearby seas.[109] The king's responsiveness demonstrates Athy's ability to influence royal decisions from afar and confirms his importance.

Edward's interest in Carrickfergus and his receptiveness to Athy's requests as constable continued through the remainder of 1319. The chamberlain of Caernarvon was ordered to send 200 quarters of corn and various other victuals to the castle with all speed, in November, in direct response to Athy's advice.[110] There is also evidence that Athy's value went beyond merely defending castles and captaining fleets. He seems to have been capable of building good relations with local native Irish leaders whose support was crucial in protecting Anglo-Irish interests in Ulster. Athy was on particularly good terms with Colman MacDuilechain of Clanbrassil, who was able to give Athy military assistance for the protection of Carrickfergus from the Scots.[111]

The details of Athy's career given here are only a glimpse of his activities

---

105 *CPR 1317–21*, p. 311; *CCR 1318–23*, p. 55.
106 *CCR 1318–23*, pp. 58–9.
107 *Irish Exchequer Payments, 1270–1446*, ed. P. Connolly (Dublin, 1998), pp. 256, 261.
108 Presumably Edward was anxious to avoid a repeat of the fall of the castle through starvation. See G. O. Sayles, 'The Siege of Carrickfergus Castle, 1315–16', *Irish Historical Studies* 10 (1956–7), 94–100.
109 *CCR 1318–23*, p. 59.
110 *CCR 1318–23*, p. 165.
111 McNamee, *Wars of the Bruces*, p. 186; *CCR 1318–23*, p. 127. MacDuilechain was one of

at a time of particular crisis. He was to remain in royal service for many years. He was later a constable of various other castles in Ulster and he held the office of admiral of the 'western sea' into the 1330s.[112] His abilities were highly valued by both Edward II and Edward III, and he was still receiving an annual pension for his good service in 1344.[113] Edward II's choice of household knights can sometimes be questioned, but in the case of John de Athy it is clear that an exceptionally reliable and competent military man was recruited and beneficially employed.

Overall, the picture we gain of Edward's abilities as a commander by looking at his management of household knights is mixed. His extensive use of household knights in 1308 and 1312 to counter the threat posed by baronial opponents shows that he looked to retainers as an important and reliable resource. However, his tendency to take a defensive posture by dispersing his household knights across the country in castles was ineffective and probably contributed to the capture and murder of Piers Gaveston in 1312. Between 1315 and 1318 his deployment of large numbers of household knights on the western and eastern Marches shows once again that he placed great faith in their military value. But again, the evidence suggests that the way in which they were employed did little to hinder the Scots. This failure probably led to discord in the ranks of the knightly retinue itself, as exhibited by the outburst of the household knight Adam de Swinburn, who criticized the King's policy in the north to his face.[114] Edward's failures, however, should not be allowed to dominate the whole picture. His use of household knights against Llywelyn Bren was imaginative and successful, and it also appears that Edward learned lessons from the set-backs he suffered at the hands of his domestic opponents in 1308 and 1312. The deployment of the knightly retinue against the Marcher lords in 1322 was masterful and their thoroughness in suppressing any lingering revolt in the months afterwards did much handicap political opposition to Edward for some years. Any assessment of Edward's military abilities based on how he managed household knights has, therefore, to concede the existence of both startling failure and remarkable success.

---

a few native Irish lords from eastern Ulster who had resisted Edward Bruce in 1315. See R. Frame, *Ireland and Britain* (London, 1998), pp. 82–3.

[112] *CPR 1321–24*, p. 121; *Irish Exchequer Payments*, pp. 309, 314, 356, 379.

[113] Ibid., p. 404.

[114] An account of this event is given in Thomas Grey, *Scalacronica*, ed. Sir H. Maxwell (Glasgow, 1907), p. 60.

6

England in Europe in the Reign of Edward II

W. R. Childs

The England of Edward II is firmly embedded in Europe in every aspect of life: territorially, dynastically, socially, culturally, religiously and commercially. Awareness of these varied European contacts is clear in the writers of the fourteenth century and among modern historians. Some facets of these contacts have been quite fully explored, but others are rarely mentioned, and there is no full study of England's European contacts in all their aspects for this period. In particular, there is no study of formal government links at the diplomatic level, beyond the obviously important negotiations within the core north-south axis of Scotland, France and Avignon. And yet Edward had diplomatic contacts as extensive as his father's, stretching from Norway in the north to Portugal in the west and through the eastern Mediterranean to the Tartar Il-Khans of Persia. This paper is an initial survey, part of continuing research, which is intended to lead to a larger study. Here I simply want to draw attention to the wide scope of these government to government diplomatic contacts. At the very least, the management of foreign relations is a part of normal government activity, and a study of diplomatic contacts beyond England's immediate neighbours and the skill with which they were conducted might possibly add to how we view Edward II's reign.[1]

The stimulus for this paper was my recent close re-reading of the *Vita Edwardi Secundi*, in which the author's main interest is clearly high domestic politics.[2] It is true that the Scottish war takes up some twenty-five per cent of the *Vita*'s space, and Edward's French visits and the French war are all mentioned, but in these the primary focus is still domestic. The relations of the king and his baronage affect the prosecution of the Scottish war and, in turn, the consequences of the war affect their relationship in England. Similarly, the preparations for the French war are a vehicle for comment on the king's wealth and his harshness at home. The highly educated author cannot but

---

1 My thanks go to all those who raised questions and commented on an early draft of this paper at the International Medieval Congress at Leeds and at the Symposium on Edward II at Nottingham. I hope they will recognize attempts to deal with some of the matters they raised.

2 My new edition is published by Oxford University Press: *Vita Edwardi Secundi*, ed. W. R. Childs, Oxford Medieval Texts (Oxford, 2005). My discussion will refer to this edition.

have been aware of the wider European world, notably in relation to the church, but even here contact with Avignon, which is frequently mentioned, is always in relation to the domestic scene – to the Ordinances, Gaveston, episcopal appointments, and Bruce. Only in the critical obituary on Clement V is there mention of the Council of Vienne and the destruction of the Templars.

This is not surprising, since the domestic drama of Edward's reign is so arresting. Most other chronicles of the reign are similarly fixed on home affairs, although some make a little more mention of European affairs, particularly of the accusations against the Templars and the Council at Vienne.[3] Almost all record the deaths of the French kings, and four pick up some details of the scandal at the French court in 1313. Seven also make some reference to imperial matters – the election or death of Henry of Luxemburg or the papal war against Louis of Bavaria and the papal preference for Robert of Sicily. Four refer to the episodes of the Pastoureaux and of the accusations against lepers and Jews in 1320. The Lanercost chronicler picked up the Saracens' defeat of the Spanish in 1319, Trokelowe picked up news of an animal pest in France, Murimuth (who probably has the widest range of European news) also noted the clash of Guelfs and Ghibillines in 1324; and the *Annales Paulini* (which also contain a wide range of European news) recorded the burning of St John Lateran in 1308 and the intense cold in Avignon in 1325. The *Flores* notes the outbreak of war between France and Flanders in 1315, and the *Annales Paulini* notes the peace between them in 1319.

Chroniclers also had an awareness of Englishness, for good or ill, in the face of Europe. The well-educated author of the *Vita* wrote interestingly (and so far insolubly) that 'In every kingdom bordering the Mediterranean you will find many of the English race (*de genere Anglorum*); it is commonly said and rumour relates that deceit (*dolus*) resides in them above all others.'[4] The possibly less cosmopolitan author of the long continuation of the *Brut* was, on the other hand, altogether more critical of foreigners and blamed the civil war of 1321–2 on the fact that

> the grete lordes of Engeland were nougt alle of o nacioun, but were mellede with othere nacions that is forto seyn, somme Britons, somme Saxones, somme Danois, somme Peghtes, somme Frenchemen, somme Normans, somme Spaignardes, somme Romayns, some Henaudes, some Flemyngus, and of othere diverse naciouns, the which naciouns acorded nougt to the kynde bloode of Engeland.[5]

However, it was not only the relatively limited geographical scope of the

3 The eleven other chronicles examined have been *Murimuth, AL, AP, Anonimalle, Brut, Flores, Geoffrey le Baker, Lanercost, Bridlington* and Henry Blaneforde and John Trokelowe (*JT*).
4 *Vita*, ed. Childs, pp. 108–9. Some English merchants were in Italy, such as Geoffrey le Lacer of London who lost £1050 of goods in Bologna in 1316, *CPR 1327–30*, p. 41.
5 *Brut*, p. 220.

contemporary political histories which struck me recently, but that of some modern writers on the political history of the reign.[6] Again, as I have said, this is not surprising, given the drama of the domestic politics and the obvious impact of the Scottish and French wars. However, the contrast with studies of Henry III and Edward I, who are viewed as European kings, is marked,[7] and it seems worth reminding ourselves from time to time of the scale of Edward II's relationships with the rest of Europe. Not only does this extend our understanding of his activities, but it also opens up wider questions. Was his activity more limited than his father's? Was there any overall pattern to his contacts abroad? Did Edward II, like his father, look for allies? Was the government active or reactive? Did Edward II, in fact, have a 'foreign policy'?

In the space allowed this paper cannot possibly be comprehensive. I shall therefore, for convenience, divide England's activities in Europe into three zones: the inner core of contiguous neighbours, the immediate circle of close neighbours, and powers in the rest of Europe and even beyond. From them I shall take some illustrative examples, before addressing some of the wider questions.

The inner core, running due north-south, comprised Scotland, France, and the Papacy at Avignon (possibly Ireland should also be included here). In both Scotland and France Edward inherited difficult territorial claims. In Scotland he also inherited a war, and in France the problems eventually led to war in 1324. The problems in both areas drew in the Papacy, which was concerned to promote peace. The narratives of these relationships are well known and will not be repeated here, but we need to keep certain points in mind which stem from these activities and affect other areas. First, from time to time Edward needed to look for allies, which he naturally did mainly within the first circle beyond the core. Second, and perhaps as important, the problems produced not only war but also a good deal of diplomatic activity, whether it was the Process of Perigueux grinding away in the early years of Edward's reign, the sharp exchange of insults when Anglo-Scottish negotiations failed in 1322 or the many negotiations in Avignon relevant to war as well as to the normal Anglo-Papal affairs. This constant exchange of messengers and envoys continued to hone English diplomatic practices and skills which had long antecedents, but which had been developing fast during the

---

6 Many of the recent studies of the reign are studies of individuals and therefore can not be expected to cover foreign relations, but even the most recent general study of the reign by Haines, *King Edward II*, does not go far beyond Scotland and France. The wider geographical contacts are of course evident in the more specialized works on trade and the church, including works by Haines himself.

7 For Edward I's early diplomacy, see M. Prestwich, *Edward I* (London, 1988), pp. 312–35.

reign of Edward I.[8] Specialists became apparent: in November 1324 the magnates' advice to the king, when he asked them whether and how to treat with France and Scotland, was to 'take advice from those treating with them before'.[9] In Castile and Aragon, Edward used Peter de Galiciano and Arnaud Guillaume of Béarn as regular envoys. They became skilled in Iberian affairs, and in 1325 Edward thanked Guillaume for his work, writing that he was sending him on another embassy to Spain 'because Arnaud has more knowledge than others of the matter and has knowledge of the magnates of those parts, and the king has faith in his prudence'.[10] The machinery of a keeper of processes and of a hierarchy of messengers, envoys, and ambassadors was also there, to be applied to any area Edward wished to deal with. Moreover, the presence of frequent envoys in Paris and their virtually permanent presence in Avignon kept the English officials at home well informed about events and people all over Christendom. But it is the circles beyond this core that I wish to examine in more detail.

In the immediate circle beyond the core were those overseas countries closest to England; on one side of France were Scandinavia and the Low Countries, on the other was Iberia. Not only might these make possible allies against Scotland or France, but they were also England's nearest trading partners, and contact was constant and rising. Europe's booming economy had greatly extended and intensified commercial contacts during the thirteenth century, and trade was an ever-increasing element in government-to-government correspondence. In a number of areas more energy was expended on sorting out trade disputes than on traditional dynastic diplomacy. In this circle I will pick out as examples Norway (which is generally ignored), Holland, Zeeland and Hainault (which is sometimes ignored until Isabella's betrothal of the young Edward to Phillippa), and Castile (more often given a passing mention because of Edward's Castilian lineage).

Of the Scandinavian countries, Norway was of most interest to England. But it played a surprisingly small political role as ally or enemy, despite its proximity to Scotland and its former importance in 1290, when Edward I had betrothed his son to Margaret of Norway, heiress of Scotland. The short-lived Norwegian-Scottish and Norwegian-Flemish alliances were not to England's liking, but there is no evidence of damage. From 1307 Edward's and Haaken's correspondence was most frequently prompted by requests for justice for their countries' merchants in matters of debt and robbery. Norway was still one of the major suppliers of timber and cod (Norwegian and

---

[8] G. P. Cuttino, *English Diplomatic Administration 1259–1339*, 2nd edn (Oxford, 1971); P. Chaplais, *English Medieval Diplomatic Practice*, 2 vols (London, 1982); P. Chaplais, *English Diplomatic Practice in the Middle Ages* (London, 2003).

[9] *The War of Saint-Sardos (1323–1325)*, ed. P. Chaplais, Camden Society 3rd s. 87 (London, 1954), p. 89.

[10] *CCR 1323–7*, p. 516.

Icelandic) to England's east coast ports, although by the 1320s it was beginning to fade in the face of strong Hanseatic competition. At Hull in *c.*1303–11
Norwegian ships and merchants accounted for some twenty to twenty-five
per cent of alien merchants' import and export values (excluding wool), and
Norwegian ships from Trondheim, Bergen and Oslo dominated the trade in
timber and stockfish there. At Lynn, before 1309, Norwegians were equally
important, and in 1305–6 some nineteen Norwegian ships had carried forty-
six per cent by value of alien merchants' exports (excluding wool).[11] English
ships and merchants sailed to Bergen and Vik frequently, and in 1312, 400
men of Lynn (presumably merchants and seamen) were arrested in Norway
with goods alleged to be worth £6,000.[12]

Relations were still covered by the treaty made between Henry III and
Magnus IV, renewed by Edward I and Magnus (1284) and now renewed
between Edward II and Haaken in 1309.[13] Normally, trade ran smoothly, but
royal letters were exchanged over trading disputes in 1308, 1310, 1312, 1313,
1316 and 1319, and envoys met to sort out conflicting claims in 1316 and
1319.[14] Letters could move fast: on 28 July 1316 Haaken had read and replied
to one of Edward's letters dated 15 July. But justice moved more slowly: in
1316 Haaken was still seeking justice in the particularly unpleasant incident,
blamed at first on the men of Lynn but apparently perpetrated by men of
Berwick, which took place in 1312, in which his bailiff and ten others had
been killed by scalding and stabbing at a dinner.[15] Although he seemed
willing enough to do what he should to help sort out the mess, in 1316
Edward clearly put Norwegian affairs well down his agenda, and on 30
October 1316 he wrote a courteous but nonetheless rather dismissive letter to
Haaken, saying that he could not reply then to Haaken's letters because he
was en route for Scotland, but he had sent Haaken's letter to his council.[16] At
this time Edward clearly neither feared Norway as a potential ally of Scotland
nor valued Norway as a potential political ally for himself. In 1325, however,
with trouble in France, he responded much more warmly to overtures from
Norway for new peace negotiations. In reply to the archbishop of Trondheim,
the king's steward, and others of the king's counsellors, he wrote on 17
February that he was eager to have peace with all the surrounding nations
and especially the king of Norway (*quod nos, quantum ad nos pertinet,*

---

[11] E 122/55/16, 17, 19, 23, 56/3, 7, 10, 11, 57/1, 93/2–4. See also W. R. Childs, 'Timber
for Cloth. Changing commodities in Anglo-Baltic Trade in the Fourteenth Century',
in *Cogs, Cargoes and Commerce: Maritime Bulk Trade in Northern Europe, 1150–1400*, ed.
L. Berggren, N. Hybel, A. Landen (Toronto, 2002), pp. 181–211 (pp. 188–97).

[12] *CCR 1307–13*, p. 554.

[13] *Foedera*, I², 640, 645; *Foedera*, II¹, 81.

[14] *CCR 1307–13*, pp. 127, 209, 325, 523, 554, 573, 576, 577; *CCR 1313–18*, pp. 80, 326, 333;
CCR 1318–23, pp. 141, 144, 145–6; *Foedera*, II¹, 293, 294.

[15] *Foedera*, II¹, 293, 294.

[16] *CCR 1313–18*, p. 439.

pacem habere appetimus cum omnibus circumpositarum populis nationum, et praecipue cum praefato rege et subditis suis); and if they would send envoys with sufficient power to re-confirm the alliances, he would send safe-conducts for them.[17]

Overall trade rather than potential alliance was at the core of Anglo-Norwegian royal exchanges. Trade and potential alliance were more evenly balanced in the Low Countries. Rulers here were potentially more effective allies in the French wars, and those with coastal areas were also strong trading partners, taking almost all of England's crucial wool exports. Edward I cultivated Low Country allies and seems to have had a clear policy in marrying his daughters to the Duke of Brabant (1290), the Count of Bar (1293), and the Count of Holland (1296).[18] Edward II also maintained steady contacts there, but local politics were volatile and relationships with each state could be very different. Relations with Flanders, for instance, continued to be bumpy. Flanders took many of England's wool exports, but it also welcomed Scottish trade. Nonetheless, when Edward was forced into the Franco-Flemish war of 1315–19 under the terms of his treaty with France, he minimised action against Flanders. Relations with Brabant were perhaps the most comfortable. This was where Edward had the closest family connections and the smoothest diplomatic relations. Duke John II was his brother-in-law, and he was succeeded in 1312 by his son, Edward's nephew, Duke John III. Edward's sister, Margaret, lived in Brabant until her death in 1318. Trade connections were close and good. Antwerp was a major destination for English wool, and the Duke frequently and successfully sought letters of protection, safe-conducts, and exemptions from general debts for his merchants.[19] Merchants on both sides seem to have worked well together, and problems on the route nearly always arose from French or Flemish actions at sea. In 1319 the Duke was very willing to oblige Edward and curb Scottish trade in his duchy.[20] It is not surprising that Edward saw Brabant as a refuge for Gaveston in 1311, and later asked Brabant, alongside Bar and Hainault (now inheritor of Holland and Zeeland) for help against the Contrariants in 1322.[21] Bar figured more rarely in Edward's correspondence, yet his knowledge of Bar and its vassals was good, as the letters for the release of the Earl of Pembroke in 1317 show. However, the marriage difficulties of Bar's sister (Edward's niece) and Earl Warenne, whose petition for annulment Edward backed, may have left Bar unsympathetic to Edward.[22]

[17] *Foedera*, II¹, 590.
[18] Cuttino, however, suggested Edward responded to offers rather than initiating them, *English Diplomatic Administration*, pp. 67–8.
[19] *CPR 1313–17*, p. 663; *CPR 1317–21*, p. 429; *CCR 1318–23*, p. 560; *CPR 1321–4*, p. 130.
[20] *Foedera*, II¹, 392.
[21] *CCR 1307–13*, p. 441; *CCR 1318–23*, pp. 521–2.
[22] Phillips, *Aymer de Valence*, pp. 111–16.

More interesting are the relations with Hainault, which grew closer when the count of land-locked Hainault inherited Holland and Zeeland in 1299. The Francophile counts were now drawn into closer contacts with England because of the trade interests with England of their new territories. The first letters between Edward II and Hainault, long before diplomatic marriages were suggested, were therefore over trade. Relations were usually good, but Zeeland merchants had been to blame for damage to English shipping during a recent conflict between Zeelanders and Flemings, and William III of Hainault, most unusually, was prepared to take personal responsibility for his merchants. A financial arrangement was made at the Stamford parliament in 1309, whereby the count, through his envoys, bound himself to pay compensation to the aggrieved English merchants. Difficulties over payment led in 1316 to William agreeing to tolls being imposed on those of his fishermen and merchants who came into English east coast ports. Edward agreed that they could be collected by William's agents (who in fact included one of the injured English merchants), and instructed English port officials to uphold the collection even in the face of opposition from certain men of Holland and Zeeland. This payment of foreign tolls in England worked, although further adjustments had to be made and the merchants had still not been fully paid by 1327.[23] Other acts of violence at sea took place, especially in 1314–15 and during the Franco-Flemish war, and resulted in further correspondence and envoys between Edward and William.[24] Letters at royal and comital level were also required in attempts to recover Elizabeth Bohun's full dower (including the town of Dordrecht) from her first marriage to the Count of Holland.[25]

Hainault's inheritance of Holland and Zeeland both enhanced its own potential power and pulled it closer to England, and it is not surprising that Edward pursued diplomatic negotiations for a marriage alliance between Prince Edward and William's eldest daughter, Margaret, between 1318 and 1321.[26] Nothing came of this (Margaret later married the emperor, Louis of Bavaria), but the suggestion foreshadowed the later marriage of Edward III to her younger sister, Phillippa. Hainault's tightening links with England are illustrated by the way both sides in the civil war looked to it in 1322: Edward wrote to ask for aid, and Hereford is rumoured to have looked on Hainault as

23 *Foedera*, II¹, 11, 79–80; *CCR 1307–13*, pp. 54–5, 66, 133–4, 153, 335; *CCR 1313–18*, pp. 37, 301, 308, 340–1, 418; *CCR 1318–23*, pp. 248–9, 327, 341; *CPR 1307–13*, pp. 12, 52, 115, 225; *CPR 1313–17*, pp. 254, 406, 511, 515, 546, 568, 594, 609, 642, 676, 679–80; *CPR 1317–21*, pp. 106–8, 112, 171, 178, 184, 284, 306–7, 365, 463, 481, 609; *CPR 1321–4*, pp. 55–6; *CPR 1324–7*, p. 140. In 1327 £223 was still outstanding, but, as nothing more is heard, the debt was presumably steadily collected. *CPR 1327–30*, p. 178.
24 *CCR 1313–17*, pp. 227, 345, 481, 571; *CCR 1318–23*, pp. 45–6, 126, 325; *CPR 1313–17*, pp. 261–2, 276, 318–19, 321–2, 324, 326, 609, 660.
25 *CCR 1313–18*, pp. 301, 454; *CPR 1313–17*, p. 332.
26 *Foedera*, II¹, 381, 437, 446.

a possible refuge (probably because of his wife's connections).[27] However, while William might look for good relations with England, he was clearly not firmly engaged to Edward personally, and his marriage to Philip IV's niece, Jeanne de Valois (cousin to Isabella) may have predisposed him to support Isabella. Although Edward and William continued to treat peaceably over trade and Edward provided safe-conducts for Hainault's merchants in 1325, already in 1324 there were rumours that Hainault was preparing ships against England for the use of Mortimer and other exiles,[28] and in 1326 it was, of course, with Hainault's help that Isabella launched her invasion of England. Edward's correspondence with William had not brought friend-ship; nor does it seem that Edward – whether through ignorance, negligence, or calculation – did anything to try to stop Hainault's support for his oppo-nents. Here, despite much contact, is a clear area of failure.

On the other side of France lay Castile, and here the pattern of activity was different and more successful (although not successful enough to defend Gascony). As Edward II was half-Castilian, Castile had a common border with Gascony, and trade between Castile and England was busy, close connection was only to be expected. Moreover, Castile was now looking like a heavy player in European affairs. The reconquest of the mid thirteenth century had brought it much territory and potential wealth; and Alfonso X (son of Fernando III and Beatrice of Suabia) had been considered suitable for election as king of the Germans. Edward I had considered a Spanish marriage for the future Edward II, and although nothing had come of this, exchanges were cordial.[29] The kingdom was powerful enough for the author of the *Vita* to list Spanish kinship as one of Edward's assets:[30] at his accession the king of Spain was Fernando IV (1295–1312), his first cousin once removed. Most governmental exchanges between England and Castile in the first years of Edward II's reign were over trade. The Basque ports and the Cuatro Villas were the busiest contact areas, and their ships came predominantly to Southampton, Sandwich, and London. In Southampton and London there is evidence of immigrant groups settling, marrying, and leasing houses. At Southampton in 1310–11 Spaniards supplied about twenty per cent by value of the alien merchants' imports. In Sandwich in the 1320s a substantial amount of the import trade was in their hands; Edward II regularly sent merchants to buy horses in Castile; and among a group of merchants impor-tant enough to hit the public records, Andres Perez of Burgos was outstanding. Perez traded with England from 1278, became a 'king's

---

[27] Maddicott, *Thomas of Lancaster*, p. 310.
[28] Chaplais, *Saint-Sardos*, pp. 59–72.
[29] *CCR 1302–7*, pp. 83, 458.
[30] *Vita*, ed. Childs, pp. 68–9.

merchant' by 1315, and became involved with Edward's diplomatic activity in Castile in 1324.[31]

Although most trade with England ran smoothly enough, there were troubles between the Basques and the men of Bayonne, just as there had been trouble in 1293–4 between the Bayonnese and the Normans. However, whereas the latter clashes had led to war because of Edward's peculiar relationship with the king of France, the simpler relationship with the king of Castile meant that both kings tried to settle the former troubles through the courts. In 1308 and 1309, amid enquiries after each other's health and citations of blood relationship and long affection, both Edward and Fernando encouraged negotiations and arbitration,[32] and the feud between their men was formally settled in 1309 (although complaints that compensation had not yet been fully paid were made, in one case until 1314 and in another until 1333).[33] Long before then, other cases were prompting letters between the two governments, but they continued to seek peaceful recompense and minimal reprisals: continued clashes between men of Castile and Bayonne led in 1315 to letters of protection for all Alfonso's merchants[34] and in 1317 Viscaya (with the support of King Alfonso, King Edward, and of Bayonne itself) successfully claimed its independent status, so that its men should not be punished for offences committed by Castilians.[35]

Despite this promising governmental cooperation over trade, closer relations proved difficult. Edward's letter to Fernando in December 1307, asking him (along with the rulers of Aragon and Portugal) not to believe the accusations against the Templars, was spitting in the wind.[36] Then, faced with domestic crisis, Edward was in no position in 1311 to respond positively to Fernando IV's request that he fulfil clauses of the treaty of 1254 and provide Fernando with a loan to help fight the Saracens. He wrote on 9 October 1311 that he was, as ever, ready to help, but was sorely pressed by the Scottish war and other hindrances (clearly a reference to the crisis over the Ordinances); but he did find time to request favour for a Spanish widow in 1312.[37] The next years were difficult in both countries. Fernando's death in 1312, leaving a one-year-old heir, propelled Castile into the problems of a long regency. This

---

31 For details of these connections see W. R. Childs, *Anglo-Castilian Trade in the Later Middle Ages* (Manchester, 1978), pp. 17–22, 229–30.

32 *Foedera*, II^1, 60, 71, 80, 88.

33 Things had reached such a stage that the Cinque Ports had to be forbidden from fitting out a fleet to help the men of Bayonne in their conflict with those of Castile. *CPR 1301–7*, pp. 460–1; *CCR 1307–13*, p. 130; *Gascon Rolls*, ed. Y. Renouard, nos 105, 211, 289, 290, 298, 336, 562; *Foedera*, II^1, 60, 71.

34 In 1315 Winchelsea also sought protection from arrest for Spanish merchants to protect the town's trade: *CCR 1313–18*, p. 231; *CPR 1313–17*, p. 303.

35 *CPR 1317–21*, pp. 53, 55; SC 8/13463.

36 *Foedera*, II^1, 19.

37 *Foedera*, II^1, 144; SC 1/16/14; C 47/27/8(13); *CCR 1307–13*, p. 457.

was at a time when Edward's concerns became wholly focused on domestic and Scottish affairs, so it is not surprising that activity faded, apart from formal requests from Edward to the Castilian government to allow the export of horses and grain to England. Closer diplomatic relations were re-opened when Hugh Despenser the Elder went to Spain in 1319, with letters dated 5 February addressed to the Infantes Pedro and Juan and to Andres Perez.[38] The addressing of the letters shows appreciation of the situation in Spain, where the two Infantes shared power as regents with Maria de Molina, Sancho IV's widow, grandmother to Alfonso XI, until they were both killed in battle in June 1319. Andres Perez was the Burgos merchant who was a 'king's merchant', and in a good position to provide support and loans en route.

Unlike the Low Countries, Castile was not asked for help against the Contrariants in 1322. Perhaps it was felt that Castile was simply too distant to send effective immediate aid, or that the regency council, now in great disarray, might take too long to respond, but when conflict with France arose in 1324 it was to Iberia, not the Low Countries, that Edward looked. The initiative clearly came from Edward (unlike in the diplomatic activity with Norway at about the same time, which seems to have been initiated by Norway). Overtures to Castile were sensible, given its proximity to Gascony, but the request was sent at a time when the regency council was still in deep disarray. After the deaths of the two Infantes in June 1319 and of Maria de Molina in June 1321, the regency council disintegrated, and from 1322 central control virtually collapsed. The three regents jockeying for position were the Infante Felipe, Alfonso XI's uncle, whose power base was largely in Galicia, Juan Manuel, nephew of Alfonso X and a cousin twice removed of Alfonso XI, and Juan (called el Tuerto), son of the former regent, Infante Juan and of his wife Maria Díaz de Haro, heiress of Vizcaya. Given the rather unexpected open conflict with France, and the disarray in Castile, Edward's knowledge of the power struggles and whom to address seems not to gave been too bad. News was available through merchants such as Perez, possibly through pilgrims passing through to Santiago, and through the Gascons, who knew what was happening over the border.

The diplomatic practice of using the same men, who thus became proficient through experience, is visible in Edward's dealings with Spain. On all the embassies to Castile at least one member was from southern Gascony – either Arnaud Guillaume de Béarn, lord of Lescun, or Master Peter de Galiciano, treasurer of the Agenais, a member of the Got family and an experienced diplomat.[39] Often both were sent. The first overtures were in April 1324, when letters of credence issued for Guillaume and Galiciano were sent to Alfonso, the three main regents (as above), Maria Díaz de Haro, lady of

[38] CCR 1319–23, p. 123; see also CPR 1317–21, p. 262. Pedro was Fernando IV's brother, uncle to Alfonso XI; Juan was Sancho IV's brother, great-uncle to Alfonso XI.
[39] Chaplais, *English Diplomatic Practice*, p. 173.

Viscaya (Juan el Tuerto's mother), as well as the archbishop of Toledo, the bishop of Burgos, and five others.[40] The inclusion of all these seems to indicate that Edward was quite well informed about the power struggles at the Castilian court, although he may not have been sure who had most influence at the time. In any case, diplomats had oral instructions, which doubtless included some discretion about whom they approached. Further letters suggest that his envoys came to see the Biscayan group as the likeliest supporters. On 30 September letters were addressed to Alfonso, and to Juan lord of Viscaya, Maria, lady of Viscaya, and Don Fernando, son of Don Diego de Haro.[41] The concentration on the Biscayan group seems to have been well chosen, since Guillaume and Galiciano reported to the earl of Kent on their return to Gascony that Juan was prepared to send 1,000 horse and 10,000 footmen if Edward would pay for their expenses. Kent sent the envoys back to Juan to continue negotiations and to ask him to work on others for similar help.[42] This was a more promising line than that of Ralph Basset, who, in December 1324, suggested mentioning the old Castilian claim to overlordship in Gascony, presumably in the hope that this would encourage Castile to fight France for a share in Gascony.[43]

The king of France naturally expressed displeasure at the attempts of Edward to win allies in Castile and Aragon,[44] but Edward persisted. On 6 January he wrote to Alfonso, 'consanguineo *and* amico suo carissimo', explaining the French king's iniquities, and asking Alfonso to let his officials draw horses and victuals for his army from Castile.[45] He continued to sort out trade problems and give safe-conducts to the men of the major Basque and Castilian ports – no doubt hoping for commercial cooperation for supplies.[46] On 18 January 1325 Guillaume and Galiciano were appointed to return, together with Sir John Stonor and John Burton, canon of Wells; on 6 February Burton was replaced by William Weston, canon of St Mary's, Lincoln and professor of civil law. These additions raised the level of the embassy, and their instructions were to ask for the help of 3,000 men and to negotiate marriages between Prince Edward and Alfonso's sister and also between Alfonso himself and Edward's daughter Eleanor. The instructions included bargaining levels over the payment for troops and the dowries for the marriages.[47] The letters of credence were addressed variously: to Alfonso, to

40 *CCR 1323–7*, p. 175; *Foedera*, II¹, 549.
41 *CCR 1323–7*, pp. 313–14. Don Fernando's father was Diego Lopez de Haro V, who had for a while usurped his niece, Mary's, inheritance, but who had agreed to her succession on his death. Fernando was therefore Mary's cousin.
42 Chaplais, *Saint-Sardos*, no. 96, pp. 109–10.
43 Chaplais, *Saint-Sardos*, no. 109, p. 118.
44 Chaplais, *Saint-Sardos*, no. 124, p. 130. For negotiations with Aragon see below.
45 C 61/37, m. 12d.
46 C 61/37, m. 12d.
47 Chaplais, *Saint-Sardos*, no. 132, p. 140.

W. R. Childs

Juan son of the Infante Juan, guardian of the king and keeper of his realm (the regent best disposed towards Edward), to the bishop of Burgos, and to Martin Ferrandez (18 January), to Juan Manuel and the lady of Viscaya (6 February), once more to all three regents, Felipe, Juan Manuel and Juan son of the Infante Juan (10 February).[48] Influence was used behind the scenes where possible, and letters dated 16 February, drafted in French but translated into Spanish for sending, were dispatched to Juan, son of the Infante Juan Manuel, and Alvaro Nuñez, steward of the Infante Felipe, urging them to trust what Andres Perez of Burgos would tell them by word of mouth – a clear instance of a merchant being used in confidential, not just routine, diplomatic work.[49] On 11 April, despite all the encouragement, Stonor reported home from Valladolid that there had been no progress because the king had been ill and the regents had not yet arrived, and it was not known when they would arrive. Nonetheless, he said, he had been told that the king was pleased they had come. On 22 May a full formal report was agreed by both sides at Valladolid and confirmed goodwill, but no progress. The Castilian negotiators stated that a new marriage was not necessary since there were already past marriage links and kinship between them; that if there were marriages, the king of England should offer more dower than the king of Castile, since the Castilian bride would not be queen for a long time, whereas the English princess would become queen immediately; that the treaty against the king of France would be a new burden to the king of Castile but make no further difference to the king of England; and that the money offered for military help was insufficient, given that such help would remove troops from the Saracen borders. In the end it was decided, since the king could not make decisions without the advice of his regents, who were not there, to wait until the following 1 November, when the king would come officially of age (at the age of 14). The parting appeared to be amicable and the meeting to be seen as simply a stage in hard bargaining. The report revealed the Castilian terms which Edward would have to address.[50] Stonor finally reached England on 27 August and, no doubt after digesting Stonor's full verbal report, on 15 October Edward replied. Acknowledging that there could be no answer while Alfonso's guardians were absent (but presumably expecting the embassy to arrive after 1 November), Edward wrote that he was sending Peter de Galiciano again, and if a marriage was agreed and a dispensation was necessary, then Galiciano would continue on to the pope to procure it. He also wrote to the bishop of Burgos and others, thanking them for their help.

48 *CCR 1323–7*, pp. 344, 350–1; *CPR 1324–7*, pp. 104–5; *Foedera*, II¹, 585–8. Ferrandez was to be one of the Castilian negotiators who sealed the joint report in May 1325.
49 C 61/36, m. 14d.
50 *The Stonor Letters and Papers, 1290–1483*, ed. C. L. Kingsford, 2 vols (London, 1919), I, no. 2; Chaplais, *Saint-Sardos*, no. 178, pp. 214–16.

By January 1326 doubts had arisen about Edward's ability to deliver on a marriage treaty: Edward wrote, denying rumours of a French marriage and again saying that Galiciano was on his way to Spain to confirm previous negotiations and proceed to the pope for a dispensation.[51] But despite difficulties, negotiations clearly continued. In April, when the king of Portugal suggested a match between the young Edward and his own daughter, Edward II wrote that the negotiations with Spain were still under way and had priority.[52] He was also still negotiating with Juan, lord of Viscaya; and wrote to him on 28 June that Arnaud Guillaume had brought Juan's letter offering troops and that he was now sending Arnaud back to negotiate, along with Oliver Ingham and Reymund Durand.[53] Given the Castilian minority and Edward's mounting difficulties in the summer of 1326, it is perhaps not surprising that little came of the proposed marriage alliance, but there were regular links, appropriate letters, and discussions of some depth, which show considerable negotiating skills being brought to bear.

Beyond Castile, on the western extremity of the first circle, was Portugal. This, like Norway in the east, could provide supplies and shipping support for Edward in small quantities, but it was not in the same league as Castile and Edward spent little effort on it. Although there had been friendly contacts since English crusaders had helped in the conquest of Lisbon, and the commercial links were growing, government contacts were sparse. In 1307 Edward and Diniz operated at the courteous level of sending good wishes; later that year, Edward wrote to Portugal as well as to all the Iberian kingdoms to express his doubt about the accusations against the Templars. In 1308 he replied to King Diniz that he intended to keep the commercial peace between the two countries, and provided safe-conducts for Portuguese merchants.[54] After this, there seems to have been a long hiatus in official government contacts until 1324, when, in January, Edward wrote to ask Diniz to prevent his admiral, Manuel Pessagno, from helping his brother, Antonio Pessagno, now out of favour with Edward and suspected of planning harm.[55] Then, in 1325, again prompted by Gascon troubles, on 7 May Edward wrote to the new king, Afonso IV, and his mother, Queen Isabella, asking them to allow one of Edward's sergeants at arms to buy corn supplies for Aquitaine. This again shows knowledge of local power structures, since the queen mother was an important political figure who had acted as mediator between

---

[51] *CCR 1323–7*, pp. 417, 515, 516, 533; *Foedera*, II¹, 617.

[52] *CCR 1323–7*, p. 556; *Foedera*, II¹, 625–6.

[53] C 61/38, m. 3d. Rather surprisingly, the enrolled letter shows the addressee as Juan Tort ('el Tuerto'), Lord of Viscaya. The use of a nickname seems rather undiplomatic, but the original may have been differently worded. Letters were corrected before being sent, Chaplais, *English Diplomatic Practice*, p. 141.

[54] *Foedera*, I², 7, 19, 58; *CPR 1307–14*, pp. 106, 138.

[55] C 61/37, m.12d.

her husband and son, and now did the same between Afonso and his rebellious half-brother. Afonso clearly responded warmly to these renewed contacts, and suggested the royal marriage mentioned above, but Edward was luke-warm and stood on protocol. While maintaining that he would like such a thing because of their earlier connections, his immediate reply in July 1325 was that the Portuguese envoys were not of sufficient status to negotiate such a business. Then, by the time more important envoys arrived in April 1326, Edward replied that he was now exploring a Castilian marriage for his son, but the prince was in France, so negotiations about any marriage were difficult. He said, however, that he would like to strengthen the agreements with Portugal even without a marriage.[56] It is clear that Portugal, like Norway, was not high on the list of allies Edward II sought, although its friendship was equally worth having.

In the outer circle, behind these close neighbours, lay the Empire, the Mediterranean powers (Aragon, Italian city states, Sicily and the dismembered Greek Empire) and the Near East. It was in this circle that Edward II began to approach his father and grandfather in the extent of his contacts, although never with the same intensity. A few examples will illustrate the range of his activities.

Edward's diplomatic links with the German Emperors were sparse. Edward I had drawn Adolph of Nassau to his side quite effectively, with money, in 1294–8, but Adolph had had reasons of his own to fight France, and Edward's £20,000 gave him the means to carry out his own wishes.[57] Edward II made no alliance with the emperor, either because he learned from Edward I's example that it would be expensive and unreliable, or because the emperors of his period were less inclined to look to the north. Edward sent politely enthusiastic congratulations in April 1313 in reply to Henry's letter telling him of his imperial coronation in 1312, but in August that year Edward expressed disapproval to the pope of Henry's war against Robert, king of Sicily.[58] Henry died, allegedly of poison, the same year, and his successor was Louis of Bavaria, elected in 1314 and with no interests in the northern areas at all. He spent his first years fighting the Habsburgs in Germany, and then turned his attention to the Tyrol and northern Italy. When Edward was looking for allies against France in the 1320s, he did not even write to Louis of Bavaria. Edward's strongest contacts with the Empire were in fact through its Low Country vassals and even more through its merchants. The towns of the Hanse (although not as tightly organized as they would be a few decades later) brought contacts from Cologne to Danzig, but

56 *CCR 1323–7*, pp. 364, 496, 556; *CPR 1324–7*, p. 260.
57 G. Barraclough, 'Edward I and Adolf of Nassau. A Chapter of Diplomatic History', *Cambridge Historical Journal* 6 (1940), 230. And see M. Prestwich, *Edward I* (London, 1988), pp. 387–90.
58 *Foedera*, II¹, 170, 210, 224.

most communication was with individual merchants through lawsuits, safe-conducts, and grants. Only occasionally did Edward address municipal governments or receive formal envoys.[59]

In the Mediterranean there was more diplomatic activity, and Edward showed generally good knowledge of complex politics and titles. For instance, his letters in 1313 were correctly addressed to Federico, king of Sicily, but his letters to Robert, king of Naples, were also consistently addressed to him, as Robert would wish, as king of Sicily and Jerusalem, although Federico of Aragon was de facto ruler of Sicily, and the kings of Cyprus had a better claim to Jerusalem and were regularly crowned as such in Famagusta.[60] Likewise, Edward showed knowledge of the political situation in Aragon, by writing to both the aged Jaime and to his son Alfonso and to a number of churchmen and nobles, but in 1325 his envoys slipped up there, and he had to apologize to the Archbishop of Zaragoza for their failure to present their letters to him as primate of Aragon.[61] Aragon received a surge of attention at the end of Edward's reign, alongside Castile, because of its proximity to Gascony, but Aragon's own interests were firmly in the Mediterranean, and its relationship there with France complicated any formal anti-French alliance with England. At this time Franco-Aragonese relations were relatively peaceful, and Aragon, even more than Castile, had no need to pick up England's burden.

There were far fewer commercial links with Aragon, although one case complicated affairs just as Edward was requesting help against France. In 1323 Aragonese merchants using two ships of Majorca (then an independent kingdom) were robbed by the English between Calais and Sandwich.[62] Letters between Edward and Jaime are particularly interesting for their exposition of the different methods of compensating injured merchants. The Aragonese expected swift letters of marque, but Edward (or his chancery) sent several letters explaining and robustly defending English legal processes, which the Aragonese merchants had not exhausted. Slow justice was therefore their own fault, because they had not properly notified the courts of the events, provided names of the guilty, or stayed for a commission of oyer and terminer, which Edward had freely offered them, although this should have been initiated by a petition from them. Whatever happened in the Mediterranean, Edward was determined to stick to English practices: he

---

[59] For details of Hanseatic trade with England at this time see T. H. Lloyd, *Alien Merchants in England in the High Middle Ages* (Brighton, 1982), pp. 135–42; T. H. Lloyd, *England and the German Hanse, 1157–1611* (Cambridge, 1991), pp. 24–9, 35–46.

[60] *CPR 1324–7*, p. 55; *Foedera*, II¹, 405, 470. Edward used Robert's support in some requests to the pope; he also received Robert's messengers in the winter of 1324–5.

[61] *CCR 1323–7*, pp. 516–17.

[62] For Majorcan trade with England see D. Abulafia, *A Mediterranean Emporium, the Catalan Kingdom of Majorca* (Cambridge, 1994), pp. 191–7.

could not, he wrote in 1324, change practices 'against the law and custom of the realm and to the prejudice of his men'.[63] Nonetheless, despite this problem, negotiations towards a marriage treaty, which had been informally broached as early as 1320, continued. Formal envoys were sent from Jaime in 1321, and talks moved slowly, through to 1324 when English envoys heard that Jaime was also discussing a French marriage for his daughter. He nonetheless continued to encourage English negotiations, and in October Edward appointed a solemn embassy to take this further. By February 1325, however, he had learned from Galiciano and Guillaume that the terms offered were not agreeable to Jaime.[64] Giving up ideas of marriage, Edward sent further envoys to discuss help in Gascony. The Infante Afonso and the nobles made available well-equipped and experienced men to serve in Gascony but, as with the offer from Juan in Castile, at a price. The returning envoys advised Edward in June 1325 that the Aragonese price was too high. Although envoys were still being exchanged in February 1326, negotiations faded away, presumably because Edward and his advisors realized that they were less likely to get effective help here than in Castile.[65] In the event, the negotiations brought no Iberian help in Gascony.

Beyond Aragon, Mediterranean contacts included Genoa, the Tuscan city states, Sicily, Cyprus, Byzantium, Armenia and, beyond that, Il-Khan Persia. Some of these links were strong, through trade and banking, others were not very robust. All are worth consideration as evidence of England's diplomatic reach, but here again, only a few examples can be chosen.

Although Edward's best known contacts with Italy were with the Florentine and Lucchese merchants who were bankers to the Crown, the Genoese were rising fast to prominence. Genoa, extremely active in the trade of the old Greek Empire, Cyprus, and the Levant, took up the challenge of direct sailing between the Mediterranean and the Channel at the end of the thirteenth century, and its galleys and dromonds were becoming familiar sights in London and Southampton. It was these newer Genoese contacts which provoked diplomatic correspondence with government. In 1309 the Genoese plundered a Bayonne cog, provoking Edward's first formal letter to the podestá and consuls of Genoa.[66] The role of Antonio Pessagno as king's merchant and major creditor brought the Genoese to the forefront of English political life.[67] Edward received Pessagno's nephew, Antonio Doria, onto his

---

63 CCR 1323–7, pp. 312–13.
64 CCR 1318–23, p. 721; Chaplais, English Medieval Diplomatic Practice, I, nos 47a, 47b, and notes 55, 58; Chaplais, English Diplomatic Practice, pp. 227–9; Foedera, II¹, 573, 589; Chaplais, Saint-Sardos, pp. 230–1
65 Foedera, II¹, 573, 621; CCR 1323–7, p. 547; Chaplais, Saint-Sardos, pp. 230–1.
66 CCR 1307–13, pp. 233, 328.
67 N. Fryde, 'Antonio Pessagno of Genoa, King's Merchant of Edward II of England', in Studi in Memoria di Federigo Melis, 5 vols (Naples, 1978), II, 159–78.

council alongside his own kinsman, Carlo Fieschi. Edward may have felt particular friendship for Genoa because of marriage links with the Fieschi family through his grandmother, Eleanor of Provence, whose uncle had married a Fieschi daughter as his second wife. The link was through marriage, not blood, but Edward willingly acknowledged it and wrote to the podestá and others of the Genoese commune in 1318 to welcome the news that they had elected his kinsman Carlo Fieschi as captain of Genoa.[68] The obvious strength of the Genoese galleys was also attractive and led to further diplomatic letters on Edward's part. The first offer of galleys, in 1315, for Edward's use against the Scots, seems to have been an entirely private affair by the Doria family, and was clearly acceptable to Edward; less acceptable to him was the offer by other Genoese merchants of galleys to help Scotland, and in 1316 Edward formally complained to the Genoese commune about that.[69] Then, in 1317, when Edward hoped to hire five Genoese galleys through Leonardo de Pessagno (Antonio's brother) for war against Scotland, he again wrote formally to the podestá, asking for Leonardo to be allowed to bring them.[70] The importance of regular Italian contacts, perhaps especially those of Genoa, was that they could easily provide up-to-date news about the constantly changing Mediterranean politics, and in 1313 Edward certainly saw the podestá of Genoa as a source of information in the attempt to free Argentein.

The episode of Giles d'Argentein's capture on his way home from the Holy Land is interesting for what it shows of the way Edward could mobilize information in order to address his letters to the right people. Argentein was captured off Rhodes and taken to Thessalonika. On 7 August Edward wrote to the Master and Preceptor of the Hospitallers, as he had been informed that the Master was the person who could help above all others. He also wrote again to the podestá and commune of Genoa, as he had heard that they knew the Master and Preceptor well. By 12 October he had received an appropriate list of those to whom to write, and his next letters went off to Andronicus, Emperor of Byzantium, whom he now knew to be the ruler of those who had seized Argentein, to Michael, his son and co-emperor, to the empress, Irene of Montferrat, whose father had had the claim to the kingdom of Thessalonika and had granted it to his daughter on her marriage to the emperor, and to the Marquis of Montferrat, her son. Letters asking them to use their influence were also sent to Federico, the Aragonese king of Sicily, and to five Genoese: to the Fieschi count of Lavagna, Carlo Fieschi, Conrad and Bernabo Doria (who later offered Edward galleys to help against the Scots) and a member of

---

68 *CCR 1313–18*, p. 589. For the complex family link see G. P. Cuttino and T. Lyman, 'Where is Edward II?', *Speculum* 53 (1978), 544. Pessagno's wife was also a Fieschi, Fryde, 'Antonio Pessagno', pp. 163–4.

69 *CCR 1313–18*, pp. 310, 422.

70 *CCR 1313–18*, p. 452 (and *Foedera*, II¹, 313).

the Spinelli family. At this time the Genoese were strong in the Greek territories, with a new quarter in Galata, their monopoly of the alum mines at Focea on Asia Minor, and their new colony on the island of Chios. The letters show a very precise knowledge of the powerful figures in Byzantium and Thessalonika and of the Genoese influence there. Argentein was home to fight and die at Bannockburn the following year. Why Argentein provoked Edward's interest in this way is not entirely clear, but his capture came just after Edward himself had agreed to take the cross with Philip IV, and perhaps Edward felt the need to have at his side 'the third best known knight of his time'.[71]

Contacts further east show Edward's faint and flickering interest in conversion and crusading plans. In November 1307 Edward recommended to Leo of Armenia a group of English Dominicans going to preach against Islam; but in March 1308 he felt unable to give any practical help to Leo, although he thanked Leo for his gift.[72] In the autumn of 1307 Edward also wrote to Oldjaitu, ruler of the Il-Khans, in response to envoys who had come to him in England confirming friendship and hopes for peace (the Il-Khans still hoped for a Christian alliance against Egypt), but he did not respond to the Tartars with envoys on the scale of Edward I's sending Geoffrey of Langley.[73] The responses suggest courtesy rather than real interest, but Edward did take the cross with Philip IV in 1313. This may have been partly in response to Clement V's call for a crusade at the Council of Vienne, and partly in response to Guillaume de Ville Neuve, who came as a messenger from the Tartars at that time. Whether Edward's interest in taking part in what Tyerman has called 'a Capetian family affair' was sincere is unclear – in any case, problems at home soon held him back.[74] He continued nonetheless to take a conventional interest, as when he wrote to the king of Cyprus in 1320, recommending three Dominicans who were passing through to the east to preach against Islam.[75]

What does this rather brisk and partial diplomatic tour of Europe tell us or prompt us to ask? There are several points to be made. First, Edward's diplomatic geographical scope was as wide as his father's, stretching from Norway to the Levant Tartars, even if contemporary chroniclers ignored it. Second, commercial links were now a much more constant element in foreign relationships. For centuries trade had drawn royal interest in tax and protection, but Edward II reigned at a time when the medieval commercial boom was

---

[71] *CCR 1313–18*, pp. 71, 76; for Argentein ('the third best known knight of his time') see J. R. V. Barker, *The Tournament in England, 1100–1400* (Woodbridge, 1986), pp. 127–8.

[72] *Foedera*, II¹, 17, 37.

[73] *Foedera*, II¹, 8, 18.

[74] *CPR 1307–13*, p. 596; J. R. S. Phillips, *The Medieval Expansion of Europe* (Oxford, 1988), p. 138; C. Tyerman, *England and the Crusades* (London, 1988), pp. 241–5.

[75] *Foedera*, II¹, 433.

reaching its peak and commercial matters bulked ever larger in government correspondence. Much could go before the normal courts and needed only internal letters in response to petitions for justice, but in more complex cases government-to-government exchanges took place. In defence of his merchants and of English justice, Edward could be robust. Even in the case of his good friend and kinsman, Brabant, Edward on one occasion wrote a strong reply. The case was somewhat complicated, and Brabant's request for justice for one of his men arrested in England was late (although not excessively so). Edward responded: 'It is not consonant with reason that what has been terminated by reasonable and due process and executed should be cancelled and revoked to the injury of another.'[76] In relation to requests from Aragon, as shown above, Edward was similarly firm, explaining that in England it was simply not done in the way the Mediterranean king demanded. Commercial contacts not only brought regular news of distant parts, but thrust some merchants close to the court as suppliers and financiers. Some of these, no doubt for their language skills, contacts, and sometimes wealth, were used in diplomacy itself. The Florentines and Genoese are the most obvious examples of court financiers who were used widely to help the king, but Andres Perez of Burgos was also used by Edward II, and the Hanseatic Steelyard could offer a wealth of information on northern and Baltic areas.

Third, the question might be asked, whether there was sufficient pattern to these contacts to suggest a 'policy'. How far medieval diplomatic activity should be called 'foreign policy' was raised in relation to France and Castile in the 1980s. Joseph Strayer commented that it was difficult, in the case of France, to decide what was 'foreign', since much of Philip the Fair's diplomatic activity involved two of his vassals – Flanders and Aquitaine – and thus could be seen as internal affairs.[77] Luis Vicente Díaz Martín similarly suggested all Iberian activity concerning Aragon, Navarre and Portugal might be seen as internal Iberian affairs. He further suggested that 'foreign policy' implies a consistent strategy, even if not consistent detailed plans, and the means to put it into practice (bribes, threats, and skilled diplomatic personnel). He doubted whether Castile had this at all during much of the reigns of Fernando IV and Alfonso XI, with their long minorities and civil disputes.[78] Using these criteria, we might ask whether Edward II had a 'foreign policy'. He certainly had means – efficient personnel, money, and trade levers. Arguments about internal and external affairs are less clear cut. If Edward I's claim to overlordship in Scotland is accepted, then perhaps

---

[76] *CCR 1313–18*, pp. 315–16.

[77] J. Strayer, *The Reign of Philip the Fair* (Princeton, 1980), pp. 314–16.

[78] Luis Vicente Díaz Martín, 'Castilla 1280–1360: Politica exterior o relaciones accidentals?', in *Genesis medieval del Estado Moderno: Castilla y Navarra (1250–1370)*, ed. A. Ruquoi (Vallodolid, 1988), pp. 125–47.

Scotland could be seen as part of domestic policy; the king of England's position of vassal to France might also be seen as a domestic affair. But in both cases Edward I and Edward II were dealing with independent kings and, in looking for allies, looked well outside their own borders. Without doubt, for all the semantic complications, the activities seem to be 'foreign'. But was there a consistent policy? In broad terms there was, especially in relation to Gascony, where English kings clearly wished to hang on to Gascony on the best terms possible.

On the other hand, tactics to achieve this end might vary. In the light of the later establishment of great power blocs and empires, webs of 'great alliances', and especially modern ideological blocs, much medieval manoeuvring does look short term and ad hoc, but this does not mean foreign affairs were chaotic. Over decades, groupings of traditional friends with similar aims developed. These might prove fickle at times, putting their own immediate concerns first, but that need not deny the term 'consistent foreign policy' to the activities which, in the main, kept them together. England had sets of traditional enemies and friends. Edward II, like his father, could look to the Low Countries and to Iberia for support against France when necessary, but he used them rather differently. In times of internal difficulty he looked to kinsmen in both the Low Countries *and* France for help against rebels: thus, in 1311 the French king sent lawyers to offer support against the Ordinances and in 1322 Edward II asked for military help from the king of France, as well as from the duke of Brabant and the counts of Hainault, Beaumont, St Pol, Aumale, Bar, Eu and Valois, all kinsmen.[79] But when it came to war with France, unlike his father, he looked only to Iberia. This was not due to a lack of previous contacts or ignorance of the Low Countries, because contacts were there. It might show a lack of the tactical flair shown by his father in the 1290s, but it could equally show an appreciation of reality. Hindsight would indicate that a pincer movement such as that planned by Edward I would be expensive and had not worked in the past; current knowledge would show that the emperor was uninterested. If Edward had wanted to try this, he had the financial means to do so, but he might well have been right in his judgement that this would not work and that the immediate need was for help focused entirely on Gascony, which was close to being over-run.

Given that Edward II did have a consistent policy of defending Gascony and holding Scotland, we might also ask whether his policy was proactive or simply reactive. Much routine diplomacy – welcoming newly crowned heads, sorting out commerce – was inevitably reaction to an event. Proactive choice is possibly visible in the requests to Low Country rulers not to help Scotland and in the request for Genoese naval help, but much of Edward's activity over the French war was reactive. In 1325 Edward was simply

---

[79] *CCR 1318–22*, pp. 521–2.

responding to overtures from Norway and Portugal for alliances; he had not (as far as we can see) sought their help, except for supplies in the case of Portugal. In Castile diplomatic activity was vigorous and well-directed from 1324, but it followed rather than preceded French action. The move to an Anglo-Aragonese marriage, on the other hand, predated the war, but it seems to have had little to do with an anti-French strategy until 1324. However, the criticism of being reactive, with its implication of being slack and unready, may be unfair. This was a period as yet without great power blocs to be constantly kept in balance. Moreover, the relationship with France was extremely difficult. English kings were in no position to take an aggressive stand against France.[80] Edward's best policy towards France was probably to sit tight and be un-provocative, and to try to be, as he said to Norway 'friends with all neighbouring peoples'.

Edward's disastrous reign has led in the past to his being roundly criticized in every sphere of activity. More recently, some successes have been identified. Michael Prestwich has pointed out that his financial success was impressive (although it brought political problems), and others have pointed out that, despite quarrels with individual bishops, he had one of the best relationships with the papacy of the middle ages. This paper is a reminder of England's (and thus Edward's) role in the larger theatre of Europe. Perhaps here, too, we should be mindful of successes. His diplomatic activity covered an area as extensive as his father's. His diplomatic correspondence shows competence, a robust defence of English merchants and of English commercial legal practices (in letters to Brabant and Aragon). His choice of Iberia over the Low Countries in 1324 shows a sense of reality (although concentration on Iberia may have led to lack of appreciation of what was happening in Hainault). Edward drew on diplomatic personnel of high quality, which his letter to Arnaud Guillaume shows he appreciated. He could draw on an extensive web of contacts who could inform them about local affairs. His negotiations in Castile, for instance, demonstrate experienced envoys, appropriate linguists, and good information on who mattered. Efforts here were successful enough to bring offers of military aid. The rescue of Argentein shows how effectively information could be mobilized even in the eastern Mediterranean. On the other hand, the French war and Hainault's backing for Isabella's invasion show break-downs in foreign relations of the highest order. Even here we could mention mitigating circumstances. The French situation was extremely volatile and a small local incident could blow up at any time – in 1323 just as in 1293 – and the royal coup in which Hainault helped his Valois wife's cousin was an exceptional circumstance, due as much to domestic failure as to diplomatic failure and perhaps more so; but

---

[80] For comment on Edward I's caution in dealing with France see Prestwich, *Edward I*, p. 326.

the fact remains that in 1326 Edward faced a French war and a foreign-backed invasion. Diplomatic mechanisms worked well, but they needed direction, and alone were not sufficient to overcome Edward's other weaknesses, which cost him Gascony and his throne.

7

The Last Refuge of a Scoundrel?
Edward II and Ireland, 1321–7

Paul Dryburgh

> ...the earl of Leicester, Roger Mortimer and John of Hainault...pursued the king, Hugh Despenser and Robert Baldock, lest they should take to the sea and cross to Ireland, raise an army and oppress England as before; the said lords feared that if the king could reach Ireland and gather an army, he might cross to Scotland and, with the help of the Scots and the Irish, invade England.

Fleeing his estranged queen and her lover, Roger Mortimer, Edward II put to sea at Chepstow on 20 October 1326.[1] In revisiting the denouement of his reign, contemporaries keenly speculate on his destination and purpose. A Franciscan friar writing on the Scottish marches fifteen years later offers this striking interpretation.[2] His is the most developed version of a story with its origins in popular rumours, as expressed by the Anonimalle chronicler, that the king 'voleit aver passe en Irland'.[3] This, though, countered general opinion. Adam Murimuth believed Edward aimed 'ad partes remotas'. Most chroniclers assume he intended flight to Wales to raise forces against the invaders.[4] Modern authorities, as Seymour Phillips notes in re-examining literary traditions surrounding Edward's relationship with Ireland, have dismissed any venture across the Irish Sea.[5] His latest biographer believes Wales was his aim.[6] Edward's failure to navigate the Severn Estuary and his capture near Llantrisant on 16 November make such rumours easy to reject. They may, moreover, reflect his literary denigration as cowardly and duplicitous, or accentuate Scottish perfidy during subsequent crises in Anglo-Scots relations. Similarly, they may mirror a historical tradition in which Ireland acts as a refuge for those fleeing persecution in England. William de Braose

---

[1] E 101/382/1; SAL, MS 122, p. 90.

[2] *Lanercost*, pp. 256–7. The chronicle dates to *c.* 1340.

[3] *Anonimalle*, p. 131.

[4] *Murimuth*, p. 49; *Brut*, p. 239; *Flores*, III, 233; *AP*, 314.

[5] J. R. S. Phillips, 'Edward II and Ireland (in Fact and in Fiction)', *Irish Historical Studies* 33, no. 129 (2002), 1–16, p. 13. Professor Phillips's article was the immediate catalyst for this present essay, though its inspiration came from Brendan Smith.

[6] Haines, *King Edward II*, p. 222.

famously retreated to the protection of William Marshal in Leinster during his dispute with John.[7] Within recent memory Roger Birthorpe had escaped to Ireland, having participated in attacks on Sempringham priory, only to become a stalwart of the Dublin government.[8] More pertinently, the warm welcome Piers Gaveston apparently received in Ireland upon his exile in 1308 long retained historical currency.[9] Nevertheless, Lanercost, a sober authority renowned for his knowledge of the Scots, and the Anonimalle chronicler, an 'informed political commentator' with court connections, should not be dismissed lightly.[10]

It is commonly assumed that Ireland receded from the compass of the English political elite in the early fourteenth century.[11] The personal maintenance of Irish estates became 'too marginal to the natural centre of gravity'[12] of many families who had shaped the 'single aristocratic world that stretched across the Irish Sea'.[13] No English king since John had established a personal presence in Ireland, creating physical and psychological distance between crown and settler community. Edward was the first monarch who had to uphold, rather than establish and extend, English hegemony across the British Isles, but he too appeared indifferent towards Ireland. Early in his reign he continued his predecessors' exploitation of manpower and financial resources in his conflict with Robert Bruce, levies being employed, for

[7] *A New History of Ireland II: Medieval Ireland, 1169–1547*, ed. A. Cosgrove (Oxford, 1987) (hereafter *NHI*), pp. 132–43.

[8] J. Coleman, 'New Evidence about Sir Geoffrey Luttrell's Raid on Sempringham Priory, 1312', *British Library Journal*, 25:2 (1999), 103–28. I am indebted to Maureen Jurkowski for this reference. For Roger's administrative activities, see: *The Administration of Ireland, 1172–1377*, ed. H. G. Richardson and G. O. Sayles (Dublin, 1963), pp. 108, 147, 156, 168.

[9] *AP*, p. 263; *Jacobi Grace, Kilkenniensis, Annales Hiberniae*, ed. R. Butler (Dublin, 1842), pp. 54–5; 'The Laud Annals' in *Chartularies of St Mary's Abbey, Dublin . . . and Annals of Ireland, 1162–1370*, ed. J. T. Gilbert (RS, 1870), II, 337–9.

[10] R. F. Frame, *English Lordship in Ireland, 1318–61* (Oxford, 1982), p. 139; *Anonimalle*, p. 20.

[11] C. McNamee, *The Wars of the Bruces: Scotland, England and Ireland, 1306–28* (East Linton, 1997), p. 16.

[12] R. R. Davies, 'The Failure of the First British Empire? England's Relations with Ireland, Scotland and Wales, 1066–1500', in *England in Europe, 1066–1453*, ed. N. E. Saul (London, 1994), pp. 121–32. More generally, see R. F. Frame, *The Political Development of the British Isles, 1100–1400* (Oxford, 1995).

[13] R. F. Frame, 'The "Failure" of the First English Conquest of Ireland', in *Ireland and Britain, 1170–1450*, ed. R. F. Frame (London, 1998), 1–13, p. 7. Gilbert de Clare (d. 1295), for example, often visited his Irish estates, but the curialist ambitions of Hugh Audley, Roger Amory and Hugh Despenser junior, co-parceners of his inheritance, shunted Kilkenny to the periphery of their thoughts: Maddicott, *Thomas of Lancaster*, pp. 203–62.

instance, in the Bannockburn campaign.[14] Edward Bruce's invasion of Ireland in 1315, which raised the spectre of Scottish liaison with disaffected native communities in Ireland and Wales,[15] first shook Edward from his complacency.[16] But, only when he became embroiled with Roger Mortimer in a struggle for England did Edward seriously try to bring Ireland closer to his kingship.

Alone among his contemporaries Roger Mortimer, lord of Wigmore, Ludlow and Ewyas Lacy on the Welsh Marches, Dunamase (Co. Laois) and the liberty of Trim in eastern Meath,[17] appreciated the vulnerability of English supremacy across the British Isles and how the proliferation of the Anglo-Scots conflict interplayed with crises in England. By autumn 1320 Mortimer was *the* political force in Ireland. Serving twice as chief governor from 1317–20,[18] he married military flair with targeted diplomacy to consolidate English dominion in Ireland and lay the groundwork for Edward Bruce's defeat at Faughart on 14 October 1318 – 'the only clear-cut English military victory during the reign of Edward II.'[19] In so doing he built upon the experience and connections he had established prior to the invasion by imposing his personal presence on his Meath estates.[20] He gained insight into a fragmentary society riven by warfare, shifting frontiers and political and tenurial relations which had to be painstakingly negotiated with settler and

14 J. F. Lydon, 'The Scottish Soldier Abroad: the Bruce invasion and the Galloglass', in *The Scottish Soldier Abroad, 1247–1967*, ed. G. G. Simpson (Edinburgh, 1992), reprinted in *Robert the Bruce's Irish Wars: the Invasions of Ireland, 1306–29*, ed. S. Duffy (Stroud, 2002), pp. 89–106.

15 J. B. Smith, 'Gruffydd Llwyd and the Celtic Alliance, 1315–18', *Bulletin of the Board of Celtic Studies* 20 (1974–6), 463–78.

16 R. F. Frame, 'The Bruces in Ireland, 1315–18', in *Ireland and Britain*, pp. 71–98; J. F. Lydon, 'The Bruce Invasion of Ireland: An Examination of Some Problems', in *Historical Studies IV. Papers read before the fifth Irish conference of Historians*, ed. G. A. Hayes-McCoy (London, 1963), pp. 111–25; J. F. Lydon, 'The Impact of the Bruce Invasion, 1315–27', in *NHI*, pp. 275–302; S. Duffy, 'The Bruce Brothers and the Irish Sea World, 1306–29', *Cambridge Medieval Celtic Studies* 21 (1991), 55–86.

17 For Mortimer's estates, see: P. R. Dryburgh, 'The Career of Roger Mortimer, first earl of March, c.1287–1330' (unpublished Ph.D. thesis, University of Bristol, 2003), pp. 254–61.

18 Mortimer served as Lieutenant (April 1317–May 1318) and as Justiciar (June 1319–September 1320). For his appointments, see: *CPR 1313–17*, pp. 563–4 (23 November 1316); *CCR 1318–23*, pp. 61, 129; *CPR 1317–21*, p. 317 (15 March 1319).

19 John Barbour, *The Bruce*, ed. A. A. M. Duncan (Edinburgh, 1997), pp. 666–74; *Grace*, pp. 93–5; *Laud*, pp. 358–9; G. O. Sayles, 'The Battle of Faughart, 1318', in Duffy, *Bruce's Irish Wars*, pp. 107–18. Few historians cast more than a cursory glance at Mortimer's governance during the Bruce invasion: A. J. Otway-Ruthven, *A History of Medieval Ireland* (London, 1969), pp. 233–7; I. Mortimer, *The Greatest Traitor. The Life of Sir Roger Mortimer, 1st Earl of March, Ruler of England, 1327–1330* (London, 2003), pp. 81–98.

20 Mortimer spent much of 1308–12 in Ireland: Dryburgh, 'Career of Roger Mortimer', pp. 13–26.

native potentates and tenants alike.[21] This paper aims to assess the impact upon the king and the political elite in Ireland of Mortimer's exploitation of this portfolio of knowledge to challenge Edward upon the fringes and at the heart of his authority. Throughout the civil war of 1321–2 and after his extrication from the Tower in August 1323, Mortimer compelled Edward to pay greater attention to Ireland's defence and to the crown's standing among its political classes. This resulted in increased dialogue between the king and a politically sophisticated community whose response possibly induced Edward to contemplate seeking refuge among them.

Despite making his name in Ireland, Roger Mortimer was principally a baron of the Welsh March. It was here that his relationship with Edward II shattered. Spring 1321 saw the formation of a bellicose Marcher faction to counter Despenser expansionism in south Wales after their acquisition of Gower.[22] Violence exploded in Glamorgan on 4 May, devastating the Despensers' estates in south Wales, Wiltshire and Dorset.[23] Neither Mortimer nor the king, however, let such mayhem blind them to the broader nature of the conflict. On 9 May Mortimer spirited away Ralph de Gorges, captain of the besieged garrison of Cardiff castle, into captivity at Wigmore.[24] Robin Frame shrewdly noted that he thereby hoped 'to seal Ireland off' from his enemies.[25]

Gorges, a long-standing retainer of Hugh Despenser senior,[26] had replaced Mortimer as Justiciar of Ireland on 1 February, ostensibly to stiffen English governmental authority.[27] Complaints had reached the king concerning the strategies Mortimer had employed in restoring order. On 11 December 1320

---

[21] Trim was Anglicised but Dunamase and Dysart (Co. Westmeath) lay *inter Hibernicos* by 1323/4: C 47/10/18 (17), C 143/168, m. 2.

[22] J. Conway-Davies, 'The Despenser War in Glamorgan', *TRHS* 3rd s. 9 (1915), 21–62. According to one authority the Mortimers had most to fear, for Despenser junior 'also ardently coveted certain castles which Roger Mortimer had a while ago of the king's gift, and so persuaded the lord king to try to get the said castles back again' (castra quedam, ex regia munificentia Rogero de Mortemer dudum collata, vehementer affectavit, et dominum regem ad repetitionem dictorum castrorum consequenter induxit). His personal animosity was such that 'he proposed to despoil the one, and had promised to avenge the death of his grandfather upon each of them' (unum spoliare disposuit et in utrumque mortem avi sui vendicare promisit): *Vita*, pp. 108, 109.

[23] *CPR 1317–21*, p. 541.

[24] W. Dugdale, *Monasticon Anglicanum* VI, ed. J. Carey (London, 1830), 352. A Tintern writer believed Gorges was delivered to Thomas of Lancaster: *Flores*, III, 345. Nicholas Trivet thought Ralph had been grievously wounded at Caerphilly: BL Cotton Nero MS D ix, fol. 111r. Wigmore was undoubtedly his place of confinement as, despite an offer of 500 marks for his ransom on 2 July, Mortimer was still holding him in December: *CPR 1317–21*, p. 596; *CCR 1318–23*, p. 505.

[25] Frame, *English Lordship*, pp. 161–2.

[26] N. E. Saul, 'The Despensers and the Downfall of Edward II', *EHR* 99 (1984), 1–33, p. 6.

[27] *CPR 1317–21*, p. 558.

Edward demanded an end to pardons for murders of Englishmen – a practice current since his father's reign – without his command.[28] This was a response to parliamentary petitions bemoaning liberal punishment of murderers by fine.[29] Shortly after his arrival as Lieutenant, Mortimer had been forbidden from pardoning homicide without the assent of the Irish Council.[30] But, in an attempt to quell internecine warfare in Munster and reinforce the loyalty of prominent lineages to the Crown, Mortimer had negotiated numerous pardons. At Martinmas 1317, for example, members of the Power, Argentein, Roche and Walsh families received the king's peace for felonies including murder.[31] Twelve days before Mortimer's removal, moreover, Edward issued a five-year mandate that all native Irishmen admitted to English law should be protected in life and limb, as this had been omitted from previous grants and many were being attacked with impunity.[32] Mortimer, though, had facilitated native access to English legal process, the denial of which had been denounced in the Remonstrance to John XXII of 1317–18.[33] He had been trapped by the dichotomy between breaking the cycle of violence and the expectations of conflicting communities and royal government. Because his actions could be deemed detrimental to peace and harmony, his replacement, which was primarily politically motivated, could be justified.

It certainly coincided with moves to marshal sentiment against Mortimer, as Edward courted three men who had been his deputy in Ireland. Ten days after his dismissal, Mortimer had negotiated a marriage alliance with Edmund Butler.[34] The leading figure in Tipperary, with Oxfordshire and Berkshire estates, Butler had served as Justiciar during Mortimer's lieutenancy.[35] Their agreement sealed a long-standing bond and implicitly assured both men of their mutual interests. Upon Edmund's death in September, however, James, his heir, became the king's ward, removing the Butlers from Mortimer's extended family and bringing them nearer to court.[36] Mortimer must also have been aware of the appointment on 23 April of Thomas fitz John, earl of Kildare, into whose hands he had committed Ireland in

---

28 *CPR 1317–21*, p. 551.
29 *Documents of the Affairs of Ireland before the King's Council*, ed. G. O. Sayles (Dublin, 1979), nos. 136, 137, pp. 99–101.
30 Sayles, *Affairs of Ireland*, no. 111, pp. 85–6 (22 April 1317).
31 Dublin, National Archives of Ireland (hereafter NAI), KB 2/12, m. 2d.
32 *CPR 1317–21*, p. 563.
33 *Rotulorum Patentium et Clausorum Cancellariae Hiberniae Calendarium*, ed. E. Tresham (Dublin, 1828) (hereafter *RCH*), p. 21, nos. 25–6 (1 January 1318); *CPR 1317–21*, p. 155 (22 May 1318). For the Remonstrance: Walter Bower, *Scotichronicon*, ed. D. E. R. Watt (Aberdeen, 1991), VI, 389–403.
34 *CCR 1318–23*, p. 360 (11 February).
35 C 135/55, mm. 1–27; Richardson and Sayles, ed., *Administration of Ireland*, p. 84 (April 1317–May 1318).
36 *CPR 1321–4*, pp. 24, 27, 241.

September 1320, to fill the vacuum during Gorges's absence.[37] Since Kildare's promotion coincided with the rebuttal of Mortimer and Hereford's demands for Despenser's commitment into Lancastrian custody, his appointment may have been intended to assuage one of Despenser's leading critics.[38] Three days on, though, Edward ordered Kildare to resume the Irish lands of Hugh Audley for repeated disobedience of parliamentary summonses, presaging the imposition of Despenser's will upon Kilkenny by eliminating his co-parceners.[39] In seizing Gorges a fortnight later, Mortimer struck at the core of the Despensers' coterie and made the government rethink its tactics. John de Bermingham was named as Gorges's successor on 21 May.[40]

Bermingham was Mortimer's closest cohort during his lieutenancy, being knighted by him after their campaign in June 1317 against the Lacys, kinsmen of Roger's wife, Joan, and rival claimants to Trim, who had allied with Edward Bruce to exercise their claim.[41] Mortimer's subsequent promotion of Bermingham's interests facilitated his establishment in Louth and strengthened English authority in an area where Bruce had exploited a vacuum in de Verdun lordship.[42] Bermingham, indeed, captained the Meath and Louth levies, triumphant at Faughart, for which he received the earldom of Louth on 12 May 1319, probably through Mortimer's influence.[43] His appointment, therefore, might have been conceived to conciliate Mortimer following Gorges's abduction. Conversely, Bermingham had been attracted to court early in 1321. Despenser needed experienced clients to extend his grasp to the periphery of his conflict with the magnates of England, and had the capacity to reward them. Who better than men who owed their prominence to one now in direct conflict with the crown and whose future might be compromised? During Edward's reign ties of service and lordship were fragile and fluid. For men such as Bermingham and Kildare, though, inducing their sovereign lord to address the penury and weakness of English authority in Ireland, regardless of the affiliations they formed, was equally important. Bermingham's appointment introduced a productive shepherding of resources.

---

[37] *CPR 1317–21*, p. 578; Richardson and Sayles, ed., *Administration of Ireland*, p. 84.

[38] *CCR 1318–23*, pp. 367–8.

[39] *CFR 1319–27*, p. 52.

[40] *CPR 1317–21*, p. 588.

[41] *Annalium Hiberniae Chronicon ad annum MCCCXLIX digessit per Frater Johannes Clyn* (Dublin, 1809), p. 15. The Lacys' desertion at Kells on 6 December 1315 cost Mortimer his lordship for over a year: *Grace*, p. 63; *Laud*, 348.

[42] B. G. C. Smith, *Colonisation and Conquest. The English in Louth, 1170–1330* (Cambridge, 1999), p. 113.

[43] *CPR 1317–21*, pp. 334–5. Mortimer was prominent at court as a permanent counsellor and secured rewards for other Faughart victors: ibid., 271, 311, 313. Mortimer, it should also be noted, was at court in May 1316, having just returned from Ireland, when John fitz Thomas received the earldom of Kildare and Arnold le Poer lordship of Castlewarden and Oughterard: *CCR 1313–18*, pp. 280, 288; C 53/102, m. 5.

Conciliation failed during the summer. Joining with Thomas of Lancaster, the Marchers secured the Despensers' exile on 14 August.[44] Edward, nonetheless, would not demur and began isolating and eliminating individuals. Striking first against his steward, Bartholomew Badlesmere,[45] he then ingeniously undermined Roger Mortimer's position, measures being timed to extinguish his legacy in Ireland as the net fell upon him in the Marches. On 30 November, as Edward launched his campaign against his opponents in England, sheriffs of south-western shires being commanded to bring their levies to Cirencester, Bermingham was commanded to empanel justices to make an eyre in Meath.[46] A week later the arrest of all leading rebels was promulgated.[47] Mortimer himself was raising an army to descend upon Gloucester on 6 December.[48] Two days earlier Edward empowered Bermingham to remove all justices and ministers in Ireland appointed by Mortimer, possibly to root out any conspiracies there, and on 8 December commissioned him to review the records and processes of all pleas and assizes over which Mortimer had presided, correcting all errors.[49] On 5 January 1322 Edmund, earl of Arundel replaced Mortimer's uncle, Roger of Chirk, as Justice of Wales.[50] Gruffydd Llwyd, leader of the Welsh of north Wales, meanwhile captured Marcher strongholds at Welshpool, Clun and Holt.[51] Pressured from every angle, on 13 January Mortimer received safe conduct to approach the king.[52] On 22 January he and his uncle acknowledged their crimes and abjectly surrendered at Shrewsbury.[53]

For over a year Edward had tried to isolate Ireland from his dispute with the English baronage and to ensure sentiment would be positively exercised in his favour. Though peripheral to the crux of the conflict – Despenser's 'evil counsel' – this was sound strategy. After the Mortimers' surrender the main body of the rebel force rallied to Lancaster, only to be routed at Boroughbridge on 16 March 1322.[54] Letters were apparently discovered in the battle's aftermath, pointing to the rebels' negotiations with Robert Bruce for the Scots' aid in England, Wales *and* Ireland.[55] It is questionable that the Contrariants could have succeeded, for in courting important figures among

44 Maddicott, *Thomas of Lancaster*, pp. 266–93.
45 Haines, *King Edward II*, pp. 132–3.
46 *CCR 1318–23*, p. 408.
47 *CFR 1319–27*, p. 85 (7 December).
48 JUST 1/1388.
49 *CPR 1321–4*, pp. 40, 43.
50 *CFR 1319–27*, pp. 86–7.
51 BL Cotton Nero MS D ix, fol. 111r.
52 *CPR 1321–4*, pp. 47, 48.
53 Conway Davies, *Baronial Opposition*, p. 561.
54 *Anonimalle*, p. 107; *Flores*, III, 204, 347; *Vita*, pp. 20–1.
55 *Foedera*, II¹, 463, 472, 474.

the aristocratic elite in Ireland, Edward ensured that his lordship would not be surrendered lightly.

Boroughbridge freed Edward from baronial constraint, which in the view of some historians ushered in years of tyranny in England.[56] Whether this applied in Ireland is debatable. Edward first turned his attention to extinguishing Roger Mortimer's legacy across the British Isles. On 23 January 1322 his Marcher lands were entrusted to royal keepers.[57] On 25 March Edmund, earl of Arundel acquired Chirk, Ceri and Cedewain, while five days later Edmund, earl of Kent, received Maelienydd.[58] Trim, too, fell into royal hands. On 28 January pleas of assize examined the warrant by which Roger and Joan claimed their liberty. Although their attorneys correctly showed that title emanated from Walter de Lacy, Joan's great-grandfather, one-time lord of Meath, the prosecutors declared the liberty forfeit, arguing disingenuously that title originated in a grant of Henry III in which liberty status had not been stipulated – Edward I had since restored it on several occasions.[59] The consequent shiring of Trim brought the whole of Meath under the administrative umbrella of the Dublin government. It could now be mined for taxation and war subsidies. Over the next eighteen months Edward also partly reshaped Meath landholding society. During his lieutenancy Mortimer created an environment in which to exercise his lordship more comfortably. Hugh Turpilton, who hailed from a hamlet beneath Wigmore castle, received lands at Tober, Martry and Old Grange near Rathwire, and Richard Ideshale, a Shropshire landowner, obtained Foxtown.[60] Turpilton was forfeited alongside Mortimer for his rebellion and his lands, along with Dysart, were granted to Milo de Verdun, an important figure in western Meath, on 26 April 1323.[61] Henry and Valentine Mortimer, Roger's kinsmen, lost their stake in Meath on 9 March 1322.[62] The culmination of these efforts came on 13 July with the order to Bermingham to re-examine all cases tried before Mortimer.[63] A day later the Mortimers were sentenced to death for having ridden against the king in war.[64]

The results of this strategy were profound. In summer 1322 four hundred soldiers, mainly from Meath and Louth, sailed from Dublin and Drogheda under the captaincy of John de Bermingham to liaise with Edward II's host, taking his war with Robert Bruce to the communities of lowland Scotland

---

[56] Fryde, *Tyranny and Fall*.
[57] *CFR 1319–27*, pp. 91, 93.
[58] *CChR 1300–26*, pp. 441–2, 446.
[59] BL Harley MS 1240, fols 118–20; Sayles, *Affairs of Ireland*, nos. 51, 58, 65, pp. 37–9, 47, 54–5
[60] *RCH*, p. 24, no. 150 (Turpilton); p. 23, no. 97 (Ideshale).
[61] *CPR 1321–4*, p. 277.
[62] *CFR 1319–27*, pp. 104–5.
[63] *CPR 1317–21*, p. 176.
[64] Ibid., p. 175.

and bringing his 'rebellion', which had flared again two weeks after Boroughbridge, to an end. Though Edward had been humiliated near Byland abbey,[65] this restoration of the military link between Ireland and England highlighted Bruce's failure to convert his martial mastery to political ends and challenge English hegemony in the Irish Sea world on a permanent basis. Scotland's western seaboard remained vulnerable, and the English Crown could again deploy Ireland's agricultural and military resources against him.[66] Therefore, although Byland paved the way for the thirteen-year Anglo-Scots truce, sealed at Bishopthorpe on 30 May 1323,[67] Edward knew that he need not concede the recognition of his personal title and the independence of his kingdom that Bruce so desired. Furthermore, the ties of patronage and service that Edward established with elements of the political community in Ireland proved vital in consolidating his kingship during renewed crises. For despite Mortimer's sensational escape from the Tower of London on 1 August 1323, which made him the most prominent surviving Contrariant, he was unable to exploit growing curial paranoia.[68] Until his liaison with Isabella he could not strike a physical blow as, despite concerns that their invasion might be marshalled upon the fringes of his authority, Edward had the whip-hand.

Mortimer fled to his cousins, the Fienles brothers, in Picardy.[69] It is revealing, however, that Edward was convinced he intended flight to Ireland.[70] Three suspicious Irish ships had been spotted off Kent, and on 26 August spies were set to ascertain their purpose. Two days later the authorities of major Irish towns, the Justiciar and the leaders of Anglo-Irish society were ordered to set spies and to pursue and arrest Mortimer if he came there.[71] Edward re-instigated the Meath eyre, which had been suspended upon the petition of the men of Drogheda, keen to cultivate good will in a community crucial to victualling his forces in Scotland.[72] This, however,

---

65 Barbour, *The Bruce*, pp. 684–90; Fryde, *Tyranny and Fall*, pp. 119–33; E 101/16/16, mm. 1, 4, 13 (Bermingham's account).

66 Huge quantities of victuals were delivered to Waterford and Drogheda for the Byland campaign: E 101/15/36, 16/6.

67 *CPR 1321–4*, p. 292.

68 *Anonimalle*, p. 107. For a comprehensive list of those executed and imprisoned after Boroughbridge, see Fryde, *Tyranny and Fall*, pp. 161–3.

69 Mortimer, *Greatest Traitor*, pp. 130–3; *CCR 1323–7*, pp. 140–1.

70 News of the escape reached Court by 6 August. Edward ordered inquiries and the setting of spies in south coast ports and in Ireland. Gruffydd Llwyd and Rhys ap Gruffydd were to raise levies and pursue him should he make for Wales: *CCR 1323–7*, pp. 13–14, 132; *CPR 1321–4*, pp. 335.

71 *CCR 1323–7*, pp. 133–4.

72 The eyre was officially prorogued on 8 November 1322 in a week when the king had forbidden anything to be taken from the citizens for the war effort, granted the burgesses licence to trade in England and awarded them the proceeds of pontage for three years: *CCR 1318–23*, p. 610; *CPR 1321–4*, pp. 215, 217, 219.

under-estimated the relative successes of the dissemination of patronage and governmental re-organization in Ireland. Mortimer's fall and the resettlement of Meath created an upper stratum of landowners owing their improved status to the king and their court connections. In 1322 the Dublin Treasurer, Walter Islip, for example, siphoned off £403 from the forfeited lands, goods and chattels found at Trim and other Mortimer manors in Meath to ensure Bermingham received his full annual fee of £500.[73]

Nevertheless, even in exile Mortimer viewed his former inheritance as one and was determined to capitalise on Edward's fears over wide areas. Within weeks of his escape, agents and letters penetrated England, the Marches and possibly Ireland.[74] In September 1323, Bermingham and the Irish Chancellor, Roger Outlaw, apparently reported in person that Mortimer's friends and relations were readying themselves for an assault on the lordship.[75] Robin Frame has rightly advised caution in accepting this at face value, as it survives in correspondence between Edward and Charles IV, king of France, in which Edward excuses himself from performance of homage for Gascony.[76] But their report dovetails with revelations in November of plotting against the king and his favourites.

Evidence submitted to royal justices by Richard Fernhale and Thomas Newbiggin, two of Mortimer's agents who had entered England on their master's bidding, only to confess all, exposed a deadly plot whose branches penetrated the British Isles.[77] Most seriously, Roger de Offeton had been sent to burn the residences of the Despensers, Arundel, Robert Baldock, and Geoffrey le Scrope, intending thereby to kill the king's *secretarii*. Several men from Wigmore and the Marches were implicated, along with prominent Londoners. In Ireland the earls of Ulster and Kildare allegedly received his letters and answered positively, while John de Barry looked forward to his coming. Walter Cusack held his war-horses and Richard Tuyt his mares and geldings. Robin Frame has dissected the Irish evidence and concludes that it constituted little more than 'tittle-tattle' designed to tap into the pervading air of paranoia at Court.[78] Their testimony is certainly tainted. After they had made their confession, Edward employed them to pursue and arrest rebels in London and the Marches 'whose names they know'.[79] Newbiggin used the opportunity to extort menaces from prominent Londoners, for which he was

---

[73] E 101/239/12.

[74] On 4 September Edward urged searchers in south coast ports to hunt more diligently for prejudicial letters, as some had already got through: *CCR 1318–23*, pp. 137–8.

[75] *The War of Saint-Sardos (1323–1325)*, ed. P. Chaplais, Camden 3rd s. 87 (London, 1954), no. 167, p. 178 (16 November 1323).

[76] Frame, *English Lordship*, p. 165, n. 47.

[77] *Parl. Writs*, II², Appendix, 244–9.

[78] Frame, *English Lordship*, p. 168. Hugh Despenser later claimed to be the victim of a witchcraft practitioner: *SCCKB*, III, 155.

[79] *Parl. Writs*, II², 247.

tried and his evidence discredited. He had, though, served in Ireland and was by no means just pulling names out of the air.[80] Walter Cusack had acted as Mortimer's steward of Trim, and Kildare as his deputy justiciar.[81] Tuyt, conversely, was an uneasy bedfellow. According to a possibly contemporaneous inquisition Bermingham had committed the custody of Mortimer's forfeited manors to him and he had split the proceeds with Alexander Bicknor, archbishop of Dublin, chief justice of the Meath eyre.[82]

What are we to make of these revelations? Perhaps they reflect genuine campaigns of terror and lobbying for support by Mortimer, making Edward's kingship tantalisingly vulnerable. In the panicky atmosphere at court, maybe they were what Despenser wanted to hear, words being put into their mouths as part of a crackdown on suspected parties across the king's dominions.[83] Richard de Burgh, earl of Ulster, for instance, owed his freedom from the stain of treachery to Roger Mortimer, and although the king attested to his good faith, suspicion may have lingered.[84] None of the accused was punished, which points to a lack of substance in the allegations. Conceivably, Mortimer's agents singled out elements in Ireland which they believed were acting against him, trying thus to implicate them and bring about their downfall, thereby highlighting the strengthened state of Edwardian authority in Ireland. Edward certainly redoubled his efforts to tackle long-term socio-economic and fiscal problems, to ensure Ireland no longer attracted Roger Mortimer's destabilising influence.

A reforming ordinance for the Dublin government was issued simultaneously to these disturbing revelations.[85] Technical legislation to ensure that writs pleadable at common law were sealed with the Irish Great Seal accom-

---

80 E 101/238/9; Frame, *English Lordship*, p. 168, n. 48.
81 Following his defeat at Kells, Mortimer entrusted Cusack with defending his liberty: *Laud*, p. 348.
82 C 49/5/11. Professor Frame dates this inquisition to summer 1326, when other inquiries were being made into the fate of Mortimer's forfeits in 1322, mainly on the grounds that allegations are brought against the then rebel Bicknor. It is possible that it had been submitted at a similar time to Newbiggin's evidence. The testimony comes from Roger de Ufton, who is probably the same man from Mortimer's Berkshire manor of Stratfield, sent to kill the king's intimates. Perhaps he too had turned king's evidence and it is his 'knowledge' of the Irish scene that Fernhale reports, in which case it may be more credible.
83 Similar allegations against Adam Orleton may have been concocted to oust an enemy from prominence in political society: R. M. Haines, *The Church and Politics in Fourteenth Century England: the Career of Adam Orleton, c.1275–1345* (Cambridge, 1978), pp. 135–41.
84 Richard had been imprisoned by the mayor of Dublin in February 1317, essentially accused of abetting his son-in-law, Robert Bruce's aborted assault on Dublin. Mortimer's first task as Lieutenant was to secure his release: *Grace*, p. 77; *Laud*, 352; Sayles, *Affairs of Ireland*, no. 111, pp. 85–6. Edward notified the community that Richard had behaved well towards him, on 19 September 1322: *CPR 1321–4*, p. 203.
85 *CPR 1321–4*, pp. 363–4 (24 November).

panied measures to combat abuses in the office of chief governor. Henceforth, no assizes of novel disseisin were to be adjourned to another county on the Justiciar's circuit, to secure swift dispensation of justice locally. No minister could purchase lands without licence, take victuals without the assent of the Irish Council, or divert shipping laden with victuals destined for England or Wales. While such changes addressed corruption by Bermingham, they also reflected Mortimer's perceived misgovernment. Shortly after arriving as Lieutenant, Mortimer had impounded the cargo of an English ship bound for Skinburness, which had been forced ashore at Malahide, to victual Dublin castle.[86] Mortimer left Ireland in 1318 owing £1,000 for provisions. Only the king's intervention in 1319 prevented him acquiring valuable estates forfeited by the Lacys at Portlick (Co. Meath).[87] A re-affirmation that pardons for murder without special royal command be forbidden, though, reflected the on-going struggle to balance prevention with cure in the maintenance of order in Ireland, a task committed to a new Justiciar, John Darcy.[88]

An experienced administrator, Darcy had few of the connections with Ireland which had tainted the lordship both before and since Mortimer's fall.[89] Darcy's task was twofold – to ensure that stability in the lordship had not been, and would not be, compromised in the whirlwind of accusations produced by Mortimer's machinations, and to preside over a restructuring of the financial relationship between Dublin and Westminster. The first steps were taken at a parliament convened in Dublin in May 1324 which was attended by the earls of Ulster, Louth and Kildare and the most prominent figures of the Midlands and south-west. There Darcy procured a repetition of the commitment made in 1310 and 1320 that those of great lineage would take responsibility for disciplining their kinsmen and followers.[90] Consequently, on 18 August Edward thanked fifty-five magnates, representative of the political community of Ireland for being 'prompt and well-wishing in all things touching the king', and urged them to continue in this vein.[91] This was the least some could expect. Milo de Verdun had the grant of Dysart extended to include the manor of Old Grange, late of Hugh Turpilton.[92] Thomas fitz John acquired custody of Mortimer's castle at Dunamase.[93]

As well as fostering and rewarding loyalty, these grants tapped into two concurrent developments in the relationship between Edward II and Ireland.

[86] E 159/90, m. 60d.
[87] *Laud*, 359; CCR 1318–23, p. 91 (5 July).
[88] *CPR 1321–4*, p. 348 (18 November).
[89] R. H. M. Mortimer, 'Lordship and Patronage: John Darcy and the Dublin Administration' (unpublished Ph.D. thesis, University of Durham, 1990).
[90] *Statutes and Ordinances and Acts of Parliament of Ireland, King John to Henry V*, ed. H. F. Berry (Dublin, 1907), pp. 306–8.
[91] *CCR 1323–7*, p. 308.
[92] *CChR 1300–26*, p. 469.
[93] *CFR 1319–27*, pp. 288–9.

First, they imposed custodians better able to defend these areas and perhaps raise greater revenue for the Dublin government.[94] The day before Borough-bridge, the Irish exchequer had been committed to Walter Islip, essentially to marshal resources against the Contrariants, which were then switched to tackling the Scots.[95] Islip therefore was to demise all lands in Ireland held in the king's ward.[96] Prior to Mortimer's escape, moreover, an ordinance provided for the extension of all lands in royal hands so that they could be farmed out. This was accompanied by measures for greater scrutiny of the procedures of the Dublin exchequer.[97] On 30 May 1324 Adam Herwynton, chief baron, received orders to survey the exchequer.[98] After repeated attempts at distraint, Alexander Bicknor, archbishop of Dublin, appeared in Westminster in 1325 for the audit of his account as Treasurer of Ireland from 1308 to 1314.[99] Serious fraud was detected and Islip, who had sealed Bicknor's account when appointed as his successor, had the veracity of his accounts questioned before being imprisoned.[100] What effect such measures had is hard to gauge, but £2,373 flowed into royal coffers from Ireland in 1323–6.[101]

Second, such rewards bound these men more intimately to court. Kildare, indeed, had already contracted for his son's marriage to Joan, daughter of Hugh Despenser junior.[102] He entered a network of contacts which potentially placed him in the vanguard of attempts to hold back an encroaching tide of rebellion and to undermine further Roger Mortimer's position across the British Isles. In 1325 the earl of Arundel, whose son had also married a Despenser bride, added the Mortimer lordships of Gwrtheyrnion and Cwmwd Deuddwr to his own patrimony in the Welsh Marches.[103] In promising Milo de Verdun £100 of land on 1 September, Edward perhaps perceived a similar opportunity to extend such influence further, across lands which had previously owed their allegiance to Mortimer.[104] Conversely, for Milo and Kildare their connection to Despenser was probably directed at

---

94 Dunamase lay in ruins by 1323: C 47/10/18 (17).
95 *CFR 1319–27*, p. 109 (15 March 1322). Islip received allowance for his expenditure in raising supplies to be sent to England: E 159/95, m. 21.
96 *CCR 1318–23*, p. 432 (14 April 1322).
97 *CPR 1321–4*, p. 332 (27/28 July 1323).
98 *CPR 1321–4*, p. 421.
99 Orders for distraint were issued on 14 April, 22 May and 8 November 1322 and 4 June 1323: *CCR 1318–23*, pp. 436–7, 610; E 368/92, m. 89d, E 368/93, m. 84.
100 E 159/102, m. 114.
101 Frame, *English Lordship*, p. 136.
102 Papal dispensation was granted on 1 June 1323: *Calendar of Entries in the Papal Registers relating to Great Britain and Ireland: Papal Letters 1305–42*, ed. W. H. Bliss (London 1895), p. 231.
103 *CFR 1319–27*, p. 353 (13 July), 369 (2 December).
104 *CFR 1319–27*, p. 359; *CChR 1300–26*, p. 469. The restoration to favour of Hugh Turpilton on the same day, however, necessitated the resumption of Milo's grants,

maintaining a share of land and influence in Ireland from the one source they could virtually guarantee, for despite Despenser's tight grip on power, he commanded the loyalty of few sections of English society and gradually became more desperate for support.[105]

In the short term, opening up such channels of patronage proved sensible. Not only did the Gascon war break out in autumn 1324, but fears grew of an invasion of England by Dutch and German mercenaries led by Roger Mortimer from Hainault.[106] His ambitions frustrated elsewhere, Mortimer had trawled Europe for support. The invasion never materialised, for in practical terms Edward had stymied any paranoia Mortimer could engender across the British Isles. Indeed, the comments of Nicholas Huggate, treasurer for the Gascon war, with reference to Mortimer's invasion and his liaison with Charles IV in the St Sardos campaign that 'le peril est toutz jours a douter', stand equally well for his actual threat in Ireland.[107]

The situation changed with Queen Isabella's adoption of Mortimer as her lover in December 1325.[108] Although incorrectly as it turned out, Edward, significantly, appears to have been concerned to address the potential threat in the Irish Sea first. Having established watches on the south coast to monitor letters streaming into England,[109] Edward implored resistance to any invaders on 8 February 1326, the day upon which he proclaimed Isabella had 'given herself up to the counsel of the Mortimer'.[110] Four days later, the treasury was ordered to ensure the castles of North Wales were adequately victualled.[111] His potential master-stroke, though, came on 26 March, in his offer of safe-conduct to Edmund Lacy to approach his court from Scotland, followed on 16 July by a like conduct to his brother, Hugh.[112] The threat of restoring the Lacys to Trim and extinguishing the Mortimer claim, allied to the potential for them to rally sympathy for the king in the event of an invasion, was obvious. They did not take up the offer, however, probably being concerned with spiralling anarchy in England and the tenuousness of their grip on Trim should Mortimer succeed.

    but the king may have intended to make up his promise from other Mortimer lands in Meath: *CPR 1324–7*, p. 165.
[105] Saul, 'Downfall of Edward II', p. 1.
[106] Chaplais, *Saint-Sardos*, no. 43, pp. 58–9; no. 44, p. 59; no. 54, p. 72 – a letter from Hugh Despenser reporting that a 'grant nombre de gentz et autres . . . quieux gentz deivent ester cheventein Sire Rogier de Mortymer et les autres bannis' planned to attack East Anglia.
[107] Chaplais, *Saint-Sardos*, no. 87, pp. 102–3.
[108] P. C. Doherty, *Isabella and the Strange Death of Edward II* (London, 2003), pp. 84–8.
[109] *CPR 1324–7*, pp. 208–12.
[110] 'sest done au consail le Mortimer': C 54/143, m. 14d.
[111] *CCR 1323–7*, p. 445. On 23 February Robert le Poer was ordered to survey repairs to Welsh castles: ibid., 450.
[112] *CPR 1324–7*, pp. 253, 296. The latter was vacated.

If so, this is symptomatic of a general collapse of law and order across the British Isles, and more particularly in Ireland, which signalled the ultimate futility of attempts to reform transmarine political relationships. The years 1325–6 witnessed increasing violence from native Irish kin-groupings; wards were established against the Ó Broin at Baltinglass and Dunlovan, and contingencies were made for campaigns in Leinster and Munster.[113] Slieve Bloom experienced campaigns led by the earl of Louth and Thomas Butler against the Uí Cerbhaill, and then raiding by Brian Ban Ó Briain and the English of Ely.[114] Much of this, though, paled in comparison with the war in Munster, which flared in the early summer of 1325.[115]

Originating in a dispute over control of the lands of the Clare inheritance in Thomond, practical, if not legal, lordship over which had been exercised by Maurice fitz Thomas, a leading landowner in Kerry, Cork and Waterford, Munster witnessed the violent determination of such claims between Maurice, his allies of the Butler and Bermingham families, and Arnold le Poer, seneschal of Kilkenny, his kinsmen and members of the de Burgh dynasty with interests in Connacht. Although at the height of the invasion scare in England, John Darcy attempted to broker a compromise, the government did little, save manipulate some of those involved.[116] On 23 April 1326 James Butler, lord of Tipperary and parts of Kilkenny, received protection to return to Ireland.[117] In the previous five months, possibly prompted by the crisis caused by Isabella's estrangement,[118] Edward had restored his inheritance and had allowed him, for a fine of 2,000 marks, to marry whomever he wished.[119] By reintroducing one who had been raised at court and was thus bound over for his future conduct, Edward may have envisaged him as taming his kinsmen. Perhaps more naturally, the government also patronised Arnold le Poer. On 1 July, in England, Arnold received a commitment of the first wardships and marriages in Ireland, valued £100.[120] Extricating him from the conflict breathed new life into peace negotiations, as on 14 July Maurice fitz Thomas and John le Poer of Donohill agreed to chastise the criminal elements in their followings, free from the chance of arrest.[121] Arnold, though, was seneschal of the lords of Kilkenny and Carlow, Hugh Despenser

---

113 P. Connolly, *Irish Exchequer Payments, 1270–1446* (Dublin, 1998), pp. 307, 310–11.
114 *Clyn*, p. 17.
115 Frame, *English Lordship*, pp. 169–73.
116 NAI, RC 8/15, pp. 690–1.
117 *CPR 1324–7*, p. 259.
118 The grant restoring Butler's lands (2 December 1325) comes on the day after Edward wrote to Isabella urging her to return to him: *CCR 1323–7*, p. 580.
119 *CFR 1319–27*, pp. 367–8; *CPR 1324–7*, p. 203. James also requested that a plea concerning his father's marriage agreement with Mortimer in 1321 be dropped: E 159/101, m. 55.
120 *CPR 1324–7*, p. 280.
121 *RCH*, pp. 33–4, nos. 20–1.

and Thomas of Brotherton, Edward II's half-brother. It is likely therefore that the court was concerned to curtail the violence by promoting the man best able to represent their interests in the area. At a time of impending crisis, with Mortimer and Isabella's forces massing on the near continent, what exactly such interests were is open to question. As his kingdom was swamped, Edward may have believed Ireland offered a realistic escape route.

*

The rapid collapse of Edward II's kingship has created an almost impenetrable fog, through which his motivations and ambitions cannot be glimpsed with any certainty. Facts are few and the surviving evidence will not allow firm conclusions. There are indications, however, that he did not intend Glamorgan as the place to make his last stand. Mortimer and Isabella landed on the Orwell estuary in Suffolk on 24 September 1326 and, seeing they met with little resistance, Edward abandoned his household and made his escape at Chepstow on 20 October.[122] First, that Edward did not realise he would be open to allegations that he had abjured his realm is hardly credible. On 26 October, a day after he had been cast ashore near Cardiff, a council convened at Bristol elected Prince Edward *custos regni*, the king having been 'eloigned' from his kingdom by Despenser.[123] To risk this on the short hop from Chepstow to Cardiff seems foolhardy in the extreme. Admittedly, he might have been making for Despenser's lordships of Glamorgan and Morgannwg to raise forces to meld with other Welsh levies, but the hasty and haphazard summonses issued only *after* his landing suggest otherwise.[124] Second, Edward's ship probably only landed in Cardiff Bay by accident. Geoffrey le Baker reasons that a storm in the Bristol Channel sent it awry.[125] One of the final payments recorded in Edward's chamber account, indeed, is 9d to Richard de Blitone, Hugh Despenser's confessor, that he might 'avower a seint Anne qe ele nous envoiast bon vent'.[126] Third, Edward fled armed with a vast cache of money, some £29,000 being surrendered to him from the Treasury by John Langton, sufficient to maintain a sizeable army in the field for some time.[127] Fourth, Edward may have had a contingency plan. On 30 September, a day before fleeing London, he commanded Robert le Poer,

[122] Haines, *King Edward II*, pp. 166–86. Edward left London on 1 October: E 101/382/1.
[123] *CCR 1323–7*, pp. 655–6.
[124] On 27/28 October commissioners were appointed to raise the people of south Wales against the invaders. On 29 October Rhys ap Gruffydd received a commission to raise the king's forces in south-west Wales and muster with the king: *CPR 1324–7*, pp. 333–4, 335.
[125] *Geoffrey le Baker*, p. 23.
[126] SAL, MS 122, p. 90.
[127] *Calendar of Memoranda Rolls (Exchequer) Preserved in the Public Record Office London: Michaelmas 1326 to Michaelmas 1327*, ed R. E. Latham (London, 1968), no. 212, p. 36.

chamberlain of North Wales, to provide for the sustenance of 100 men-at-arms in Conwy castle for six months.[128] On 20 October, moreover, William Ercalowe replaced Aline Burnell as custodian.[129] This could simply have reinforced the Principality against a future assault by Mortimer. Equally, Conwy might be a bolthole from which to jump to Ireland, or a conduit through which an invading force from Ireland might funnel.[130] Mortimer brought it under his aegis by 20 November, thereby swiftly securing the approaches to north Wales.[131]

None of this proves that Edward hatched an Irish escape plan. His relationship with Ireland was more complex, however. On 5 October 1326 the Dublin government warned Nicholas de Verdun and Richard Tuyt to desist from provoking 'tumult'. We are not told where they had been causing trouble, but they had gathered a multitude of armed men, to the terror of the local population.[132] The association of this command with the payment of Tuyt's fee as keeper of Athlone may imply nothing more than personal irritation. Athlone, though, had been in the custody of Roger Mortimer during his periods in government and it is tempting to link the tumult with a reaction to his arrival in England some eleven days earlier.[133] Tuyt had benefited from Mortimer's fall and he had reason to fear his return. An inquisition taken at Trim in 1322 demonstrated that Mortimer had unjustly disseised Tuyt from the manor of Demor, a decision Mortimer quickly overturned when he came to power.[134] More pertinently, Tuyt had been placed in charge of Mortimer's stock and had shared the proceeds of his downfall.[135] Both men, moreover, had been thanked in August 1324 for their good services, and so perhaps were displaying their dismay at Mortimer's potential return.[136] Did they have prior information as to the invasion? Letters were sent to Irish magnates in August 1326 by Elizabeth de Burgh, dower landlady of Kells in Meath and one third of Kilkenny.[137] Though primarily concerned with managing her son, William's inheritance of the earldom of Ulster after the death of his

---

128 *CFR 1319–27*, p. 418.
129 *CFR 1319–27*, p. 421.
130 Mortimer himself had employed Conwy as a conduit to visit Trim: BL MS Harley 1240, fol. 54v (31 August 1310). The Scots appreciated its important position in the Irish Sea too. In September 1315 John de Hothum, the king's special envoy to Ireland, had to sail from Chester as the route via Conwy and Anglesey had been blockaded by Thomas Dun, Bruce's lieutenant in the Irish Sea: E 101/309/19 (3).
131 E 371/85, m. 16.
132 *RCH*, p. 34, nos. 26–7.
133 *CFR 1307–19*, p. 393.
134 E 163/3/12. Edward III overturned its findings in Mortimer's favour on 17 February 1328.
135 C 49/5/11.
136 *CCR 1323–7*, p. 308. See p. 130 above.
137 E 101/91/12, m. 3d.

grandfather, Richard, on 29 July,[138] Elizabeth received intelligence from the exiles throughout the summer of 1326 and entertained members of the rebel court upon their landing. Such letters may therefore have conveyed a sense of impending chaos.

The most tantalising glimpse of this chaos came on 12 December 1326. The Irish Council revealed to the sheriffs of Cork, Limerick, Tipperary and Waterford that certain magnates had risen up 'to perpetrate evils against the faithful people'.[139] Among those urged not to indulge were Maurice fitz Thomas, Arnold le Poer, John and William de Bermingham and John fitz David de Barry. Frame speculates that although such disquiet ought to be ascribed to a continuation of local power struggles, there is a chance that these men 'had been preparing for the arrival of the fugitive court.'[140] Arnold might have been party to Edward's plans, having visited the court recently. The others were not usual bedfellows, but the Berminghams had plenty to fear from Mortimer, they having equally benefited from his fall.[141] Professor Phillips has, indeed, identified counties Carlow, Wexford, Waterford and Kilkenny as likely areas where the fugitive king might receive a ready welcome.[142] While this may somewhat stretch credulity, his underlying assertion that there were parties in Ireland willing to succour Edward II is appealing.

Perhaps the most controversial but potent source of succour, however, came from the Scots. It is apparent from the conducts issued to the Lacys that Edward had been in contact with Robert Bruce during 1326. Evidence that serious discussions had occurred came on 29 August. Power was granted to Robert de Welle to agree to arrangements for an Anglo-Scots assembly to treat for peace.[143] Three days earlier, John Jordan, who had reached Edward with Bruce's letters, was allowed to return to Scotland with a reply.[144] Had he negotiated for a conjunction between Edward II and the Scots in Ireland along the lines suggested by Lanercost? As the reconfigured English political elite gathered for the coronation of Edward III on 1 February 1327, the late king was moved into captivity at Kenilworth and the British Isles ushered in Mortimer lordship, the ties binding England, Ireland, Wales and Scotland through Edward II cast an ominous shadow over the tottering English crown.

Somewhat incongruously, the loss of Ireland sat alongside the loss of Scotland in the condemnation of Edward II at the Westminster Parliament of

---

138 *Clyn*, p. 18; *Grace*, p. 103; *Laud*, 364.

139 *RCH*, p. 35, no. 60.

140 Frame, *English Lordship*, p. 177.

141 See above, pp. 124, 126–8.

142 Phillips, 'Edward II and Ireland', p. 14.

143 *CPR 1324–7*, p. 315.

144 *CPR 1324–7*, p. 313. On 30 August Jordan received a gift of 40s, having been 'misso in negociis Regis privatis usque ad partes Scocie': E 101/382/6, m. 3.

February 1327. While the cycle of violence and criminality could not be stemmed, Bruce's failure to subvert the bonds of lordship between England and Ireland had, to some extent, consolidated them. This condemnation may reflect Mortimer's own perspective, opinion having been exercised against him since 1322. The phrasing of an ordinance issued at the Westminster Parliament of 3 February, that restorations of Contrariants' land be made 'as well in Ireland and Wales as in England' speaks volumes.[145] His new regime, moreover, was frozen out in Ireland. Despite the proclamation of Edward III's authority on 29 January 1327 and the appointment of Thomas fitz John as Justiciar on 13 February, not until 13 May did Edward's writ run officially in Ireland.[146] John Darcy clung tenaciously to the levers of power until he felt there was no chance of another regime change. He also clung tenaciously to Mortimer's former castle of Trim and the manor of Moylagh, which he had held since 26 August 1324.[147] More sinisterly, he sent the Franciscan, Henry Cogery, to Scotland to expedite 'certain confidential business touching the lord king', by whom he meant Edward II.[148] What this 'business' was is not clear, but it may have been connected with the renewed vigour with which Robert Bruce explored his options across the British Isles.

On the day of Edward III's coronation the Scots attacked Norham castle.[149] Defensive measures were hastily enacted. On 10 February Anthony Lucy secured custody of Carlisle castle, and three days later Henry Percy contracted to keep the northern marches of England with 100 men-at-arms, 100 hobelars and as many foot-soldiers as necessary.[150] On this latter day, as seen, the earl of Kildare was appointed as Justiciar to impose Mortimer's authority on Ireland. Letters were also sent to the leaders of Anglo-Irish society, informing them that power no longer resided with Edward II and requesting them to 'continue their faithfulness to the king's royal house.'[151] Mortimer himself took the justiceship of Wales on 20 February, evidence of a more integrated approach to dealing with a Scottish threat transcending national frontiers.[152] The necessity for such a strategy was highlighted only a week after the English government had called a muster at Newcastle for 18 May on 5 April.[153] Around 12 April Robert Bruce landed at Larne, intending 'ex consensu quorundam hibernicorum ulterius in Wallie processisse et

---

[145] *CCR 1327–30*, p. 101.

[146] *Foedera*, II², 683, 688–9.

[147] Payments to Darcy as custodian are recorded from August 1325 to April 1327: *RCH*, p. 36, no. 98. For Moylagh, see: *CFR 1319–27*, p. 297.

[148] *RCH*, p. 36, no. 77 (payment of 40s on 6 February 1327); Frame, *English Lordship*, p. 140.

[149] *Lanercost*, p. 258.

[150] *CPR 1327–30*, p. 6 (Lucy); *CPR 1327–30*, p. 18 (Percy).

[151] *Foedera*, II², 688–9 (14 February).

[152] *CFR 1327–37*, p. 19.

[153] *Foedera*, II², 702–3.

ibidem cum exercitum applicuisse et terram vestram Anglie more guerrero invasisse . . .'[154]

This claim came in an inquisition taken in 1331 to discover exactly what John Jordan had undertaken during 1327. John, the jury testified, had dissuaded Bruce from his plan. One might say the better the story, the better the reward.[155] But, this verdict correlates with Lanercost, and the government took it seriously. Robert le Poer, chamberlain of north Wales, rendered his Easter account by proxy as Mortimer testified 'Robert's presence is very necessary in those parts for their safety.'[156] Whether Bruce actually had the capacity to affect such a scheme is doubtful, although there were those in Ireland who could only have feared Mortimer rule. Bruce probably hoped to exploit the Ulster power vacuum to ratchet up the pressure.

Despite a realisation of the fragility of English authority, which led to William de Burgh, grandson of the last earl, being granted wardship of Ulster on 5 February 1327, the arrangements for his expedition could not be accelerated.[157] Bruce spent over three months in Ulster and on 12 July extracted a truce from Henry Mandeville, steward of the earldom, with a commitment to render annual tribute to the Scots and to allow Bruce to receive the submission of any Irishmen who wished to be his men ['*estre les soens*'].[158] The Dublin government was sufficiently concerned to send the chancellor, Roger Outlaw, 'to treat with the men of Ulster and examine their hearts regarding resistance to the Scottish enemies and rebels . . .'[159] Although this seems to have curtailed the threat, Bruce used Ulster to strike psychologically at Roger Mortimer. All the Bruces' previous forays into Ireland, even the Faughart campaign, had been launched from Ulster with Mortimer out of Ireland and they had repeatedly raided Trim and Meath.[160] Moreover, in involving Wales they revived threats of encirclement and held out the possibility of a union with communities who, in 1322, had demanded the Mortimers' execution.[161] Bruce intervened further in Welsh politics too. On 26 June the sheriff of Shropshire and the mayor of Shrewsbury were ordered to arrest James

---

[154] C 47/10/19 (8); R. G. Nicholson, 'A Sequel to Edward Bruce's Invasion of Ireland,' *Scottish Historical Review* 42 (1963–4), 30–40.

[155] The council advised he be given £100 of land for having gone into hostile territory.

[156] *Memoranda Rolls, 1326–7*, no. 1289, p. 192. Mortimer himself was briefly absent from court, possibly to survey Welsh defences: C 53/114, mm. 29–34.

[157] *CFR 1327–37*, p. 28.

[158] E 30/1536, m. 1.

[159] E 101/239/5; Frame, *English Lordship*, p. 141. In the previous year Edward had pardoned Alan fitz Warin and two Savage brothers, Ulstermen, for adhering to Bruce during his invasion: *CFR 1319–27*, p. 373; *CPR 1324–7*, p. 212; *CCR 1323–7*, pp. 534–5.

[160] They had rested at Trim on their famine-ravaged retreat from Munster in April 1317: *Grace*, p. 83.

[161] *Calendar of Ancient Petitions Relating to Wales from the Thirteenth to the Sixteenth Century in the Public Record Office, London* (Cardiff, 1975), [6], no. 255.

Trumwyn and his confederates, who were attempting 'to do what evils they can against the king and his subjects' in the Welsh Marches.[162] Trumwyn had recently returned from Scotland with Donald, earl of Mar, and they were suspected of raising forces to release Edward II, then at Berkeley, with Bruce's approval.

Ultimately, Mortimer and Isabella became persuaded of the need for a final peace settlement.[163] The Treaty of Edinburgh of 17 March 1328 restored Scottish independence and recognised Bruce claims to the Scottish throne, overturning all Edward II had struggled to uphold. This gave Mortimer latitude to assault royal prerogative in Ireland and accumulate an array of estates circling Dublin.[164] In order to achieve this, however, he needed to impose himself upon the political community in Ireland from a distance, and to bring those men whom Edward II had courted back to his authority. In so doing he loosed competitive forces that looked to his court in their struggles over regional supremacies, which proved impossible to restrain, bequeathing Edward III an unenviable legacy.[165] Edward, nevertheless, respected the ties binding England and Ireland and it is no irony that it was to the lordship that he turned for *his* first campaign.[166]

It is difficult to conceive of the reign of Edward II without reference to the margins of his kingdom and kingship. While his energies were largely focused on slaying his demons in England, the roots of his most serious crises consistently lay elsewhere. Robert Bruce's genius was to explore every angle so as to exert the maximum pressure, a strategy Roger Mortimer wanted to adapt when trying to wrest hegemony from his perceptibly tyrannical and incompetent sovereign. Edward's sensibility to the imperial dimensions of his kingship should not be under-estimated, though. Resolute in his will not to cede ground, in Ireland at least, inspired by Mortimer and encouraged by Despenser, he resourcefully cultivated reciprocal shoots of patronage and service. Even in his darkest hour, while he perhaps realised the ultimate futility of battling Bruce, Edward may have believed his best hope of salvation lay in harvesting these shoots. His probable intention to flee to Ireland, therefore, implies not just desperation, but also a calculated decision to risk all for his crown.

---

162 'ad mala que poterunt contra nos et nostros facienda': C 54/146, m. 18d.
163 S. Cameron and A. Ross, 'The Treaty of Edinburgh and the Disinherited (1328–1332)', *History* 84 (1999), 237–56.
164 Dryburgh, 'The Career of Roger Mortimer', pp. 138–43, 259–61.
165 Frame, *English Lordship*, pp. 174–96.
166 The campaign planned for 1332, however, was aborted after Edward Balliol's triumph at Dupplin Moor: Frame, *English Lordship*, pp. 196–208.

8

Edward II:
The Public and Private Faces of the Law

Anthony Musson

In terms of legal theory, the king was regarded as God's representative on earth: he was responsible for promulgating just laws, he headed the judicial system (the writs and courts sessions operating in his name) and was held to be the fount of justice.[1] At his coronation he undertook to uphold the laws and customs of the realm and do justice to all.[2] This paper engages not simply with the monarch's theoretical duties and the restraints upon his executive power,[3] but with his real life actions, his inaction, and the 'virtual reality' of kingship. Rather than focusing on the institutions of government and the operation of the legal system, therefore, it examines Edward's personal role in the administration of justice and the impact of the king's physical presence (or absence) in particular situations. At his deposition Edward was charged with a failure to do justice and there were allegations that he had been counselled to disregard the laws.[4] Public perceptions of Edward's attitude towards the law are examined and the paper seeks to revise existing views on the extent to which he was involved in or even cared about judicial matters. In so doing, recourse has been made to both textual sources (the various chronicles of the reign and surviving legal records) and visual images (as found in chronicles, genealogies, treatises and statute books).

Given the conventions of 'administrative kingship', that the king delegated his power and did not normally become personally involved in judicial matters, there is a difficulty in pin-pointing from the records the extent to which Edward actually gave attention to legal issues and whether he dealt personally with the matters with which the king is credited. As Fryde pointed out, 'In the case of the king himself, personal evidence which might explain

---

[1] Henry de Bracton, *De Legibus et Consuetudinibus Regni Angliae*, ed. S. E. Thorne, 4 vols (Cambridge, MA, 1968–77), III, 22–3; E. Powell, 'Law and Justice', in *Fifteenth-Century Attitudes: Perceptions of Society in Late Medieval England*, ed. R. Horrox (Cambridge, 1994), pp. 29–33.

[2] H. G. Richardson, 'The English Coronation Oath', *Speculum* 24 (1949), 43–75. For *Vita's* comments on the coronation oath see p. 10.

[3] J. Watts, *Henry VI and the Politics of Kingship* (Cambridge, 1996), pp. 16–28.

[4] *AP*, 317; C. Valente, *The Theory and Practice of Revolt in Medieval England* (Aldershot, 2003), pp. 27–8.

political decisions is distressingly scanty . . .'[5] Indeed, there is a distinct 'shortage of intimate royal correspondence which might give us a better understanding of some of the motives and ideas of the king himself'.[6] To a limited extent, this is made up for by the surviving writs, plea rolls, petitions and memoranda that make up the business of justice from which one can occasionally glimpse (sometimes obliquely) Edward in action. Edward's involvement in the exercise of justice will be analysed initially with regard to his handling of petitions in parliament, his apparent administrative direction in legal matters, and his personal presence at judicial hearings. Finally, I shall discuss perceptions of Edward as being above the law and the extent to which the person of the king made a difference to the practical realities of the judicial system.

*

Private petitions for redress of grievances were submitted to the king in parliament, often as a last resort where the common law could not provide remedy or where the king's special grace was required. They were a natural part of royal business and a great number were submitted at a parliamentary session, requiring their filtering and sorting by panels of auditors. The majority of bills directed to the king or to king and council, if not rejected, were hived off to the relevant administrative or judicial departments.[7] The author of the *Vita* couches his account of the events of 1321 in such a way that he effectively accuses the king of being unwilling to fulfil his duty to hear individual grievances in parliament and determine petitions according to the laws or (in another passage) 'satisfy their (the barons') petitions according to justice' and indeed 'do justice to all'.[8] These comments should perhaps be seen in their wider political context, yet if they are supposed to imply a laxity or general reluctance to engage with private petitions on Edward's part, then it is not borne out by the records of parliament or the endorsements on petitions themselves. While there were a number of issues that the auditors of petitions could deal with on their own authority, there were instances where the active participation of the king was required. Endorsements show variously that the king himself needed to be consulted[9] and nothing could be done further in the matter without the king's input,[10] 'the king will tell them

---

5 Fryde, *Tyranny and Fall*, p. 9.
6 Ibid., p. 8. See also the paper by Hamilton in this volume.
7 A. Harding, *Medieval Law and the Foundations of the State* (Oxford, 2002), pp. 178–82; G. Dodd, 'The Hidden Presence: Parliament and the Private Petition in the Fourteenth Century', in *Expectations of the Law in the Middle Ages*, ed. A. Musson (Woodbridge, 2001), pp. 135–49.
8 *Vita*, p. 112.
9 For example: SC 8/3/145 (c.1320), SC 8/5/218 (1322).
10 SC 8/5/216 (1322).

of his will',[11] or that he had already entertained the petition (either personally or through a senior official acting in his name) and further advice was required.[12] Surviving schedules from 1318 indicate how the petitions that had been presented in parliament were categorised according to their appropriate destination. A group of petitions was listed as being for the king's personal consideration.[13] In the case of *La Warre v. Bishop of Coventry* (1318) concerning presentment to an advowson, the prospect of further royal deliberation was explicitly mentioned in the response.[14] Consultation with the king, therefore, appears to have been a normal feature of the process: 'the lord King having been more fully consulted touching these matters both through himself and through his Council, he may make such declaration in the premises as shall fall in with his careful discretion . . . the king having been consulted thereof when it shall please him . . .'.[15] Achieving a hearing of such matters obviously depended in reality upon the king's demeanour and availability, but it was not considered to be unforthcoming or an unlikely event.

In the case of certain high status petitioners, Edward communicated with them personally, face-to-face. Roger Brabazon, the chief justice, for instance was summoned into the king's presence,[16] while the archbishop of York was told the king wished to consult him personally or would certainly speak with him when he (Edward) next came to Yorkshire.[17] Contemporaries commented on the king's active participation in the parliament of October 1320. The bishop of Worcester noted in a letter to Pope John XXII that 'our lord the king, in the parliament summoned to London bore himself splendidly, with prudence and discretion . . . Present almost every day in person, he arranged what business was to be dealt with, discussed and determined.

---

11 SC 8/4/154, SC 8/4/156 (1320).
12 For example: SC 8/4/151 (c. 1320), SC 8/4/188 (1322), SC 8/4/199 (1321–2).
13 *Rotuli Parliamentorum Anglie Hactenus Inediti, 1279–1383*, ed. H. G. Richardson and G. Sayles, Camden 3rd s. 51 (London, 1935), pp. 65–6, 71–3.
14 *Year Books of Edward II: 11 Edward II*, ed. J. P. Collas and W. S. Holdsworth, Selden Society 61 (London, 1942), 312 (from record at CP 40/222 r. 194 *Shropshire*). 'The said bishop, by his petition which was laid before us and our council, prayed that a remedy be applied to him; we therefore wishing to provide, as we are bound, a legal remedy . . . do command you that, having heard the arguments of the aforesaid parties and inspected the aforesaid bishop's petition . . . and having carefully considered the articles contained in the same petition, you make thereof fulfilment of justice to the aforesaid bishop; and if it should happen that doubt arise, whereby it should seem to you impossible to proceed to render judgment thereof without consulting us, then you are to inform us of this, according to your discretion, so that we may then further cause to be done that which we from our deliberation shall seem to be necessary.' [Witness myself at Westminster – 25 May 1318]
15 *Year Books of Edward II: 8 Edward II*, ed. W. C. Bolland, Selden Society 41 (London, 1927), p. 78.
16 SC 8/2/88 (c.1315).
17 SC 8/5/222, SC 8/5/224.

Where amendment proved necessary he ingeniously supplied what was lacking . . .'.[18] In another letter (this time to Cardinal Vitale Dufour) he wrote with similar sentiment: 'All those wishing to speak with reasonableness he listened to patiently, assigning prelates and lords for the hearing and implementation of petitions, and in many instances supplying ingeniously of his own discernment what he felt to be lacking.'[19] 'Trivet' equally recorded that the king demonstrated prudence in answering the petitions of the poor, and balanced severity with clemency in judicial matters, to most people's amazement.[20] In other words, from his general demeanour, Edward exhibited an inclination to do justice and some aptitude in his task.

In addition to his demonstrable attention to petitions (at least during the years 1318–22), Edward's contribution to the administration of justice can be ascertained from the instructions he issued personally for the instigation of judicial inquiries, the holding of special sessions and for dealing with certain legal matters. It is understandably difficult to separate out policy decisions and identify a personal hand in instructions effected through officials and messengers.[21] The individuals concerned, the nature of the case or the particular problem can sometimes indicate possible direct royal involvement, as too can the witnessing formula and the type of seal affixed to the commands.[22] Decrees concerning the punishment of those who had destroyed Piers Gaveston's property, for example, or orders causing it to be proclaimed that Piers had been illegally banished and had returned by the king's command, were likely to have originated with the king.[23] Similarly, the concern for increased precautions for the arrest of Roger Mortimer, the appointment of Hugh Despenser the elder to attend to his arrest, and the setting of a price on Mortimer's head (dead or alive) were matters directly of concern to Edward as well as the realm.[24] A proposal to the king of France for the settlement of disputes between the two countries and the request for a personal interview, even if diplomatic positioning, suggest a willingness to involve himself.[25] As, too, does the order from the king for Amarenus de Lebret (on account of his special affection) to appear in England 'in nostra

---

18 *Register of Thomas de Cobham, Bishop of Worcester, 1317–27*, ed. E. H. Pearce, Worcestershire Historical Society 39 (1930), p. 97.
19 Ibid., p. 98. For a context for and interpretation of these letters see Haines, *King Edward II*, pp. 45–6.
20 *Nicholai Trevet Annales*, ed. T. Hog (London, 1845); Maddicott, *Thomas of Lancaster*, p. 257.
21 Conway Davies, *Baronial Opposition*, pp. 150–63.
22 J. H. Trueman, 'The Privy Seal and the English Ordinances of 1311', *Speculum* 31 (1956), 611–25.
23 *Foedera*, II^1, 67 (1308), 153 (1312).
24 *Foedera*, II^1, 530 (1323), 644 (1326).
25 *Foedera*, II^1, 122 (1310), 145 (1312).

presentia' for the settlement of disputes between him and John de Ferrers, seneschal of Gascony.[26]

More incisive evidence of Edward's direct involvement comes from the period 1323–4. The chronicler Henry de Blanford (although writing after events) recorded for the year 1323 that the king made a determined effort on the state of public order, asserting that all disturbers of the peace were to be punished according to their deserts, and the law of the land observed in all places.[27] This perception of royal energy is born out in surviving instructions to Henry le Scrope, in which Edward castigates the chief justice of king's bench and expresses a desire for wrongs to be punished according to law. Towards the end of January 1323, Henry le Scrope received the following communication from the king:

> We marvel that, whereas you, Henry, hold our place in hearing such pleas and should supply our presence therefore in the places through which you travel in our realm, you do not make inquiry or do further what is fitting about prises of corn, victuals and other goods taken from our subjects against their will, conspirators, trespassers, informers who make false plaints, conventicles and confederacies illegally made. Wishing therefore to punish such evils as is fitting, we order you, firmly enjoining that you are to inquire at once into such prises, conspirators, trespassers, informers who make false plaints, conventicles and confederacies in every place through which you travel, as well within liberties as outside them, with all the diligence and in all the ways you can, and you are to punish all those who may happen to be lawfully convicted thereof in accordance with the terms of the statutes and articles promulgated thereon and the law and custom of our realm, so conducting yourself in this matter that complaint thereon may not come yet again to us. Witness myself at Newark the thirtieth day of January in the sixteenth year of our reign.[28]

The implication here from this unusual documentary evidence is that Edward had been made aware on several occasions of Scrope's inefficiency or lack of drive in pursuing the king's business.[29] Clearly, Edward felt that as his chief judicial representative (supplying 'our presence'), Scrope's lack of enthusiasm reflected directly on royal endeavours. Whether as a result of further complaint or not, Henry le Scrope was replaced as chief justice of king's bench in July 1323 by Hervey Stanton.[30] It is noticeable that during the

---

[26] *Foedera*, II¹, 177 (1312); see also ibid., II¹, 221 (payment to Lebret on advice of the king of France).

[27] *JT*, p. 139.

[28] KB 27/251 m. 30; printed in *SCCKB*, IV, 110–11. See also Oxford, Bodleian Library, MS Holkham Misc. 29, fol. 43.

[29] A petition purportedly from the community of the realm made direct complaint in 1320 (SC 8/3/129).

[30] *SCCKB*, IV, xiii, xl.

autumn of the same year, Edward issued under the privy and secret seal a steady flow of letters (jointly and separately) to royal justices Hervey Stanton, William Herle and Geoffrey le Scrope,[31] to Master Robert de Aylestone (keeper of the privy seal engaged in judicial work),[32] and the barons of the exchequer.[33] The activity was presumably related to the instructions issued for the Michaelmas term to the court of king's bench to travel to the north-west to inquire concerning new articles and hear and determine misdeeds committed in Lancashire, Derbyshire and Staffordshire during the period of rebellion.[34] Edward's concern with punishing offenders and with securing the royal dues from the goods and chattels of rebels comes across in the commissions and is evidenced by the scale of planned judicial investigation.[35]

There is evidence from the chroniclers, the formal records of parliament and documents relating to the court of king's bench to suggest that Edward was physically present or personally involved in dispensing justice on several occasions. This intervention came about because of either the serious nature of the case (for which a reaction from the king was expected), or the king's proximity to the event (it occurred while he was travelling the kingdom), or because it appealed to him to pursue the matter. In 1318, for example, a young man (John of Powderham)[36] who claimed openly that he was the true son and heir of Edward I and that the present king was 'but a carter child sotily broute into the qween', went into the King's Hall in Oxford (recently taken over by the Carmelite friars) and allegedly tried to take seisin there.[37] There are variations in detail as to whether it was the mayor of Oxford, or the chancellor of the university and bailiffs of the town jointly, who arrested the man and sent him to the king at Northampton. In the *Vita*, word reached Edward and the pretender was arrested on the king's orders and brought before him ('domino regi presentatur'). According to the contemporary Pauline Annalist he was led before the king on a number of occa-

---

31 For example: E 101/379/19 fols 1 (23 October, 30 October, 4 November 1323), 1v (9 November), 2 (24 November, 26 November), 5v (3 and 4 January 1324).

32 E 101/379/19 fols 1 (23 October and 30 October 1323), 7 (20 January 1324).

33 E 101/379/19 fol. 2 (27 November 1323).

34 KB 27/240 mm. 40, 40d; KB 145 2/1/1 mm. 52–65; *SCCKB*, IV, pp. xl–xlii, 132–3. For proceedings in Lancashire see *South Lancashire in the Reign of Edward II*, ed. G. Tupling, Chetham Society 3rd s. 1 (1949).

35 See for example: JUST 1/425 m. 13. Note also the appointment of sub-keepers in Lancashire in November 1323: E 101/379/19 fol. 1v; *CPR 1321–4*, p. 382; A. J. Musson, 'Peace-Keeping in Early Fourteenth-Century Lancashire', *Northern History* 34 (1998), 41–50.

36 For an analysis of this event see W. R. Childs, ' "Welcome, my brother": Edward II, John of Powderham, and the Chronicles, 1318', in *Church and Chronicle: Essays Presented to John Taylor*, ed. I. N. Wood and G. A. Loud (London, 1991), pp. 149–63.

37 *Vita*, pp. 86–7; *AP*, pp. 282–3; *Anonimalle*, p. 95; *Bridlington*, p. 55; *Chronicle of England of John Capgrave*, ed. F. C. Hingeston (London, 1858), pp. 185–6; *Chronicon Monasterii de Melsa*, ed. E. A Bond, 3 vols (London 1866–8), II, 335–6.

sions ('ductus, et coram rege muiltipliciter aggressus'). In spite of questioning, the young man still maintained that he was the rightful heir and the present king ruled without justification, though he produced neither evidences nor proof to back up his claims. Given the words 'coram rege' (used here) it is obviously ambiguous as to whether the pretender came before the king himself, members of the king's council or the king's bench (though the court was located at Westminster during the Trinity term).[38] Edward is credited with taking advice on the matter and, following consultation, the pretender was adjudged the penalty for traitors. This may well have been Edward's decision, though in the *Vita* the judgment was said to have been relayed through the court ('ex decreto curie'). The implication is, therefore, that in spite of the king's direct involvement in the case, the alleged traitor went through the formal adjudication process, rather than being tried summarily. The case is not enrolled on the king's bench plea rolls,[39] but an order for delivery from Northampton gaol was made on 20 July 1318.[40] A general delivery of all prisoners in the gaol took place on 24 July (before Spigurnel and Boudon),[41] but there is no mention of John, suggesting the special delivery had occurred earlier.[42] On another occasion, this time in 1321, whilst at Gloucester, Edward is said to have ordered into his presence ('jussit suae praesentiae sisti') three knights, Roger de Elmrugg, Nicholas Lavin and Nicholas Torville, who had allegedly behaved traitorously and disloyally.[43] Here there is no mention of a formal trial and no record has survived, so they may well have been tried summarily before the king. They received the punishment of being drawn behind horses and hanged for their treachery, though the continuator of the *Flores Historiarum* alleges unjustly so.[44]

[38] Both Denholm-Young, *Vita*, p. 88, and Wendy Childs in her re-edited and revised translation of the *Vita Edwardi Secundi* (Oxford, 2003), pp. 148–9, translate 'coram rege' as 'face to face with the king'.

[39] The Trinity legal term ended on 19 July.

[40] *CPR 1317–21*, p. 273. William Montecute, John Botetorte and Hugh Beaufiz were commissioned to deliver the gaol of 'John de Exon'. Montecute was steward of the household. One of the few surviving rolls for the court of the verge, over which Montecute presided, coincides with this regnal year (E 37/4 m. 1). Although allegations of treason could not be entertained by the court, it is interesting that there are no entries between 21 July (when the court was at Northampton) and 26 July (by which time the court had moved to Oxford): ibid., m. 3.

[41] JUST 3/51/1 m. 12.

[42] Possibly 22 July, as the day after was a Sunday. According to *Lanercost* Montecute presided at the trial (Childs, ' "Welcome my brother" ', pp. 152–3).

[43] The *Vita* only mentions 'a certain Herefordshire knight', though it is apparent from the description (noting that he had been sheriff of Herefordshire) that is was Roger de Elmrugg (pp. 119–20).

[44] *Flores*, III, 202–3. This stance would be understandable if, as Antonia Gransden argues, this chronicle was commissioned by Queen Isabella to justify her invasion and Edward's deposition (A. Gransden, *Historical Writing in England, c. 1307 to the Early Sixteenth Century* (London, 1982), pp. 17–18). The *Vita* indicates that the king

The issue of treason or lese-majesty brought the bishop of Hereford, Adam Orleton, initially before the king's bench and then (maintaining that the substance of the articles alleged against him was so serious that he ought not to answer them in court) before the king himself in full parliament in February 1324.[45] The bishop was duly arraigned before the king in parliament, the chronicler Blandford describing Edward's participation here in terms of his taking on a judicial or inquisitorial function ('Rex . . . quasi ex officio judicis').[46] The king's personal cognisance of another treason case, concerning adherents of Roger Mortimer, is suggested by a writ dated 10 March 1324 that mentions that the sheriffs and coroners of London are making accusations and petitioning 'in istandi parliamenti' concerning Thomas Newbiggin and Richard Fernhale.[47] Appended is a schedule of statements containing their confessions taken 'in the presence of the lord king' before John Stonor and his associates and released 'in curia hic' [on Friday 16 March 1324] by Master Robert de Ayleston, keeper of the privy seal.[48] Although it is unlikely that the confessions were heard literally in Edward's presence, as this phrase is intended to denote the court of king's bench in session, their subject-matter did concern a plot against the king and members of his council, and so the case and this record may well have come before him at some stage.

The ambiguity of the terminology denoting sessions held before the king 'in presencia domini regis', like 'coram rege' or 'coram ipso domino rege', clearly presents problems when assessing Edward's personal involvement. An assault occurred in the Guildhall at York on 22 November 1322 'in presencia regis',[49] but was Edward actually present at the time? He was in definitely in York on the 25th of that month, and recorded as being there

---

softened his approach to the punishment, as the penalty for treason was remitted (p. 120) and there is an order to restore the issues of the manor of Risley in Herefordshire (which had previously been taken into the king's hand) to Agnes, lately wife of Richard de Elmrugg (*CCR 1318–23*, p. 582). Elmrugg is listed in the *Flores* and other chronicles as among those executed after the battle of Boroughbridge (see Childs, *Vita Edwardi Secundi*, p. 204, n. 422). This may be a retrospective listing of his death or an indication that he lived on for another year.

45 Essentially, he was accused of being an ally and adherent of Roger Mortimer, whose villainy and treachery had already been investigated. The background and initial stages are recorded in the king's bench: KB 27/255 m. 87d (Hilary 1324); printed in *SCCKB*, IV, 143–6; see also R. M. Haines, *Church and Politics in the Fourteenth Century: the Career of Adam Orleton c.1275–1345* (Cambridge, 1978), pp. 140–51. Haines highlights Orleton's legal objections and the glaring procedural errors.

46 *JT*, pp. 141–2. Orleton was claimed as a clerk by the archbishop of Canterbury, though a jury found him guilty.

47 KB 145/1/18 m. 223. See also Dryburgh's paper in this volume.

48 KB 145/1/18 mm. 224–6. This information is endorsed on the final sheet of the schedule (m. 226d).

49 KB 27/250 m. 85d; *SCCKB*, IV, lxxiii.

earlier,[50] but it still does not explain whether he was in audience at the sessions. A more tantalising prospect is afforded by a writ sent under the privy seal addressed to Hervey Stanton 'et ses companions justices de nostre Baunk por le Roy'.[51] It is dated 20 January 1324 and includes a schedule on which is endorsed a statement from Adam Leonard, cursitor, that this writ had been released to Hervey Stanton at Hereford on the evening ('hora vespera') of 5 February.[52] The schedule is headed 'Ces pointz sont reconez en la presence le Roy' and concerns an examination conducted, as it suggests, in the king's presence at Gloucester. The prior of Llanthony Abbey, near Gloucester, the main subject of the investigation, was suspected of aiding the king's enemies. The court of king's bench, headed by Stanton, was based at Hereford before it moved on to Gloucester.[53] The king appears to have been ahead of the court as he was already in Gloucester on 19 January and at Berkeley on 5 February.[54] Given the gravity of the case, Edward may well have decided to question the prior himself.

As in the above instances, the king's personal intervention is often only discernible from the chance survival of memoranda denoting his intentions or recording his instructions.[55] For example, on 10 October 1320 'the king in his full parliament at Westminster . . . delivered with his own hands to Henry Scrope a schedule in the following form and ordered execution to made thereof in accordance with the law and custom of the realm'.[56] This particular schedule is headed: 'Inquisiciones capte coram domino rege ipso agente in comitatu Berk' mense Augusti anno regnis suo quarto decimo' and consists of three inquests held at Sandleford before the lord king on Sunday 31 August and Monday 1 September 1320, looking into the death of Robert Ileslee (Ilsley).[57] The king's privy seal was located at Sandleford on these two days.[58] The schedule is recorded on the king's bench plea rolls. Sayles notes that it was very unusual for the court of king's bench to have sat outside term in such an obscure location.[59] It is intriguing to surmise who was heading or carrying out this examination, especially as the king later handed the record personally to his chief justice.

---

[50] Hallam, *Itinerary*, p. 235.

[51] KB 145/1/18 m. 276.

[52] KB 145/1/18 m. 277d.

[53] *SCCKB*, IV, appendix 3 (travels of the court of king's bench), cii. No precise dates are given by Sayles, but the court was sitting in Gloucester on 8 February 1324 (KB 27/255 *Rex* m. 24d).

[54] Hallam, *Itinerary*, pp. 252–3.

[55] I am indebted here to the references mentioned by Sayles in his volumes of *SCCKB* and J. Conway Davies in his 'Common Law Writs and Returns: Richard I to Richard II', *BIHR* 23 (1963), 125–55.

[56] KB 27/242 *Rex* m. 3; *SCCKB*, IV, lix.

[57] KB 27/242 *Rex* m. 3, 3d.

[58] Hallam, *Itinerary*, pp. 201–2.

[59] *SCCKB*, IV. p. lii.

Edward's receipt and examination of indictments is possibly observable again during the burst of activity associated with the itinerant king's bench in 1323–4. Indictments taken before Henry le Scrope and Master Robert de Ayleston at Ightenhill (including schedules containing lists of names) are noted as having been sent 'per dominum Regem coram Rege hic per manus predicti Magistri Roberti'.[60] The king was present at Ightenhill at the time.[61] An order 'per ipsum Regem' for the determination of indictments made in Lancashire (issued at Up Holland, and dated 12 October 1323) shows Edward was actively encouraging justice: 'we already being in parts of the same county, because we wish that the matters be determined before us (*coram nobis*) command that you have all inquests made before you on the matters before us wherever we shall be in England without delay . . .'[62] A list of thirty-three names (those indicted as well before the king as before Master Robert de Ayleston and Henry de Waldene) is appended.[63] Indictments made in the king's bench at Wigan were especially noted as being 'in the presence of the king and by his order'.[64] In November 1323 the treasurer and barons of the exchequer were ordered (under the secret seal) to send without delay (to wheresoever we will be in England) indictments concerning the goods and chattels of enemies and rebels of the king in their custody, so that they could be determined according to the law and custom of the realm.[65] It may well be that these were destined for and determined by king's bench justices, but Edward seems to have taken some executive action in directing or encouraging his servants in the pursuit of justice and royal financial benefit.

Much royal activity is hidden from view because it occurred in private or was effected through oral communication to the chancellor, royal justices, members of the household and local officials.[66] Nevertheless, some indication of the Edward's involvement in judicial business can be gleaned from instructions and directions conveyed obliquely through messengers or intermediaries. He appears to have intervened in 1312, at the instigation of Nicholas de Percy, in the suit that Walter Foliot and his wife, Ada, were pursuing to recover lands rightfully her inheritance. The justices were ordered to act 'with as much haste as you can in accordance with the law and custom of our realm' and 'to show as much grace and favour as you lawfully can' to the complainants. The record states that Edward had notified the justices of king's bench by word of mouth via Hugh Despenser not to proceed further

---

60 JUST 1/425 m. 22.
61 Hallam, *Itinerary*, p. 249. The Privy Seal was at Ightenhill 4–10 October.
62 JUST 1/425 m. 13. See Hallam, *Itinerary*, p. 249. The terms of the writ itself were fairly standard.
63 JUST 1/425 m. 12d.
64 KB 27/254 m. 41.
65 E 159/102 m. 104. It transpired that many of these indictments had already been enrolled with extents of lands and so could not easily be separated.
66 Conway Davies, *Baronial Opposition*, p. 175.

except to adjourn the parties. At later stages the king's subsequent instructions were again relayed by Hugh le Despenser (with Aymer de Valence on one occasion and on another with Bartholomew de Badlesmere).[67] In the case of William Gentilcorps, which was reviewed in the court of king's bench in 1318, we learn that the defendant was imprisoned in Rochester Castle in September 1312 'by our special command' ('per speciale preceptum nostrum') under a privy seal writ, having been accused of the rape and death of Alice de Beauchamp. The king's bench was alerted following a petition from Gentilcorps, heard in early 1315, complaining that he had been detained for two years without standing trial. A search of the rolls and records of the sheriffs and coroners of Buckinghamshire (where the alleged attack took place) revealed no indictments or appeals or other process affecting him there. The justices of king's bench were clearly puzzled as to why Gentilcorps should have been arrested and detained for such a period and resolved that they should be certified of the king's will in the matter and the reason for the commands issued. It is recorded that the justices had a discussion with Edward at York on 16 November 1318 concerning the manner and cause of Gentilcorps' arrest and 'the king told the justices by word of mouth that they should proceed to release William in accordance with the law and custom of England, notwithstanding any previous order from the king'.[68] Oral orders ('oretenus') were also given by Edward to justice Henry Spigurnel to associate with him a Staffordshire knight (John Hastang) and try at Stafford the case of John, son of Roger Swynnerton (and others), who had previously come before the king's bench by way of appeal for the death of Robert de Esnyngton, but on default of the appellatrix were being tried at the king's suit.[69] In 1326 Edward personally charged the mayor, sheriffs and alderman of the city of London to keep the peace in the city of London when they appeared in his chamber in the Tower of London.[70]

In addition to his responsibility for justice, the king possessed the prerogative of mercy. Edward exercised his prerogative through the issuing of pardons[71] and in various personal acts of clemency. Robert Poun, for example, allied with the earl of Hereford in the civil war of 1321–2, was pardoned on the king's oral instruction.[72] Other rebels also received lenient treatment.[73] Following the king's siege of Leeds Castle in October 1321 and the eventual surrender of it to him, he reacted violently against Bartholomew Badlesmere's supporters, ordering at least six to be hanged outside the walls

---

[67] KB 27/210 m. 59 (Michaelmas 1312); printed in *SCCKB*, IV, 37–43.
[68] KB 27/233 m. 105 (Trinity 1318); printed in *SCCKB*, IV, 84–6.
[69] *William Salt Archaeological Collections*, X (1889), 18–19.
[70] *CCR 1323–7*, p. 563.
[71] Though he was said to have granted charters of pardon 'unwillingly' to those involved in the destruction of the Despensers' manors in 1321 (*Vita*, p. 116).
[72] Conway Davies, *Baronial Opposition*, p. 174.
[73] Fryde, *Tyranny and Fall*, p. 62.

of the castle.[74] The trial in Canterbury Castle of those taken as prisoners, however, was halted and abandoned on the instructions of the king, just as the justices were about to pass sentence.[75] This may seem like undue interference in the course of justice, which on one level it was, but on another, the king was upholding his original promise of mercy to those who had surrendered the castle, even if a little late on the call. Similarly, although Edward did not intervene at any point during Thomas of Lancaster's trial,[76] his remission of Lancaster's sentence to be drawn and hanged is significant even if it may not seem much of an act of clemency. The substitution at Edward's behest of beheading, because of the earl's royal blood,[77] enabled Lancaster to die in a more honourable way; a method of death contemporaries regarded as befitting a nobleman.[78]

*

Throughout his reign, Edward II appears to have been aware of the power of a visual display of authority. Lancaster's death would not have been lost on contemporaries and Edward was concerned to punish and indeed make an example of offenders. He was keen for punishment to be witnessed and that justice be seen to be done. Thomas Lercedekne having allegedly gone beyond the form of his commission of purveyance in Cornwall was warned that if he did not make redress the king would make an example of him.[79] This is readily apparent in the case of former servants turned traitors, such as Gilbert de Middleton and Andrew Harclay, but also with regard to those who displeased the king or defied him, such as Walter Culpepper and, more obviously, those who ended up on the wrong side after the battle of Boroughbridge. In the case of Middleton, Harclay, Lancaster and his many supporters, trials were duly held, but examples were made of the offenders accordingly, in the regions where they had held jurisdiction, their lifeless bodies prominently displayed.[80] The chroniclers' highlighting of such events

---

74 *AP*, p. 299; *Vita*, p. 116; *Anonimalle*, pp. 102–3.
75 Haines, *King Edward II*, pp. 132–3.
76 Whatever the political motive, there was legal justification for the trial (see M. Keen, 'Treason Trials under the Law of Arms', *TRHS* 5th s. 12 (1962), 83–103), though its unusual nature and the course followed were highlighted by chroniclers (*Brut*, p. 222; *Lancercost*, p. 244) and supposedly Lancaster himself: he was not allowed to speak in his defence or in mitigation and apparently proclaimed 'This is a powerful court, and great in authority, where no answer is heard nor any excuse admitted' (*Vita*, p. 126).
77 *Vita*, pp. 125–6; *Bridlington*, p. 77; see also *RP*, III, 3–4.
78 E. Cohen, 'Symbols of Culpability and the Universal Language of Justice: the Ritual of Public Executions in Late Medieval Europe', *History of European Ideas* 11 (1989), 410.
79 SC 8/4/186.
80 *CPR 1321–4*, pp. 148–9; *JT*, pp. 100–1; *Bridlington*, p. 83; *AP*, pp. 299, 302–3; *Flores*, III, 180, 206–8; *Meaux*, II, 342–3, 347.

and their detailed descriptions of the deaths were, like the punishment itself, concomitant with the desire to warn and deter others.[81] Spectacles of executions, as Spierenburg notes, 'served a double function': they 'warned potential transgressors of the law that criminal justice would be practised and . . . warned everyone to remember who practised it'.[82] The spectacle for on-lookers and vivid descriptions for chronicle readers may equally have had the effect of feeding a perception of tyrannous and arbitrary behaviour,[83] though it is noticeable that dissatisfaction with the trials of 1322–3 and complaint against treason 'on the king's record' did not really emerge until after Edward's deposition (or perhaps 1326 at the earliest).[84] Other than the use of public spectacle, there is no special evidence to suggest that Edward deliberately used images of justice personally for propaganda purposes.[85]

In the absence of specific royal-inspired iconography it is necessary to examine illuminated chronicles, law books and treatises for perceptions of Edward's rule and attitudes towards it. The image of a king enthroned is intended to convey his majesty and the attributes of kingship (which included his responsibility for law and justice).[86] The conventional imagery employed in day-to-day contexts on charters, royal seals and coins may have maintained to a large extent the perception of royal authority and the king as fount of justice.[87] The iconographic evidence, however, reflects the mixed views on his reign, naturally depending upon the date of the manuscript and when the art work was drawn up. Where we can be sure that a distinct image programme was intended (for instance, where Henry III is pictured with Westminster Abbey or Edward I is shown smiting the Scots and Welsh)[88] it is possible to gauge something of the expectations arising from Edward II's accession and the response to his reign (whether a general one or personal to

---

[81] The *Vita* has a passage giving historical examples of treason as a warning (pp. 98–9) and specifically states, with reference to the execution of Bladesmere's followers, 'For the king wished to make an example of them, so that no one in future would dare to hold fortresses against him' (p. 116).

[82] P. Spierenburg, *The Spectacle of Suffering* (Cambridge, 1984), p. 55.

[83] Compare these proceedings with the political expedience, vengeance and general 'aura of lynching' in 1326 (Valente, *Theory and Practice of Revolt*, p. 155).

[84] J. G. Bellamy, *The Law of Treason in England in the Later Middle Ages* (Cambridge, 1970), pp. 44–53.

[85] J. Watts, 'Looking for the State in Later Medieval England', in *Heraldry, Pageantry and Social Display in Medieval England*, ed. P. Coss and M. Keen (Woodbridge, 2002), pp. 243–67 (especially p. 267).

[86] See, for example, pictures of Solomon enthroned holding a sword and scales of justice: Cambridge, Emmanuel College, MS 67 fols 162, 253v.

[87] M. T. Clanchy, *England and Its Rulers, 1066–1272* (Oxford, 1983), p. 156.

[88] Oxford, Bodleian Library, MS Rawlinson D 329 fols 5v, 6. Contrast with genealogies where the images of kings are uniform and rarely have separate attributes (e.g. Bodleian, MS Ashmole Rolls 21, MS Hatton 53) or where the chronicle or list has been continued and roundels have been drawn but no image has been included (e.g. MS Bodley 912 fols 229, 229v).

the illuminator) as encapsulated in the image. There can be problems in the 'reading' and interpretation of such images. Is Edward dressed in a long, purple, fur-trimmed robe as a sign of imperial aspirations (whether real or manifested here as a reflection of political prophecy)?[89] Why, in the same image, does Edward not have his hand on his heart (as other kings pictured do), but is shown covering his genitals? Does it imply a lack of trustworthiness?

The detail of the representation (the absence of certain props or its variation from the standard icon) can perhaps convey to the viewer personal attributes or qualities. In iconographical terms the sword is regarded as a significant prop. Employed in connection with images of kings, it symbolises not only might and skill in war, but also the power of justice and the consequent ability (or willingness) to punish wrong-doers.[90] The images portraying Edward II usually depict him empty-handed or holding a rod.[91] It is rare to find him shown holding a sword. Given the apparent standardisation of both the sword imagery and that of Edward holding a rod, is it fanciful to suggest therefore that there was a notion that Edward II did not warrant a sword (or the symbolism it conveyed)? This emasculation of the royal image was, of course, familiar from pictures of Henry III, and had carried with it overtones of the arbitrary actions and injustices carried out in Henry's name.[92] The notion should not necessarily be taken too far, as it may have been a matter of compositional form: where there is a series of images of kings (in a genealogy or chronicle) some element of iconographic contrast may have been deemed appropriate. Edward I is normally depicted holding a sword (upright or pointing with it),[93] yet there are some images of him holding a sceptre or fleur-de-lys ended rod.[94] The examples I have found depicting Edward II with a sword may in fact be the exceptions that prove the proposition. One derives from the figure of a king in an illuminated initial

---

[89] BL MS Cotton Julius E iv fol. 6v. This may of course be a reflection of the artist's palette, but Richard II is similarly attired (fol. 7v) and was known to enjoy imperial epithets, if not harbour imperial aspirations. *Adam Davy's Dreams about Edward the Second*, ed. F. J. Furnivall, Early English Text Society, o. s. 69 (London, 1978), p. 13; J. R. S. Phillips, 'Edward II and the Prophets', in *England in the Fourteenth Century, Proceedings of the 1985 Harlaxton Symposium*, ed. W. M. Ormrod (Woodbridge, 1986), pp. 189–201 (pp. 189–94); N. Saul, 'Richard II and the Vocabulary of Kingship', *EHR* 110 (1995), 854–77.

[90] P. Binski, 'Hierarchies and Orders in English Royal Images of Power', in J. Denton (ed.), *Orders and Hierarchies in Late Medieval and Renaissance Europe* (Manchester, 1999), pp. 76–7.

[91] For example: Bodleian MS Rawlinson C 292 fol. 9; MS Rawlinson D 329 fol. 7; BL MS Cotton Julius E iv fol. 6v.

[92] Binski, 'Hierarchies and Orders', p. 79.

[93] See for example: BL MS Cotton, Vitellius A xiii fol. 6v; MS Royal 20 A ii fol. 9v; Bodleian, MS Rawlinson C 612B fol. 7.

[94] Bodleian, MS Bodley 912 fol. 209; MS Rawlinson C 454 fol. 19.

'E' (for Edward) in a Liber Custumarum (dated to c.1320–30),[95] another from a genealogical roll (dated to c.1310)[96] and another from the Treatise of Walter de Milemete (dated to c.1326–7).[97] All three instances are explainable from the context (and date) of the manuscript. In the first, the kingly icon is expected to endorse the charters or legal rights enshrined in the text. It is a standard convention. In the second, the kingly figure (inscribed with 'Edward his son') had only recently come to the throne and in an initial contemporary reaction, the illuminator clearly believed or wished to promote the notion (in keeping with those who wrote or had knowledge of the political prophecies of the time)[98] that Edward II had inherited the same kingly qualities as his father. In the third example, the treatise on kingship presented to the young Edward III,[99] an old king is pictured seated and holding a sword. He appears to be disputing across the text with a young king, who is also seated and holding a sword. Given Milemete's agenda to instruct the young Prince Edward, this may represent the giving of advice from a paradigmatic forebear (such as Edward I or Edward the Confessor). On the other hand, it may represent the prince's father, Edward II, with the implication being that the future (new) ruler should not follow the example of the present (old) one.

*

Towards the end of his account of Edward's reign, Capgrave states that there were 'open cries throughout the realm that the king should come home, and take the rule of his people, on that condition, that he should be ruled by his own laws'.[100] Similarly, during his account for 1325, the author of the *Vita* comments on the present dire political situation and closes the passage with a paraphrase of the well known maxim from Justinian: 'Sic voluntas hodie vincit rationem. Nam quicquid regi placuerit, quamvis ratione careat, legis habet vigorem' (Thus today will overcomes reason. For whatever pleases the king, although lacking reason, has the force of law).[101] Written contemporary to events and almost certainly before 1326, this is a forcefully expressed opinion. To what extent was there a distinct perception during his reign that Edward acted above the law?

---

[95] Bodleian, Oriel College MS 46 fol. 111. This image has also been attributed to Edward I, but the gesture with two fingers (horizontally outstretched and slightly apart) of the left hand suggests that he is indicating that he is 'the second'.

[96] Bodleian, MS Ashmole Rolls 38.

[97] Oxford, Christ Church College, MS 92 fol. 39.

[98] See L. A. Coote, *Prophecy and Public Affairs in Later Medieval England* (Woodbridge, 2000), pp. 83–91.

[99] For background to this treatise see M. Michael, 'The Iconography of Kingship in the Walter of Milemete Treatise', *Journal of the Courtauld and Warburg Institutes* 57 (1978), 35–47.

[100] *Capgrave*, p. 196.

[101] *Vita*, p. 136.

It was certainly something that was aired in the courts and bandied around in jurisprudential terms amongst judges and senior lawyers. Various judges maintained that 'against the king who is above the law you cannot rely on legal principles . . .' and that 'the king's charter cannot be judged by other than the king, for he is without peer and is above all law etc'. Herle, before his elevation to the bench, pleaded in response that 'the king ought not to force you into doing aught that is inequitable, for he is the maintainer of the law of the land . . .'.[102] In the case of *Scoland v Grandison* (heard in the Kent eyre of 1313–14) the legality of the king overriding existing statute was raised by John Stonor, counsel for Grandison.[103] As a way of arguing that his client should not answer the writ, Stonor pointed out that there was legislation limiting the submission of writs during an eyre visitation to a given day and that the writ in this case had been delivered a month after the relevant date. To entertain the writ would be to go against statute, which no man could do. The judges hearing the case, Hervey Stanton, William Ormesby and Henry Spigurnel, countered respectively that the writ was entertained in response to a direct command from the king and that to ignore it would be 'tantamount to challenging and disputing the king's authority', which they could not do. Indeed, in another (fuller) version of the report the judges contended that the subsequent warrant from the king was equally binding with the statute ('nous avoms garrant du Roy plus tardif quest auxi haut com est lestatut') and they could legitimately entertain it because they held the sessions under the king's commission.[104] Not to be deterred, another serjeant pleading on behalf of Grandison maintained that since the statute had been made by 'comun conseil du Roialme', it could not be overridden by a simple command of the king: the plain words of the statute should therefore stand. The contrast made between the king's will and the tenor of the statute and the apparent illegality of their position was again countered by the justices, who stated that it must be presumed that the authority of the king's commands was equatable with those made 'par comune consail' and, moreover, that no one could argue against an act of the king. Grandison's attorney then raised the fact that this seemed to go against one of the provisions in the Ordinances that the law should not be changed through the king's mandate (issued under the privy seal) to the detriment of justice.[105]

Another case raising concern at the legality of the king's intervention arose immediately after the promulgation of the Ordinances, when they were prob-

---

102 *YB 8 Edward II*, 74–5.
103 I have collated Stonor's arguments from the two versions of the report.
104 The justices contrast the effect on the writ if the sheriff had received it after the eyre proclamation (in which case it would be void).
105 *Year Books of Edward II: The Eyre of Kent 6 & 7 Edward II, A. D. 1313–14*, ed. F. W. Maitland, W. C. Bolland et al., Selden Society 24, 27, 29 (London, 1909–13), I, 161, 175–6.

ably very much in mind. In 1311, when the abbot of Croyland, in response to a writ of cosinage brought against him by Thomas de Horneby and others, proffered a writ of protection, it was claimed in response that he could not thereby make default and there was no reason by virtue of the protection that he should be quit of all pleas. For, it was argued, since the king was not attesting that the abbot was in his service or on affairs of state, but merely given leave to go abroad for a year, the protection ought not to delay the plea, as to do so would be against the 'new ordinances' (c. 6) and clause 29 in Magna Carta (1225) 'to no man will we sell or deny right or justice'. Chief Justice Beresford considered that because the justices were acting in the king's name (stead) due weight should be given to his orders. The king having personally instructed them by writ that the abbot should be quit of all pleas and plaints (with certain exceptions), they had warrant for the decision to allow the protection.[106] The king's apparent awareness of this and rehearsal of the import of the clause in the Ordinances is seen in a later royal writ that states the approved line:

> Because we wish that full justice be done to each and every man wishing to pursue right in our court, according to the law and custom of our realm, we do firmly . . . command that because any messages hitherto sent to you under our great or little seals, or henceforth to be sent, you in no way omit to do justice for us and others pursuing their right before you in the aforesaid Bench, according to the law and custom of our realm, by denying or delaying right or justice to anyone. [Witness myself at Windsor 22 November 1317][107]

It should be noted that while the above cases consider various constitutional principles, they do so in an abstract way that is not personal to Edward II. They also occur early in Edward's reign and therefore may well have been a continuation of the constitutional debates of his father's reign, which were able to flourish in an intellectual atmosphere unaffected by the person of the king. The cases do have implications for how historians view the king's commands and his personal intervention in and support of litigation. The king's position as head of the judicial system obviously brought ambiguity and paradox in cases where the crown was a party to litigation, notably in cases involving rights and franchises (*quo warranto*) and those concerning the presentation to benefices (*quare impedit*).[108] There is a differentiation in approach between cases where the king was a party and normal litigation, both in the advantages in pleading which the crown enjoyed (for example, claims could be made by the crown in the name of its ward that could not be asserted by wards in their own name) and in the language used by the

[106] *Year Books of Edward II: 5 Edward II*, ed. G. J. Turner and T. F. T. Plucknett, Selden Society 63 (London, 1947), 6–8.
[107] *YB 11 Edward II*, 315.
[108] See for example: *YB 5 Edward II*, xviii–xxxvii, 166–8; *YB 11 Edward II*, 84–91.

serjeants when arguing against the crown, which was less forthright and more deferential, suggesting that the king might not really wish to take such a course of actions (with reasons given).[109] In practical terms, however, there were limitations as to how much the king could affect the operation of justice in his own cause.[110] Moreover, when engaged in litigation in his own courts, the king had to abide by the judgments made in his name through his judges, or else risk loss of confidence and dissatisfaction with the whole system.

Perceptions of a lack of concern for the law of the realm may have derived from Edward's encouragement of training in the 'learned laws' (canon and civil laws) and his resort to Roman civil law (and possibly canon law) principles, thereby stepping outside of the common law, in his attempt to use legal argument to overturn the Ordinances and the banishment of the Despensers. His foundation of King's Hall within the University of Cambridge, set up by writ in July 1317, initially as the Society of the King's Scholars, provided students with a programme of civil law studies and perpetuated the first institutional link between the royal household and an English university. Winning the support of the new pope, Edward received confirmation and an augmentation of the privileges accorded to Cambridge. His dedication to the foundation is evidenced first, by the fact he had clearly planned for it to gain collegiate status from the very beginning, and second, in the way he personally supervised the appointment of the new Scholars. He also requested that the privilege 'ius ubique docendi' that had been conferred on the University of Paris be granted to the University of Oxford.[111] The establishment of a college for the education (and presumably advancement) of civil lawyers was probably not, however, an attempt to inculcate the theocratic notions of kingship that perpetuated in Roman law.

Edward appears to have called upon the services of civil lawyers to refute the legality of the barons' actions with regard to the introduction of the Ordinances. Two French lawyers (probably supplied by the French king) provided reasoned objections to the Ordinances in 1312, pointing out inconsistencies in the logic and promoting the abstract principles they felt had been overridden.[112] The methods by which the Ordainers were chosen were questioned, and the lawyers also rejected the validity of the document on the grounds of historical precedent: Louis IX's rejection of the Provisions of Oxford (at the Mise of Amiens), which received papal confirmation by both Urban IV and Clement IV. The lawyers also argued that in legal terms the Ordinances contained elements that were not only against law and reason, being contrary to Magna Carta and the Charter of the Forest, but also in dero-

---

[109] *YB 5 Edward II*, xxxvii; *YB 8 Edward II*, xiii.

[110] For the king's impotence in relation to his favourites see below.

[111] A. B. Cobban, *The King's Hall with the University of Cambridge in the Later Middle Ages* (Cambridge, 1969), pp. 9–10, 12–13, 20, 28, 32, 151.

[112] See *AL*, 211–15.

gation of the rights of the king and his Crown.[113] The barons' response underlined England's reliance on 'ancient and approved laws and customs' rather
than the written law of the jurists.[114]

Edward presumably sought and obtained legal advice for the compilation
of a defence against the Despensers' sentence of exile, though it is not clear
which branch of law he relied upon. This was entrusted to the earls of Richmond and Arundel and Robert Baldock, the latter having legal training, who
were required to 'explain ... by word of mouth' the points to the prelates at a
provincial council in December 1321.[115] Who drafted it is unknown, but it
bears the hallmarks of careful legal construction, as it was based on allegations of procedural error (some sounding in natural justice). The advice highlighted the Despensers' lack of ability to defend themselves, that their
behaviour had not been criminal, the allegations did not amount to felony or
treason and so the punishment was not commensurate, that the process was
not in line with the king's record, and had been undertaken without common
assent since the clergy were absent. It stressed that armed entry to parliament
in the king's presence negated the legitimacy of the move against them and
those undertaking the judgment bore enmity to the accused. Indeed, it was
stated that the majority were motivated by 'asperity', and that the judgment
did not carry the agreement of the king and so Magna Carta had been
ignored and greater excommunication incurred.[116] The defence, although
retrospective, indicates Edward's employment of legal argument (rather than
mere royal will) to try and vindicate his (and his favourites' position).

While there is no contemporary talk of 'tyranny' and neither the political
commentators nor the deposition theory precedents use the language of it,
during Edward II's reign there is an increasing concern exhibited for legitimate channels of power and due legal process. To some extent Edward's
exercise of power and influence over the judicial system may have been
circumscribed, given his close relationships with first Gaveston and then the
Despensers. How much influence in the judicial arena did any of them wield?
Naturally, there were contemporary suggestions that the king's favourites
regarded themselves as rulers and exercised kingly power. It was said, for
instance, that those requiring the king's special grace were sent to Piers and
that whatever he said or commanded was soon carried out and the king
accepted it.[117] Similarly, it was alleged of the Despensers that they did not
permit the king to hear complaints himself nor do justice, because justice

---

[113] See *JT*, pp. 77–8; Haines, *King Edward II*, p. 90; E. A. Roberts, *Edward II, the Lords Ordainers and Piers Gaveston's Jewels and Horses, 1312–13*, Camden Society Miscellany (London, 1929), pp. vi–vii; Richardson, 'English Coronation Oath', 69–70.

[114] Maddicott, *Thomas of Lancaster*, p. 136.

[115] *CCR 1318–21*, p. 410; *CPR 1321–4*, p. 37; Phillips, *Aymer de Valence*, pp. 218–19.

[116] See *Bridlington*, pp. 70–71 (pardon), 72–3.

[117] *AP*, 259.

could only be channelled through them.[118] Edward's concern for his favourites and their close relationship may be realised visually for posterity (as an image encapsulating his reign) through the depiction of the king with two dogs situated either side of his throne.[119] Thus, in the early years of Edward's reign it was said that two kings co-existed in a single kingdom and correspondingly, after 1322, there were in fact three kings in England at the same time.[120] The similarity of the statements and their satirical capacity or value (carrying resonances with political figures in modern times) suggest this was a recognised image of political commentary. Modern commentators have distinguished between Gaveston's exercise of authority and that of his successors in royal affection.[121] The allegations drawn up against the Despensers, not surprisingly, couch their behaviour in terms recognisable as treason relative not only to the person of the king and the crown ('vobis regalem potestatem attrahentes'),[122] but also with regard to his duty in upholding the laws of the land ('mes par poer, en contre la ley de la tere, en crochant a vous real poer et conseilant le rey a desheriter et defere ses leys').[123] Their giving of advice is criticised, but how far did this actually go in terms of using royal power over the legal system? Did they systematically corrupt justice? Did Edward allow the Despensers free reign of the legal system? How much did they exercise legal instruments and mechanisms in his name or for their own benefit? There are some examples cited in the sentence against them,[124] and numerous petitions alleging lands had been wrongly seized by them,[125] though these should be taken in the context of the opportunistic complaint and rhetoric of treason that emerged in the wake of Edward's deposition. Certainly, the 1321 eyre of London, an attempt to assert royal authority over the increasing independence of the city, was an overtly political and intimidatory use of judicial machinery for which the Despensers were blamed.[126] Equally, the Despensers' concern to obtain the lordship of Gower and their consequent lack of respect for the law and customs of the

---

[118] *Bridlington*, pp. 68–9.

[119] Bodleian, MS Rawlinson D 329 fol. 7. Alternatively or additionally this may represent (using the Latin *domini canes*) his support for the Dominicans.

[120] *Bridlington*, pp. 32–3; *AP*, p. 259; *Geoffrey le Baker*, pp. 15–16.

[121] For discussion of recent historiography see Haines, *King Edward II*, pp. 67–8, 158–60.

[122] *Bridlington*, pp. 87–9 (quotation at p. 88) (sentence on Hugh, the younger). See also *Chronicon Henrici Knighton*, ed. J. R. Lumby, 2 vols (London, 1889–95), I, pp. 437–8.

[123] *AP*, pp. 317–18 (quotation at p. 317) (sentence on Hugh, the elder).

[124] *CCR 1318–23*, pp. 492–5 (at p. 494).

[125] For example: *RP*, II, 20–40. It would have been easy to lay at the Despensers' feet the blame for the advantage taken of the social conditions arising from the civil war. See also S. L. Waugh, 'The Profits of Violence: the Minor Gentry in the Rebellion of 1321–1322 in Gloucestershire and Herefordshire', *Speculum* 52 (1977), 843–69.

[126] *Year Books of Edward II: The Eyre of London 14 Edward II A.D. 1321*, ed. H. M. Cam, Selden Society 85–6 (London, 1968–9), xv–xix; D. Crook, 'The Later Eyres', *EHR* 97 (1982), 248–9; Fryde, *Tyranny and Fall*, pp. 169–71. Complaint against the instigation

March (the citation of which the *Vita* says they equated with treason), not to mention the rights of those who stood in their way, demonstrate an arrogance and an ability to manipulate the legal system to their advantage.[127] It is difficult to tell how widespread and calculated their misdeeds were, especially in terms of the routine administration of justice.[128]

In reality, there was a limit to the king's capacity for personal intervention and a discrepancy between the public face of the crown and the private wishes of the king when it came to the judicially-sanctioned downfall of his favourites, Gaveston and the Despensers. Edward (grudgingly) accepted their banishment,[129] but was unable to interfere personally in the process leading to their demises. Even though 'his own personal feelings were deeply involved'[130] in both cases the situation was out of Edward's immediate control. Their executions themselves appear to have had public participation and widespread approval.[131] Indeed, the events following Gaveston's capture and imprisonment in Warwick Castle in June 1312 take on a strange quality, since they were enacted in the name of the king, but clearly occurred without his will or direct command. Although the order for his death was said to have come from Thomas of Lancaster,[132] the majority of chroniclers accord to Guy, earl of Warwick and other earls accompanying him the judgment passed on Gaveston (in a sense, then, still lawful judgment by his peers).[133] The Bridlington chronicler, however, states that he was presented before the royal assize justices, William Inge and Henry Spigurnel, who were supposedly delivering the gaol at Warwick at that time,[134] and they adjudged him to be beheaded as an outlaw and traitor to the king and the realm.[135] The execution

of the eyre by evil counsellors was included in Lancaster's Sherburn petition of 1321 (Maddicott, *Thomas of Lancaster*, pp. 276–9).

[127] *Vita*, pp. 108–9; Fryde, *Tyranny and Fall*, pp. 38–45, 109–16; Phillips, *Aymer de Valence*, pp. 199–200, 234–8.

[128] S. L. Waugh, 'For King, Country and Patron: The Despensers and Local Administration 1321–1322', *Journal of British Studies* (1983), 23–58; N. Saul, 'The Despensers and the Downfall of Edward II', *EHR* 99 (1984), 1–33.

[129] *Vita*, pp. 113–15. Both Gaveston and the Despensers returned from their exile.

[130] Phillips, *Aymer de Valence*, p. 214.

[131] Maddicott, *Thomas of Lancaster*, pp. 280, 288.

[132] *Vita*, p. 28; *JT*, pp. 69–74, 77.

[133] For example: *Flores*, III, 152–3;

[134] No records survive for gaol deliveries or assizes held at Warwick in this year. Spigurnel was operating in the nearby counties of Nottinghamshire (17 May 1312) and Derbyshire (22 May) and was certainly in Warwickshire around the time of Gaveston's supposed trial, as he presided over assizes at Stratford on 22 June (JUST 1/1350 mm. 39, 42, 42d), but there is no evidence from commissions or sessions linking him with Inge or for Inge's whereabouts. The gaol delivery commissions for Warwick listed in the patent rolls for the second part of 5 Edward II give the names of Cantilupe and Langley (local men) as the justices (C 66/137 mm. 8d (18 April 1312), 5d, 3d).

[135] *Bridlington*, pp. 43–4. Hamilton, *Piers Gaveston*, pp. 97–9.

was then carried out in full view of a host of men. Whether or not the continuance of the Ordinances in Warwickshire was a fiction and whether the trial in the presence of royal justices even occurred, in the knowledge that legal grounds for the prosecution of Gaveston were insubstantial and unlikely to succeed, the barons went to a lot of trouble to justify their proceedings.[136]

Similarly, the executions of the two Despensers were public affairs, and carried out after trial before a tribunal comprising William Trussel and various leading earls and other lords sitting judicially ('justitialiter sedentibus') and with the sentences duly recorded.[137] They were presumably acting under royal aegis, but were beyond the king's personal control. Following the siege of Bristol,[138] Hugh the elder was drawn, hanged and beheaded and his severed head sent to Winchester (the seat of his earldom).[139] The king himself was already in flight and so was unable to intervene. By the time the king and the younger Despenser had been apprehended, Prince Edward had been declared keeper of the realm and the king himself was under house arrest at Kenilworth. He was in no position to stop the death of his favourite, who, after trial at Hereford, was publicly humiliated, dragged through the city, hanged and then beheaded. His head was then sent to London and affixed for public display onto London Bridge.[140] The overlap of public and private elements at play here is eloquently captured in visual terms in an illustration accompanying the 'St Alban's Chronicle' which depicts the deaths of the two Depensers, with the king on horseback watching.[141] The picture conflates the two events, as the deaths were both geographically and chronologically separate and, moreover, Edward himself was not in the vicinity. Nevertheless it provides a strong sense of the king's impotence, yet tacit acquiescence as to their fates, as head of the legal system. It also presents the artist's view that things were (or should have been) under the auspices of royal justice.

At other times, too, the operation of justice appears to have been conducted not solely under the king's auspices, or outside of his control. Adam Banaster, who rebelled against Thomas of Lancaster, was allegedly put to death on the command of the earl and his steward (Robert Holland) in 1315, although there is little to suggest that Lancaster was personally

---

136 Maddicott, *Thomas of Lancaster*, pp. 127–8, 151.
137 *AP*, pp. 317–20; *Bridlington*, pp. 87–9.
138 *Murimuth*, pp. 47–8; C. D. Liddy, 'Bristol and the Crown, 1326–31: Local and National Politics in the Early Years of Edward III's Reign', in *Fourteenth Century England III*, ed. W. M. Ormrod (Woodbridge, 2004), pp. 47–9.
139 *Chroniques de London*, ed. G. J. Aungier, Camden Society 28 (London, 1844), p. 55; *Capgrave*, pp. 196–7.
140 *Flores*, III, 234–5; *Knighton*, pp. 436–8; *AP*, pp. 319–20, 322. See also G. A. Holmes, 'The Judgment on the Younger Despenser, 1326', *EHR* 70 (1955), 264–7.
141 London, Lambeth Palace Library, MS 6 fol. 197v.

involved.[142] The younger Despenser similarly had Llywelyn Bren executed for his rebellion against the Marcher lords in 1318 (even though Llywelyn had surrendered and been imprisoned in the Tower of London for two years).[143] The citizens of London equally exercised justice, whether by rightful claim to jurisdiction or the demands of circumstances. This can be seen in their popularly inspired 'execution' of Bishop Stapledon, accompanied by the rallying cry of 'traitor',[144] and their forcible abduction of Robert Baldock when imprisoned in Orleton's London home (having been sentenced to perpetual internment) so that they could 'try' him in the rightful gaol of the city, Newgate.[145] Ironically, the bishop's execution sparked off riots and looting in London, to the extent that (according to the chroniclers) the London courts were closed and justice was unable to be administered. The court of Arches, the consistory court of the diocese of St Paul's and the archdeacon of London's courts were not held and no business was transacted. The mayor's and the sheriffs' courts in the city of London were not convened.[146] The king's departure for Wales and his abandonment of responsibility had a direct effect on the administration of justice. Not only did Edward and his chancellor make off with the Great Seal, impeding the business of the royal courts, but the Westminster courts themselves were unable to sit and judges went in fear of their lives. Symbolically (and paradoxically, considering the cases of Gaveston and the Despensers above), justice had ceased to operate.[147]

*

In this essay there are two questions essentially being posed. How serious was Edward in undertaking what was expected of him? To what extent is it possible to observe a distinction between the crown and the person of the king in the operation of justice? Clearly, the king was not required to dispense justice personally in a routine way, although there were expectations that he would be able to solve particularly intractable or high profile disputes. It is noticeable that in high profile cases, or instances where a response from the king was required, on the whole Edward proved himself ready and capable, though his lack of intervention at the trial of Thomas of

---

[142] *Vita*, pp. 65–6; Tupling, *South Lancashire*, pp. xli–xlviii (see especially p. xlvii n. 1).
[143] *Vita*, pp. 66–9; Fryde, *Tyranny and Fall*, pp. 39, 48.
[144] *AP*, p. 316; *Chronique de London*, p. 52.
[145] *AP*, pp. 320–1.
[146] *AP*, pp. 321–2; *Chronique de London*, pp. 54–5.
[147] The illuminated miniature in BL MS Royal 20 A ii fol. 10, which shows an enthroned king handing a crown to a young boy dressed in a toga, was at one time identified as Edward II with the Prince Edward (the former apparently symbolically divesting himself of the right to rule), but is more likely to be Edward I investing his son as Prince of Wales. I am grateful to Michael Prestwich and Seymour Phillips for their views on this.

Lancaster (or in commuting his sentence to exile) is significant and appears deliberate. As regards law-giving and the king's responsibility for just laws there is at least an expressed concern that Magna Carta be followed, observable in symbolic recitations before parliament and great councils, in the rhetoric used in the royal courts on the king's behalf, in the arguments of legal counsel (against the Ordinances) and in its insertion in legal judgments. In discerning a divergence between the crown and the king himself, it is noticeable that Edward maintained throughout that Gaveston's execution was illegal and that despite royal assent the Ordinances should be regarded as having no force in law.[148] Arguably, the Ordinances were never properly implemented during the period 1311–22, merely, attempts were made to enforce them. Moreover, there is evidence to show that although the law was not always his prime concern in terms of detailed royal attention, he did have bursts of enthusiasm and adopted a 'hands on' approach at times, on occasion at least before the 1320s, but increasingly so after 1322. While we do not know the extent of his interventionism, whether what we have is the tip of the iceberg or not, the surviving memoranda at least suggest a keener interest than was probably realised by contemporaries and is currently accepted.

The reign exhibits many of the problems and ambiguities of perceptions of law and justice. Contemporaries probably judged Edward by the standards set up during his father's reign. In many ways he inherited a legacy of constitutional and administrative problems that inevitably resurfaced.[149] It was perceived that there was an increase in lawlessness during the opening decades of the fourteenth century, but in many respects this can be regarded as symptomatic of the climate of the times, exacerbated by the political and military situation.[150] In many instances, dissatisfaction stemmed from difficulties in bringing offenders to justice or achieving satisfactory results from protracted legal inquiries.[151] Such problems were part and parcel of a system undergoing experimentation and change, they cannot be laid solely at Edward's feet. There was, of course, an expectation that the king should rule in accord with justice and be prepared to do justice, but if he intervened too much or made examples of people too frequently, then abstractly and in hindsight his role as lawgiver could be seen to lose a sense of proportionality and fairness. Arguably, there were enough special circumstances arising during the reign to warrant the king's personal attention. Edward thus

---

148 Maddicott, *Thomas of Lancaster*, p. 151.
149 Conway Davies, *Baronial Opposition*, pp. 72–3; M. Prestwich, *War, Politics and Finance under Edward I* (London, 1972), pp. 272–7.
150 A. Musson and W. M. Ormrod, *The Evolution of English Justice: Law, Politics and Society in the Fourteenth Century* (Basingstoke, 1999), pp. 76–85, 102–6.
151 See, for example, the earl of Pembroke's problems following the attack on Painswick in 1318 (Phillips, *Aymer de Valence*, pp. 261–6) and the attack on William de Burgh's house in London in 1315 (Fryde, *Tyranny and Fall*, p. 168).

became involved in justice in a way that would not routinely be required of kings. It was the unusualness of such intervention that was being emphasised by the chroniclers, rather than the constitutional propriety of his actions. Treason as a serious criminal act and a direct threat to the person of king was the predominant trigger for royal involvement and, as a result, was constantly being redefined during his reign.[152] From another angle, the judges were present at major trials and pronounced on the fates of Lancaster and the Despensers alike. Whether they passively accepted this role without questioning or criticising the political nature of their judgments is not recorded. There is a suggestion from one of the reporters of the Kent eyre (1313–14), however, that even at an early stage in the reign they were afraid of the king ('quia fecerunt ad terrorem') and acted out of a concern to maximise the profits of justice rather than maintain the laws.[153] In the end, divorcing Edward from his own mechanisms was essential so that the legal system could function, albeit through fictions and illusory continuities. Even in the fourteenth century, therefore, justice was still regarded as stemming from the real presence of the king.[154]

[152] Wendy Childs notes contemporary awareness of 'a hairline division between lawful and unlawful action' and the conflicting loyalties sometimes felt in differing measures to crown, king and lord (*Vita Edwardi Secundi*, pp. liii–liv).

[153] *Eyre of Kent*, I, 104.

[154] For a discussion of this theme in relation to the outlaw literature see W. M. Ormrod, 'Law in the Landscape: Criminality, Outlawry and Regional Identity in Later Medieval England', in A. Musson (ed.), *Boundaries of the Law: Geography, Gender and Jurisdiction in Medieval and Early Modern Europe* (Aldershot, 2005), pp. 7–20.

9

Parliament and Political Legitimacy in the Reign of Edward II*

Gwilym Dodd

Half as many parliaments met under Edward II as under Edward III, and a fraction of parliamentary records survive for the earlier reign compared to the latter, and yet it is the development of parliament under Edward II that has really caught the attention and fired the enthusiasm of twentieth-century constitutional historians.[1] This is because scholars have looked to the reign of Edward II to identify the first signs of a fundamental change that overtook parliament in the first half of the fourteenth century; namely, the emergence of the representatives as a permanent and important force in English politics.[2] The paucity of parliamentary records under Edward II has shrouded these developments under a veil of uncertainty and ambiguity. One of the consequences has been a great body of historiography which attempts to draw broad conclusions about the political significance of the early fourteenth-century parliament but which uses only a handful of key texts associated with landmark parliamentary events – or, at least, political events that took place within a parliamentary context. These include the Ordinances of 1310–11, the Statute of York of 1322, Edward's deposition in 1327 and, finally, the tantalisingly enigmatic *Modus Tenendi Parliamentum* (*circa* Edward II's reign). The history of parliament under Edward II proves the maxim that a dearth of evidence will often generate greater volumes of historical writing than subjects for which there is an abundance of documentation, for where information is scarce there is greater scope for speculation, conjecture and disagreement. The early decades of the English parliament's history are

* I am very grateful to Claire Valente and John Maddicott for reading and commenting on an earlier draft of this article, as well as the feedback generously offered by the other contributors to this volume. All errors are my own.

1 For a list of parliaments held in both reigns see *Handbook of British Chronology*, ed. E. B. Fryde et al. (3rd edn, London, 1986), pp. 552–64.

2 See H. G. Richardson and G. O. Sayles, *The English Parliament in the Middle Ages* (London, 1981), chapter 21; G. L. Harriss, 'War and the Emergence of the English Parliament, 1297–1360', *Journal of Medieval History* 2 (1976), 35–56; idem, 'The Formation of Parliament, 1272–1377', in *The English Parliament in the Middle Ages*, ed. R. G. Davies and J. H. Denton (Manchester, 1981), pp. 29–60.

therefore probably not only the most widely written about, but also the most hotly contended. At no other point in the historiography of the late medieval English parliament have historians argued at such length about the fundamentals of the institution, a point amply illustrated by the classic debate between the irrepressible Richardson and Sayles on the one hand, and J. G. Edwards on the other hand, over what constituted the defining 'essence' of parliament's function in the late thirteenth and early fourteenth centuries.[3]

Recent historiography on parliament under Edward II, not least the work done by Harriss and Prestwich that has treated parliament directly, and the aristocratic biographies written by Maddicott and Phillips that have considered parliament more incidentally, has gone far towards establishing these fundamentals.[4] But the waters are still clouded with uncertainty. Some problems will be familiar, particularly those concerning the political significance of the parliamentary representatives. How much power did MPs possess in the reign of Edward II? How politically homogeneous were they as a body of men (and what role did common petitions and taxation play in forging a political 'agenda' in the lower house?)? If the representatives gradually gained political prominence under Edward II by becoming recognised as the true representatives of the 'community of the realm' (thereby eclipsing the nobles' traditional role) how should we account for this change? Was it a process so gradual that it was hardly perceptible to the contemporary eye, or was it part of a deliberate stratagem pursued by MPs to grab a share of political power for themselves? Indeed, was their elevation the result of royal policy, or a policy promoted by the opposition to the king? Other aspects of parliament under Edward II have received less attention. Perhaps the most neglected area is the king's own relationship with the institution. Beyond Natalie Fryde's comment that Edward considered parliament in the 1320s to be 'a highly regrettable necessity',[5] few other scholars have directly considered how we might define the relationship between king and parliament and how this relationship changed over the course of Edward's reign. How much control did Edward have over parliament? What purpose or use did parliament hold for the king (e.g. was taxation the only real benefit the crown gained from the institution?)? What was the king's attitude towards legislation and how willing was he to enact statutes in response to the community's grievances? There are other issues. Modern research has gone far in scotching

---

3   The views of both sides are summed up in Richardson and Sayles, *English Parliament*, chapter 16, p. 133; J. G. Edwards, *Historians and the Medieval English Parliament* (Glasgow, 1960), p. 24.

4   G. L. Harriss, *King, Parliament, and Public Finance in Medieval England to 1369* (Oxford, 1975); M. Prestwich, 'Parliament and the Community of the Realm in Fourteenth Century England', *Historical Studies* 14 (1981), 5–24; Maddicott, *Thomas of Lancaster*; Phillips, *Aymer de Valence*.

5   Fryde, *Tyranny and Fall*, p. 66.

the old 'constitutional' interpretation of the opposition to Edward II, whereby a group of magnates led by Thomas of Lancaster supposedly took steps to replace a 'household system' of government with an institutional or conciliar form of government;[6] but how far, if at all, this opposition affected the way parliament was organised is still a matter for conjecture. Traditionally, the clerks and bureaucrats of parliament are supposed to have suffered a backlash as a result of the baronial opposition of the 1310s, but we may wonder whether those responsible for the humdrum workings of the institution were quite as vulnerable to the political volatility of the period as this theory supposes.

In a paper of this length these questions (and others) cannot possibly be answered exhaustively, so the aim of the discussion is more general. It is to explore the place that parliament held in Edward II's polity. The aim is, in as sense, to 'join up the dots' by considering some of the principal parliamentary themes and events of the period as part of an overall picture rather than as isolated or self-contained episodes. This broad brush-stroke approach should, it is hoped, establish a better context in which to understand how parliament was regarded and how it developed in these crucial early decades of its existence. The *Modus Tenendi Parliamentum*, while clearly of critical importance to understanding contemporary perceptions of parliament, is not addressed directly in the present discussion because it raises a number of well-known methodological problems which are best left for detailed consideration in a separate study.[7]

*

The single most important event that took place within parliament during the reign of Edward II was the king's own deposition in January 1327. The parliamentary setting for Edward's political demise has not gone unnoticed by historians, but its true significance has been rather understated, particularly in light of the great historical controversy surrounding the later deposition of Richard II in 1399. On this later event G. L. Lapsley, H. G. Richardson and others argued at length about the role of parliament in the transfer of power between Richard II and Henry IV, for seemingly what was at stake was the very nature of the medieval constitution itself. How far could a late medieval king depend on parliament for his position and authority in the polity? Did parliament depose Richard II? Did Henry IV have a 'parliamentary title'?[8] In

---

6 For a useful outline of historiographical trends see Fryde, *Tyranny and Fall*, chapter 1 and M. Prestwich, 'The Ordinances of 1311 and the Politics of the Early Fourteenth Century', in *Politics and Crisis in Fourteenth-Century England*, ed. J. Taylor and W. Childs (Gloucester, 1990), pp. 1–18.
7 I hope to have a reassessment of the *Modus*, in which I offer a new explanation for its date and purpose, published in due course.
8 G. Lapsley, 'The Parliamentary Title of Henry IV', *EHR* 44 (1934), 423–449, 577–606; H. G. Richardson, 'Richard II's Last Parliament', *EHR* 52 (1937), 39–47. Lapsley

fact, Lapsley demonstrated that the new regime of Henry Bolingbroke took great care to classify the assembly that witnessed Richard II's abdication as an assembly of 'estates' rather than a conventional parliament, for to have done otherwise, Lapsley pointed out, would have 'created a precedent most damaging to the accepted view of [the Commons'] position and responsibility in parliament'.[9] No such constitutional angst, however, seems to have attached itself to the proceedings of 1327. As Claire Valente has demonstrated, although the decision to end Edward II's rule was taken by the magnates and prelates in a meeting held outside a parliamentary context, nevertheless, some of the principal acts of the deposition took place within parliament and with the full support of the knights and burgesses in the lower house.[10] On the second day of parliament, 13 January, the articles of deposition were read out to, and accepted by, the assembled MPs, who then went on to acclaim the succession of Edward III. The deputation that travelled to Kenilworth a few days later to withdraw homage from the king was not exclusively parliamentary in its make-up, but it contained enough parliamentary members to suggest a very definite link with the institution – enough to persuade some chroniclers that the renunciation was made on parliament's behalf.[11] But perhaps the most important point is that, unlike Henry Bolingbroke, the regime of Isabella and Mortimer took no steps to disavow the role of parliament in the deposition. In fact, parliament had been called by Isabella and Mortimer precisely to take centre stage in the deposition process. It was only when MPs balked at the charge given them by Orleton on the first day – when they were asked whether they preferred Edward II or his son to be king – that the process was temporarily taken out of parliament and into a special meeting of the barons on the evening of 12 January.[12] When the new regime came to recast the events as an abdication rather than a deposition, in the document known as the *Forma deposicionnis Regis Edwardi*, still no attempt was made to deny parliament a role in the proceedings: indeed, the whole account centres on the events that took place *in parliament* on 13 January.[13] On top of all this is the remarkable fact that parliament continued in session throughout the drama of Edward II's deposition and remained in session for the first six weeks of Edward III's reign. This made it the only assembly in the late medieval period to outlive a king and see in his successor, a phenomenon that not only confused contemporaries,

---

responded to Richardson in 'Richard II's "Last Parliament" ', *EHR* 53 (1938), 53–78. See also Bertie Wilkinson's attempt to resolve the debate in, 'The Deposition of Richard II and the Accession of Henry IV', *EHR* 54 (1939), 215–39.

[9]   Lapsley, 'Richard II's "Last Parliament" ', p. 65.

[10] For the remainder of this paragraph see C. Valente, 'The Deposition and Abdication of Edward II', *EHR* 113 (1998), 851–81 (pp. 862–68).

[11] M. Clarke, *Medieval Representation and Consent* (New York, 1964), p. 191.

[12] Valente, 'Deposition and Abdication', p. 853.

[13] The *Forma* is printed in Fryde, *Tyranny and Fall*, Appendix 2.

who did not know to which king they should address their petitions, but has been the source of considerable perplexity to modern historians.[14]

All of these points, and particularly the last, clearly have important implications for our understanding of the place of parliament in the medieval constitution (implications I hope to address in due course); but our more immediate concern is to explain why attitudes towards parliament were so different in 1327 as compared to 1399, and to identify more general developments in parliament under Edward II that might account for the institution's key role in the king's downfall. By far the most obvious point is that, unlike Henry Bolingbroke, Edward III's political legitimacy rested on the unassailable fact of his direct royal lineage. In a sense, Edward III could afford for his succession to be associated with parliament because all contemporaries realised that it was not parliament that gave the king his political legitimacy, but his royal blood. For Bolingbroke the issue was not so clear cut. In the absence of a convincing hereditary claim, the role of parliament in the transfer of royal power took on far greater significance: it was not a case of parliament providing convenient (but non-vital) popular endorsement; now, parliament potentially became the focus itself of royal legitimacy. The fear for Bolingbroke and his advisors, to paraphrase Lapsley, was that by making the deposition and succession a *parliamentary* process this would empower the Commons and undermine the authority of the crown. After three decades of outspoken and emboldened criticism of the government by the Commons, perhaps this fear was not unfounded.[15] In 1327, however, the position of the representatives was very different. At this point knights and burgesses had been routinely attending parliament for barely a decade; before 1311 more assemblies under Edward II had sat without representatives than those with them.[16] By the end of the 1320s it is true that the representatives were beginning to find their collective voice, by presenting lists of common grievances on matters of general concern, but this did not indicate that they had come of age in a political sense.[17] Arguably, they were first and foremost lobbyists at

---

14 Dr Shelagh Sneddon has discussed these petitions in her paper 'Words and Realities: Some Problems with the Language and Dating of Petitions, 1326–7', given at the International Medieval Congress, Leeds, 2004. For the reluctance of modern historians to regard Edward II's deposition as 'parliamentary', see Lapsley, 'Parliamentary Title', pp. 582–3 and Wilkinson, 'Deposition of Richard II', p. 224.

15 Excellent introductions to the political context of the parliamentary opposition of the 1370s and 1380s can be found in G. Holmes, *The Good Parliament* (Oxford, 1975) and A. Tuck, *Richard II and the English Nobility* (London, 1973).

16 These were the assemblies which met in April 1308, October 1308, July 1309 and February 1310. The record of attendance by representatives in the latter part of Edward I's reign (from 1294) was admittedly better: out of twenty assemblies only six were unattended by any representatives: *Handbook of British Chronology*, pp. 552–6.

17 For this development the key work is D. Rayner, 'The Forms and Machinery of the

this time: their role at parliament, besides granting taxation, was to represent the views of their constituents by means of the petition.[18]

The representatives were given a prominent role in the deposition of 1327 partly, it could be argued, because there was nothing to indicate to Isabella and Mortimer that they were anything other than a relatively benign political force. Looking back over the preceding two decades, Isabella and Mortimer would quickly have appreciated that all the trouble that had been caused in parliament had emanated almost exclusively from the barons. The crisis of 1310–11 had largely come about as a result of the denial to the king *by the barons* of the taxation granted in the parliament of April 1309, and it was at a meeting of magnates at Stamford in July that the main tenets of the opposition agenda were first set out (i.e. the Stamford Articles). The Ordinances of 1311 incorporated some clauses that appealed to a populist agenda, but there is no evidence that the Ordainers either needed or wished for the input of the parliamentary representatives in the formulation of their political programme.[19] Indeed, the knights and burgesses were not even present at the key parliamentary meeting of March/February 1310 when the Ordainers were appointed and when their intention to force reforms on Edward's government first became obvious. In the 1310s it was not the parliamentary representatives who used taxation to defend and uphold the terms of the Ordinances, it was the barons. Edward II had to wait for three parliaments to pass (August 1312, March 1313 and July 1313) before finally, in September 1313, he received a grant of a fifteenth and twentieth to spend on an expedition to Scotland. This grant had been directly linked to the king's willingness to pardon Lancaster, Hereford, Warwick and other barons for their involvement in Gaveston's murder; only when the king accepted their submission did the barons release the funds. In the next grant of taxation, made in January 1315, the price of supply (another fifteenth and twentieth) was the king's reaffirmation of the Ordinances and a year later, in January 1316, the king received a fifteenth from the shires and a foot soldier from every vill in

---

"Commune Petition" in the Fourteenth Century', *EHR* 56 (1941), 198–233, 549–70. The emergence of the common petition in parliament was almost certainly a direct consequence of the consistency with which MPs attended parliament from 1311 onwards.

[18] For the issues which particularly vexed the representatives in the 1310s see Harriss, *King, Parliament, and Public Finance*, pp. 109–10. For the 1320s see W. M. Ormrod, 'Agenda for Legislation, 1322–c. 1340', *EHR* 105 (1990), 1–33. The important point about MPs' attendance of parliament under Edward II (which marked a crucial change from Edward I) was that they now attended assemblies when no taxation was granted, suggesting that their role at parliament had come to be seen as extending beyond merely fiscal considerations. I am very grateful to J. R. Maddicott for generously making this point to me.

[19] Prestwich, 'Ordinances of 1311', p. 13. Harriss offers a more upbeat assessment of the representatives' involvement in the Ordinances: *King, Parliament and Public Finance*, pp. 109–12.

return for the appointment of a baronial committee to amend the condition of the household and kingdom. In short, this was a period when high politics in parliament was overwhelmingly an activity for the king and barons. By this time the knights and burgesses had won the right to consent to taxation (this they had probably achieved by the beginning of Edward I's reign);[20] but in political terms taxation was a weapon that still resided in the armoury of the barons.[21] It is interesting to conjecture that this made parliament much more difficult for the crown than in later years when taxation was more firmly under the control of MPs. In the 1310s the barons ruthlessly exploited the king's obligation to organise the defence of the realm by withholding finance in order to extract political concessions:[22] it is hard to find a comparable example in a later period where the Commons displayed the same audacity in the face of a serious military threat.[23]

In the 1320s, when the baronial opposition had largely dissipated, the representatives faced the king in parliament alone; but even here there is no indication that the representatives tried to make political capital out of their new position. More recent historiography has implied that in this situation the knights and burgesses put up a stout defence against the demands of the crown for financial aid.[24] Certainly, after the parliament of November 1322 Edward did not receive any further parliamentary subsidy; but whether this indicated the existence of an entrenched, recalcitrant body of parliamentary representatives is a moot point. If the crown really had asked for aid in February 1324 and November 1325, its reluctance to pay anything more than lip service to the common petitions that were presented in these assemblies suggests that its need for funds cannot have been particularly pressing. This is perhaps understandable in the context of February 1324, when the crown

---

20 J. R. Maddicott, 'The Crusade Taxation of 1268–1270 and the Development of Parliament', in *Thirteenth Century England II*, ed. P. R. Coss and S. D. Lloyd (Woodbridge, 1987), pp. 93–117 (p. 116).

21 The opposition to Edward II was probably the most aristocratic for over a century: see C. Valente, *The Theory and Practice of Revolt in Medieval England* (Aldershot, 2003), p. 139. For discussion of the knights' involvement in the crisis years of 1258–67, see P. Coss, *The Origins of the English Gentry* (Cambridge, 2003), pp. 127–35.

22 This echoed earlier instances in 1300 and 1301 (and 1309) when parliament had withheld taxation in the face of compelling pleas of urgent necessity by the crown: Harriss, *King, Parliament, and Public Finance*, p. 108.

23 The obvious occasion when the Commons *appear* to have withheld funds at the time of a genuine military crisis was in the early 1380s, when a series of parliaments ended apparently with no grant of direct taxation forthcoming. Elsewhere, however, I have questioned whether these instances really constituted 'refusals' by the Commons when there is little evidence to show that the crown actually asked for taxation: G. Dodd, 'The Lords, Taxation and the Community of Parliament in the 1370s and Early 1380s', *Parliamentary History* 20 (2001), 287–310 (pp. 297–8).

24 M. C. Buck, 'The Reform of the Exchequer, 1316–1326', *EHR* 98 (1983), 241–60 (pp. 252–4); Ormrod, 'Agenda for Legislation', pp. 8–9.

apparently requested a lay subsidy to raise finance for the ransom of the earl of Richmond – hardly a matter of national emergency.[25] In 1325 the evidence for parliament considering (and rejecting) a grant of taxation is tenuous indeed. Had there truly been a tussle between the crown and representatives over funds, it was remarkably short-lived, for parliament lasted a mere nine days, in which time we know much other business was discussed.[26] Nor can it be said that the representatives resisted the crown's demands for aid in November 1325, in the face of an imminent threat to the kingdom's security. It is true that rumours abounded that the queen planned to invade England and depose the king, but these rumours had been circulating since 1324 and there is no evidence to suggest that there was any more substance to them in late 1325 than at any other point during Isabella's two-year exile.[27] So it is true that Edward did not tyrannise parliament in the 1320s and could not compel its members to grant him taxation; but equally, it is debatable how far the resolve of these representatives to resist subsidies was tested, if tested at all. Certainly, the author of the *Vita Edwardi Secundi* was not much impressed with parliament's resilience in this decade.[28] After 1322, Edward began to accumulate a vast personal fortune, much of it appropriated from the unspent lay subsidy of November 1322 and two clerical taxes of 1323 and 1324, so there was no real need for the crown to have further parliamentary supply, even when war broke out with France in June 1324.[29] In the final years of his reign, neither Edward's domestic nor his foreign policies placed him financially at the mercy of parliament. He may have tried his luck to gain parliamentary funds, but the implementation of his plans did not depend on whether such funds were forthcoming.

The mantle which the knights, burgesses and clerical proctors had assumed by the early fourteenth century as the representatives and *defenders* of the 'community of the realm' thus took some time to translate into actual political power.[30] Edward II's reign could be seen as a half way house where, although the rhetoric of 'community' had transferred from barons to knights, burgesses and lower clergy, the power that went with it eluded them for the time being. If we are to find an explanation for this we must look to the

---

[25] Buck, 'Reform of the Exchequer', p. 254.

[26] The main topic discussed in this parliament was whether the king should go to Gascony in person. Eventually, it was decided he should not, on the basis that the Despensers objected: Buck, *Politics, Finance*, pp. 154–5.

[27] Haines, *King Edward II*, pp. 168–76.

[28] '[P]arliaments, colloquies, and councils decide nothing these days [i.e. 1325]. For the nobles of the realm, terrified by threats and the penalties inflicted on others, let the king's will have free play', in *Vita*, p. 136.

[29] Fryde, *Tyranny and Fall*, pp. 94–5.

[30] Prestwich, 'Parliament and Community of Realm', passim; W. A. Morris, 'Magnates and Community of the Realm in Parliament 1264–1327', *Mediaevalia et Humanistica* 1 (1943), 58–94.

healthy state of royal finances in the 1320s, which negated the opportunity for the representatives to bargain with the crown over redress and supply, and we might also look to the strength and dominance of the barons in their opposition to Edward – there is no evidence to indicate that the barons countenanced relinquishing any significant role to the representatives in their campaign to bring the king to heel (as late as 1317 Lancaster still did not consider the presence of representatives to be intrinsic to a parliamentary session).[31] But equally, we might look to the parliamentary representatives themselves, who were not yet ready or able to forge a coherent political programme in their own right. The lower house under Edward II was an immensely unwieldy and cumbersome body of men that contained not only representatives from the counties and towns, but also large numbers of lower clergy.[32] Besides the obvious practical difficulties that such numbers created in conducting discussion and reaching collective decisions, the presence within the lower house of both lay and clerical representatives was hardly conducive to generating political single-mindedness. The lay and clerical representatives separately granted taxation (the latter jealously resisting any parliamentary jurisdiction over their grants) and they also articulated their collective grievances separately, as (lay) common petitions and (clerical) *gravamina*.[33] Though the lower clergy sat with the knights and burgesses they almost certainly were not enthusiastic members of parliament, which they considered to be a secular court that ought not to have any hold over them. Their political predilection was to distance themselves from the knights and burgesses and assert their self-sufficiency, rather than to exploit common ground in order to bring overwhelming pressure to bear on the crown. These were the conditions that would shortly lead to the establishment of convocation as the principal forum for clerical representation.[34] In essence, in 1327 the lower house was still a collection of disparate and politically uncoordinated men from the localities. They did not constitute 'the Commons', with its association of institutional continuity and internal cohesion brought about by a common secular agenda, but rather a collection of self-contained and relatively independent 'estates'. The term, and indeed the phenomenon of, the 'Commons' was a development of Edward III's reign.[35]

---

31 Maddicott, *Thomas of Lancaster*, p. 202.
32 J. H. Denton and J. P. Dooley, *Representatives of the Lower Clergy in Parliament 1295–1340* (Woodbridge, 1987); J. H. Denton, 'The Clergy and Parliament in the Thirteenth and Fourteenth Centuries', in *The English Parliament in the Middle Ages*, ed. R. G. Davies and J. H. Denton (Manchester, 1981), chapter 4.
33 For the *gravamina* see W. R. Jones, 'Bishops, politics and the two laws: the *gravamina* of the English clergy, 1237–1399', *Speculum* 41 (1966), 209–45 (pp. 222–7). See also J. H. Denton, 'The "Communitas Cleri" in the Early Fourteenth Century', *BIHR* 51 (1978), 72–8.
34 Denton, 'Clergy and Parliament', pp. 100–101.
35 Prestwich, 'Parliament and Community', p. 14. The term 'Commons', to denote all

*

Though the role of the representatives in 1327 was important, it was parliament as a whole that enjoyed acclamation as a result of the events of the deposition. Again, it is possible to see this as a legacy of developments that had taken place in parliament over the course of Edward II's reign. Arguably, parliament acquired a very special status in the polity as a result of the emphasis that the baronial opposition placed on its role in the political life of the kingdom. This is seen most obviously in the Ordinances of 1310–11 which imposed a series of important limitations on the king's actions and used parliament as the context in which these limitations were to be enforced. Thus, the king could not make war, leave the realm, make grants, appoint chief ministers or even make changes to the royal council without first seeking the consent of the barons in parliament.[36] It was not that the Ordainers were 'constitutionalists': even William Stubbs could find little to say that was complimentary about the barons' attitude towards parliament.[37] The point was that parliament provided the best way of imposing a new system of

elements within the lower house in parliament, did not enter regular usage until the parliament of October 1339, when it was applied on eighteen separate occasions in the official record of this assembly (note, however, that the absence of rolls for the series of parliaments which met between 1334 and 1339 makes it likely that the new terminology appeared some time before 1339). There appears to have been a 'one-off' employment of the term in January 1327 (item 13) in a petition presented by the community, but the more usual application was in petitions which used the word to refer to the 'common people', and also when parliamentary clerks referred to the 'knights of the counties and the commons' to describe those people at parliament who were not members of the Lords. Presumably, in this context, 'commons' referred primarily to the urban representatives in parliament. This happened in the parliaments of March 1332 (item 5), September 1332 (item 3), December 1332 (item 1) and January 1333 (item 6). In compiling this survey I have greatly benefited from the electronic searching facilities now available as part of *PROME*. I am grateful to the editors for allowing me access to this resource ahead of its publication.

[36] *English Historical Documents, 1189–1327*, III, ed. H. Rothwell (London, 1975), 527–39.

[37] Stubbs had little sympathy for the Ordainers because no role was accorded to the parliamentary representatives in their reform programme: the Ordinances made no mention of the role of representatives in parliament. Thus, '[t]he earl of Lancaster had never understood the crisis through which the nation was passing ... [because] his idea was to limit the royal power by a council of barons ... [and] not to admit the three estates to a just share in the national government': W. Stubbs, *The Constitutional History of England in its Origins and Development*, 3 vols (1891–1903), II, p. 366. Bertie Wilkinson was less reticent, describing the Ordainers as 'parliamentarians'. However, he does not explain what this term means other than that parliament was used extensively by the Ordainers to push through their reforms: B. Wilkinson, *Constitutional History of Medieval England 1216–1399*, 3 vols (London, 1952), II, p. 14. Note that the Ordainers had originally intended to have a committee of barons appointed in each parliament to oversee royal expenditure, but they changed their minds, presumably because of the constitutional implications such a measure would have

government in which executive power was to be shared out amongst the leading nobles of the realm. Parliament provided the means by which decisions affecting the state and condition of the kingdom, and also (and perhaps most importantly) the particular circumstances of individual noblemen, were taken out of the private context of the king and his court and placed into a public arena where a degree of consensus, transparency and accountability – at least amongst the barons – could be achieved. The importance of parliament from the point of view of the opposition lay in the fact that the king could not select only those he favoured to attend it: the nobility were 'summoned by right and not by the king's grace'.[38] If a parliament was summoned, then all spiritual and lay lords were entitled and expected to attend. This automatically limited what the king could do, how he could do it and when it could be done. In this sense, parliament played into the opposition's hands, for it provided a constitutional framework that made it very hard for the king to rule to the total exclusion of those nobles he disliked.

The inclusive nature of parliament's membership was the keystone to the strength of the opposition that Edward II faced; this is why the writs of summons became such a hot topic in the period (in March 1313, for example, Warwick and Lancaster refused to attend parliament because they felt the writs of summons had been drafted in an irregular form)[39] and why such opprobrium was attached to the idea of the king holding 'secret' parliaments with limited membership (some of the principal nobles of the realm refused to attend a *'Secretum Parliamentum'* arranged by the king to meet in October 1309;[40] and in December 1320 Lancaster refused to attend a parliament held *in cameris*).[41] It also explains why Lancaster adamantly refused to attend meetings of the council that were organised by the king to meet at Clarendon, Westminster and Nottingham in 1317 in order to settle the realm.[42] To have attended would have undermined a central tenet of the Ordinances by tacitly acknowledging Edward's ability to make policies outside parliament at times and with advisors of his own choosing. Ultimately, of course, one of the results of this emphasis on the inclusive nature of parliament's membership (in the upper house) was the emergence of the peerage – a term first coined, it seems, in the course of negotiations between the king and barons in 1312.[43] In the early fourteenth century the essence of the parliamentary peerage was not

---

had: see M. Prestwich, 'A New Version of the Ordinances of 1311', *BIHR* 57 (1984), 187–203 (pp. 190–1).

38 Clarke, *Medieval Representation*, p. 199.

39 *AL*, pp. 225, 227.

40 *The Chronicle of Walter de Guisborough*, ed. H. Rothwell, Camden Series 99 (London, 1957), pp. 384–5.

41 *Vita*, pp. 103–4.

42 Maddicott, *Thomas of Lancaster*, pp. 190–201.

43 Prestwich, 'Parliament and Community', p. 7. The term appears in the document known as the *Prima Tractatio*.

its exclusivity (as it was to become in later decades) but its inclusiveness. The momentum to expand and standardise the list of barons and bishops eligible to receive personal summons to parliament and, indeed, the appearance in 1315 of the 'Great Council' to oversee matters of importance in parliament,[44] derived in the first instance from an attempt to make government as collective and collaborative an undertaking as possible. It was in the period when parliament was either directly or loosely controlled by the opposition to Edward II in the 1310s that the list of barons receiving personal writs of summons to parliament finally solidified, so that the same names and the same number of individuals were summoned time and time again when parliament was called.[45]

But parliament, for the opposition, provided much more than accountability, transparency and protection: it also provided the crucial element of political legitimacy. For Lancaster and his allies the strength of parliament lay in the representative quality that its inclusive membership furnished on their activities. By acting through parliament, it was a logical step to claim to be acting in the interests of the realm. Thus, the parliamentary representatives may not have had much practical input into the Ordinances of 1310–11 but it was absolutely imperative for the barons to invoke popular support by claiming the endorsement of the 'community of the realm' to their opposition programme. Had they not done so, had parliament not been used as a forum in which the king was brought to account and the baronial reform plan implemented, the barons would have had little to counter the charge that they were acting out of ambition and self-interest. Thus, whereas the source of a king's authority came naturally from the inherent representative quality of his office, the barons had to manufacture an alternative (and artificial?) structure of political legitimacy that only parliament could generate effectively. This is why so many of the political acts of the opposition to Edward II occurred in a parliamentary setting and it is why Thomas of Lancaster, in particular, was most powerful politically when he controlled parliament and got the institution to adopt his policies. This occurred most obviously (because there are unusually good records for the assembly) in the Lincoln Parliament of January 1316, when he secured confirmation of the Ordinances and a commission of reform to look at Edward's household.[46] Such concessions could have been extracted from the king by military force alone, but having the stamp of parliamentary approval made Lancaster's position and

---

[44] G. O. Sayles, *The King's Parliament of England* (London, 1975), pp. 99–100.
[45] It was from the parliament of March 1313 that the list of those individuals eligible for a personal summons (numbering eighty-nine barons) came to be used as a blueprint for future assemblies: J. E. Powell and K. Wallis, *The House of Lords in the Middle Ages* (London, 1967), p. 310. There was some considerable, though temporary, disruption to the lists in the mid 1320s as a result of the war of Saint-Sardos.
[46] Maddicott, *Thomas of Lancaster*, pp. 180–2.

his programme more secure, and it made Edward's task to undo this programme far less straightforward.

At the very least, by using parliament as a source of political legitimacy for their actions, the opposition virtually ensured that Edward would have to act through parliament himself if he wished to mount an effective and credible political counter-attack. This situation was explicitly recognised by Walter Stapledon, who advised the king in January 1322 that the only credible way to reverse the sentence of exile imposed on the Despensers was to hold a parliament, since the original process had been passed by parliament.[47] Throughout the 1310s, Lancaster and his allies were well aware that the king's platform of political support was too narrow for him to be able to do this successfully, which is why their opposition proved to be so effective. Implicit in their actions was an assumption that the legitimacy expressed through parliamentary acts was just as powerful, and perhaps even more so, than the legitimacy expressed through royal acts. In other words, parliamentary acts enjoyed a certain degree of constitutional protection. This was the implication of the barons' insistence in 1313 that the royal pardon they wished to have for Gaveston's death should only be granted in parliament: in any other context such a pardon could never be relied upon.[48] And it was the implication of this principle for royal authority, and the sense in which the king was in some way beholden to the institution of parliament, which explained why Edward was so angry in 1322 when Stapledon told him that he must go through parliament if his acts were to enjoy full political legitimacy.

What emerges, then, is a sense in which parliament was set up to rival, and in some areas even replace, the king as the centre or focus of political life in the 1310s. In a period when the barons could no longer look to kingship to provide a stable and secure political system, indeed when kingship was itself undermining this very system, parliament was being used as an alternative institutional framework through which a new set of political ground rules, based on the Ordinances, was to shape the nature of the polity. That Edward was not able to resist this assault on his position was a reflection, above all, of Lancaster's power; but this power derived in large part from the success with which Lancaster usurped Edward's position as the source of political legitimacy by challenging the king through the institution of parliament. Indeed, parliament was so important to Lancaster and Lancaster's programme, that on several occasions in the 1310s he took his armed retinue to Westminster to ensure that his will was done: it did not matter to the earl how decisions were reached in parliament, so long as they were parliamentary decisions that

---

[47] This is discussed by Buck, *Politics, Finance*, pp. 138–9, and Fryde, *Tyranny and Fall*, p. 52.

[48] Maddicott, *Thomas of Lancaster*, p. 148.

served his interests.[49] Thus, almost uniquely in the medieval period, parliament in the 1310s had ceased functioning as the king's parliament. Between 1310–21 it was rare indeed for the king to summon parliament when he wished to do so, and rarer still for parliament to transact (political) business that served primarily the king's own interests.[50] The refusal of the earls to attend the parliament of March 1313, because of alleged irregularities in the summonses that had been sent out by chancery, underlined the principle that parliament did not function as part of the patrimony of the king, but existed outside the royal orbit as an institution that belonged to the political nation and whose self-styled guardians were the barons who watched over and protected its constitutional integrity. It may have been this principle which provided constitutional justification for the summoning of the 'pseudo-parliaments' of the north in 1315 (at Doncaster) and in the summer of 1321 (at Sherburn), which were called by, and met under the presidency of, Lancaster.[51] How far these meetings were deliberate attempts to undermine the king's prerogative is debatable, but Edward II's reign is unique in witnessing the convocation of assemblies, apparently independently of the king's wishes, that had many of the trappings of conventional parliamentary meetings at Westminster. If not explicitly, then implicitly, they represented a fundamental challenge to the king's sovereign power and his status as head

---

[49] These were the parliaments of February 1316, October 1318 and May 1319. In June 1318 the king's council accused Lancaster of coming to parliaments *a force e armes*: Maddicott, *Thomas of Lancaster*, pp. 43–4, 53–4. Lancaster, with Warwick and Hereford, also arrived at the parliament of September 1312 fully armed, and there are indications that the barons attended the assembly of April 1308 (which passed sentence of exile on Gaveston) also arrayed for war: Haines, *King Edward II*, p. 88; Hamilton, *Piers Gaveston*, p. 50. Prohibitions not to bring arms to parliament were issued on at least five occasions in the first half of the reign – October 1308, February 1310, November 1311, August 1312 and September 1313: Maddicott, *Thomas of Lancaster*, p. 53, fns 5 & 6.

[50] The assemblies of February 1310 and August 1311 met in the context of the political opposition expressed in the Ordinances; political deadlock shaped the meetings of August 1312, March 1313 and September 1313 when the king and barons tried to come to terms; the parliament of September 1314 met in the aftermath of Bannockburn, when the king was forced to reconfirm the Ordinances and to agree to the removal of royal nominees holding the principal offices of state; the session of January 1315 similarly reconfirmed the Ordinances and also instigated the removal of two royal nominees from the council (Despenser and Langton); the parliament of January 1316 once again reconfirmed the Ordinances, and also implemented a commission of reform to examine the royal household; the parliament of October 1318 was dominated by the discussion and confirmation of the terms of the Treaty of Leake; the parliaments of May 1319, January 1320 and October 1320 were relatively benign, politically speaking, for the king; but in July 1321 the king faced a full frontal attack by Lancaster and his allies, who succeeded in having Despenser exiled from the kingdom.

[51] Clarke, *Medieval Representation*, pp. 161–7; Maddicott, *Thomas of Lancaster*, pp. 167–6, 268–79.

of the body politic. These assemblies, and the baronial control of parliament in general, enabled the well-known baronial declaration of 1308, which distinguished between the crown and the king's person, to be translated into tangible and sustainable political action.[52]

And so, in 1327, providing a *parliamentary* context for the transfer of power between the king and his son may have been regarded as a very natural extension to the processes that had been set in train in previous years. Under Edward II parliament had developed facets that could be extremely useful for a new regime struggling to justify its violent interruption of the natural line of royal succession. Acting through parliament allowed Isabella and Mortimer to cloak the overthrow of Edward under a veil of 'Lancastrian Constitutionalism' (à la Thomas of Lancaster, not Henry Bolingbroke), with all the trappings of institutional regularity, broad based political consensus and transparency that Lancaster himself had promoted in his own opposition programme. The removal of parliament from the control of the king and its operation against royal interests for much of Edward's reign provided a very solid foundation for Isabella and Mortimer to take the process one stage further and (possibly following the precedent set by the meeting at Sherburn in 1321) hold a parliament in the absence of the king in order to use the institution to remove him from office. But whilst Isabella and Mortimer's actions in relation to Edward II exploited and emphasised the separateness of king and parliament, this was not what they had in mind for his successor. In the reign of Edward II the basis of royal authority had been very effectively challenged on the grounds that the kingdom ought to be ruled through parliament rather than by the king, because parliament (and the barons summoned to it) was more effective in representing the common interest than the king himself. Involving parliament in ridding the realm of a failing king and installing his successor was a fitting end to this unfortunate chapter; but it was also a very appropriate way of reinstating and reinforcing the indivisibility of king and parliament under the new monarch, Edward III. There can have been few more effective ways to set a precedent for the future unity and cooperation of king and parliament than for parliament itself to provide the institutional context for the king's accession to power. If nothing else, parliament was now complicit in the whole dubious affair and nobody would now be able to claim that the regime of Isabella and Mortimer did not have the support of the community of the realm.

---

[52] See E. Kantorowicz, *The King's Two Bodies* (Princeton, 1957), pp. 364–72; Haines, *King Edward II*, pp. 59–60. The declaration of 1308 featured prominently in the indictment against Despenser which was prepared at the meeting held at Sherburn: Maddicott, *Thomas of Lancaster*, pp. 278–89.

Gwilym Dodd

*

Isabella and Mortimer were not the first to attempt to establish a new relationship between parliament and the crown. Arguably, this was one of the central motives for Edward's promulgation of the Statute of York in 1322. This legislation has been the subject of intense scholarly debate, not least because at the end of the statute Edward seemed to acknowledge the centrality of parliament and the importance of parliamentary representatives – the 'community of the realm' – in the formulation of new statutory legislation.[53] Much of this older 'whiggish' writing, which interpreted the statute as providing the 'Commons' with very real political power, has been discredited and the legislation is now rightly seen as a very conservative assertion of royal hegemony over parliament.[54] Too much focus on the final clause of the statute has obscured the fact that its overriding purpose for the king was to rid the realm once and for all of the despised Ordinances of 1310–11. The statute was not a royal manifesto setting out a new populist programme. Rather, it was an attempt to re-establish the old political order in parliament with an assertion that the political initiative should lie exclusively with the king who alone could 'establish' things for his estate and the 'estate of the realm'. His subjects were expected passively to witness these decisions and give them their approval. Edward's acknowledgement of the 'community of the realm' did, nevertheless, indicate that he and his advisors had come to appreciate the huge power that could be harnessed by someone who controlled parliament and who pursued a political programme with parliamentary endorsement. By acknowledging that the 'estate of the king . . . shall be treated, agreed and established in parliaments', albeit at the behest of the king, Edward was engaging with recent developments which had seen parliament become a major source of political legitimacy. Parliament had provided a constitutional platform for the baronial opposition to circumvent royal authority; now the institution would provide a means for the king to re-impose his position as the head of the body politic.

So Edward was not handing power over to parliament or to the representatives within it; by the terms of the Statute of York the king acknowledged that he could no longer ignore parliament and that he would have to embrace it in order to prevent the institution ever from falling back into the hands of a

---

53 The text of the Statute of York can be found in *English Historical Documents*, III, 543–4. For a useful discussion of the historiography on the Statute (though not necessarily a convincing explanation) see J. H. Trueman, 'The Statute of York and the Ordinances of 1311', *Medievalia et Humanistica* 10 (1956), 64–81.
54 J. R. Strayer, 'The Statute of York and the Community of Realm', *American History Review* 47 (1941), 1–22. The other point of contention has focused on the significance of the phrases 'estate of the king' and 'estate of the crown', for which see G. Post, *Studies in Medieval Legal Thought: Public Law and the State, 1100–1322* (Princeton, 1964), pp. 368–414.

180

baronial opposition. Perhaps it was this realisation that provided some of the impetus behind the emergence of the common petition in these years. It has long been recognised that Edward II's reign witnessed the first significant step towards the lower house forging a collective and cohesive identity, because it was in these years that lists of petitions were produced by MPs that truly represented national concerns. But the question why this development should have occurred has never been thoroughly explored. More recent commentators are inclined to see it as the result of initiative shown by the representatives, stressing the undoubted fact that the compilation of such lists of common grievances required a large degree of cooperation and coordination on the part of MPs.[55] But this rather overlooks the fact that in order for common petitions to 'work', the parliamentary representatives depended even more so than previously on the cooperation of the crown. The king and council had always dealt with isolated petitions from the community of the realm; but the introduction of regular *schedules* of common petitions was an altogether different matter and had many important implications for the structure of parliamentary meetings, the business that parliament dealt with and (last but not least) the *time* to which the king and council were now committing themselves by taking on these expanded lists of general grievances. It seems hardly plausible that Edward and his advisors would not have been fully aware of these ramifications, nor that they were not fully concordant with a development which projected the common petition to such a prominent place in the order of parliamentary business.

We know from the pioneering researches of Doris Rayner that petitions in the name of the community of the realm had been presented in parliament individually for almost as long as parliamentary records survive, but it is not until the 1320s, and specifically the parliament of February 1324 – the next assembly to meet after the Statute of York had been promulgated – that the first *schedule* of common petitions survives.[56] This may simply be coincidence (we cannot be certain that schedules were not produced before this date); but the timing does add credence to the hypothesis that the systematisation of common petition procedure was encouraged and even initiated in the first instance by the crown. Neat schedules of common petitions for presentation to the king and council had obvious bureaucratic advantages; but we may also see this as part of the process by which the king wished to draw parliament closer into the royal orbit. The rhetorical strength of the barons in the 1310s, as we have seen, was their claim to represent, and act for, the interests of the community of the realm. What better way was there for the crown to

---

[55] For example, see W. M. Ormrod, *Political Life in Medieval England, 1300–1450* (Basingstoke, 1995), p. 34.

[56] Rayner, 'Forms and Machinery', pp. 551–7. For the forerunners of the common petition, see G. L. Haskins, 'Three Early Petitions of the Commonalty', *Speculum* 12 (1937), 314–18.

undermine this stratagem than by procedurally separating the barons from the 'community of the realm' and by giving the latter their own independent and institutionalised voice in parliament? Edward and his advisors might well have mused on the significant advantages such a development could hold for the crown. First of all, and most importantly, the barons could no longer so easily speak for the community of the realm, thus significantly weakening their position in parliament. At the very least, recalcitrant barons like Lancaster would now have to act through the common petition (and therefore through the lower house) in order to assume the mantle of defender of the common interests. Second, by shifting the emphasis in such a way as to give the parliamentary representatives procedural precedence in representing the wider realm, the crown had reduced the potential for the 'community of the realm' to challenge its authority. This was not only because the parliamentary representatives carried far less political weight than the barons; it was also because the crown now controlled how the community of the realm expressed its views. Common petitions passed along a channel that was, at all points, monitored and regulated by the crown, and we know from later periods that common petitions could be suppressed and omitted from the record if they were deemed by royal agents to be inappropriate, awkward or embarrassing for the crown.[57] And finally, but no less importantly, all this could be achieved whilst maintaining the impression of a parliament-friendly crown.

In practical terms, common petitions made very little difference to the power of parliamentary representatives in parliament. It was still too early for statutory legislation to be routinely linked with issues raised by petitions presented to the institution (again, this would occur only in the course of Edward III's reign, when taxation became a more regular aspect of the business of parliament). The evidence from the statute roll suggests that Edward himself had a very fixed and narrow understanding of the legislative process. True to the principles expressed in the Statute of York, in the remaining years of the reign only those statutes devised by the crown made it onto the statute roll. More pertinently, a large proportion of this legislation was made *outside* parliament. A series of measures to improve the governance of Ireland, for example, was discussed and made into ordinances by members of the king's council who met at Nottingham in November 1323.[58] The series of reforms to the exchequer in the 1320s also took place in a non-parliamentary context and is a classic example of the government taking responsibility for its own amendment; only the first of these reforms was recorded on the statute roll after the king and his council sent letters from Cowick (Essex) in June 1323

---

[57] W. M. Ormrod, 'On- and Off-the Record: The Rolls of Parliament, 1337–1377', in *Parchment and People: Parliament in the Middle Ages*, ed. L. Clark (Edinburgh, 2004), pp. 39–56 (pp. 46–7).
[58] *SR*, I, 193–4.

instructing chancery to this effect.[59] The legislation of February 1324, which granted the Templars' lands to the Hospitallers, demonstrated a different aspect to this royal control of the legislative process: on this occasion the statute was apparently discussed in parliament, but not in order for the king to listen to his subjects' views, because the legislation was passed in spite of a common petition requesting that the lands should revert to the crown.[60] Edward's responses to the earliest common petitions of the mid 1320s were recorded not on the statute roll, as was later to become the custom, but on the list of petitions itself or, in the case of November 1325, in the close rolls.[61] It was almost as though Edward, in the 1320s, perceived the legislative process as existing exclusively to serve the royal whim. At this time, the statute roll was a record of *royal* legislation: its purpose was not to make a note of legislative changes made at the behest of the political community, but to record the reforms initiated by Edward and his advisors.

How far we should see this reassertion of royal authority over parliament as a programme actively pursued by the king himself or as one he adopted as a result of the cajoling of his counsellors is a moot point, and one that strikes at the very heart of any assessment that is made of Edward's character and his abilities (or failings). There is no doubting that the king was surrounded by some extremely talented administrators and reformers in the 1320s, and it is possible that their achievements extended to the reconfiguration of parliament into a royal talking shop.[62] Edward also had the advice of Hugh Despenser the elder, amongst others, to draw on. Despenser's closeness and loyalty to the king is usually interpreted as a measure of his self-interest and political ambition, but Martyn Lawrence's discussion of Despenser's early career usefully reminds us that he was also a very capable servant of the crown, having seen extensive military and diplomatic service in the 1290s and 1300s.[63] He was heavily implicated, on the crown's behalf, in the crisis of 1297–8 and, significantly, it was Despenser whom Edward I entrusted with the mission to secure the pope's annulment of the Confirmation of the Charters which had been passed by the political community in the parliament of September/October 1297. Is it too fanciful to suppose that part of the

---

59 *SR*, I, 190–2; Buck, 'Reform of the Exchequer', passim.
60 *SR*, I, 194–6; Buck, *Politics, Finance*, p. 145. For the common petition, see SC 8/108/5398.
61 The four common petitions of February 1324 were endorsed 'those who are aggrieved should present themselves and the king will see that justice is done': SC 8/108/5398. The eighteen petitions of October 1324 have responses recorded underneath each request: C 49/5/25, printed in Ormrod, 'Agenda for Legislation', Appendix C. For the six common petitions of 1325 see SC 8/8/392; and for the crown's responses (to five of these petitions) see *CCR 1323–7*, pp. 539–40. For general discussion of these petitions see Rayner, 'Forms and Machinery', pp. 552–6.
62 Tout, *Place of Edward II*, pp. 142–83; Buck, 'Reform of the Exchequer', passim.
63 See Martyn Lawrence in this volume, pp. 205–19.

impetus behind the reassertion of royal authority in parliament in the early 1320s came from this royal favourite, whose link with Edward's father provided a real sense of validation and continuity to the regime's political agenda? We should also not dismiss the possibility that Edward himself took some role in the process. Elsewhere in the volume it has been suggested that Edward took a rather more active interest in legal affairs than his reputation for being a lazy king has previously allowed, and in the context of the activities of the exchequer it has also been suggested that Edward was remarkably proactive.[64] Edward's invigorated interest in the workings of his government may also have extended to parliament. This much is suggested by the famous letter of 1320 from bishop Cobham of Worcester to the pope, in which he remarked that the king was rising unusually early and was actively contributing to the discussions of parliamentary business.[65] It is quite possible that Edward was well aware of the benefits the institution could bring to the crown if managed carefully. It is interesting in this respect to note that Edward is known to have possessed a copy of *de Regimine Principum*.[66] Much has been made of the influence that this work had on Richard II's sense of the inalienability of the royal prerogative and, whilst all the usual caveats apply to reading too much into book ownership, one wonders whether similar conclusions cannot also be drawn with regard to Edward II.[67]

Whatever we may conclude about Edward's political drive, or lack thereof, he did not need an ideology as such to understand the trouble which parliament had caused him for much of his reign. There is every possibility that his attitude towards parliament, and his apparent unwillingness to allow the knights and burgesses to participate in the statutory process, was determined simply by his unhappy experiences in parliament in the first decade of his reign, when legislation had become an essential tool of his enemies, allowing them to express and publicise a dissenting agenda.[68] Either statutes had been imposed on Edward by the sheer weight of opposition he faced in parliament (Ordinances of 1310–11 and the statutory exile and disinheritance of the Despensers in August 1321), or else they were a price the crown had to pay in order to secure much-needed funding (the Statute of Stamford of 1309; the pardons given to the Ordainers in September 1313; and the *Articuli Cleri*

---

[64] See Anthony Musson's chapter in this volume, pp. 140–64. For the exchequer, see Buck, *Politics, Finance*, pp. 166–7.

[65] *Register of Thomas de Cobham, Bishop of Worcester, 1317–27*, ed. E. H. Pearce, Worcestershire Historical Society (1930), pp. 97–8. See also the quotations on Edward's assiduousness to attending petitionary business in Musson's discussion above, pp. 142–3.

[66] M. T. Clanchy, *From Memory to Written Record: England 1066–1307* (Oxford, 1993), p. 162.

[67] See N. Saul, 'The Kingship of Richard II', in *Richard II: The Art of Kingship*, ed. A. Goodman and J. L. Gillespie (Oxford, 1999), pp. 37–57 (pp. 44–5).

[68] For what follows see *SR*, I, 153–84.

of January 1316, negotiated in return for *clerical* taxation granted in convocation).[69] Until May 1322, when Edward statutorily revoked the process of exile against the Despensers, only a handful of statutes had been passed since the accession that could be said to have been either favourable to the king or at least politically neutral: one was the statute forbidding the presence of armed men in parliament, made in September 1313; there were a couple of statutes regulating the appointment and actions of sheriffs; and in 1318 the parliament at York passed a number of fairly routine legal reforms. In legislative terms, Edward II was looking backwards to the reign of Edward I, when statutes were primarily the expression of royal prerogative power,[70] rather than forwards to the reign of his son, when the legislative process was to become much more of a partnership between the crown and the political community.

In this sense Edward II was seriously disadvantaged. In one of the first parliaments of his reign, that of April 1309, Edward had a wonderful opportunity to engage the political community and respond to its concerns by enacting legislation that dealt with some or all of the eleven articles of complaint that had been submitted to that assembly.[71] Had Edward done so he would have set a new tone for crown–parliament relations and would immediately have cast himself in a very favourable light compared to his father, whose autocratic tendencies towards parliament were still a fresh memory. Edward III would probably have been pragmatic, reasoning that for the sake of a much-needed grant of taxation it was worth enacting legislation that satisfied the kingdom's needs but which probably did not impinge too much on the crown's interests.[72] But Edward II dug his heels in and, according to the chronicles, undertook to remedy none of the concerns which had been raised in these articles.[73] The scene was thus set for the show-down of July, which resulted in the Statute of Stamford, and following this, the political meltdown of 1310–11 that resulted in the Ordinances. There is no obvious reason to explain Edward's refusal to address these articles so early on in his reign, many of which hardly constituted a serious imposition on the

---

69 K. Edwards, 'The Political Importance of the English Bishops during the Reign of Edward II', *EHR* 59 (1944), 311–347 (p. 331).
70 T. F. T. Plucknett, *The Legislation of Edward I* (Oxford, 1947); M. Prestwich, *Edward I* (London, 1988), chapter 10.
71 The fullest discussion of this parliament is given by Maddicott, *Thomas of Lancaster*, pp. 97–102
72 In fact, Edward III *was* pragmatic. As Mark Ormrod has demonstrated, much of the legislative programme of Edward III's early years very deliberately focused on long-standing grievances aired by the representatives in the final years of Edward II's reign ('Agenda for Legislation', pp. 11–15). Actually, many of these grievances can be traced even further back than the 1320s and some were present amongst the articles of 1309.
73 For references see Maddicott, *Thomas of Lancaster*, p. 97, n. 3.

royal prerogative.[74] Perhaps Edward had inherited from his father an innate sense of political conservatism which viewed 'bargaining' for taxation in return for royal concessions to be distasteful and a serious affront to the royal dignity. Perhaps he feared setting an unwelcome precedent for the future, in which the political community would hold the crown to ransom with even harsher conditions attached to its grants of taxation. Or it may simply have been that medieval kingship was not yet ready to engage in the sort of political dialogue that was to become the norm for parliamentary sessions later in the fourteenth century and that the crown had not kept pace with an increasing expectation from the political community that parliament was there to serve its own needs as well as those of the king. In each of these cases the result was the same: Edward's disengagement from parliament, almost from the beginning of his reign, pushed the institution into the hands of the baronial opposition, who used it with deadly effect as a weapon *against* the king and royal interests.

*

So the lesson of Edward II's reign was that a king ignored parliament at his peril. Parliament may (indeed) have been 'a highly regrettable necessity'[75] in the 1320s, but for the king it was a necessity nonetheless. Its value lay not so much in the access it provided to the nation's wealth or the administrative and legal role it served by dealing with hundreds of complaints each year from disgruntled subjects. These functions, though undoubtedly vital, were transitory – the king, as we have seen, could survive without parliamentary aid if he had sufficient funds of his own, and the crown's attitude towards the dispatch of petitions (private or common) was, to say the least, apathetic. By the end of Edward II's reign the indispensability of parliament lay rather in the authority the institution could lend to political action. The turbulent politics of Edward II's reign demonstrated that whoever controlled the proceedings of parliament and cultivated the support of MPs within it also gained access to an enormous and almost irresistible reserve of political legitimacy. The barons understood this principle very early in the reign and exploited it fully in their attempts to bring Edward to heel; Edward, for his part, endured ten years of humiliating political subjugation before accepting, in the Statute of York, that parliament could serve a useful political purpose for the crown; Isabella and Mortimer regarded parliament as a positive asset because it provided a veil of legality to their illegal act of deposition. Both the barons

---

[74] Amongst the articles raised were: a complaint that constables of royal castles illegally held common pleas before the gates of their castles; a call for the abolition of the new customs of 1303; an end to the depreciation of the coinage; a request for receivers to deal with unanswered private petitions handled in parliament; and more vigorous regulation of pardons granted to criminals: *RP*, I, 443–5.

[75] Fryde, *Tyranny and Fall*, p. 66.

and Edward II had come to understand the importance that parliament now had in the polity, but their reasons for valuing the institution could not have been more different: the barons saw parliament as providing a safety valve on royal misgovernment as well as legality to their own political programme; the king saw parliament, above all, as an instrument of royal authority and a means of injecting the king's policies with the flavour of popular consent. These conflicting perspectives were to resurface in future periods of heightened political tension between the king and the political community, most obviously in the reign of Richard II, when parliament once again acted as a vehicle both for political opposition and for resurgent royal authority.[76] It was a situation that demonstrated that parliament was not exclusively or without qualification 'the king's parliament'.[77] Parliament, if it 'belonged' to anyone, in the sense that it was controlled and dominated by a discreet political body, was the institution of those who could claim the largest share of political legitimacy for their actions. Mostly this was the king; occasionally, at times of crisis (such as the 1310s), this was dissenting members of the Lords; and very rarely (such as in the Good Parliament of 1376) it could be the representatives. Parliament's nature and purpose never stood still, but changed constantly according to the ebb and flow of political fortune.

The winners of the struggle between the barons and the king in Edward II's reign were, in the short term, the lay representatives, whose position in parliament was elevated almost by default as first the barons and then the king sought to make political capital by embracing their interests. As we have seen, it was the crown's attempt to repossess parliament from the opposition that might have provided the initial impetus behind the emergence of the common petition in the 1320s. However, neither the king nor the barons contemplated a politically independent and assertive lower house and it was to be some time before the representatives gained the sort of prominence in parliament that they were accorded in the *Modus Tenendi Parliamentum* – a point that serves to illustrate how ahead of its time this treatise was. Ultimately, however, the real winner was parliament itself. The prolonged period of political instability caused by the failings of Edward II's kingship had thrust parliament into the limelight, and by the end of the reign it had reached a stage in development that was far removed from the position it had occupied in 1307. This was one of the most constructive periods of parliamentary development in late medieval English history.[78] The events of Edward

---

[76] For the parliamentary opposition of the 1380s see Tuck, *Richard II*, pp. 87–137 and N. Saul, *Richard II* (New Haven and London, 1997), pp. 148–96. For Richard II's recapture of the political initiative in parliament in the 1390s, see G. Dodd, 'Richard II and the Transformation of Parliament', in *The Reign of Richard II*, ed. G. Dodd (Stroud, 2000), pp. 71–84.

[77] A reference, of course, to the title of Sayles' monograph, *King's Parliament*.

[78] It is interesting to reflect that a similar period of political vacuum was responsible for

II's reign had demonstrated that parliament's potential to harness popular support made it too valuable, but also too dangerous, for the crown to neglect, for it was no longer simply an extension of the king's council (as we might think of it under Edward I), but was an institution in which the political community as a whole now had a stake. Irrespective of whether the king needed taxation or how many petitions (common or private) were being presented in parliament, by the end of Edward II's reign the institution had attained a virtually unassailable position in the polity because it had become a principal means to advertise – or expose – a medieval king's willingness – or unwillingness – to rule for the common interest.[79] Used wisely, parliament offered a medieval king immeasurable benefits; misused or ignored, parliament could become the source of unrelenting political misery for the ruling monarch.

This, it should be emphasised, is not to advocate a return to a history of Edward II's reign that places premium on the role of administrative systems[80] or the idea of 'Edwardian constitutionalism'[81] or the notion that the Ordainers were 'parliamentarians'.[82] The prominence of parliament under Edward II arguably owed much more to the political pragmatism and opportunism of the protagonists than to deeply held or enduring political principle. At its most fundamental level, it can be said that rule through parliament was not considered by either the barons or the king to be an end in itself, but the means to an end: namely, the enhancement of their political authority. But if parliament was not held with the same constitutional reverence by Edward and his barons as it was by early twentieth-century historians, there is no denying that it was still absolutely critical in shaping the conflict of Edward II's rule, and to this extent an institutional perspective still has an important and valuable place, alongside the role of personalities, in our explanation of the crisis which faced the political community in the 1310s and 1320s.

Before finishing on what, at least for Edward II, is a relatively negative assessment of parliament's value, it is worth considering one final point.

---

propelling the Scottish parliament into the limelight and making it, in effect, a consistent and permanent feature of the Scottish constitution. This occurred during the period of Guardianship between 1286 and 1291, when parliament substituted for the king in providing legitimacy and consensus to the collective rule of the leading Scottish magnates: see A. A. B. McQueen, 'Parliament, the Guardians and John Balliol, 1284–1296', in *Parliament and Politics in Scotland, 1235–1560*, ed. K. M. Brown and R. J. Tanner (Edinburgh, 1988), pp. 29–49 (pp. 32–8); A. A. M. Duncan, *The Kingship of the Scots, 842–1292: Succession and Independence* (Edinburgh, 2002), p. 336.

[79] I therefore disagree with Fryde's comment that 'these last years of Edward II's reign show that the very existence of parliament was precarious'; *Tyranny and Fall*, p. 4.

[80] Conway Davies, *Baronial Opposition*.

[81] Tout, *Place of Edward II*, p. 30.

[82] Wilkinson, *Constitutional History*, II, 14.

Surveying the political landscape of Edward II's reign, one might easily infer that parliament spelled nothing but trouble for the king: that it not only facilitated the opposition against his authority, but also provided a constitutional framework that enhanced and prolonged the life of this opposition. But it is worth considering how else the political opposition to the king would have manifested itself had parliament not been taken up and used in this way. To what extent might the absence of parliament have pushed the baronial opposition more quickly and readily towards a decisive and catastrophic military confrontation in order to resolve the problem of a king who showed no interest in ruling by political consensus? It is true that parliament was extremely effective as a vehicle for placing restrictions on the king's authority; but it is also true that parliament was key in providing a framework which allowed the energies and resources of the king's opponents to be channelled towards finding a political solution to the crisis facing the polity. Edward II had every reason to resent the damage that parliament had caused to his authority and prestige, but the irony was that parliament may also have been his greatest political asset for preserving his rule for so long in the face of such overwhelming and determined opposition.

10

The Childhood and Household of
Edward II's Half-Brothers,
Thomas of Brotherton and Edmund of Woodstock

Alison Marshall

Thomas of Brotherton and Edmund of Woodstock – the youngest sons of Edward I by his second wife, Margaret of France – were born on 1 June 1300 and 5 August 1301 respectively.[1] Between 1301 and 16 December 1312 (on which latter date Thomas was created earl of Norfolk), the two young princes were brought up within a royal household which had been created by the king in order to cater for their needs.[2] Since this household was subject to audit on a regular basis, a considerable number of its financial and administrative records have survived amongst the governmental documents of the period. Although the existence of these records (which number about forty in total) has been known of for many decades, they have never previously been systematically analysed as a whole.[3] The intention of the present article is, therefore, to use this series of documents in conjunction with contemporary correspondence and chronicles to investigate three particular areas of the childhood and household of Thomas of Brotherton and Edmund of Woodstock: the structure and organization of their hospicium; the character of their early relationships with their father and half-brother; and the nature of their upbringing and life-style.

The documents pertaining to Thomas and Edmund's household were never, of course, intended to be used as a social record of their upbringing, but nevertheless they are invaluable in the details they provide as to the

---

[1] *Flores*, III, 109; See entries under 'Thomas, first earl of Norfolk (1300–1338)' and 'Edmund, first earl of Kent (1301–1330)' by S. L. Waugh in the *New Oxford Dictionary of National Biography* (Oxford, 2004).

[2] The bestowal of the earldom of Norfolk upon Thomas is recorded in CChR 1300–1326, pp. 205–6.

[3] The documents were listed in an article by Johnstone in 1925: H. Johnstone, 'The Wardrobe and Household Accounts of the Sons of Edward I', *BIHR* 2 (1925), 37–45. Some use of the records has been made since then, particularly in works on medieval childhood and courtly culture. See for instance: N. Orme, *Medieval Children* (New Haven, 2001), p. 190; M. Vale, *The Princely Court: Medieval Courts and Culture in North-West Europe 1270–1380* (Oxford, 2001), pp. 50, 105–9, 143–4, 171, 237, 245, 266.

structure of the household itself, as well as the kinds of necessities and luxuries provided for the two princes. The most informative of the extant documents are the wardrobe books and household rolls, both of which would have been presented for audit at the end of the financial year and which – in combination – were intended to provide a full record of the receipts and expenditures of the wardrobe and household for the relevant period. In format these documents seem to have been closely based upon the records used in the king's wardrobe. The household rolls record the total expenditures of each of the household departments on a daily basis (with weekly and monthly totals provided at appropriate intervals), and usually note the location of the household or the arrival of visitors on a given date in order to account for any increases in expenditure.[4] The wardrobe books (of which four have survived), detail individual items of receipt and expenditure listed under a series of headings or tituli.[5] In addition to the household rolls and wardrobe books a number of other useful household records exist, including rolls of liveries and indentures for money or victuals.

The records of the household begin in early 1301 and reveal that Thomas, and soon thereafter Edmund, were placed within their own household at a surprisingly young age. Edward I's marriage to his second wife, Margaret, had taken place at Canterbury on 10 September 1299 in partial conclusion of the peace treaty arbitrated by Boniface VIII between England and France.[6] Although Edward I's primary aim was undoubtedly to secure the return of his Gascon duchy, he had much else to gain from the marriage alliance. His first wife, Eleanor of Castle (who died in 1290), had dutifully borne her husband at least fourteen children, but by 1299 only five of these were alive and – most importantly – only one of his surviving children was male.[7] While there is no evidence to suggest that Edward of Caernarfon was in poor health, it must have seemed a sensible precaution to take a second wife, with the expectation that she would produce more sons.

At sixty years of age Edward I seems not to have been displeased with his seventeen-year-old bride, as she was soon expecting her first child, Thomas, who was born at Brotherton, near Pontefract in Yorkshire, on 1 June 1300 and who was apparently named in honour of St Thomas Becket, to whom the

---

4   For a typical household roll in good condition, although covering only a short period from 11 October to 19 November 1301, see E 101/360/12.

5   The four wardrobe books relate to the following periods: 13 February to 19 November 1305 (BL MS Add. 37656); 20 November 1305 to 19 November 1306 (E 101/368/12); 30 September 1310 to 29 September 1311 (BL MS Add. 32050); and 30 September 1311 to 29 September 1312 (E 101/374/19).

6   *The Chronicle of Bury St Edmunds 1212–1301*, ed. and trans. A. Gransden (London, 1964), pp. 152–3.

7   Edward I's children by Eleanor of Castile are listed in M. Prestwich, *Edward I* (London, 1988), pp. 125–7.

queen had prayed to ease her labour.[8] Edward I, who had been making his way north towards Scotland, is described as having flown 'like a falcon before the wind' towards Brotherton upon hearing the news of his son's birth.[9] An indenture of goods delivered to the queen and her son soon after his birth records that Thomas was provided with two cradles, each furnished with 13 ells of cloth, one in scarlet and the other in blue. At the specific order of the king his chamber was adorned with striped drapes, as well as golden cloths and hangings decorated with heraldic arms.[10] Similar luxuries were also bought for Edmund following his birth a little over a year later at Woodstock on 5 August 1301, when merchants avoided the surrounding area because of the extensive purveyances being made for the queen's household.[11]

Despite the comforts provided for the young princes within the queen's household subsequent to their birth, it would seem that a separate *hospicium* had been created for Thomas by January 1301, when he was little more than six months old, and by the end of that year Edmund had also been placed in the care of this establishment.[12] The provision of separate households for heirs to the throne was not a new development – the future Edward I had been provided with his own court in about 1254, and he in turn created households for his eldest sons and heirs.[13] As younger sons of the king, it would not have been inappropriate for Thomas and Edmund to have been left in the care of their mother or to have been placed in the charge of Edward of Caernarfon's household, but these possibilities were presumably disregarded because of Edward I's frequent campaigns in Scotland during the early 1300s on which he was often accompanied by his wife and eldest son. The establishment of a separate household for Thomas and Edmund also held the advantage that it unequivocally demonstrated their status.

In terms of structure and administration, Thomas and Edmund's household was organized along similar lines to those of the king and queen, although on a smaller scale. It was divided into departments (the chamber, wardrobe, chapel, hall, kitchen, pantry, scullery, saucery and stables), which

---

[8] *Rishanger*, II, 438–9.
[9] *Langtoft*, II, 323–5.
[10] E 101/357/20.
[11] For the various items bought for Edmund in August 1301 see BL MS Add. 7966A, fol. 161v; C. M. Woolgar, *The Great Household in Late Medieval England* (New Haven, 1999), p. 98.
[12] On 6 January 1301, the king ordered that twenty tuns of wine be delivered to 'the household of Thomas, the king's son': *CCR 1296–1302*, p. 416. The following day various items were also delivered for Thomas's chapel, and a chaplain was appointed to the household: E 101/360/15; for a transcription of the latter document also see Vale, *Princely Court*, p. 357.
[13] N. Orme, *From Childhood to Chivalry: The Education of the English Kings and Aristocracy 1066–1530* (London, 1984), p. 14.

were run by a host of officials and servants of varying status and importance. At the apex of the household hierarchy were the keeper of the wardrobe, the steward, the household knights and the boys' *magistra*. The keeper of the wardrobe throughout the period from 1301 to 1312 was a certain Master John de Claxton, who had the unenviable task of organizing all financial matters relating to the household. His demanding duties often seem to have necessitated his absence – he was regularly called to London to account to the king's wardrobe or to the exchequer, and at other times travelled ahead of the rest of the household to ensure that the manors which they intended to visit were prepared for the arrival of the princes and their court.[14] Between 20 February and 19 November 1305 John de Claxton was absent from the household for a total of 102 days because he was attending to such duties on behalf of Thomas and Edmund, and this high figure may not have been unusual.[15]

The steward of the household, Sir John de Weston, also served throughout the period from 1301 to 1312. In his youth he had been a ward of the crown and had consequently been one of Prince Henry's companions in the early 1270s.[16] Edward I must have regarded him as a capable figure, since his duties as steward would have been wide ranging, including the responsibility for the general welfare of his two charges as well as the running of, and discipline within, the household itself. In addition to acting as steward, John de Weston is also listed in the records as one of the household knights, of whom there were usually two or three within the household at any given time. The second household knight during the years 1301 to 1306 was Sir Stephen de Venuse, whose place was taken in later years by Sir Walter de Norwich and Sir Richard de Bourhunt.[17]

An interesting figure within the household is that of Sir Stephen de Venuse's wife, Lady Edeline, who is frequently referred to in the sources as 'magistra dominorum filiorum Regis'.[18] She played an active role in the upbringing of Thomas and Edmund (far more so – it would seem – than her husband, who is rarely mentioned in the records in comparison), often making offerings on their behalf at masses, buying luxurious goods for their chamber, or ordering various items of clothing for them.[19] She would, no doubt, also have been responsible for the other female members of the house-

---

14 E 101/374/19, fol. 4v; BL MS Add. 32050, fol. 6r.

15 BL MS Add. 37656, fol. 7v.

16 H. Johnstone, 'The Wardrobe and Household of Henry, Son of Edward I', *Bulletin of the John Rylands Library* 7 (1923), 384–420 (pp. 389–90).

17 The latter had previously acted as the sheriff of Somerset and Dorset during the reign of Edward I: *CCR 1307–1313*, p. 209.

18 See, for instance, BL MS Add. 37656, fol. 2r. It is difficult to find an appropriate English term for Lady Edeline's position: a literal translation of 'mistress' implies a certain subservience on the part of Thomas and Edmund which had no reality, while 'governess' has too many connotations of Victorian private education.

19 E 101/363/14.

hold, who included wet-nurses and berceresses, or rockers. Thomas and Edmund would almost certainly have been weaned by the age of three,[20] and so is interesting to note that Thomas's wet-nurse, Mabille de Raundes, and Edmund's rocker, Perrette de Porssy, were retained until at least 1306, which suggests that they continued to play an important care-giving role even after their primary services were no longer needed.[21] A number of other chamber girls and a washerwoman (whose task, given the quantities of linen bought for the boys' use, must have seemed never-ending), were also employed within the household.[22]

Also further down the hierarchy within the household were the clerks and the squires. The main departments of the hospicium – such as the chapel, the pantry and the wardrobe – were served by clerks who recorded the day-to-day business conducted in these offices. The squires were a diverse group, consisting both of men of good birth, who served in capacities such as marshal, usher of the chamber or serjeant-at-arms, and of men of lesser birth, but whose status within the household was nevertheless high because they served as the heads of departments such as the kitchen or the pantry. A more numerous group than both the clerks and the squires were the yeomen of the chamber and other various officials, who performed services as diverse as candle-making, tailoring or delivering letters. At the lowest level within the household were the serving boys and stable hands.[23]

The rewards for serving in the princes' household were by no means large. Servants could expect an annual fee (which in the case of the knights was 10 marks),[24] and an allowance for robes and shoes either once or twice yearly, depending upon the status of the individual. Occasionally gifts or favours might also be bestowed upon members of the household by the royal family. For instance, in October 1305 the queen gave monetary gifts to Lady Edeline, Mabille de Raundes and Perrette de Porssy,[25] while in 1310 Edward II pardoned Sir Richard de Bourhunt of a debt of £79 7s. 9½d. 'in consideration of his good service to the late king and to Thomas and Edmund'.[26] Such rewards do not, though, seem to have been made with any particular frequency. The maintenance of Thomas, Edmund and their court was expensive enough without such favours. The two princes needed to be clothed, mounted and provided with other necessities appropriate to their status; offi-

---

[20] Orme has suggested that weaning usually occurred between the ages of one and three years old: Orme, *Childhood to Chivalry*, p. 66.

[21] E 101/368/12, fol. 8r.

[22] E 101/368/12, fol. 8r.

[23] An idea of the social structure and membership of the household as described above can most easily be gleaned from the rolls of liveries, such as those for 1303 and 1304: E 101/365/15, /367/2.

[24] BL MS Add. 32050, fol. 12r.

[25] They were given 10 marks, £4, and 11s, respectively: BL MS Add. 37656, fol. 4v.

[26] *CCR 1307–1313*, p. 209.

cials and servants had to be fed and given their allowances; carters had to be hired regularly to transport the chapel and wardrobe around the countryside according to the household's perambulations; and there were numerous other day-to-day expenses.[27]

Given these various expenses it is interesting to consider the means by which the household was financed. For the first ten years money and victuals seem to have been obtained in rather a haphazard manner from a variety of sources. The main supplier was no doubt the king's wardrobe, but the household was also maintained by local officials and townsmen, who in return received tallies for presentation at the exchequer, where they would be reimbursed or where the corresponding sum would be deducted from the amount they owed to the crown. For instance, in 1301 the mayor and burgesses of Northampton were supplying money and victuals to the household,[28] while a series of indentures dating from 1303 to1305 (during which period Thomas and Edmund were often resident at Windsor) suggest that the sheriff of Berkshire was the main source of funding during these years.[29] With such varied and uncertain sources of income it is unsurprising that John de Claxton found it necessary to spend so much time in London and elsewhere organizing the household's finances. In 1310, though, Edward II came up with a much more practical solution to the problem. In July of that year he assigned the revenues of various lands which had previously been held by the (now deceased) earl of Norfolk, Roger Bigod, to Thomas and Edmund for their sustenance. Edward II also appointed two officials to manage these farms on behalf of the princes – John de Thorp became keeper of the lands in Norfolk and Suffolk, while Robert Darcy was made custodian of Chepstow Castle.[30] John de Claxton still had to account to the king's wardrobe, but he now had a predictable source of income with which to work.

So what was the actual cost of the upbringing of Thomas and Edmund? During 1305 and 1306 the annual expenditure of the household seems to have been around £800, while the wardrobe spent another £500, making a total yearly expenditure of roughly £1,300.[31] Unfortunately, there are no records between 1307 and 1309 to show whether Edward II reduced or increased the amount given to his brothers for their expenses when he initially came to the throne. However, when the records resume again in 1310 it seems that the total expenditure of the household had in fact increased by about £200 to

---

27 The costs of carriage could be considerable. When the household moved by boat from Westminster to Kennington and then by land to Banstead in late April and early May 1305, it was at a cost of 33s. 4d.: BL MS Add. 37656, fol. 2r.
28 E 101/360/13.
29 E 101/582/7.
30 *Flores*, III, 334; *CCR 1307–1313*, p. 279; *CFR 1307–1319*, p. 67; E 101/374/19, fol. 3v.
31 E 101/367/4, /369/15, fol. 7r, /368/11; BL MS Add. 37656, fol. 8r (in the case of the latter document, allowance has been made for the fact that the account only covers 8 months rather than a year).

£1,500.[32] This tallies well with the amount that the household was now obtaining in receipts from the lands that had been granted to Thomas and Edmund, which from 30 September 1310 to 29 September 1311 amounted to £1,428 16d.[33] It would therefore seem that, far from reducing his brothers' expenditure, Edward II increased the amount that they received in order to allow for their growing needs.

These figures suggest that the household of Thomas and Edmund should not be unfavourably compared to other roughly contemporary royal households. For instance, the household of Prince Henry (who was born in 1268) numbered only around thirty to forty persons, whilst his annual expenses amounted to a meagre £355.[34] Initially this household would appear to have been surprisingly small, but – as Johnstone has pointed out – it must be taken into account that the majority of Prince Henry's short life was spent either at the garrisoned castle of Windsor or in the company of his grandmother, Eleanor of Provence (who had a large following of her own), therefore negating the need to retain a military element within his hospicium.[35] In contrast, Edward of Caernarfon (born in 1284) travelled a great deal together with the considerable number of young nobles (including his four elder sisters and wards of the crown) who were resident with him in his household. This helps to explain the fact that in the 1290s Edward of Caernarfon's court seems to have had outgoings of well over £3,000 and that in 1300 household liveries were granted to 140 individuals.[36] The household of Thomas and Edmund – with its annual expenditure during 1310–11 of £1,500 and an estimated familia at this time of around fifty-five to seventy individuals – would seem therefore to represent a reasonable middle ground between these two extremes.[37]

Edward I's interest in his sons' welfare was by no means, however, purely financial. Edward I has typically been seen as a rather irascible figure – especially during his later years – whose relationship with his elder children by Eleanor of Castile was occasionally fiery (the occasions on which he threw his daughter Elizabeth's coronet into the fire and tore out clumps of Edward of Caernarfon's hair are well known and need not be repeated here).[38] In many ways the extant correspondence between Edward I and his younger sons does little to dispel this image of austerity, and it is clear that he had high

---

[32] E 101/374/19, fol. 2v; BL MS Add. 32050, fols 2r–3r.

[33] BL MS Add. 32050, fol. 3v.

[34] Johnstone, 'Wardrobe and Household of Henry', pp. 384–92.

[35] Ibid., p. 392.

[36] Johnstone, *Edward of Carnarvon*, pp. 9–12.

[37] The estimated size of their familia is based on the number of individuals listed as receiving wages and livery in the following documents: BL MS Add. 32050; E 101/374/19.

[38] For a discussion of the king's temper and the incidents mentioned above see Prestwich, *Edward I*, pp. 111, 127.

expectations of Thomas and Edmund. In September 1302, for instance, he sent instructions to John de Weston that Thomas and Edmund were to attend a mass at Canterbury and to make an offering of 7s. each, after which Weston was to report on how well they had attended to the service – despite the fact that they were little more than two and one years old respectively at the time.[39] In another letter, sent in 1305, the king commanded his sons to make sure that the park at Kennington was well-enclosed so that his hunting would be successful when he came to visit them there, and they were to be prepared to look after him as well as Prince Edward had done at Langley.[40] Although the king would by no means have expected Thomas and Edmund to oversee the repair of the fences themselves (John de Weston would have deputed others to do this on their behalf) the tone of the letter suggests that Edward I was keen to encourage his sons to take an interest and pride in the running of their household.

Nevertheless, on occasion Edward I also demonstrated a more affectionate paternal interest in his sons' well-being and seems to have been eager to hear news of them. On 21 September 1306, the king gently reprimanded a certain Margery de Haustede for not having informed him of his children's welfare, and demanded to know of 'lor estate e coment il cressent e coment il sont juantz, vistes, legiers e menantz'.[41] It was not uncommon for the king to send orders that a particular castle or manor was to be repaired in preparation for the arrival of his sons so that they would be appropriately housed, or to issue highly specific commands as to how much charcoal and brushwood should be supplied for their fires.[42]

Following Edward I's death on 7 July 1307, Thomas and Edmund became dependent upon their elder half-brother for their continuing prosperity and welfare. Their relationship with Edward of Caernarfon prior to 1307 does not seem to have been particularly close, perhaps partially because he was already sixteen years of age by the time Thomas was born in 1300, and so was in fact much closer in age to Thomas and Edmund's mother, Margaret.[43] They corresponded (as one would expect), but given that the prince was frequently on campaign in Scotland with his father during this period and that his preference was to stay at Langley when not involved in other affairs, it is unsurprising to find that he only seldom visited his brothers. His rare visits were, though, cause for great preparation and excitement within Thomas and

---

39 SC 1/14/88; P. Chaplais, 'Some Private Letters of Edward I', *EHR* 77 (1962), 79–86.
40 SC 1/63/51; Chaplais, 'Private Letters', pp. 81–5.
41 Ibid., p. 86.
42 *CCR 1302–1307*, pp. 291, 386, 400.
43 Edward II and Margaret do seem to have had a good relationship. They shared a household for a time in 1299 before Margaret was assigned her own lands, and in early January 1303 the prince sent her a gold ring set with a ruby as a New Year's gift: Haines, *King Edward II*, p. 2; H. F. Hutchison, *Edward II: The Pliant King* (London, 1971), p. 36.

Edmund's household – the wardrobe book for 1305 reveals that various luxuries (including various types of sugar, dill, dried ginger and electuaries of pine seed and sandalwood) were bought from apothecaries of London and Florence in expectation of a visit from the prince and their sister, Mary.[44] The equivalent household roll notes with anticipation, in the margin, that the household was awaiting their arrival on 23 August, although they did not arrive until four days later on 27 August and stayed only two days.[45]

When Edward II succeeded to the throne in 1307 he had a duty to look after his younger brothers, not only out of filial piety, but also out of respect for his father's wishes and affection for Margaret. His apparent failure to do this has earned him some criticism from both contemporary chroniclers and modern historians. The chroniclers commented that Edward II preferred Gaveston 'to all the other nobles of the country, whether of his own kin or otherwise',[46] and asserted that the favourite's unpopularity was due in part to the fact that 'the lord king Edward the elder had decided that the earldom of Cornwall should be conferred upon one of his sons Thomas or Edmund', but that Edward II decided instead to promote 'the stranger over his brother' by giving the earldom to Gaveston.[47] Historians have also commented that 'the earldom [of Cornwall] had been intended for the late king's second son, Thomas of Brotherton, but Edward [II] disregarded his young half-brother's interest',[48] and that when the king went to France for his marriage in January 1308 'he could have given the regency to Thomas or Edmund' rather than to his favourite.[49]

It may be the case, though, that Edward II's apparent disregard for his younger brothers' interests has been overstated. It is certainly true that the earldom of Cornwall had traditionally been held by members of the royal family, and that it would have been more appropriate – and certainly more popular – had Edward II given it to one of his brothers rather than to Piers Gaveston. However, on 1 August 1306 Edward I issued a document which stated in detail the future estates that Thomas and Edmund should receive when they reached a suitable age, and this document made no mention of the earldom of Cornwall. In fact, Thomas was bequeathed the earldom of Norfolk (valued at six thousand marks) together with other unspecified lands and rents to the value of four thousand marks, while Edmund was simply bequeathed unspecified lands to a total value of seven thousand marks.[50]

---

44 BL MS Add. 37656, fols 2r–2v.
45 E 101/367/4.
46 *Lanercost*, p. 184.
47 *Vita*, pp. 15–16.
48 I. Mortimer, *The Greatest Traitor: The Life of Sir Roger Mortimer, 1st Earl of March, Ruler of England, 1327–1330* (London, 2003), p. 32.
49 Chaplais, *Piers Gaveston*, pp. 30–5.
50 *Foedera*, II¹, 998.

Furthermore, while it would have been acceptable for Edward II to have left either Thomas or Edmund as regent in January 1308 instead of appointing Gaveston, this would hardly have been practical, given their immaturity. Edward II may also have felt that it would be unwise to push his younger brothers into the spotlight at a time when he had no heir and his nobles were showing increasing signs of dissatisfaction with his rule. It is clear from the grants of estates made to Thomas and Edmund in 1310 and from occasional gifts bestowed upon them, such as firewood for their hearths,[51] that Edward II was not unconcerned with their welfare, and so perhaps – for once – he has been criticized too harshly.

Although Edward I and Edward II may have taken an interest in the upbringing of Thomas and Edmund, it is difficult to discern from the records what arrangements – if any – they made for the princes' education. The only books recorded as being bought for their household are a Bible and a missal for the chapel, from which scant evidence it is impossible to determine whether or not Thomas and Edmund were taught to read or write.[52] Neither is there any reference in the household documents to a magister or tutor, although it does not necessarily follow from this that no such individual was appointed. The name of Edward II's tutor, Sir Guy de Ferre, is known only because he had the misfortune to break a silver dish, for which he had to pay compensation, and as Johnstone has pointed out, 'scribes writing the records of a household were apt either to speak merely of "the magister", taking for granted that everybody concerned knew who he was, or else to give his personal name, taking for granted that they knew what post he occupied'.[53]

The education of the upper classes during the Middle Ages was not, though, purely (or even largely) a matter of being taught to read or write. The most important task of the tutor was to help his ward to achieve the attainments needed for courtly life – skills such as riding, hunting, military training, religious devotion, music and perhaps even dancing. Thomas and Edmund would certainly have been taught to ride at an early age and they had their own palfreyman, William Boreward, from 1301 onwards.[54] By 1310 they had a palfreyman each, and in the summer of 1312 they were provided with new mounts – Thomas received a dapple-grey palfrey at a cost of 60s., while Edmund's palfrey was a bay costing 66s. 8d.[55] Intriguingly, no items of a military nature are recorded as having been bought for Thomas and Edmund before December 1312, and nor is there any reference to hunting in the documents. According to Shahar's research into childhood during the medieval period, young noblemen did not begin serious military training

---

51 *CCR 1307–1313*, pp. 295, 304.
52 BL MS Add. 32050, fol. 6r; E 101/360/29.
53 Johnstone, *Edward of Carnarvon*, pp. 14–15.
54 E 101/360/28.
55 E 101/374/19, fols 6r–6v.

before the age of twelve, while other strenuous pursuits such as wrestling and riding might be put off until the age of fourteen.[56] The evidence from the upbringing of Thomas and Edmund would seem to corroborate this.

With regard to other educational activities, Thomas and Edmund were taught to play the drum – a pursuit for which they seem to have had some enthusiasm, given that the instrument had to be repaired in July 1305 and November 1306.[57] Thomas and Edmund also played chess and a game called 'tables'.[58] It should be noted that chess was not merely seen as a recreational pastime in the Middle Ages. Its educational use was valued not only because of the logic needed to play successfully, but also because 'its pieces were seen as emblematic of society: king, queen, knights, judges, rooks . . . and common folk, each having its own function and all being effective when working together'.[59] Both Edward I and Queen Margaret played chess and owned expensive boards, and so it may be that the princes' parents encouraged them in this activity.[60]

Another area of Thomas and Edmund's upbringing which can be discussed in some detail is their religious education. From their earliest days, Thomas and Edmund were raised to be pious and God-fearing. In January 1301 William de Lorri was appointed as Thomas's chaplain and almoner, while his chapel was equipped with all the necessary items (including a variety of altar cloths, chalices and vessels for holding holy water).[61] Thomas and Edmund attended high masses from a very early age and usually gave offerings on these occasions. Easter seems to have been a particularly important celebration within the household, on which occasion a servant would be instructed to distribute cloth, shoes and money to twenty-six paupers on behalf of the two princes.[62] Another important religious occasion within the household was the feast of St Nicholas (6 December), which is of particular interest, given that saint's connection with children. The wardrobe books show that the established custom whereby a boy was appointed to act as bishop on this feast day was followed in Thomas and Edmund's court. For instance, on 6 December 1311 the wardrobe account records that the appointed boy-bishop sang a canticle to the princes in their chamber.[63]

With the exception of St Nicholas, neither Thomas nor Edmund seems to have had a preference for any one particular saint, although it was the images

---

[56] S. Shahar, *Childhood in the Middle Ages* (London, 1990), pp. 209–12.

[57] BL MS Add. 37656, fol. 1r; E 101/368/12, fol. 3.

[58] Edmund lost 2s. playing tables with one of his squires in May 1311: BL MS Add. 32050, fol. 6r. A chess board was bought for them in June 1312 at a cost of 4s.: E 101/374/19, fol. 5v.

[59] Orme, *Medieval Children*, p. 178.

[60] Prestwich, *Edward I*, pp. 114–15.

[61] E 101/360/15; Vale, *Princely Court*, p. 357.

[62] E 101/363/14, /374/19, fol. 3r; BL MS Add. 32050, fol. 4r.

[63] E 101/374/19, fol. 3r. Also see Vale, *Princely Court*, pp. 244–5.

of three female saints – the Virgin Mary, Catherine and Margaret – which were bought for their chapel at Hampstead Marshall in December 1311.[64] With regard to friars, however, the Franciscans rather than the Dominicans dominate the records, with quite regular payments being made to the Friars Minor for performing religious services on behalf of the young lords. Two individuals in particular stand out in the documents – Brothers Robert de Mugginton and John de Dunstaple, Friars Minor of Reading – who frequently stayed within the household for short periods, and from 1310 onwards a Franciscan clerk seems to have been permanently resident in the household.[65] Given that Edward I seems to have favoured no particular order of friars and that Edward II patronized the Dominicans, it would seem a likely assumption that this preference was influenced by Queen Margaret, whose own confessor was a Franciscan.[66]

Moving on from Thomas and Edmund's education and religious upbringing, what can be said of their life-style? Certainly, that it involved a great deal of travelling – an itinerant life-style was a necessity of all noble households during the Middle Ages because of the need to administer widespread estates and because of the burdens placed on the surrounding neighbourhood by the purveyance of food and other essentials. During 1303 and 1304 Thomas and Edmund seem to have been resident at Windsor for the majority of the time (presumably because it was impractical for the household to travel great distances before the princes were able to ride),[67] but from 1305 they began to travel frequently around the south-east and south-west of England.[68] They tended to spend the summer and winter months in one place, often either at Windsor or at Ludgershall in Wiltshire (although after they were granted Roger Bigod's lands in 1310, Chepstow in south-east Wales and Framlingham in Suffolk became preferred destinations). The rest of the year was spent travelling to and from these locations, and this often involved short stays at royal manors such as Fulham or Staines, which were within easy distance of the city of London and the royal family. The household roll for 1305 provides a good example of their itinerary. At the end of April 1305 the princes were lodged in manors close to London at Fulham, Isleworth and Kennington, and then moved through West Sussex to Ludgershall and Amesbury in Wiltshire, where they spent the majority of

64 E 101/374/19, fol. 4r.
65 BL MS Add. 32050, fol. 4r; E 101/374/19, fol. 3r.
66 Margaret's confessor is named in the king's wardrobe book for 20 November 1300–19 November 1301: BL MS Add. 7966A, fol. 32r. For the friars favoured by Edward I and Edward II see Johnstone, *Edward of Carnarvon*, p. 10; Prestwich, *Edward I*, p. 112.
67 E 101/363/14; E 101/366/15.
68 They tended to travel no further north than Northampton, where they were staying in September 1306 according to the letter discussed above from Edward I to Margery de Haustede: Chaplais, 'Some Private Letters', p. 86.

June, July, August and September. In October they made their way back to
Isleworth and Staines, and by the end of November were resident at Windsor
for the winter.[69]

Despite their perpetual journeying, Thomas and Edmund were by no
means removed from noble society and its gatherings. On one occasion in
April 1312 they travelled to Cardiff to attend the baptism of John de Clare, the
son of Earl Gilbert of Gloucester, who seems to have died shortly thereafter.[70]
More commonly, visits were paid by various members of the nobility to
Thomas and Edmund. Their most frequent visitor was undoubtedly their
half-sister, Mary (a nun of Amesbury), who called upon them a total of eleven
times between 27 June and 4 October 1305, sometimes staying for periods of
up to five days.[71] Other noble guests included the earl of Richmond, Peter of
Savoy, the countess Marshal and the bishop of Chester, whilst the list of
lesser members of the nobility and clergy is much more extensive.[72] On the
occasion of such visits, the princes and their guests were often entertained by
minstrels playing a diversity of instruments including the drum, trumpet,
violar and cyther.[73] The princes do, though, seem to have largely lacked the
company of other children of their own age, and herein lies one of the most
obvious distinctions between the household of Thomas and Edmund and
that of their elder half-brother, Edward of Caernarfon. Whilst numerous
wards of the crown were placed within Edward's household, the only children of the nobility within the comitiva of Thomas and Edmund were their
young niece, Margaret de Bohun (who stayed with them from 1303 to 1305),[74]
their younger sister, Eleanor (who died relatively young and lived with them
only briefly, from 1305 to 1306),[75] and in later years Edward Balliol, the son of
the deposed king of the Scots.[76]

Despite being mere children in the company of aristocratic adults, the
elevated status and magnificent life-style of Thomas and Edmund would
have been immediately apparent to anyone meeting them, from the manner
of their dress. This was extremely diverse, with a variety of types and colours
of cloth cut in different styles by their tailor, Stephen. They possessed mantles
and tabards in russet or in mixed colours, silk and woollen cloaks, as well as
robes lined with fur and adorned with silver buttons. To keep them warm in
the winter they had gloves and hats made from beaver skins, as well as shoes,

[69] E 101/376/4. I am grateful to Paul Dryburgh for his assistance with this document.
[70] E 101/374/19, fol. 5r.
[71] E 101/367/4.
[72] E 101/367/4, /374/19, fol. 8r.
[73] E 101/363/14, /374/19, fols 8r–8v.
[74] Margaret was attended by her own valet, nurse, rocker and tailor: E 101/365/15,
/366/15, /367/2, /367/3.
[75] E 101/369/15.
[76] Edward Balliol was first placed in their household in late 1310 and stayed with them
for a number of years: BL MS Cotton Nero C viii, fol. 31v, Add. 32050, fol. 4r.

boots and galoshes.[77] Vale has noted that the liveries issued to members of Thomas and Edmund's household adhered to the strict hierarchy within the court – the squires were issued with lambswool robes, which lacked the grandeur of the liveries of the knights, which were lined with fur and silk. The garments made for the brothers, though, were more opulent still, enabling them to exude 'a state of appropriately princely magnificence'.[78]

The diet enjoyed by Thomas and Edmund was every bit as varied and luxurious as their clothing. The provision of meat, fish, and vegetables to eat and wine to drink were a staple part of this diet: in October 1305 Edward I ordered the constable of Wallingford Castle to provide sufficient wine and fish for the pending arrival of Thomas and Edmund, while the wardrobe book for the same year notes that a ferret was bought for their gamekeeper, with which to catch rabbits in addition to other types of game.[79] More exotic foodstuffs were also bought on quite a regular basis for consumption by Thomas and Edmund, such as rice, cloves, saffron, almonds, ginger, cinnamon, pepper, figs, dates and raisins.[80]

Given the princes' warm clothing and excellent diet, they must have enjoyed a much healthier life-style than many of their less fortunate contemporaries. Thomas seems to have enjoyed good health throughout his childhood, with the exception of a period directly after his birth, when Rishanger records that he was unable to digest his milk. This was blamed on his French wet-nurse, and the prince apparently recovered when she was replaced by an Englishwoman.[81] In contrast, Edmund is quite frequently described as *infirmatus* in the household records.[82] His specific ailments are never described in the sources, but among the provisions bought for him are listed cow's milk, fresh fruit, and twisted sticks of sugar.[83] In 1301 and 1302 a physician by the name of Master Ralph was receiving wages from the wardrobe, and this same individual seems to have been responsible for burning down the house of a certain Nicholas de Winterburn in Devizes while preparing remedies for the princes.[84] Subsequently, however, no physician or apothecary seems to have been permanently resident within the household and instead, physicians, such as Master Robert de Reynham of London, were summoned when the need arose.[85] It would therefore seem logical to assume that Edmund's illnesses were not generally deemed to be life-threatening.

77 E 101/374/19, fols 3v–5r; BL MSS Add. 32050, fol. 8v, Add. 37656, fol. 2v.
78 Vale, *Princely Court*, pp. 105–8.
79 *CCR 1302–1307*, p. 291; BL MS Add. 37656, fol. 2v.
80 E 101/368/12, fol. 7r, /374/10, fol. 1, /374/19, fol. 14r.
81 *Rishanger*, II, 438–9.
82 E 101/363/14; BL MSS Add. 37656, fol. 1r, Add. 32050, fols 4r, 7v.
83 E 101/363/14; BL MS Add. 37656, fol. 2v; E 101/368/12, fol. 1r.
84 E 101/360/28; Vale, *Princely Court*, pp. 42–3.
85 Master Robert de Reynham, who attended Edmund in September 1303, was paid 20s. for his services: E 101/363/14.

No doubt in some part thanks to their privileged life-style, both Thomas and Edmund survived into adulthood. After the earldom of Norfolk was granted to Thomas on 16 December 1312 the household no longer needed to account to the king's wardrobe, and as a consequence the two princes all but disappear from the records for a number of years. There is, though, an interesting document dating from 11 November 1313, which records that a sum of £61 10s. was given to 'Mr John de Claxton, treasurer of Thomas and Edmund the king's brothers, for expenses from 8 July–7 November [1313] of Edward de Bailiolo, staying in their hospice'.[86] This would suggest that Thomas and Edmund continued to live together in the company of Edward Balliol, and that John de Claxton was still acting as the keeper of their wardrobe. Thomas and Edmund's upbringing may well, therefore, have continued along much the same lines as before.

To conclude, it is hoped that this study of the childhood and household of Thomas of Brotherton and Edmund of Woodstock has demonstrated the fascinating insights which can be gleaned from the analysis of financial and administrative documents of the medieval period. In terms of size and expenditure their court rivalled the households of the greatest magnates of the kingdom and in many ways they seem to have led a remarkably adult existence – travelling, for instance, quite considerable distances, entertaining members of the nobility, partaking in traditional religious celebrations and even gambling. However, the fact that nurture was also deemed to be an important element within their upbringing is suggested by the employment of Lady Edeline and by the retention of the services of their wet-nurse and rocker until at least 1306. Above all, nearly every aspect of their household and childhood was intended to visibly display their status to the outside world and to enable them in later life to achieve the high expectations of their father, Edward I, by providing them with the resources and skills that they would need to function within early fourteenth-century aristocratic society.

---

[86] *Calendar of Documents Relating to Scotland Preserved in the Public Record Office and the British Library* (London, 1887), p. 237.

11

Rise of a Royal Favourite:
The Early Career of Hugh Despenser the Elder

Martyn Lawrence

It was the complaint of a great many medieval chroniclers and moralists that monarchs too often chose inappropriate favourites. The chroniclers, as innately conservative as the barons themselves, wrote of men 'raised from the dust' to dazzling pre-eminence against all the strictures of the establishment.[1] Walter of Guisborough used just this language when he referred to Piers Gaveston having been 'raised up as if from nothing'.[2] It was also a common refrain that kings spurned the counsel of the hoary heads. Both Edward II and Richard II were likened to King Rehoboam, who 'followed the counsel of youths [and] lost the kingdom of Israel'.[3] The Kirkstall chronicler drew an explicit comparison between the two men, when he wrote that Richard ignored mature advice in favour of inexperience, 'rather like Edward of Caernarvon'.[4] Indeed, the reign of Edward II is the most commonly cited example of a reign in which too little recognition was given to the needs of the realm and too much to the intimates of the king. Looking back on the reign from the vantage point of the seventeenth century, men such as Sir Francis Hubert, Sir Robert Howard and Nathaniel Crouch wrote histories of royal favourites, 'that swarm of Sycophants that gap'd after greatness, and cared not to pawn their Souls to gain promotion'.[5] Pamphlet wars during the 1640s led

---

1 The phrase was coined by Orderic Vitalis: *Historia Ecclesiastica*, ed. M. Chibnall (Oxford, 1968–80), VI, 16; see also R. V. Turner, *Men Raised from the Dust: Administrative Service and Upward Mobility in Angevin England* (Philadelphia, 1988), pp. 1–19; J. A. Green, *The Government of England under Henry I* (Cambridge, 1986), pp. 139–43.
2 *The Chronicle of Walter of Guisborough*, ed. H. Rothwell, Camden Society 89 (1957), p. 382.
3 *Vita*, pp. 18, 36; *The Chronicle of Adam Usk 1377–1421*, ed. C. Given-Wilson (Oxford, 1997), p. 76. J. Ferster, *Fictions of Advice: The Literature and Politics of Counsel in Late Medieval England* (Philadelphia, 1996), pp. 123–6, examines the tradition of using Rehoboam as a warning.
4 *The Kirkstall Abbey Chronicles*, ed. J. Taylor, Thoresby Society 42 (1952), p. 83.
5 Seventeenth-century commentary appeared in three swathes: the Buckingham regime (1620s), the Civil War (1640s) and the Glorious Revolution (1680s), although earlier works were often republished as situations required. A selection of works on Edward II is as follows: M. Drayton, *Piers Gaveston Earle of Cornwall, His Life, Death and Fortune* (London, [1593]); F. Hubert, *The Deplorable Life and Death of Edward the*

to the publication of a narrative of the Appellant Parliament (1386), as well as the reproduction of Bishop Merk's parliamentary speech from 1399 during which the fate of Richard II was debated (the note on the title page reads, 'Thought seasonable to be published to this murmuring age').[6] On the stage, Christopher Marlowe and Ben Jonson both paraded the theme of a favourite being brought low.[7] It is argued with some validity that these books and plays, which used the situations of their time to contextualise events long past, could not have carried such weight had their audience not been convinced that they too were living in an age of over-mighty favourites.[8] The authors wrote what they saw in the European courts: Howard concocted a vehement defence of the Glorious Revolution under the guise of a medieval history, and Hubert drew explicit comparison between the England of Edward II and the France of Henry III. Yet it is equally true to say that the examples of Piers Gaveston, Robert de Vere and the younger Hugh Despenser could never have found

---

Second, King of England, together with the Downfall of the two Unfortunate Favorits, Gavestone and Spencer, Storied in an Excellent Poem (London, 1628); E. Cary, *The History of the Life, Reign and Death of Edward II, King of England and Lord of Ireland, with The Rise and Fall of his Great Favourites, Gaveston and the Spencers, Written by E. F. in the year 1627* (London, 1680), quotation at p. 49; C. Caesar, *Numerus Infaustus: A short view of the unfortunate reigns of William the Second, Henry the Second, Edward the Second, Richard the Second, Charles the Second, James the Second* (London, 1689); R. Howard, *Historical observations upon the reigns of Edward I. II. III. and Richard II., With remarks upon their faithful counsellors and false favourites* (London, 1689); R. Howard, *The History of the Reigns of Edward and Richard II, with Reflections, and Characters of their Chief Ministers and Favourites, As also a Comparison between those Princes Edward and Richard the Second, with Edward the First, and Edward the Third* (London, 1690); N. Crouch, *The Unfortunate Court-Favourites of England* (London, 1695). French polemicists also used Gaveston and Despenser as examples of gross folly when warning of Richelieu, Mazarin and the duc d'Epernon: J. Boucher, *Histoire tragique et mémorable de Pierre de Gaverston* (n.p., 1588); Anon., *Histoire Remarquable de la Vie et Mort d'un Favory de Roy D'Angleterre* (n.p., 1649); D. Teasley, 'The Charge of Sodomy as a Political Weapon in Early Modern France: The Case of Henry III in Catholic League Polemic, 1585–89', *The Maryland Historian* 18 (1987), 17–30.

6 T. Fannant, *A historicall Narration of the manner and forme of that memorable Parliament, which wrought wonders: begun at Westminster 1386, in the tenth year of the reigne of king Richard the Second* (n.p., 1641); Anon., *A pious and learned speech delivered in the High Court of Parliament, 1 H. 4, by T. Mercks, the Bishop of Carlisle, wherein he gravely and judiciously declares his opinion concerning the questions what should be done with the deposed King, Richard the Second* (London, [1642]).

7 Marlowe in *Edward II* and Jonson in his uncompleted *Mortimer His Fall*. To these can be added the anonymous *Woodstock* and (to a lesser extent) Shakespeare's *Othello* and *Richard II*, which were influenced by Marlowe. For discussion of the favourite in Renaissance texts, see B. Worden, 'Favourites on the English Stage', in *The World of the Favourite*, ed. J. H. Elliot and L. W. B. Brockliss (New Haven, 1999), pp. 159–83; C. Forker, 'Sexuality and Eroticism on the Renaissance Stage', *South Central Review* 7 (1990), 1–22.

8 J. H. Elliot, 'Introduction', in *The World of the Favourite*, ed. Elliott and Brockliss, p. 2.

such resonance in later centuries had they not scored so deep a mark in the English consciousness while they were alive.

By contrast, the early career of Hugh Despenser the elder (to 1321) has been too often overlooked by historians and playwrights anxious to focus on the controversy over Gaveston and the younger Despenser's brutality and vindictive dominance. In *Edward II*, Marlowe grants him just three brief appearances, and he speaks less than twenty lines. Nevertheless, in reality the elder Hugh excited great animosity amongst the baronage and in 1321 Edward II was accused of raising him beyond his means.[9] Indeed, right from the outset of the reign he may be found, together with the earl of Arundel, Thomas de Vere and Roger Mortimer of Wigmore, carrying the *scaccarium*, on which were laid the royal coronation robes, down the aisle of Westminster Abbey.[10] Walter of Guisborough remarked with some bitterness that ceremonial duties had been given to the king's friends, rather than to those who had the right to this honour.[11] Yet not many men could say that they attended both Edward's marriage and his coronation and were still at his side twenty years later.

Hugh Despenser senior laid the foundations for his son's rise to power in Edward I's campaigns of conquest. In order to understand more fully how the family fits into Edward II's reign, it is important to grasp the significance of the elder Hugh's political power, administrative ability and sense of history. To do so, we must look first at the Barons' Wars of the 1260s, where Despenser's father, also Hugh Despenser, was a great friend of Simon de Montfort. He sided with the earl after the Provisions of Oxford (1258) and was rewarded with the post of chief justiciar in 1260, an office he held on three occasions over the next five years. He was a great administrator and diplomat: according to I. J. Saunders, 'all surviving evidence indicates that de Montfort and Despenser controlled the government [in 1264–65]'.[12] Hugh Despenser the justiciar fought at Lewes in 1264 and, after the battle, was responsible for preparing the peace treaty and negotiating terms with the king. He was killed in the slaughter at Evesham the following year. The chronicle accounts are unanimous in recording that, as Prince Edward's troops surrounded the town, de Montfort turned to his justiciar and offered

---

9 *SR*, I, 181.

10 *Parliamentary Writs and Writs of Military Summons*, ed. F. Palgrave, 2 vols in 4 (London, 1827–34), II², 10; *CCR 1307–13*, p. 53.

11 *Walter of Guisborough*, pp. 381–2. This language later found its echo in Shakespeare's *Othello* (Act I, Scene i):
   Tis the curse of service
   That preferment goes by favour and affection
   And not by old gradation where each second
   Stood heir to the first.

12 *Documents of the Baronial Movement of Reform and Rebellion 1258–1267*, ed. R. E. Treharne and I. J. Saunders (Oxford, 1973), p. 297, n. 7.

him the chance to escape.[13] Unlike Thomas of Lancaster's men, who in 1322 deserted on the eve of Boroughbridge, Hugh refused to abandon his lord.[14] A recently discovered manuscript in the College of Arms recounts the conversation as follows:

> And to Sir Hugh Despenser he said: 'My lord Hugh, consider your great age and look to saving yourself; consider the fact that your counsel can still be of great value to the whole country, for you will leave behind you hardly anyone of such great value and worth.' Straightaway Sir Hugh replied: 'My lord, my lord, let it be. Today we shall all drink from one cup, just as we have in the past.'[15]

Loyalty to their cause was a characteristic that was to return in later Despenser generations. Yet these events were to cast a long shadow over the next two generations of the family, and consequently the first part of Hugh the elder's career was all about rebuilding. If the family were regain any of their former prominence it was essential to prove their willingness to conform to accepted patterns of service. If they could not, they would join the long list of middling noble families who passed largely unnoticed off the political stage.

Hugh Despenser the elder first appeared at a tournament at Compiègne in 1278 and three years later, aged twenty, took livery of his late mother's lands.[16] Since he was, technically, under-age William Beauchamp, earl of Warwick, was awarded Hugh's marriage, but Despenser bought this from him the following year for 1,600 marks.[17] In 1286 he married Warwick's widowed daughter Isabel, without royal licence. Edward I confiscated their estates for eleven months and fined the couple 2,000 marks, a sum that was later rescinded, although in the meantime it raised almost £1000 for the crown.[18] To what extent this was a genuine reaction or simply a legal fiction designed to swell the royal coffers is difficult to say. Marriage into a comital family brought Despenser considerable wealth. He was already a major landowner in the Midlands and a close neighbour and tenant of Thomas of Lancaster, and now received considerable estates in South Wales and Gloucestershire that had been held by Isabel's late husband, Patrick

---

13 A similar offer of escape was made to others: *Rishanger*, pp. 36–7.
14 Maddicott, *Thomas of Lancaster*, pp. 295–6.
15 O. de Laborderie, J. R. Maddicott and D. A. Carpenter, 'The Last Hours of Simon de Montfort: A New Account', *EHR* 115 (2000), 378–412, p. 410.
16 P. R. Coss, *The Knight in Medieval England 1000–1400* (Stroud, 1993), p. 85; *CCR 1279–88*, p. 88; *GEC*, IV, 262.
17 *CPR 1272–81*, p. 439; *CCR 1279–88*, p. 184.
18 E 159/60, m. 16; *CCR 1279–88*, p. 462; S. L. Waugh, 'The Fiscal Uses of Royal Wardships in the Reign of Edward I', in *Thirteenth Century England I*, ed. P. R. Coss and S. D. Lloyd (Woodbridge, 1986), 53–60, p. 54.

Chaworth.[19] The marriage produced two sons and five daughters, which later enabled Despenser to create a network of men bound to him by marriage. However, it was in the wars of the 1290s that he began to reclaim the prominence his father had once held.

Although he fought under Edmund, earl of Cornwall in the second Welsh war of 1283,[20] Hugh's military career began in earnest in 1294, the year that Edward I faced a three-pronged threat from Scotland, Wales and France. The discontent that had been rife since John Balliol was installed on the Scottish throne was exacerbated when Philip IV declared Edward's duchy of Aquitaine confiscate.[21] In September, as troops were mustered to sail for Gascony, a national revolt broke out in Wales.[22] Although the Lanercost chronicler was scornful of 'the miserable Welsh',[23] the rebellion was the greatest threat to English supremacy for a decade, and the army destined for Gascony, which had included the elder Hugh, was redirected to Wales.[24] Despenser himself, however, was detached from the army and dispatched to the continent to recruit allies against the French.[25] This was the first of a long series of diplomatic missions on which he was sent. Perhaps Edward, having

---

[19] Fryde, *Tyranny and Fall*, p. 29, confuses Patrick Chaworth with his older brother Payn, who was a Marcher royalist in 1264–65. For the family: M. T. W. Payne and J. E. Payne, 'The Wall Inscriptions of Gloucester Cathedral Chapter House and the de Chaworths of Kempsford', *Bristol and Gloucester Archaeological Society Transactions* 112 (1994), 93–102. A late thirteenth century effigy, possibly of Patrick Chaworth, is in the church of Neuvillette-en-Charnie, five miles west of Sources: E. F. F. Hucher, *Études sur l'histoire et les monuments de département de la Sarthe* (Paris, 1856), pp. 195–201.

[20] *Foedera*, I², 630; *Parl. Writs*, I, 246. J. E. Morris was unaware that Despenser was involved before 1294 (*The Welsh Wars of Edward I* (Oxford, 1901), p. 247), probably because he received no letters of protection, nor appeared on the roll for valuation of horses (C 67/8; C 42/2/7).

[21] The outbreak of war with France is best summarised in F. M. Powicke, *The Thirteenth Century*, 2nd edn (Oxford, 1962), pp. 644–50. For Philip's declaration, see *Foedera*, I (ii), 800. For a recent discussion of the 'unofficial diplomacy' behind these events, see W. M. Ormrod, 'Love and War in 1294', in *Thirteenth Century England VIII*, ed. M. C. Prestwich, R. H. Britnell and R. Frame (Woodbridge, 2001), pp. 143–52.

[22] Morris, *Welsh Wars*, pp. 240–70; R. R. Davies, *The Age of Conquest: Wales 1063–1415* (Oxford, 1991), pp. 382–6.

[23] *Lanercost*, p. 107.

[24] For Despenser's involvement: *Parl. Writs*, I¹, 261; *Rôles Gascons*, trans. and ed. F. Michel and C. Bemont, 3 vols in 4 (1885–1906), III, no. 3449.

[25] *CPR 1292–1301*, pp. 72–3, 76; *Treaty Rolls Preserved in the Public Record Office*, ed. P. Chaplais and J. Ferguson, 2 vols (1955–72), I (*1234–1325*), 89–90, 98–100, 102. For the general diplomatic activity of 1294–8, see Powicke, *Thirteenth Century*, pp. 658–69; G. P. Cuttino, *English Medieval Diplomacy* (Bloomington IN, 1985), pp. 67–8; G. Barraclough, 'Edward I and Adolf of Nassau: A Chapter in Medieval Diplomatic History', *Cambridge Historical Journal* 6 (1940), 225–62; M. C. Prestwich, 'Edward I and Adolf of Nassau', in *Thirteenth Century England III*, ed. P. R. Coss and S. D. Lloyd (Woodbridge, 1991), pp. 127–36.

witnessed 'a total failure of intelligence' up to this point, remembered the legal mind of Hugh's father.[26] Unlike other men similarly employed, such as Aymer de Valence, Despenser had no foreign estates, and his inclusion must have been on merit rather than because of any vested interest.[27] In any case, the mission was clearly successful. By October, the support of Adolf of Nassau, king of the Romans, his sons-in-law Henry, count of Bar and John, duke of Brabant, and Florence V, count of Holland, was assured. It was a mission that caught the attention of Pierre Langtoft, who described Despenser as a *baroun renomez*.[28] Despenser and his companions returned to England, where he and fifteen men-at-arms met Edward I at Chester and travelled into Wales with the king.[29]

Although the Welsh threat was suppressed with ease, the next few years saw a host of separate campaigns in Scotland and France. This provided Despenser with an ideal opportunity to prove himself to the king: over the next decade, hardly a year went by without a summons for military service, appointment to a diplomatic mission, or both. Hugh served in Scotland in campaigns during 1296, 1298, 1299–1300, 1301, 1302 and 1307, with increasingly larger retinues and greater responsibility.[30] He was also sent to Rome, Avignon, Paris and Cologne in 1295–96, 1296–97, 1300–1, 1302, 1305 and 1307, and in 1296 was temporarily sworn into the king's council to assist in trying a case.[31]

However, it was between 1296 and 1298, and particularly during the crisis of 1297, that Despenser's service made most impact on Edward I. Following the Dunbar campaign of 1296, with the English coffers perilously low, Despenser, with the bishop of Coventry, Amadeus of Savoy, Otto Grandison

---

26 M. C. Prestwich, *Armies and Warfare in the Middle Ages* (London, 1996), p. 217.
27 Seymour Phillips has suggested that Pembroke's links with France 'considerably added to his value as a diplomat': Phillips, *Aymer de Valence*, p. 8.
28 *Langtoft*, II, 204.
29 C 67/10, m. 2 (protection). Despenser was one of the king's twelve companions: Morris, *Welsh Wars*, 248. Michael Prestwich notes that he spent some time 'presumably in Wales' with his stepfather, Roger Bigod, in 1295: *War, Politics and Finance in the Reign of Edward I* (London, 1972), p. 64.
30 1296: C 67/11, m. 2 (protection); Morris, *Welsh Wars*, p. 64 (retinue of 25). 1298: *Parl. Writs*, I, 311 (summons); C 67/13, m. 1 (protection); Morris, *Welsh Wars*, p. 64 (retinue of 50); E 101/354/5a, fols 7v (restoration of horses, £208 15s 3½d), 9r (wages of war, £172 15s 10d). 1299–1300: *Parl. Writs*, I, 323 (summons); C 67/14, mm. 17, 10, 9 (protection and retinue of 25). 1301: *Parl. Writs*, I, 347 (summons); C 67/14, mm. 5–2 (protection); BL MS Additional 7699a, fols 75v (restoration of horses, £26 8s 4d), 83v (wages of war, £84 3s; retinue of 4 knights and 21 men-at-arms). 1302: *Parl. Writs*, I, 366 (summons); C 67/15, m. 5 (protection), 9, 14 (retinue of 4). 1307: C 67/16, mm. 12–5 (protection and retinue of 30, including Hugh the younger for the first time).
31 J. F. Baldwin, *The King's Council in England during the Middle Ages* (London, 1913), p. 91; *Langtoft*, p. 205.

and John of Berwick, was ordered to Paris to seek peace with Philip IV.[32] This trip had an air of desperation about it: the envoys also received separate letters authorising them to discuss peace with the papal legates, Adolf of Nassau, the Burgundian nobility, and 'any nobles whatsoever'.[33] Although ultimately unsuccessful in staving off military action, this mission has been described as 'the turning point in the diplomatic war',[34] resulting on 7 January 1297 in the permanent alliance between Edward I and count Guy of Flanders.[35] This union was to be sealed by the marriage of the Prince of Wales to the count's daughter, Isabella, and on 2 February Hugh Despenser and Walter Beauchamp, having been involved in the negotiations, were chosen to attest to Edward's faith in the marriage.[36] Although the marriage was never consummated, it is a strong indication of how far Hugh had risen in the king's opinion.

Meanwhile, Edward I's domestic crisis intensified.[37] When archbishop Winchelsey assembled the clergy at St Paul's on 13 January 1297, Despenser and Berwick were the royal representatives sent to the convocation. After Winchelsey had read out the papal bull *Clericos laicos*, Despenser spoke up on behalf of the king, earls and barons, demanding payment of the clerical tenth. He then informed the exchequer that no clergy without royal letters of protection should be permitted to plead exemption.[38] During the next six months he acted as messenger to the Exchequer barons, and was appointed proctor to the convocation that assembled in March.[39] He also did much to supervise the crown's wool policy, which included the heavy *maltolt* on exports and the forced sale of wool in April and July.[40] It indicates Edward's desperation that a man heavily involved in the Flanders marriage negotiations should also be required to do this, but it clearly underlines the king's increasing regard for his service. This was made further apparent when Hugh voluntarily crossed to Flanders with the king's forces in August, after many of the magnates had

---

[32] *Treaty Rolls 1234–1325*, pp. 120–5. By this time the men were becoming regular companions.

[33] Five separate letters in all: *Foedera*, I², 848–9.

[34] Barraclough, 'Edward I and Adolf of Nassau', p. 244.

[35] *CPR 1292–1301*, pp. 232–3. This must have been established from England, since Despenser was emissary to the clergy on 13 January.

[36] *Foedera*, I², 856.

[37] For detailed discussion of the 1297 crisis: G. L. Harriss, *King, Parliament and Public Finance in Medieval England to 1369* (Oxford, 1975), pp. 49–74; Prestwich, *War, Politics and Finance*, pp. 247–61; M. C. Prestwich, 'Introduction', in *Documents Illustrating the Crisis of 1297–98 in England*, ed. M. C. Prestwich, Camden 4th s. 24 (London, 1980), pp. 1–37. For the perspective of the clergy, see J. H. Denton, *Robert Winchelsey and the Crown 1294–1313* (Cambridge, 1980), pp. 53–135.

[38] *Documents*, ed. Prestwich, no. 1.

[39] *Documents*, ed. Prestwich, nos 23, 64, 150; Denton, *Winchelsey*, pp. 108, 124–5.

[40] *Documents*, ed. Prestwich, nos 45, 71, 79.

chosen to boycott the campaign.[41] Rishanger recorded that Hugh had personally accompanied the king.[42] Although the Flanders campaign was abandoned
in September 1297 when the Scots defeated Warenne's army at Stirling Bridge,
those who had stood shoulder to shoulder with the king were remembered.
After landing at Sandwich in March 1298, Hugh rode north to Scotland with
the king and fought in Edward's battalion in the victorious battle at Falkirk.[43]

Serving the king in these years launched Despenser as one of Edward I's
most loyal and capable followers. The Caerlaverock poet echoed this
language when he wrote of 'the good Hugh Despenser, who loyally on his
courser knows how to break up a mêlée'.[44] Despenser came on the scene at a
time when Edward 'felt he had been tricked by his cousin of France, treacher-
ously attacked by the Scots, and stabbed in the back by men at home to whom
he looked for friendship and counsel',[45] and in a short time had repaid the
king's trust. In 1300, when Edward received orders from Boniface VIII to
leave Scotland, the envoys of 1296–97 were dispatched to Rome with letters
which stated explicitly that their involvement was due to previous successful
negotiations.[46] In April 1302, Despenser and seven others were sent to Paris
to conclude peace with France, and were given the same powers they had
received in 1296–97.[47] After William Wallace's execution in 1305, his name
appears on the ordinance for the government of Scotland.[48] Almost without a
break, he was sent to Avignon to discuss a possible crusade to the Holy Land
and obtain the annulment of the Confirmation of the Charters (1297).[49] It was
another diplomatic success for the commission, but for Hugh it held personal
consequences of immeasurable import. Directly after they returned home,

41 SC 1/47/76; *Parl. Writs*, I, 282, 288, 293; C 67/12, m. 3d; N. B. Lewis, 'The English
    Forces in Flanders, August-November 1297', in *Studies in Medieval History presented
    to F. M. Powicke*, ed. R. W. Hunt, W. A. Pantin and R. W. Southern (Oxford, 1948),
    310–18, p. 312 n.4 (Despenser's retinue of seven); *Documents*, ed. Prestwich, no. 166.
42 *Rishanger*, pp. 412–14.
43 For the king's companions at Falkirk: BL MS Harley 6589, fol. 9r; Morris, *Welsh Wars*,
    Appendix IV.
44 *The Siege of Caerlaverock*, ed. N. H. Nicholas (London, 1828), p. 28. The Caerlaverock
    campaign is notable because only three men who received summons actually served
    in person: Despenser, John Hastings and the earl of Gloucester (Prestwich, *War, Poli-
    tics and Finance*, pp. 68–70). For the repeated failure of summonses to muster suffi-
    cient men in 1299, see ibid., pp. 94–7; Morris, *Welsh Wars*, p. 298.
45 Powicke, *Thirteenth Century*, p. 696.
46 *Foedera*, I², 922–23; *Treaty Rolls 1234–1325*, p. 146; *CPR 1292–1301*, p. 543.
47 *Foedera*, I², 940; *Treaty Rolls 1234–1325*, pp. 152–3; *CPR 1301–1307*, p. 30. When Hugh
    returned home, he and his men received wages totalling £444 6s 9d (BL MS Add.
    7966a, fol. 34v), and Despenser received a gift of a roan palfrey, worth 20 marks (BL
    MS Add. 8835, fol. 42r).
48 *Anglo-Scottish Relations 1174–1328*, ed. E. L. G. Stones (Oxford, 1970), p. 121.
49 *Foedera*, I², 974; *CPR 1301–1307*, pp. 382, 387; *Letters*, ed. Johnstone, pp. 144, 150, 151,
    153; G. P. Cuttino, *The Gascon Calendar of 1322*, Camden 3rd s. 70 (London, 1949), no.
    398.

Edward I bought the marriage of Hugh the younger for £2,000, and thus allied the Despensers to one of the most powerful baronial families in England. Eleanor Clare was the king's favourite granddaughter and the eldest daughter of one of the most powerful men in the kingdom. Although this marriage would later have a catastrophic effect on the balance of power in the March, in 1306 it must be seen as a very public statement of the elder Despenser's abilities. Two consecutive generations of Despensers had now married upwards into comital families, and having achieved his purpose of dynastic continuity, Hugh never married again.

It has been suggested that the Scottish wars under Edward I provided 'inadequate inducement for men to fight with the consistent determination required for victory'.[50] It is interesting, however, to set this beside the service of Hugh Despenser. Although there is nothing to suggest he was an extraordinarily skilled warrior, his loyalty – particularly in 1297 – ensured that he regained the standing that his father had lost after Evesham. Edward needed negotiators as well as soldiers in those difficult years, and it was in this field that Despenser seems to have flourished. He rebuilt the family reputation and, in doing so, came to the attention of the young Edward of Caernarvon, who came to value this devotion even more than his father had done.[51] The two regularly corresponded in 1304 and 1305, the prince's letters beginning 'A son cher amy, saluz, e bon amur'.[52] Hugh also began to witness Edward's charters in 1306.[53]

At the same time, Despenser had not been idle on his estates. There is substantial evidence to suggest that he was deliberately bolstering claims on the properties surrounding his estates in the Midlands, with a number of piecemeal enfeoffments in Winterburn Basset, Compton Basset, Berwick Basset and Wootton Basset (Wilts.), and Wycombe (Bucks.).[54] In 1297 he obtained the manor of Greenhampstead (or 'la Musard') from Malcolm Musard; the following year, Musard's father, Nicholas, relinquished all claims in the manor.[55] In 1303 Hugh purchased land adjacent to Green-

---

50 M. C. Prestwich, *The Three Edwards* (London, 1980), p. 78.
51 Johnstone, *Edward of Caernarvon*, p. 102. On 22 March 1307 the ailing Edward I requested that Despenser and his usual diplomatic companions, together with the bishop of Worcester, accompany Prince Edward into France (*Foedera*, I², 1012). This was presumably to conclude the negotiations for the prince's marriage to Isabella, although it coincided with Gaveston's first exile and the famous incident when the king reputedly tore handfuls of hair from his son's head and drove him from his presence (Johnstone, *Edward of Caernarvon*, pp. 121–4).
52 *Letters*, ed. Johnstone, pp. 19, 81, 97, 123; and see Hamilton's paper in this volume.
53 *CChR 1327–41*, p. 212.
54 E 401/132 *sub* 12 October 1294; E 401/138 (no date); E 401/139 (no date); E 401/140 *sub* 8 October, 20 October 1295; E 401/144 *sub* 4 October 1298; E 401/145 *sub* 25 May 1299.
55 *A descriptive catalogue of ancient deeds in the Public Record Office*, 6 vols (London, 1890–1915) (hereafter *CAD*), A927, 934.

hampstead from his Cornish retainer Henry Pembridge and in 1307 obtained the neighbouring manor of Winston from Geoffrey Pulham, and Stoke Mandeville from Drogo Barentyne.[56] He also made a series of canny exchanges with families that held reversions of the Basset lands in the West Midlands.[57] Despenser's administrative abilities appear to have been reflected in his estate management. Two of his chief Wiltshire residences, Vasterne and Wootton Basset, both in Kingsbridge hundred, had been jointly valued at £53 11s 8¼d in 1281. After coming into Despenser's ownership, they were separately valued at £60 10s and £56 respectively.[58]

A continual trickle of wealth marked the elder Hugh's increased reputation at the highest level. In 1296 'for good service' he obtained the manor of Kirtlington from his stepmother, the countess of Warwick, to be held in fee simple.[59] Two years later the earl of Gloucester demised to Despenser the Northamptonshire manors of Rothwell and Naseby, and in 1302 he entered a bond with Robert Kaynes in which he was to receive Tarrant Kaynes and Combe Kaynes (Dorset), together with other Northamptonshire and Warwickshire manors.[60] Most interesting of all was the decision in 1304 by John of Pontoise, bishop of Winchester, to grant Despenser all his French lands.[61] Presumably an ally from his frequent missions abroad for Edward I, the bishop also made Hugh an executor of his will.[62] He then obtained the manor of Doddington (Oxon.), which he gave to his clerk Robert Harwedon whilst keeping the reversion for himself.[63] Despenser also handed some East Anglian properties to his second son, Philip, but, significantly, kept his ancestral inheritance to himself.

When Edward II ascended the throne, Hugh the elder was in a position of great influence in the realm, a king's man in every sense of the word. He was 46 years old in 1307, and it is not unreasonable to see him as something of a father figure to the new king, some twenty years his junior. Despenser

---

56 Oxford, Bodleian Library, Wiltshire Charter 34; *CAD*, A943, 946, 4839.
57 The most notable was Hugh's forceable disseising of John Meysy from his manor of Marston Meysy (Wilts.) in 1305 or 1306: CP 40/360/94; J. S. Bothwell, *Edward III and the English Peerage: Royal Patronage, Social Mobility and Political Control in Fourteenth-Century England* (Woodbridge, 2004), pp. 119–20.
58 E 142/33, m. 5; *VCH: Wilts.*, IX, 194. Their value may explain why they were sacked in 1321 (ibid., 190), but the fact that Despenser owned a prison in Vasterne hints at something more sinister (*RP*, II, 416). A further example of Despenser's estate management is in WARD 2/28/94E/75 (dated 1300).
59 *CPR 1292–1301*, p. 206. The reversion was due to one John Page of Curtlington, but was not recovered until 1326: Fryde, *Tyranny and Fall*, p. 30.
60 *CPR 1292–1301*, p. 351; *CAD*, A5848.
61 *Registrum Johannis de Pontissara, Episcopi Wyntoniensis, A.D. 1282–1304*, ed. R. Deedes, Canterbury and York Society 30 (London, 1924), II, Appendix 2.
62 *Registrum Henrici Woodstock, Dioc. Wyntoniensi, A.D. 1305–1316*, ed. A. W. Goodman, Canterbury and York Society 44 (Oxford, 1941), II, 902–3, 906.
63 Fryde, *Tyranny and Fall*, p. 30.

accompanied Edward II to Boulogne for his wedding to Isabella of France, and was one of the two courtiers on the royal barge when the newly married couple arrived at Dover on 7 February 1308.[64] Later that month he attended Edward's coronation at Westminster. Because Despenser had been in France for the king's wedding, he had taken no part in the earls' discussions over the fate of Piers Gaveston, nor had he put his seal to the written agreement made by the leading magnates.[65] Although he was not entirely alone, he was the most high-ranking dissenter to the exile of Edward's favourite.[66] The comment of the *Vita* that Hugh deserted the barons 'more from a desire to please and a lust for gain than any creditable reason' is somewhat unjustified; his loyalty was only an extension of his service in the previous reign.[67] It is probable that Despenser's unpopularity stemmed in part from his involvement in the implementation of the *maltolt* in 1297, which had led many magnates, as wool producers, to suffer loss of income, and in part from the award of the Clare marriage.

Although the elder Hugh was isolated by his stance over Gaveston, Edward granted him custody of the castles of Devizes, Marlborough, Strigoil and Chepstow. A decision was made that no wardships were to be signed away until Despenser was fully satisfied of £2,544 he was owed by Edward I,[68] and he was appointed justice of the forests south of the Trent, a position that held great authority.[69] It says much about the relationship between the two men that Edward II was not only prepared to fly in the face of baronial opinion not only over Gaveston, but over Despenser as well. Edward even went so far as to award him the wardship and marriage of Sir John Moriet, which Piers had intended for his own retainer, John Darcy. According to a

64 *Parl. Writs*, II², 9. The other was the lord of Castillione (Gascony): *CFR 1307–19*, 14. For the wider implications of the marriage: E. A. R. Brown, 'The Political Repercussions of Family Ties in the Early Fourteenth Century: The Marriage of Edward II of England and Isabelle of France', *Speculum* 63 (1988), 573–595; 64 (1989), 373–9.
65 *AP*, pp. 262–4; *Walter of Guisborough*, pp. 381–2.
66 Jeff Hamilton has shown that a handful of other barons remained loyal to Edward: Hamilton, *Piers Gaveston*, p. 146, n.104. Despenser was in the king's chamber when Gaveston surrendered Knaresborough Castle and other lands before his exile, and witnessed the sealing of the letters patent which appointed him lord of Ireland: *Parl. Writs*, II², 14–15. However, not even Despenser witnessed the charter which granted Gaveston the earldom of Cornwall: Chaplais, *Piers Gaveston*, pp. 27–33.
67 *Vita*, p. 4. Gaveston and Despenser had first come into contact in the troubled Flanders campaign of 1297 (BL MS Add. 7965, fol. 76r; E 101/6/37, m. 1), and it is possible that this created a lingering bond.
68 *CFR 1307–19*, 17; *CPR 1307–13*, pp. 51, 76. According to a petition presented by Hugh after 1322, this debt was still not satisfied: SC 8/42/2093.
69 *CPR 1307–13*, p. 183; Tout, *Place of Edward II*, pp. 318–21. He was confirmed as justice for life in August 1309, and there are numerous references to his activities as justice scattered throughout the Patent Rolls. For complaints against and condemnation of his behaviour as justice, see *Vita*, pp. 111, 114; *CPR 1313–17*, p. 407.

letter written to Darcy on 1 April 1308, this had been granted away by the king three days before Gaveston asked for it.[70] The very fact that the decision was not reversed in Gaveston's favour speaks volumes about Despenser's prominence, since any lesser man would surely have been pushed aside. The king's affection was well rewarded: Hugh similarly refused to set his seal to the Ordinances (1311), for which he was driven from the council.[71] After Gaveston's summary execution in 1312, it was Despenser who acted as Edward's intermediary with the barons, beginning a period of intense hatred between the Despensers and Thomas of Lancaster, the king's cousin, which did not end until 1322. If we are correct in reading the *Vita Edwardi Secundi* as a contemporary journal, the public perception of Hugh senior was changing.[72] The author describes how 'Sir Hugh Despenser, who was perhaps even less deserving than Piers, lurked with the king'.[73] Perhaps this comment was made in the light of the birth of Prince Edward in 1312, as Hugh was chosen as one of his godfathers. Seven are listed in all, including the bishops of Poitiers, Worcester and Bath and Wells, the count of Evreux and the earls of Richmond and Pembroke.[74] There are significant omissions here, not least the earl of Gloucester, who was a major voice of moderation. Gaveston's death clearly left something of a void that Edward chose to fill – temporarily – with Despenser, a veteran councillor with vast experience.

Opportunities for military service under Edward II were considerably less auspicious than prior to 1307. While Edward I's occupation of Scotland depended to a great extent on occupation of castles – a tactic which by its very nature required constant campaigning – his son embarked upon only four major forays north of the border throughout his entire reign (1310–11, 1314, 1319 and 1322).[75] Of these, the first appears to have been to avoid the censure of the Ordinances. The second, however, ended in the ignominious defeat at Bannockburn, the third likewise at Berwick, and the fourth at Byland Abbey. Indeed, the king's two major debacles in 1314 and 1322 both

---

[70] Maddicott, *Thomas of Lancaster*, pp. 78–80, Appendix 1.

[71] It is interesting to note that the criticisms of royal government which the Ordinances supposedly addressed were rooted in the 1290s, the same time that the elder Despenser's influence is first noticed: M. C. Prestwich, 'The Ordinances of 1311 and the Politics of the Early Fourteenth Century', in *Politics and Crisis in Four-teenth-Century England*, ed. J. Taylor and W. R. Childs (Gloucester, 1990), pp. 1–18.

[72] C. Given-Wilson, '*Vita Edwardi Secundi*: Memoir or Journal?', in *Thirteenth Century England VI*, ed. M. C. Prestwich, R. H. Britnell and R. Frame (Woodbridge, 1997), pp. 165–76.

[73] *Vita*, p. 30.

[74] *CCR 1307–13*, p. 558.

[75] Hallam, *Itinerary*, passim. The reign is a catalogue of repeated military summonses and unfulfilled musters: M. C. Prestwich, 'Cavalry Service in Early Fourteenth Century England', in *War and Government in the Middle Ages: Essays in Honour of J. O. Prestwich*, ed. J. Gillingham and J. C. Holt (Cambridge, 1984), pp. 147–58.

happened with a Despenser at his side.[76] However, by this time the elder Hugh was reaping the rewards of the recognition he had gained under Edward I. After 1308, Edward II left England on only seven occasions, and Despenser accompanied him each time.[77] Edward's desire for Hugh's counsel meant that in sharp contrast with the previous reign he was rarely sent on missions away from the king. His appointment for life as justice of the forests doubtless focused much of his time on domestic affairs, and – early in the reign, at least – he clearly acted as a man of trust and discretion in the law courts.[78] In fact, Despenser was one of the senior administrators of the early fourteenth century. Having been made a permanent member of Edward I's Great Council in 1305,[79] he witnessed more than half of Edward II's charters prior to Bannockburn, including 67 out of 68 in 1312–13.[80] For a man who never held any office higher than justice of the forests, his proximity to the king was clearly worrying for the barons and, unsurprisingly, they demanded his removal from court. He witnessed only one charter in 1318–19, supporting the comment of the *Vita* that he chose to go on pilgrimage to Santiago as he was afraid to face Thomas of Lancaster at the York parliament in 1319.[81]

Despenser's only major foreign mission was in 1320, when he was sent to Gascony and Avignon. He had originally received protection to travel with the king,[82] but Edward was still in London when Despenser, Bartholomew Badlesmere and Edmund of Woodstock sailed for Bordeaux on 19 March, accompanied by the bishop of Hereford.[83] Despenser and Badlesmere were to inquire into the excesses of the seneschal and his officers in Gascony, and to make changes if necessary.[84] It is a sad indictment upon Edward's ability to choose his followers that there were nineteen seneschals of the duchy in as many years. Despenser and Badlesmere wrote to the king in May, explaining

---

76 The elder Despenser at Bannockburn (*Lanercost*, p. 208); the younger at Byland Abbey (BL MS Stowe 553, fol. 61v).

77 (1) To Scotland, September 1310 until August 1311; (2) to Paris, May–July 1313; (3) to Boulogne, December 1313; (4) to Scotland, June–July 1314; (5) to Scotland, September 1319; (6) to Amiens, June–July 1320; (7) to Scotland, August–September 1322.

78 See, for example, *SCCKB*, IV, 32, 40.

79 E 175/1, no. 20.

80 J. S. Hamilton, 'Charter Witness Lists for the Reign of Edward II', in *Fourteenth Century England I*, ed. N. E. Saul (Woodbridge, 2000), p. 5.

81 *Vita*, p. 93; *CCR 1318–23*, p. 123.

82 *CPR 1317–21*, p. 426.

83 *Foedera*, II¹, 418; *Treaty Rolls 1234–1325*, pp. 234–35. Edward was possibly delayed by illness: the wardrobe book records the payment of expenses to an apothecary who treated the king and Eleanor Despenser during the year (BL MS Add. 17362, fol. 18r).

84 *Catalogue des Rolles Gascons, Normans et François*, ed. T. Carte, 2 vols (Paris, 1743), I, 55. Various letters of credence to rulers and bishops in France survive, dated February/March 1320: SC 1/32/78–82, 84, 88; C 47/24/3/12, no. 1. I am grateful to Professor David Smith for the Chancery reference.

the appointment of a new castellan at Montfaucon, which could imply that the mission was proceeding successfully.[85] However, the fact that another commission had to be charged with exactly the same duty four years later suggests otherwise. The envoys later travelled to Avignon to negotiate with John XXII,[86] before returning to Edward II, who by this time had arrived at Amiens with the younger Hugh. Despenser senior received £404 expenses for the trip, and six of his servants were given gifts, suggesting that the king was pleased with the outcome of the expedition.[87] However, not long after their return to England the country descended into civil war.

By 1321 it was hard to differentiate between the two Despensers. The articles of exile laid the blame for all the problems in the realm squarely on the shoulders of both men.[88] Both were accused of extortion, law-breaking and, above all, usurping the role of the barons in counselling the king. Hugh senior was singled out as a bad justice who breached the law in the royal forests, disinherited families, extorted unjust ransoms and 'collected a thousand librates of land by means of threats',[89] while Hugh junior, as chamberlain of the household, was blamed for bringing his father into the king's inner circle. Together, the two Despensers were guilty of the standard charges faced by any royal favourite: they redirected patronage and flaunted their wealth, whilst their honeyed speech contrasted with the barons' bluntness and polarised the court. Yet Hugh Despenser the elder held an almost unique position in politics. Whilst the barons were swift to criticise his proximity to Edward II, it was a position in which he prospered for over a decade. For the most part, and certainly before 1312, few men were as faithful in orthodox service as the elder Hugh: chroniclers remarked on his integrity and skills in diplomacy, soldiering and administration.[90] Neither could the barons argue that he was 'raised from the dust'. Unlike Gaveston, who came from nowhere and returned to nowhere within a generation, the Despensers existed as a

---

85 SC 1/37/7.

86 SC 1/32/122 (Edward's letter to the pope); *Catalogue des Rolles Gascons, Normans et François*, II, 9.

87 BL MS Add. 17362, fols 11r, 31r–32r.

88 The articles have been examined in detail, and a number of different texts survive: B. Wilkinson, 'The Sherburn Indenture and the Attack on the Despensers, 1321', *EHR* 63 (1948), 1–28; Maddicott, *Thomas of Lancaster*, pp. 279–87; Fryde, *Tyranny and Fall*, pp. 45–8; *Parliamentary Texts of the Later Middle Ages*, eds. N. Pronay and J. Taylor (Oxford, 1980), pp. 157–8; M. C. Prestwich, 'The Charges Against the Despensers, 1321', *BIHR* 58 (1985), 95–100; C. Valente, *The Theory and Practice of Revolt in Medieval England* (Aldershot, 2003), pp. 127–8, 137–41. The 'official' version is printed in *SR*, I, 181–4; an additional sixteenth-century French copy is in BL MS Sloane 1301, fol. 242.

89 *Vita*, p. 114.

90 For example: *Geoffrey le Baker*, p. 6. This is not to ignore the fact that Gaveston was an able warrior (Hamilton, *Piers Gaveston*, pp. 29–30), or the younger Despenser a competent household administrator, albeit for his own ends (M. C. Buck, 'The Reform of the Exchequer, 1316–1326', *EHR* 98 (1983), 241–60).

powerful noble family before Edward II's reign, and returned to prominence and greater acceptance not long after his death. Despenser's problems began when he came to exercise his newly-found authority. Power made him cruel, greedy and corrupt, and his easy familiarity with the king made the barons incandescent with rage. In calling for his exile, they took the opportunity to exorcise a grievance that had troubled them for fourteen years. Ultimately, Hugh Despenser the elder matched the stereotype of the royal favourite because he forgot how he had risen to favour in the first place. His political career – a sound beginning, ruined by a farrago of loyalty, ambition, folly and corruption – was a microcosm of Edward II's reign.

12

The Place of the Reign of Edward II

J. R. S. Phillips

To put it mildly, Edward II has received a bad press from his own day to the present. His name is a byword for incompetence and neglect of duty; and he has been used in England (and sometimes also in France) to demonstrate the folly of allowing power to accrue to irresponsible favourites and chief (or prime) ministers.[1] Seemingly the only good thing to be said about Edward II was Tout's remark that Edward's very ineffectiveness was almost a blessing since 'a strong successor to Edward I might have made England a despotism; his weak and feckless son secured the permanence of Edwardian constitutionalism'.[2]

During the latter part of the twentieth century Edward II also became an icon for the gay community through, for example, Derek Jarman's very explicit 1992 film version of Christopher Marlowe's play *Edward II*.[3] In the late 1980s the English composer Peter Tranchell (1922–93) projected an opera on Edward II;[4] David Bintley's ballet *Edward II*, was first performed by the Stuttgart Ballet in April 1995, and then by the Birmingham Royal Ballet in October 1997. The music for the ballet was composed by John McCabe, who also reworked the score in his symphony no. 5, *Edward II* (completed in April 1997). Edward's musical associations also extend to a 'folk/reggae' band, *Edward II*, active since the late 1980s, one of whose albums has the evocative title of *Edward II and the Red Hot Polkas*. In a sense, Edward II has become everybody's property,[5] making an assessment of him and his reign even more problematic.

A very good example of the tendency among historians to interpret anything and everything to Edward's discredit can be found in the

---

1   For a more detailed treatment of the subject see references above, p. 1.
2   Tout, *Place of Edward II*, p. 30.
3   Jarman gave further emphasis to this approach by his simultaneous publication of a book on the making of the film, *Queer Edward II* (London, 1991).
4   Cambridge University Library, Ms. Tranchell 1.15. The opera would presumably have given emphasis to the relationship between Edward and Gaveston under the conventions of that time.
5   A good illustration of this can be seen in the Museum of Treasures in Waterford, Ireland, where an animated cartoon depicts a foppish Edward II 'road-testing' the latest fashion in shoes with long pointed toes.

well-known letter addressed by him as Prince of Wales in May 1305 to count Louis of Evreux.[6] 'We send you a big trotting palfrey which can hardly carry its own weight, and some of our bandy-legged harriers from Wales, who can well catch a hare if they find it asleep, and some of our running dogs, which go at a gentle pace; for well we know that you take delight in lazy dogs.[7] And dear cousin, if you want anything else from our land of Wales, we can send you plenty of wild men (*gentz sauvages*)[8] if you like, who will know well how to teach breeding to the young heirs or heiresses of great lords.'[9] This has variously been described as displaying petulance or frivolity on the part of Edward,[10] but what it really shows is that Edward had a wry affection for Wales and, above all, that he had a sense of humour, which he expressed in a letter to someone he clearly knew well. As this paper will attempt to suggest, this is not the only occasion on which Edward has been under-rated, if not positively misunderstood.

Another example is the long-held belief that Edward of Caernarfon's formal education was inadequate and that, in particular, he was 'illiterate' in the sense of knowing little or no Latin.[11] This conclusion rests largely on two pieces of evidence. The first is the fact that in 1308 Edward took his Coronation Oath not in Latin but in French, a form allegedly devised for a king who did not know Latin.[12] From this circumstance and from evidence that in 1300 a primer was bought for Edward from William the Bookbinder of London at

---

6   Louis of Evreux (1276–1319) was the half-brother of Philip IV of France and became Edward's uncle when his sister Margaret (1282–1318) married Edward I in 1299. There is evidence both here and elsewhere that Edward was on close and friendly terms with Louis, who was perhaps almost a father figure at a time when Edward was on bad terms with his own father. In 1305 Louis was visiting England, together with his mother, Marie, the queen mother of France, at about the time of the start of Edward's quarrel with his father: Johnstone, *Edward of Carnarvon*, p. 99.

7   Edward may well have been thinking of the two greyhounds sent to him by the constable of Conway in 1300: Johnstone, *Edward of Carnarvon*, p. 10, n. 4, citing *Liber Quotidianus Garderobae, 28 Edward I*, ed. J. Topham (London, 1787), p. 166 (this is an edition of Society of Antiquaries MS 119).

8   Literally this means 'men of the woods': 'homines silvatici', and by extension 'wild men'. The 'wild man' was a familiar theme in medieval tradition and folklore: see J. R. S. Phillips, 'The Outer World of the European Middle Ages', in *Implicit Understandings: Observing, Reporting, and Reflecting on the Encounters between Europeans and Other Peoples in the Early Modern Era*, ed. S. B. Schwartz (Cambridge, 1994), p. 48.

9   Johnstone, *Edward of Carnarvon*, p. 64, citing *Letters*, ed. Johnstone, p. 11.

10 Johnstone, *Edward of Carnarvon*, p. 64; M. Prestwich, *Edward I* (London, 1988), p. 227. In her introduction to the *Letters*, p. xxxvii, Johnstone made the very odd remark that the letter 'seems to suggest that Edward himself was far from content with his position and his sporting equipment'. In fairness, her translation of the letter on this occasion (1931) is much less considered than in *Edward of Caernarvon* (1946).

11 For a valuable summary of the debates on Edward's education see Johnstone, *Edward of Carnarvon*, pp. 18–21.

12 Ibid., p. 19.

a cost of £2, V. H. Galbraith concluded damningly that 'It was thus stupidity or laziness, and not want of opportunity to learn Latin, that made it necessary for Edward II to take his coronation oath in French.'[13] The second piece of evidence is the letter of 1317 in which Pope John XXII thanked the archbishop of Canterbury for translating a papal letter from Latin into French 'so that what is the better understood may bear the richer fruit'.[14] Such evidence may seem conclusive, but it is seriously misleading and has been substantially undermined by more recent scholarship.[15]

The damage caused to Edward's posthumous reputation by the Coronation Oath was brought about by a roll produced at Canterbury in 1311 and still preserved there. In it there are two versions of the oath, the first, in Latin and headed 'if the king shall be literate', and the second in French and headed 'if the king shall not be literate'.[16] The implication seems clear enough, and the appropriate conclusions were drawn by scholars from William Stubbs to Vivian Galbraith. However H.G. Richardson and G. O. Sayles, writing in 1938–39, concluded that the references to literacy and illiteracy had been added as a gloss by the clerk who produced the roll and were of no authority, and that Edward took the oath in French in order to use 'the common idiom of all those assembled in the abbey'.[17] This is clearly correct. The Canterbury clerk, who presumably was highly educated in Latin, was being too clever. French was the spoken language of the upper levels of English society as well as a language of record, and it was entirely appropriate that it should be used on a great public occasion such as a coronation. Richardson and Sayles also pointed out, quite properly, that if Edward had needed to take the oath in Latin, he could easily have been taught the appropriate responses, whether he knew Latin or not. (Just as Prince Charles was coached in Welsh before he was inaugurated as Prince of Wales in 1969.) Later kings, from Edward III in 1327, also took their oath in French, but have

---

13 Ibid., p. 18, citing *Liber Quotidianus Garderobae, 28 Edward I*, p. 55; V. H. Galbraith, 'The Literacy of the Medieval English Kings', *Proceedings of the British Academy* 21 (1935), 201–38 (p. 215).

14 Ibid., pp. 19–20.

15 Ibid.

16 'Si Rex fuerit litteratus talis est' & 'si Rex non fuerit litteratus': Roll K 11 in the Canterbury cathedral archives: this text was used by the editors of the Statutes of the Realm: *Statutes of the Realm*, I, p. 168. In the official records of the coronation, the Latin version of the oath appears on the Coronation Roll and the French as a schedule to the Close Roll, which implies that they were regarded as equally authentic: see *Select Documents of English Constitutional History, 1307–1485*, ed. S. B. Chrimes and A. L. Brown (London, 1961), pp. 4–5. The Close Roll text is omitted in the calendared version (*CCR 1307–13*, p. 12) but is printed in *Foedera*, II¹, p. 36.

17 Johnstone, *Edward of Carnarvon*, p. 19; citing H. G. Richardson and G. O. Sayles, 'Early Coronation Records', *BIHR* 16 (1938–39), 129–45 (p. 140); and H. G. Richardson, 'The English Coronation Oath', *TRHS*, 4th s. 22 (1941), 129–58 (pp. 135, 144–5).

not been charged with illiteracy.[18] It is worth adding that, in the absence of any records of Edward I's coronation in 1274, it is unknown whether he also took the oath in French; and also that the Canterbury roll containing Edward II's Coronation Oath included the text as a postscript to the Ordinances of 1311, another great public document which was, of course, also composed in French.[19] The language of the Coronation Oath of 1308 thus has no bearing whatsoever on Edward's knowledge of Latin.

Pope John XXII's letter to the archbishop of Canterbury in 1317 is equally fragile as evidence.[20] The fact that the pope was writing to persuade Edward II to engage himself more seriously in his duties as king has probably made the translation of his words from Latin into French seem even more pointed to modern observers. However, none of this necessarily proves that Edward knew little or no Latin. As Hilda Johnstone wisely remarked, 'the stately periods of the papal chancery were no easy reading, even for a scholar'.[21] The problems of comprehension were not, however, confined to Edward II alone, since in 1326 he wrote to John XXII in Latin rather than in French, on the assumption that the Pope, as a speaker of the *langue d'oc*, would find Latin easier to understand. In 1323 the pope had also written to Charles IV of France telling him that he had had a recent letter translated from French into Latin because his reading knowledge of the French vernacular was inadequate, and asking him to write in Latin in future.[22]

---

18 Johnstone, *Edward of Carnarvon*, p. 19. Edward III took the same oath as his father, both in language and in content: *CCR 1327–30*, p. 100; *Foedera*, II¹, 36.

19 *SR*, I, 157–67.

20 Johnstone, *Edward of Carnarvon*, pp. 19–20, citing fol. 218 of the still unpublished Register of Archbishop Walter Reynolds in Lambeth Palace Library. The register is, however, the basis of a major study by J. R. Wright, *The Church and the English Crown, 1305–1334* (Toronto, 1980). See also P. Chaplais, *English Medieval Diplomatic Practice* (London, 1982), I, p. 22, n. 126.

21 Johnstone, *Edward of Carnarvon*, p. 20. The specialised language of papal documents was devised as a way of ensuring that papal letters could not readily be forged, but also as a way of couching what was sometimes a blunt message in diplomatic language. A good example is another letter sent by John XXII to Edward II in 1318, in which he asked Edward to remedy the grievances of the Irish against English rule: *Cal. Papal Letters, 1305–42*, p. 440; A. Theiner, *Vetera monumenta Hibernorum et Scotorum historiam illustrantia* (Rome, 1864), p. 201. A more recent example, which shows how readily an unpractised reader or hearer could lose the message of a complicated document is Henry VIII's proclamation of 20 February 1537 which began by rehearsing the many reasons why there should be a legislative union between Wales and England. Only towards the end does it become apparent that the 'Act of Union' of 1536 which provided for this, was in fact being suspended: *Tudor Royal Proclamations*, I, *The Early Tudors, 1485–1553*, ed. P. L. Hughes and J. F. Larkin (New Haven and London, 1964), no. 172, p. 254.

22 Chaplais, *English Medieval Diplomatic*, pp. 21–2, n. 126. Another instance of a text being tailored to the particular language skills of John XXII is the abbreviation in Provencal of the *Topographia Hibernie* of Giraldus Cambrensis, which was taken to

With the grosser charges of illiteracy out of the way, it is arguable that Edward's level of education has been under-estimated. Although the belief that Walter Reynolds, the future archbishop of Canterbury, who was a prominent member of Edward's household from 1297 to 1307, was his intellectual mentor has long since been disproved,[23] there is evidence to suggest that Edward's education was given special attention, especially by his mother, Eleanor of Castile. She was brought up in her native land in an atmosphere of learning. Her half-brother, Alfonso X of Castile, was deeply interested in literature and in law, and fully merited his nickname 'the Wise'.[24] She herself may have been educated by Dominican friars at the court of her father, Ferdinand III, and it has been suggested that she may have 'developed a command of the written word that went beyond the decorative or pious accomplishment it is often said to have been for medieval women of rank'.[25] She appears to have tried to pass on something of her own education and cultural appreciation to her children: her daughters Eleanor and Mary, for example, were probably both literate.[26] There is no reason to suppose that she treated the young Edward in any different manner. In 1290 she sent one of her scribes, named Philip, to join Edward's household at Woodstock. If Philip transcribed books for the use of his royal master, some attempt was presumably made to put them to practical use, perhaps under the guidance of the Dominican friars who were already in Edward's household in 1289–90.[27] It is also likely that one of the tasks of Edward's *magister*, Guy Ferre, an experienced administrator who must therefore have been literate himself, was to ensure that his royal charge acquired some degree of learning along with the ability to ride a horse.

Avignon in 1324–5 by Edward II's envoy, Philip of Slane, the Dominican bishop of Cork, to help the pope with his deliberations on a proposed reorganisation of the dioceses of the Irish Church. This is now in the British Library as Additional Ms. 17920: see J. A. Watt, *The Church and the Two Nations in Medieval Ireland* (Cambridge, 1970), p. 192.

23 Johnstone, *Edward of Carnarvon*, pp. 20–1. In 1297 Reynolds was responsible for purchasing supplies for the household, of which he was joint controller from 1301 to 1307: ibid., p. 21. Although he was not a university graduate, Reynolds was a patron and promoter of learning and was certainly not illiterate, as his enemies claimed: see J. R. Wright, *The Church and the English Crown*, pp. 250–7; idem, 'The supposed illiteracy of Archbishop Walter Reynolds', *Studies in Church History* 5 (1969), 58–68.

24 See *The Worlds of Alfonso the Learned and James the Conqueror: Intellect and Force in the Middle Ages*, ed. R. I. Burns (Princeton, 1985).

25 J. C. Parsons, *Eleanor of Castile* (New York, 1995), p. 9.

26 The Wardrobe Book of 14 Edward I (1285–86) records the purchase of 'writing tablets for Eleanor the king's daughter': Galbraith, 'Literacy of Medieval English Kings', p. 215. This immediately follows Galbraith's remarks about Edward's laziness and stupidity and makes Edward's lack of education seem even more improbable.

27 Parsons, *Eleanor of Castile*, pp. 41–2, 271, n. 120; and J. C. Parsons, 'Eleanor of Castile (1241–1290): Legend and Reality through Seven Centuries', in *Eleanor of Castile, 1290–1990*, ed. D. Parsons (Stamford, 1991), pp. 38–40.

A reasonable conclusion as to Edward of Caernarfon's educational achievements is that, like his father Edward I, 'his main language was . . . French, more specifically the Anglo-Norman dialect, but [that] he had some understanding of Latin and could speak English'.[28] Although, again like his father, there is no certainty that Edward learned to read, it seems probable that he did.[29] Neither is it known whether, like his son Edward III, he could write, but again the possibility should not be ruled out.[30] Edward did not need to achieve the heights of scholarship of a university master or the skills in reading and writing of an experienced royal clerk, but there is little doubt that he had sufficient education to perform his duties as king. He was, in

[28] Prestwich, *Edward I*, p. 6. I have deliberately quoted this description of Edward I since even less is known of his education than of his son's, yet it has never been assumed that he was ignorant and untrained. The most thorough discussion of the languages spoken in thirteenth-century England is in M. Clanchy, *From Memory to Written Record: England, 1066–1307* (2nd edn, Oxford, 1993), pp. 197–211. On the ability of Edward I and of some of his leading officials to speak English see J. R. S. Phillips and E. L. G. Stones, 'English in the Public Records: Three Late Thirteenth-Century Examples', *Nottingham Medieval Studies* 32 (1988), 1–10; see also N. Denholm-Young, *History and Heraldry, 1254–1310* (Oxford, 1965), p. 54, on Edward I and English as well as his knowledge of Latin and French. It is not at all surprising that Edward I and Edward II should have known English in a country most of whose population spoke it as their first language; what is surprising, in a country whose records were invariably kept in either Latin or French, is finding written evidence that they could do so.

[29] It is interesting that Galbraith argued that from the time of Henry II 'all our kings were taught letters in their youth, and their literacy, as distinct from their culture, has no particular importance . . . How far they were literate, in the strict sense of the word, that is to say to what extent they were Latin scholars, is hard to know; but, and this is much more important, we can hardly doubt that henceforth they could all read French': 'Literacy of Medieval English Kings', p. 215. He also notes (p. 234, n. 35) that from the time of Edward I, for about a century, wills were normally written in French. It is worth adding, in relation to Edward II, that of the 719 items in his roll of letters in 1304–5, 676 were in French and only 43 in Latin. 'A form of French, perfectly comprehensible to both Frenchmen and Englishmen alike, was the normal language of secular correspondence.': M. Vale, *The Angevin Legacy and the Hundred Years War, 1250–1340* (Oxford, 1990), pp. 43–4. The relaxed tone of the language of Edward's letters also suggests that, although he would have had clerks to do the actual writing, he understood perfectly what was set down in his name.

[30] As with a knowledge of English, so with writing: the problem is 'catching them at it'. It is only through the chance survival in the Vatican Archive of the young Edward III's 1330 letter to the pope with the words 'pater sancte' written in his own hand that we know he could write. It is also possible that Edward III wrote the response to a petition of 1350 in his own hand: Galbraith, 'Literacy of Medieval English Kings', pp. 222–3 and p. 236, n. 47. It seems to me, at any rate, unlikely that Edward III possessed a skill, even in a very basic form, which his father had not also possessed. For the text and comment on the 'pater sancte' letter see Chaplais, *English Medieval Diplomatic*, no. 18, pp. 21–3. The original document is Archivio Segreto Vaticano, A.A., Arm. C, fasc. 79.

other words, probably no better and no worse educated than his predecessor and successor on the English throne. There is also some evidence of Edward II's ability to speak effectively in public. He gave a powerful speech at Amiens in June 1320, when he bluntly refused the French suggestion that he should perform liege homage for Gascony;[31] he gave another speech concerning Gascony to an assembly of knights, prelates and magnates in London in October 1324;[32] and according to the *Vita Edwardi Secundi* (143–5), he delivered a speech before the Westminster Parliament of November 1325 concerning Isabella's refusal to return from France.[33]

Like his father, Edward I, and his son, Edward III, Edward of Caernarfon was probably 'a man of unsophisticated piety'[34] and 'conventional and predictable in his personal devotions'.[35] It is known, for example, that he inherited a very large collection of relics from his father and passed them on intact to his son.[36] Edward II does not appear to have added significantly to this collection, unless we include the ampoule containing the Holy Oil of St Thomas of Canterbury; but even this had originally belonged to Edward I and was simply brought to greater public attention by his son.[37] On the other hand, there is no reason to believe that Edward II's devotion to relics and belief in their power was any different from his father's or his son's.

As one would expect, the records of Edward's household, both in childhood and in adult life, contain many references to conventional acts of piety: his attendance at masses on saints' days and other religious festivals, his feeding of the poor and his donations to religious houses. Edward's religious formation, like his education, was probably begun by the Dominican friars whom his mother sent to join his household in 1290. She had a particular devotion to the Dominicans, to whom she gave generous endowments in her lifetime and in her will, and whose religious practices, including the saying of

---

[31] Vale, *Angevin Legacy*, p. 51.

[32] E 30/1582, edited in *Rotuli Parliamentorum Hactenus Inediti*, ed. H. G. Richardson and G. O. Sayles, Camden Third Series, 51 (London, 1935), pp. 94–8, where it is wrongly dated to June 1325. For the latest edition see *PROME*, October 1324.

[33] *Vita*, pp. 143–5.

[34] M. Prestwich, *Edward I* (New Haven and London, 1988), p. 111. For a discussion of Edward I's religious proclivities and practices see ibid., pp. 111–14, and, in more detail, M. Prestwich, 'The Piety of Edward I', in *England in the Thirteenth Century*, ed. W. M. Ormrod (Woodbridge, 1986), pp. 120–8.

[35] W. M. Ormrod, 'The Personal Religion of Edward III', *Speculum* 64 (1989), 849–77 (esp. p. 853).

[36] Ibid., pp. 855–6, where the most important ones are listed. The details are derived from the list of royal relics in 1331–2 preserved in E 101/385/19, f. 10r. It is unlikely that so early in his reign Edward III would have made many additions of his own.

[37] J. R. S. Phillips, 'Edward II and the Prophets', in *England in the Fourteenth Century: Proceedings of the 1985 Harlaxton Symposium*, ed. W. M. Ormrod (Woodbridge, 1986), pp. 196–201.

the rosary, she followed.[38] In 1300, just before his sixteenth birthday, Edward was given an expensive Primer, at a cost of £2. This has sometimes been interpreted as a textbook for Edward to learn Latin but it was probably a book of devotions. The book is no longer extant, so it is impossible to say whether the prayers which it contained would have been in accordance with his mother's wishes and those of her Dominican mentors.[39] Both Eleanor of Castile and her husband Edward I had Dominican confessors in their households, and this practice was followed by their son, Edward of Caernarfon.[40] Edward sometimes used Dominicans, such as John of Wrotham in 1311 and Nicholas of Wisbech in 1317–18, for particularly delicate royal business at the papal curia. The records of Edward's household are full of gifts and donations made to individual Dominicans or to their houses, notably the house at King's Langley which he founded and where the body of Edward's favourite, Gaveston, was finally buried in 1315.[41]

As early as 1305 Edward had expressed in a letter to the mayor of Northampton, on behalf of the local Dominicans, that he had 'a great affection for the order of friars preacher, for many reasons', and had shown his affection for them in practical ways both then and on many other occasions during his life.[42] It is not surprising that in 1327 Dominicans were involved in plots to release Edward from captivity, first at Kenilworth and then at Berkeley, or that in later years they were instrumental in spreading tales of Edward's sanctity. Edward's most striking involvement with the order was the episode of the Holy Oil of St Thomas of Canterbury between 1317 and 1319, when Nicholas of Wisbech, a former confessor to Edward's sister Margaret the duchess of Brabant, persuaded Edward to ask the pope to allow him to be anointed with the oil, in the hope that the ceremony would end the political troubles in which he was them immersed. Not surprisingly, the pope refused to sanction what would, in effect, have been a second coronation, and

---

38 Parsons, *Eleanor of Castile*, pp. 41–42, citing C 47/4/5, ff. 13, 29. See also Parsons, 'Eleanor of Castile (1241–1290)', pp. 38–40, and p. 51, nn. 64, 65.

39 Johnstone, *Edward of Carnarvon*, p. 18; cf. Galbraith, 'Literacy of Medieval English Kings', p. 215.

40 Parsons, 'Eleanor of Castile', p. 38. The role of Dominicans as confessors to English kings has been studied by R. D. Clarke, 'Some secular activities of the English Dominicans during the reigns of Edward I, Edward II and Edward III, 1272–1377' (unpublished M.A. Thesis, University of London, 1930). See also W. A. Hinnebusch, *The Early English Friars Preachers* (Rome, 1951).

41 For Edward's confessors see, for example, Lenham: E 101/359/5, f. 5v; 376/7, f. 4; and 363/18, f. 6. When Lenham was dying in August 1316 Edward took particular care for his comfort: E 101/376/7, f. 5v; SAL, MS 120, f. 8v. Wodeford and Duffeld: ibid., f. 11v; BL Add. Ms. 17362, f. 5; Add. Ms. 9951, f. 2. Wrotham: BL, Cotton MS Nero C.VIII, f. 54v; E 101/373/26, f. 90. For royal gifts in aid of building work at Langley see BL, Add. MS 35093, f. 8v (1307); BL, Cotton MS C.VIII, f. 51 (1311); for the burial of Gaveston see Phillips, *Aymer de Valence*, p. 63.

42 *Letters*, ed. Johnstone, pp. 1 and 21. A number of examples are cited.

the attempt ended in the imprisonment and subsequent flight of Nicholas of Wisbech, and in the deep embarrassment of Edward himself. These events, however, suggest that in religious matters Edward possessed both a simple piety and a certain gullibility when dealing with holy men. In a remarkably frank letter, which he addressed to the pope early in 1319, Edward admitted that through his own 'imbecility' he had allowed the unscrupulous friar to take advantage of his 'dovelike simplicity'.[43]

Little is known about Edward's personal devotions. His name saint and that of his dynasty, St Edward, was of course central to the abbey of Westminster and also figured prominently in the ceremonial of Edward's coronation in 1308.[44] The feast of St Edward the Confessor was also routinely observed by Edward and his household. In 1312–13 (probably in the summer of 1313) Edward ordered the refurbishment of the chapel of St Edward in Windsor castle, which had been built by his grandfather Henry III between 1240 and 1245/6. Edward ordered that four chaplains should be appointed to serve in the chapel and that two masses should be said daily, one for the Blessed Virgin Mary and the other for the soul of Edward I. The king's chancellor was to inspect the chapel and its fittings once a year. The chapel was also the scene of the baptism of the future Edward III, who was born at Windsor on 13 November 1312 and baptised there on 16 November.[45]

If Edward had a particular devotion to the cult of a saint other than St Edward, it seems to have been to that of St Thomas of Canterbury, a practice he inherited from his father, Edward I, who visited the shrine of St Thomas at Canterbury on six occasions between 1279 and 1305.[46] Edward himself was there in July 1293 on the feast of the translation of St Thomas, for the second marriage of Edward I and Margaret of France in September 1299, and on sixteen occasions between December 1307 and April 1323.[47] A life of St Thomas was one of the manuscripts which Edward later borrowed from Canterbury and failed to return.[48] More significant, however, was Edward's choice of the martyrdom of St Thomas as the theme of the painting he

---

43 For details see Phillips, 'Edward II and the Prophets', pp. 196–201; C 70/4 m. 6d.

44 J. C. Parsons, 'Rethinking English Coronations, 1220–1308'. I am grateful to Professor Parsons for allowing me to see this unpublished paper.

45 *Foedera*, II¹, p. 193; *CCR 1307–13*, pp. 586, 588; *The History of the King's Works: The Middle Ages*, ed. R. A. Brown, H. M. Colvin and A. J. Taylor, 2 vols (London, 1963), I, 94–125; II, 868–9.

46 A. J. Duggan, 'The Cult of St Thomas Becket in the Thirteenth Century', in *St Thomas Cantilupe, Bishop of Hereford: Essays in his Honour*, ed. Meryl Jancey (Hereford, 1982), p. 31.

47 1293: E 101/353/18, m. 6. His visits to Canterbury as king are listed in the Index of Places, in Hallam, *Itinerary*. It does not, of course, follow that Edward went to St Thomas's shrine on each of these occasions but it is likely that he made a considerable number of visits.

48 M. McKisack, *The Fourteenth Century, 1307–1399* (Oxford, 1959), p. 2, citing M. R. James, *Ancient Libraries of Canterbury and Dover* (Cambridge, 1903), pp. xlv–xlvi, 148.

commissioned from William of Northampton in April 1301 for the chapel of Chester castle shortly after he became Prince of Wales.[49] Although there are many surviving representations of Becket, this appears to be the only recorded medieval reference to an actual commission.[50] The later episode of the Holy Oil of St Thomas and Edward's attempt to make use of it and the accompanying legend for his own propaganda purposes is another highly significant example.[51] Had Edward II been successful in obtaining papal permission for a re-anointing with the oil, he would have made an important addition to the sacred and miraculous character of the monarchy of which he was the current representative

These examples suggest that Edward II was very conscious of the sacred character of monarchy and of the indefinable yet very real power which he derived from it. This was inherent in the ceremony of coronation which he had undergone in March 1308 and was always a bulwark against the power of his opponents. Only in the exceptional circumstances attending Edward's deposition in 1327 could this first and last line of defence of his royal power be breached, and even then with dubious legality. It should not be thought, for example, that when Edward sought to be anointed with the Holy Oil of St Thomas he was acting simply out of political weakness. There is little doubt that he genuinely believed that the oil had the powers ascribed to it.

A plausible case can be made for Edward II as a literate ruler and a religious man; but can anything be done to salvage his poor reputation as a ruler? Many of the political problems of the reign were certainly caused by Edward's perceived willingness to let others exercise power in his name. The evidence for this in the case of Piers Gaveston, at the beginning of the reign, is, however, more apparent than real. He behaved with circumspection when he was briefly acting as *custos regni* during Edward II's absence in France in January 1308. Gaveston's real causes of offence came through his personal arrogance towards the other magnates and through his influence over the distribution of royal patronage.[52] The behaviour of the Despensers at the end of the reign was, however, on an entirely different level. There is no doubt that both men, and more especially Hugh Despenser the Younger, exercised

---

49 William was asked for 'a picture of blessed Thomas the martyr with the four knights who slew him': Johnstone, *Edward of Carnarvon*, p. 61, citing the account roll of William Melton, Chamberlain of Chester, now preserved among the NLW Wynnstay MSS. Text edited by R. Stewart Brown in Lancashire & Cheshire Record Society, XCII, Appendix. The painting is no longer extant.

50 This was the opinion expressed to Professor Johnstone by Professor C. T. Borenius, the author of *St Thomas Becket in Art* (London, 1932). The Chester painting was not, however, previously known to him and does not figure in the list of English wall-paintings of the martyrdom in ibid., pp. 98–9.

51 Phillips, 'Edward II and the Prophets', pp. 196–201.

52 Hamilton, *Piers Gaveston*, pp. 45–6, 74–6.

real day-to-day administrative and political power.[53] Edward's own lack of interest in affairs of state business is apparently well illustrated by his letter to the earl of Lincoln in November 1309 concerning the planning of the February 1310 parliament, in which Edward stated that he would not find it convenient to stay at the meeting for more than ten or twelve days. Again, in June 1311, Edward wrote from Berwick-on-Tweed to his councillors in Westminster, ordering them to have important items of business 'in such array that the king can have good deliverance of them when he comes to London to Parliament'.[54] If Edward was expecting the business of parliament to be concluded swiftly, he was of course soon disabused on each occasion, first through the demands for the appointment of the Ordainers in 1310 and second through the drafting and final publication of the resulting Ordinances in 1311.[55] Edward could, however, on occasions display signs of energy and initiative. The well-known letter written by Thomas Cobham, bishop of Worcester, at the time of the parliament of October 1320 noted that the king was rising unusually early and was contributing to the discussions of parliamentary business, while the unpublished chronicle attributed to Nicholas Trivet adds that Edward 'showed prudence in answering the petitions of the poor, and clemency as much as severity in judicial matters, to the amazement of many who were there'.[56] Edward II's lack of interest may, however, be more apparent than real. The evidence in relation to 1310 and 1311 could also be interpreted either as a demand for the efficient conduct of business or as an unwillingness to be tied down indefinitely by the demands of his political opponents. The 1320 evidence does seem to reflect a new energy on Edward's part, an energy which he had already shown in his encounter with Philip V of France at Amiens in June 1320 and which he continued to display during the struggle with the opponents of the Despensers in 1321 and the resulting civil war in 1322. On the other hand, the comments of the bishop of Worcester need to be viewed with some degree of caution, since Cobham had an axe to grind, having been deprived of the see of Canterbury in 1313 in place of Edward II's own preferred candidate.

At a critical point in the reign, the period between the death of Gaveston in June 1312 and the political agreements with the magnates in the autumn of 1313, Edward had shown considerable political skill in wearing down his opponents and in obtaining the support of the French Crown and of the

---

[53] The letters to and from the Younger Despenser which are edited by Pierre Chaplais in *The War of St Sardos (1323–1325)*, Camden 3rd s. 87 (London, 1954), give a very clear indication of his power.

[54] Conway Davies, *Baronial Opposition*, pp. 548–9, no. 7 (citing E 159/83, m. 10d); *Calendar of Chancery Warrants, 1244–1326* (London, 1927) p. 369 (C 81/79/2138).

[55] For details of the parliaments of 1310 and 1311 see the Introductions in *PROME*.

[56] *Register of Thomas de Cobham, Bishop of Worcester, 1317–27*, ed. E. H. Pearce, Worcester Historical Society (Worcester, 1930), pp. 97–8; BL, Cotton MS Nero D.X, f. 110v.

English Church until he achieved the settlement he wanted.[57] Again, between 1316 and 1318, he succeeded in mobilising support for himself among many of the leading magnates. This, together with the mediation of the Church and two papal envoys, helped to undermine the demands of Thomas of Lancaster to such an extent that the settlement finally achieved in the summer and autumn of 1318 in practice gave the king much more than it did Lancaster.[58] Unfortunately, Edward also had an even greater skill at throwing away the fruits of victory, as he was to do with disastrous consequences for himself and his kingdom after the civil war of 1321–22.

At first sight, any attempt to salvage Edward II's reputation as a military leader may seem to be a hopeless task, given the disastrous English defeat at Bannockburn in 1314 and the humiliations at Myton in 1319 and Byland in 1322, not to mention the repeated Scottish raiding of northern England, the Scottish invasion of Ireland in 1315, and the final disaster in the autumn of 1326.

Although the young Edward of Caernarfon seems in fact to have been strong and athletic, and also to have been a good horseman, the need to preserve his life remained paramount. This may, in part, explain why, unlike his father in his own youth or his first cousins Thomas and Henry of Lancaster, he is never known to have taken part in a tournament.[59] Lack of interest or aptitude may also have been a reason, as is usually assumed, but it is just as likely that it was simply too dangerous to risk the life or health of the heir to the throne, and hence also the life and health of the kingdom itself, in such a dangerous sport. The death of duke John I of Brabant, the father-in-law of Edward's sister Margaret, in a tournament in 1294 was a close family example of what might so easily happen. On the other hand, Edward was equipped for war and took part in several of his father's campaigns in Scotland between 1300 and 1307. While he does not appear to have achieved much in his own right, he did at least learn something about the realities of war. When it came to his own reign, he was quick to take up Robert Bruce's challenge in 1314 and was eager to campaign against the Scots in 1319 and 1322. If his behaviour at Bannockburn is any guide, Edward does not seem to have lacked physical courage, whatever else he may have lacked in judgement. Edward was unsuccessful against the Scots in Scotland and in England, but he and his advisers should be given some credit for the eventual defeat of Edward Bruce in Ireland through sending John de Hotham and Roger Mortimer to organise the defence of the lordship on land and John of Athy to organise the naval war in the Irish Sea.[60] Successful precautions were also taken in 1317 to prevent the Irish war from spilling over into Wales. In

---

[57] See, for example, Phillips, *Aymer de Valence*, pp. 38–69.
[58] Ibid., pp. 136–77.
[59] Johnstone, *Edward of Carnarvon*, p. 17.
[60] For the war in Ireland see J. R. S. Phillips, 'Edward II and Ireland (in Fact and in

1321–22 Edward II also showed great determination in the organising and prosecution of the campaign against Thomas of Lancaster and his allies.

Edward's plans did not, of course, always work out as intended. The defeat of the army commanded by William Melton and John de Hotham at Myton-on-Swale in Yorkshire in September 1319, while Edward continued his siege of Berwick, is usually put down to foolishness on Edward's part in leaving inexperienced men in charge.[61] In fact, Hotham had the earlier experience of successfully organising the defence of Dublin and of the lordship of Ireland from December 1315 to January 1316, against the same Scottish enemies and some of the same Scottish commanders, such as Thomas Randolph, earl of Moray. Edward's gamble did not succeed, but it was not an act of stupidity.[62]

Edward II took an even bigger gamble in the autumn of 1326 when he fled to Wales, hoping that support from his Welsh allies would help to defeat Roger Mortimer, as it had done in 1322. When events moved too quickly, he then tried to cross to Ireland. That too failed, because of contrary winds, but if he had reached Ireland, there was a good chance that he would have found support there. He also had a large sum of money, amounting to £29,000. Had he reached his lordship of Ireland, he could not have been accused of abandoning his dominions, as he was in the articles of deposition in January 1327. There is no knowing what might have happened in England, with a legitimate king at large and with the resources to mount an invasion of his own.[63]

So what in the end can we make of Edward II? It is fair to say that he was probably under-rated in his own time and has certainly been under-rated since. His personality was complicated, which made (and makes) it all the more difficult to assess him fairly. He was not stupid; he was probably at least as well educated as his father, Edward I, and his son, Edward III; he was religious in a conventional way in much of his life. But there was also something of the holy man about him which made the later story of his wanderings around Europe in the guise of a hermit, and the attempt by Richard II to

Fiction)', *Irish Historical Studies* 33, no. 129 (May 2002), 1–18, especially 9–11, and sources cited there.

61 See, for example, Hugo Schwyzer, 'Northern Bishops and the Anglo-Scottish War in the Reign of Edward II', in *Thirteenth Century England, VII*, ed. M. Prestwich, R. Britnell and R. Frame (Woodbridge, 1999), pp. 249–50, where Hotham and Melton are described as having no previous experience of military command or of organising a defence.

62 See J. R. S. Phillips, 'Documents on the Early Stages of the Bruce Invasion of Ireland, 1315–1316', *Proceedings of the Royal Irish Academy*, 79 (1979), 247–70 (p. 247); and idem, 'The mission of John de Hothum to Ireland, 1315–1316', in *England and Ireland in the Later Middle Ages*, ed. J. Lydon (Dublin, 1981), pp. 62–85.

63 See the discussion in Phillips, 'Edward II and Ireland', pp. 13–15. This is of course speculative, but the situation in England was so volatile in 1326–7 that the possibility of a recovery of power by Edward II should not be ruled out.

have him canonised, at least seem plausible.[64] He was not lacking in physical or moral courage. Throughout his reign, Edward also stubbornly insisted on defending the rights and privileges of the crown. This may sometimes have been politically unwise, but also shows a king who took the authority and powers of his office very seriously.

As a king, he was too able to be ignored but with too many weaknesses of character and behaviour to be a success. His ultimate legacy lay not in any constitutional formulae[65] or in any growth in the importance of parliamentary institutions,[66] but rather in the precedent set by his deposition, which poisoned English politics for generations to come.[67]

[64] See J. R. S. Phillips, ' "Edward II" in Italy: English and Welsh Political Exiles and Fugitives in Continental Europe, 1322–1364', in *Thirteenth Century England X*, ed. M Prestwich, R. Britnall and R. Frame (Woodbridge, 2005), pp. 209–26.

[65] The events of the reign had finally shown that the finely wrought programmes of reform and high-sounding declarations of principle, which had punctuated the political history of England since 1307 and which have so fascinated historians down to the present, counted for nothing when there was deep distrust and even loathing between the opposing sides.

[66] For a recent assessment of the role of parliament during the reign of Edward II see, for example, the Introduction to the Parliament of January 1327 in *PROME*. The deposition of Edward II in 1327 was essentially the work of the magnates, whatever attempt there may have been to obtain as broad a range of consent (and complicity) as possible.

[67] See J. R. S. Phillips, 'Simon de Montfort (1265), the Earl of Manchester (1644), and Other Stories: Violence and Politics in Thirteenth- and Early Fourteenth-Century England', in *Violence in Medieval Society*, ed. R. W. Kaeuper (Woodbridge, 2000), pp. 79–89.

INDEX

York Studies in Medieval Theology

I   *Medieval Theology and the Natural Body*, ed. Peter Biller and A. J. Minnis (1997)

II   *Handling Sin: Confession in the Middle Ages*, ed. Peter Biller and A. J. Minnis (1998)

III *Religion and Medicine in the Middle Ages*, ed. Peter Biller and Joseph Ziegler (2001)

IV   *Texts and the Repression of Medieval Heresy*, ed. Caterina Bruschi and Peter Biller (2002)

York Manuscripts Conference

Manuscripts and Readers in Fifteenth-Century England: The Literary Implications of Manuscript Study, ed. Derek Pearsall (1983) [Proceedings of the 1981 York Manuscripts Conference]

Manuscripts and Texts: Editorial Problems in Later Middle English Literature, ed. Derek Pearsall (1987) [Proceedings of the 1985 York Manuscripts Conference]

Latin and Vernacular: Studies in Late-Medieval Texts and Manuscripts, ed. A. J. Minnis (1989) [Proceedings of the 1987 York Manuscripts Conference]

Regionalism in Late-Medieval Manuscripts and Texts: Essays celebrating the publication of 'A Linguistic Atlas of Late Mediaeval English', ed. Felicity Riddy (1991) [Proceedings of the 1989 York Manuscripts Conference]

Late-Medieval Religious Texts and their Transmission: Essays in Honour of A. I. Doyle, ed. A. J. Minnis (1994) [Proceedings of the 1991 York Manuscripts Conference]

Prestige, Authority and Power in Late Medieval Manuscripts and Texts, ed. Felicity Riddy (2000) [Proceedings of the 1994 York Manuscripts Conference]

Middle English Poetry: Texts and Traditions. Essays in Honour of Derek Pearsall, ed. A. J. Minnis (2001) [Proceedings of the 1996 York Manuscripts Conference]

Lightning Source UK Ltd.
Milton Keynes UK
UKOW06n1340240717
305942UK00001B/59/P